T0304047

ROUTLEDGE LIBRARY EDITIONS:
THE ECONOMICS AND BUSINESS OF
TECHNOLOGY

Volume 4

FINANCE, INVESTMENT AND INNOVATION

FINANCE, INVESTMENT AND INNOVATION
Theory and Empirical Evidence

Edited by
MICHELE BAGELLA

Taylor & Francis Group

LONDON AND NEW YORK

First published in 1997 by Ashgate Publishing Ltd

This edition first published in 2018
by Routledge
2 Park Square, Milton Park, Abingdon, Oxon OX14 4RN

and by Routledge
711 Third Avenue, New York, NY 10017

Routledge is an imprint of the Taylor & Francis Group, an informa business

British Library Cataloguing in Publication Data
A catalogue record for this book is available from the British Library

ISBN: 978-1-138-50336-6 (Set)
ISBN: 978-1-351-06690-7 (Set) (ebk)
ISBN: 978-1-138-47852-7 (Volume 4) (hbk)
ISBN: 978-1-351-06828-4 (Volume 4) (ebk)

Publisher's Note
The publisher has gone to great lengths to ensure the quality of this reprint but points out that some imperfections in the original copies may be apparent.

Disclaimer
The publisher has made every effort to trace copyright holders and would welcome correspondence from those they have been unable to trace.

Finance, Investment and Innovation
Theory and Empirical Evidence

Edited by
MICHELE BAGELLA

ASHGATE

Published by
Ashgate Publishing Ltd   Ashgate Publishing Company
Gower House   Suite 420
Croft Road   101 Cherry Street
Aldershot   Burlington, VT 05401-4405
Hants GU11 3HR   USA
England

Ashgate website: http://www.ashgate.com

British Library Cataloguing in Publication Data

Finance, investment and innovation: theory and empirical evidence
1. Corporations - Finance 2. Technological innovations - Finance
I. Bagella, Michele
338.6041

Library of Congress Catalog Card Number: 96-80278

ISBN 1 85972 588 6

Reprinted 1998, 2001

Printed in Great Britain by Biddles Limited, King's Lynn.

Published by
Ashgate Publishing Ltd
Gower House
Croft Road
Aldershot
Hants GU11 3HR
England

Ashgate Publishing Company
Suite 420
101 Cherry Street
Burlington, VT 05401-4405
USA

Ashgate website: http://www.ashgate.com

British Library Cataloguing in Publication Data

Finance, investment and innovation : theory and empirical
  evidence
  1. Corporations - Finance 2. Technological innovations -
  Finance
  I. Bagella, Michele
  338.6'041

Library of Congress Catalog Card Number: 96-80378

ISBN 1 85972 568 6

Reprinted 1999, 2004

Printed in Great Britain by Biddles Limited, King's Lynn.

Contents

v

Acknowledgements

All the papers collected in this book are the result of research supported by the "*Consiglio Nazionale delle Ricerche*", CNR (National Council for Research), in the framework of the "*Strategic Project on Technology and Innovation*", directed by Pasquale Lucio Scandizzo of the University of Rome Tor Vergata and realized at the "*Istituto di Studi per la Programmazione Economica*", ISPE ("Italian Institute for Studies on National Economic Policies, Rome").

To Pasquale Lucio Scandizzo and to ISPE my best thanks for their very useful suggestions and active collaboration. I want moreover to express my gratitude to Luigi Paganetto, the Dean of the Faculty of Economics of the University of Tor Vergata, for his contribution to the discussions of many issues explored in this book. Finally my thanks to all researchers and colleagues of CEIS (*Center for International Studies on Economic Growth*, University of Tor Vergata) who, with their enthusiasm and hard work, permitted the realization of this book. A special thanks to the President of ISPE, Fiorella Padoa-Schioppa, that allowed its publication.

Introduction

Michele Bagella

1. Finance and innovation are the fundamental terms of a relationship that is becoming ever more crucial in the reality of market economies. The choice of financing forms which may be of help in diversifying risk connected with high-tech investments is at the first point of the agenda of companies and financial intermediaries.

Starting from this fact this book tries to provide a few insights on the issue following four main paths.

These paths are represented by: i) theoretical analyses of informational asymmetries and coordination failures between investors and financiers in cases of venture capital financing (the problem of informational asymmetries between investors and financiers in cases of bank and stock market financing being widely explored by the existing literature); ii) comparative empirical analyses of financial constraints on firm investments (with the opportunity of comparing the relative efficiency of different country systems of innovation and investment financing); iii) direct tests of firm financial constraints based on qualitative data which may be used to check traditional results from traditional indirect tests of financial constraints (based on balance sheet data); iv) the effect of particular forms of market financing that may be of particular help in supporting innovation.

The comparative advantage of the book is that of being directly focused on one of the main unsolved issues in monetary and financial economics: the relative effectiveness of national financial systems in supporting innovation. The book proposes various theoretical and empirical contributions that, taken together, allow an evaluation of the relative effectiveness of some of the most important country systems such as Japan (an example of an intermediate and integrated system), the UK (an example of a market oriented system) and Italy (an example of a bank oriented system with imperfect capital markets).

2. The survey in the first paper "Relative effectiveness of national systems of finance, investment and innovation: a review of the literature and a proposal for a comparative approach" describes the asymmetric information problem between investors and financiers and the role of "Financial Intermediaries" in reducing this asymmetry showing that country specific features of financial systems for investment and innovation financing are nonneutral with respect to the solution of the problem.

Opinions on the relative effectiveness of the two "archetypal structures" of financial systems (the "market oriented" and the "intermediated") are mixed. Intermediaries may reduce monitor free riding problems of individual lenders, may avoid "short termism" by creating long-term relationships with borrowers, but close integration between intermediaries and firms may generate severe agency costs. The effectiveness of "market oriented systems" may be, on the other hand, understated. The market for corporate control, not only provides alternative forms of monitoring and control on managers activities, but is also an important source of internal funds for managers.

In addition to it, even though it is argued that multilateral banking may promote information sharing (and then technological spillovers) across firms, it seems that diffusion of information and better opportunities for mergers and acquisitions are a comparative advantage of "market oriented" systems.

The microempirical survey analyses the results of liquidity constraints and average announcement effects of equity/bond issues as tests of the relative performance of national financial systems. These results seem to confirm that "bank oriented" systems have an informational comparative advantage over "equity oriented" systems. The survey also stresses which methodological problems have to be solved in order to improve the quality of comparative analyses.

The survey on aggregate empirical papers show that this type of contributions seem not to solve interpretational ambiguities related to the endogeneity problem and to the direction of the causality links between finance and innovation, or the monetary and the real sector. With regard to the comparative evaluation of financial systems, it seems to show that both of them possess inherent causes of fragility ("market oriented" systems are more exposed to financial crises generated by the interaction of agents having different informational sets and "intermediated systems" amplify the real effects of monetary restrictions through the "credit view"). An implicit suggestion of these models is that the integration of the two systems may partially solve at least the "credit view" problem.

As a conclusion, this survey identifies three main paths among those less explored in the literature on finance, investment and innovation. These paths are represented by: i) theoretical analyses of informational asymmetries and coordination failures between investors and financiers in case of venture capital financing (the problem of informational asymmetries between investors and financiers in case of bank and stock market financing being widely explored by the existing literature); ii) comparative empirical analyses of financial constraints on firm investments (with the relative opportunity of comparing the relative

3

efficiency of different country systems of innovation and investment financing); iii) direct tests of firm financial constraints based on qualitative data which may be used to check traditional results from traditional indirect tests of financial constraints (based on balance sheet data); iv) the effect of particular forms of market financing that may be of particular help for supporting innovation. The aim of the following papers of the book is then that of proposing contributions in the four indicated directions.

3. The empirical evidence on the relationship between finance and innovation shows that for small and new innovating firms asymmetric information may impose severe agency costs on equity and bond financing so that it would be expedient to resort to a form of venture capital financing where a financing partner with some technological skills relaxes the innovator cash constraint in exchange of a participation to future profits from the innovation.

Recently, though, we witnessed a decline of this form of innovation financing with the tendency of venture capital units to prefer pure financial investments to the provision of technology financing in favour of small innovative firms. The model presented in the second paper "Equity dilution, small ticket problem and coordination inefficiency in venture capital financing of innovation" provides a formal framework capable of explaining all these phenomena and connecting these explanations to the rationales often quoted in literature. The possibility for the innovating unit to be financed maintaining full property rights on the venture is precluded by the "small ticket" problem of the financier (its informational costs prevent him from obtaining profits when the innovator has full property rights). On the other side, the division of property rights between the two units causes an "equity dilution" effect reducing incentives to innovate and the expected value of the innovation. A further insight of the model is that, adopting a coordination failure approach, it shows that two levels of coordination

4

inefficiency may occur in the game between one financer and one innovator. This is because, when property right shares are bargained ex ante, an umbalance between relative bargaining strenghts and relative contributions to the venture generates an inefficient division of property rights with a divergence between private and social optimum. The model also indicates as a normative prescription that an increase in the number of financiers may partially solve these inefficiencies explaining why these policies start being adopted in some industrial countries.

The third paper "Venture capital and innovation in Europe", confirms this policy option evidencing the role assumed by the Corporate Finance in financing the innovation.

The continuous evolution of technology created the necessity to operate on more research fronts; it is not therefore convenient for the firm to take on high costs of structure, but it is preferable to entrust different projects to companies which in being concerned with specific niche of the market, dispose of more project specific competence. Moreover the minor companies take advantage of channels of distribution that allow them to work on volumes that guarantee times of development and recovering of research costs.

Stock options can contribute in facilitating innovation the financing; the issue of stock option can be useful in avoiding principal-agent problems in the relationships between entrepreneur and venture capitalist when the propriety of the project is divided between the two, particularly when the majority of the shares is owned by the second. In this case, there could be the incentive for the entrepreneur not to adopt all the necessary measures to keep costs under control and to protect the interests of other possible shareholders.

The easiest way to channel resources of the institutional investors towards the innovative sectors, respecting their natural risk aversion but guaranteeing a certain stability to the innovative companies, consists in gathering such resources through closed-end funds.

4. Another approach to first risk matching is followed in the next two papers based, the first "The optimal financing strategy of Japanese High-Tech firms: the role of warrants", on the analysis of the bond warrant and the second on the introduction of stock price option "Effects of options introduction on stock price volatility: an empirical testing on High-Tech firm equities based on SSC-GARCH models. The main conclusion of this last paper is that a "Bond-Warrant" financing strategy is widely adopted by high-tech firms that have good intermediate research results and want to subordinate their opportunity to delay a following investment stage to obtain further positive results in research activities. This instrument often has the advantage of reducing the underlying asset volatility but is sensitive to nondiversifiable risk and to adverse selection issuing costs, as several warrant financing strategy failures that occurred in the nineties have recently shown. The solution for the adverse selection problem is the reinforcement of the signal through the introduction of put options in issued warrants. In addition, the exposition to nondiversifiable risk should be reduced if firms are given the opportunity of hedging against it by purchasing stock index futures when a market where these derivatives are traded exists.

The chapter adopts a methodology for the analysis of structural breaks on stock price volatility based on eight different models of conditional volatility. It applies them to 22 equities of industrial firms listed in five European markets (France, Germany, The UK, The Netherlands, Switzerland) to test option introduction effects on firm specific risk.

The methodology adopted tries to amend two main shortcomings of previous analyses on structural breaks induced by the introduction of derivatives: i) the adoption of measures of unconditional volatility such as the simple standard

6

deviation; ii) the limitation of the analysis to shifts in the intercept when measures of conditional volatility are considered.

Empirical results suggest that market characteristics, especially the informative structure, could be an important determinant of option trading effects on prices volatility. An explanation of this could be the possibility, for small traders with private information on news that are expected to raise the firm's market value (insider traders), to speculate taking risky positions in derivative markets. This new information is biased, because option trading conveys in the market not only insiders with good information, but also noise traders (an alternative way of seeing it is to suppose that secondary traders can only observe a noisy signal of the new information), that can destabilise the market lowering the informational content of the prices for already existing traders. This effect can counteract the stabilising effect of the risk sharing property of secondary markets, raising price volatility.

5. The analysis of the econometric results obtained in the sixth paper "Finance, investment and innovation: a theoretical and empirical comparative analysis in Japan and the UK", together with the knowledge of the institutional systems and the hypotheses supported in the theoretical model allow us to formulate some tentative conclusions on the comparative efficiency of the UK and the Japanese "national models" of finance, investment and innovation.

In "thick markets" where financial markets are well developed and different types of financial intermediaries exist but information is nonetheless imperfect and costly, the empirical relation between investment and liquidity shows, both from estimates in levels and in differences, that large and high-tech firms benefit more from the advantages of the systems reducing their cash constraint problems. The groups that are more penalised from imperfect information and financial constraints are those of small and new firms, firms

7

belonging to declining sectors and low-tech sectors, firms that have a higher bankruptcy risk and less capacity to provide collateral. This hypothesis seems to be confirmed by the results on UK firm data.

In "horizontally integrated markets", like the Japanese one, the share participation between banks and real investors seems to reduce the agency costs imbalance across groups of firms divided in terms of size and different measures of financial wealth. The cost differential between internal and external financing appears to be quite small and seems to be reduced. This might be explained by the fact that the "preference link" between firms and banks in Japan includes a closer relationship with some advantages such as extensive formal and informal monitoring of banks on firm activities and presence of bank personnel among firm key executives.

These empirical results seem to provide the following implications: i) the increase in the quantity and in the quality of financial intermediaries may reduce informational asymmetries for those groups of firms that benefit from the information provided to investors by the stock market; ii) "horizontal" (firm-firm cross holdings) and "vertical" (bank-firm cross-holdings) integration may equate agency costs across firms reducing the costs of external financing. This last empirical finding is consistent with the assumption of the "short-termist" hypothesis saying that "greater information asymmetries with respect to long-term business performance induce US stock market participants to attach greater importance to current-term results than their foreign counterparts".

6. The degree of information asymmetry between borrowers and lenders differs across classes of borrowers. Innovative firms undertake high-risk-high-return projects which are likely to be little understood by financial intermediaries. As a consequence, they may end up allocating too large a share of funds to traditional, low-risk-low-return projects. This proposition finds some support in a cross-

section of Italian manufacturing firms, "High-Tech firms, asymmetric information and credit rationing". Using several proxies to classify firms into high-tech and low-tech groups and direct information on each firm's access to bank credit, high-tech firms are found to be more likely to be credit constrained than low-tech firms. These results suggest that the responsiveness of R&D expenditure to cash flow found in the literature is likely due to pervasive credit constraints on innovative firms rather to cash flow proxying for future expectations. The paper also sheds light on the main factors affecting the probability of a firm being liquidity constrained.

7. The eighth paper collected in this book "New technology investment and financial development: cross-country evidence" analyses several different ways of measuring how financial development affects investments in new technology. Data on adoption of specific technologies and data sets on Total Factor Productivity at national and sectorial level all indicate that there is a positive relationship between finance and technology. Some new panel data work is also proposed, but not yet carried out. The paper also discusses some statistical biases that may arise because of reverse causation-feedback effects from technology to finance at firm level and at country level.

Exploring along this line the relationship between High-Tech firm investment and credit rationing in Italy, we reconstruct series of capital investment for High-Tech sectors in Italy by using the most recent statistical techniques. It was possible therefore to analyse the relationship between capital and R&D investments and the financial support of state subsidies. Results obtained in the ninth paper "Financing technological innovatio in Italy: sources, governmental support and productivity growth" confirm that state financial support is an important determinant of R&D investment in the imperfect Italian financial system lacking both the advantages of "market oriented systems"

9

(closed-end funds, specialised high-tech venture capitalists, opportunities of ad hoc financial issues from high-tech firms) and of "integrated systems" (closer bank-firm integration and long term relationship between innovator and financier).

The last paper, called "The structure of financing and intellectual property rights", demonstrates the importance of the financial structure of the firm and its influence on the incentives to undertake risky projects. This paper elaborates on the effects of the so called "agency costs" arising from possible conflicts of interest among different stakeholders, with special emphasis on the case of intellectual property (IP) rights. The paper shows that a leveraged firm may be very sensitive to the mix of financing in deciding the relative weight of R&D and other IP projects with respect to the firm's other activities. The presence of outstanding debt, in particular, causes a bias in favor of riskier IP activities and against *ex ante* protection of related property rights.

1 Relative effectiveness of national systems of finance, investment and innovation: a review of the literature and a proposal for a comparative approach

*Michele Bagella and Leonardo Becchetti**

1. Introduction

An analysis of the relationship between finance, investment and innovation is of great relevance in a non neoclassical world, where the performance of high-tech sectors is crucially influenced by the institutional organization and the effective functioning of the interaction between financial and innovative sectors. In times of innovation and integration of financial systems, a clear-cut prescription of the direction to take in the institutional reform of financial markets and institutions is urgently needed. What can help policy makers in decisions over financial institution reform is the evaluation of the performance of four major financial systems in supporting investment and innovation: i) the "German system" in which major banks, directly or through administrating portfolios of individual savers, have a large share participation in innovating industries[1]; ii) the Anglo-Saxon "atomistic" system in which the role of financing innovation is played, in the presence of a relatively lower bank-firm participation, by closed-ended funds and venture capitalists in a fully developed financial market (Edwards-Fisher, 1993); iii) the "Japanese" system in which large conglomerates determine a high degree of concentration and integration between financial and innovating sectors[2]; iv) the "bank-dependent" Italian system: a) where a "liquidity-volatility" dilemma and costs of information disclosure prevent small and medium firms from being listed on the domestic exchange and determine an

11

abnormally small stock market capitalisation over GDP and where b) bond financing is crowded out by public debt and is therefore not a substitute for bank financing. A short description of these systems is provided by Tables 1.1a-1.1c. Table 1.1a provides an overall picture of corporate governance and industrial structure of these systems showing that the United States is nearer to the "abstract" model of a "market oriented" system (strong separation between firm ownership and control, low ownership concentration, high independence of management, low role of financial intermediaries and high role of financial markets). The German system is nearer to the "abstract" model of a "bank oriented" system (weak separation between firm ownership and control, high ownership concentration, low independence of management, high role of financial intermediaries and low role of financial markets in corporate monitoring, very weak constraints on bank ownership of firm equity). The Japanese system is close to the German "bank oriented" model but with some crucial distinctions on cross-shareholding which are larger and intra-group relationship which are stronger. The Italian system has something in common with the US (strong constraints on bank ownership of firm equity) and much more in common with the German system even though the role of financial intermediaries in corporate monitoring is much lower and the system of cross-shareholdings, inter and intra group participation is much more widespread for large firms listed in the stock exchange.

Table 1.1b clearly shows how financial markets are more developed in "market oriented" systems such as the United Kingdom and the US than in "bank oriented" systems where stock market capitalisation and internationalisation are relatively low and firm access to direct market financing through equity or bond issues is relatively lower.

Table 1.1c shows instead the different cultures of national financial systems in supporting innovation. On one side, Italy and France have a strong tradition of state subsidies although France puts much more emphasis than Italy on advisory and consultancy services. On the other side is the United States where state support is clearly accompanied by advisory and consultancy activities and where attention is paid to programme monitoring and evaluation, and to the creation of closer links between universities and the private sector. The extreme case here is that of the United Kingdom's experience which is similar to that of the United States in the above described features, with the exception that the role of the state is not that of providing direct financial support but just that of promoting the diffusion of technological information, improving links between innovators and private consultants.

These four models of interaction between financiers and investors originated as endogenous responses to "country fundamentals" (national, social and legal norms) and are now evolving to face new challenges.

One of the primary benchmarks that may be considered as a reference for a comparative evaluation of their evolution is the "short termist" hypothesis which assumes that *"equity oriented" systems provide less support to innovation than "bank oriented" ones* (Cosh-Hughes-Singh, 1990; Hamid-Sing, 1992) *because of their lower relative capacity of reducing agency costs between investors and financiers ("arm's length relation between financier and investor"*; Mayer, 1985*)*. This view is partially confirmed by recent empirical studies, showing that the Japanese stock market incorporates information earlier than the US stock market (Aaker-Jacobson, 1993).

A huge branch of literature on financial and monetary economics is now interested in testing this working theory in order to provide an evaluation of the comparative effectiveness of financial systems in supporting the real side of the economy.

In an attempt to follow a comparative evaluation approach, this chapter intends: i) to present the puzzle of descriptive statistics on a firm's internal and external financing choices in six different countries; ii) to highlight and to comment on the main empirical and theoretical results obtained so far in analysing finance and innovation interaction; iii) to describe the methodological problems arising from this comparative research; iv) to propose a theoretical framework - which will be the reference for theoretical and empirical analyses presented in the following chapters - that may explain why different financial systems have originated in different countries, and how these systems are actually evolving. The chapter is divided into two parts.

In the first (and introductory) section, descriptive statistics and a survey of recent contributions constituting the basis of the present research are provided. Four sub-branches of analysis have been pinpointed: micro-theoretical, micro-empirical, macro-theoretical (intended as a theoretical analysis which, even being microfounded, pays particular attention to the aggregate consequences of its models and in particular to business cycle movements and growth effects) and macro-empirical (see Table 1.2). The first sub-branch presents a vast number of contributions. These contributions investigate the effects of informational asymmetries in the relationship between finance, investment and innovation and highlight the actual and potential roles of national financial systems in the reduction of such informational asymmetries. The second sub-branch examines the most recent micro-empirical results as tests of the relative effectiveness of national financial systems in dealing with investments and innovation. The section also presents a critical evaluation of the methodological issues involved in comparative empirical analyses. The remaining sub-branches show how the macro-theoretical approach is made up, to a large extent, by endogenous growth models, and the fourth macro-empirical branch by attempts to estimate macro-theoretical hypotheses through cross-country analyses.

The brief survey on the existing literature highlights the need for a comprehensive microfounded approach which is outlined in the second section. By this approach it is possible to compare the different "archetypes" of national systems of innovation financing. Its final aim is that of showing how these systems represent endogenously developed optimal responses to the same problem, according to differences in "country fundamentals".

The second section surveys models which may provide a framework for this comparative microfoundation (Becchetti 1993; Aghion-Tirole, 1994), by describing the interaction between financial and innovative units in a technological area with a coordination failure model.

In the conclusion of the chapter, preliminary policy suggestions are advanced based on the current state of research. The main conclusion is that *national financial systems play a crucial role in determining the "optimal" interaction between finance and innovation and have spontaneously adapted to the challenge of financing risky innovative ventures:* i) "equity oriented" systems creating a favourable environment for the creation of FI specialised in financing innovation such as industry funded venture capitalists; ii) "bank oriented" systems trying to reinforce the long-term reputable links between banks and firms. Both systems need to reduce existing agency problems (mainly "equity dilution syndrome" in the first case and mainly moral hazard in the second case) and to reinforce systems of penalties and incentives by which investors can finance themselves directly on the market with a strategy which is alternative to searching for a unique specialised FI.

2. Some stylised facts on firms' choices of external and internal finance under different financial systems

A first relevant empirical fact in firm financing choices is that, in different financial systems, a significant share of firm R&D is financed by governments or by foreigners. R&D state subsidies or state sponsored R&D play a relevant role in the US as well as in France and in Italy Tab 1.2). The fact that part of the research is financed abroad suggests that some of the limits of domestic financial systems may be overcome if firms are able to finance themselves on the international capital market (Table 1.3-1.4).

Several methodological difficulties arise when comparisons of firm financing choices under different financial regimes are attempted. When national statistics are used (Mayer, 1985; Stiglitz, 1994) large statistical discrepancies arise but a clearer picture of the relative effectiveness of national systems in granting external finance to firms is provided. Company account flow of funds data provide, on the contrary, homogeneous data within countries but include funds raised from overseas as well as from domestic financial markets.

Mayer (1985) interprets the results from national flow of funds data by arguing that "market oriented systems" (the US and the UK) seem to have a relative comparative disadvantage in providing external finance as compared with more "intermediated systems". This seems to support the opinion that sophisticated and well developed financial markets, where financiers have no long term relationship with investors and innovators, are less supportive of the growing effort of the real sector of the economy. But Mayer's analysis (based on 1970-1985 average data) does not track recent important changes in firm choices of internal and external finance (Table 1.5).

Company accounts flow of funds data from OECD and Datastream, including results from the last decade, provide a quite different picture.

OECD data (Table 1.6a-1.6f) have the disadvantage of presenting a firm's internal cash-flow before depreciation and provision and may overstate its role in investment financing, but nonetheless they outline some interesting stylised features: i) the weight of internal finance as a source of UK firms' investment has sharply declined in the last decade; ii) US and French firms seem to have the highest share of internally financed investments; iii) a consistent share of investment is financed externally in Italy, Japan, the UK and (presumably) Germany[3]; iv) France and Italy have the lowest share of physical investment on total investment (physical plus financial investment).

The "added value" of Datastream data (Table 1.7a-1.7d) is represented by the provision of several ratios of internal and external finance over firm investments allowing a comparison between financing choices of firms in high-tech sectors and in the overall industrial sector. The limit of this dataset is that it includes (for any country considered) only firms listed in the domestic stock exchange market.

Greater detail and a sufficient level of comparability are provided for three countries (France, the UK and the US). Japanese data is good in detail but insufficient in comparability with other countries because of differences in valuation rules, consolidated methods and interpretation of earnings from normal business activities. Data for Italy refers to the small group of high-tech companies listed in the stock market, while data for Germany is clearly not sufficient.

In spite of these problems some interesting facts common to most analysed countries seem to emerge from this data: i) on average, high-tech sectors have a higher capacity of financing investments (however they are measured) with internal finance as compared with all other firms listed in the domestic stock exchange; ii) investment financing requirements of the Pharmaceutical sector are, on average, more easily covered by internal finance than those of other high-tech

15

sectors; iii) internal finance covers a lower share of investment needs in the Electronic sector than in the average of the other high-tech sectors (in France and in the US only). Descriptive statistics on firm internal and external financing in six countries with different industrial and financial structures is quite puzzling for several reasons. First, almost insuperable measurement problems emerge from this introductory picture: different valuation rules with regard to consolidated methods, treatment of foreign currency translation and goodwill intangibles reduce comparability between countries. Second, descriptive statistics are a-theoretical. They "loom" firms' financing patterns but do not explain the cause of their choices. They cannot tell us, for example, if a large part of firm investments is internally financed because external finance is simply not needed or because of firm financial constraints. Empirical data needs then to be interpreted through theoretical and econometric analysis in order to ascertain for the relevance of the positive cost differential between external and internal finance in different national financial systems.

Third, several crucial issues remain almost untouched by this data. What happens to small firms which are not listed in the stock exchange? Can some distinctive financing forms (venture capital, bond plus equity warrant issues) be of particular help in supporting innovation? How much innovating knowledge is accumulated through interfirm agreements (mergers and acquisitions, limited participation agreements, etc.) and in which way do they indirectly represent an important form of internal finance?

The introductory survey and the following chapters of this dissertation aim at providing an additional contribution to the analysis of these issues both on the theoretical and on the empirical side, in the attempt to overcome, on the empirical side, the methodological difficulties which clearly arise from simple descriptive statistics.

3. The micro-theoretical approach

The most important task of micro-theoretical studies is to demonstrate the cost differential among different financing sources at firm level making it clear that: i) the link between finance, investment and innovation is crucially affected by the problem of imperfect information (on ex ante firm's prospects or on ex post realised returns); ii) the remuneration of financial intermediaries in terms of extra costs arising from external financing is justified by their informational economies of scale (Diamond, 1984; Ramakrishnan-Thakor, 1984).

The advantage of the imperfect information approach over the Modigliani-Miller approach[4], seems to be its "external consistency" and its capacity of giving a consistent explanation to some relevant empirical features of modern corporate finance such as, for instance: i) the downward inflexibility of dividend policy in relation to financing requirements; ii) the variations in stock prices occurring when peculiar events like equity, bond or convertible issues are announced; iii) the existence of credit rationing.

The basic idea is that managers have superior information on firm financial and economic perspectives and that market agents can infer this information from some aspects of managers' decisions such as dividend policies and financing strategies[5]. Managers are aware of this and their decisions on firm policies must take into account the indirect "signalling" effects of a given choice that, in some cases, are conflicting with the perfect information effects of the choice itself (this may occur for example in the dilemma between dividend distribution and internal financing).

The perverse effect of imperfect information is that it creates, through adverse selection, a positive cost differential between external and internal financing sources (Myers-Mayluf, 1984; Stiglitz-Weiss, 1981).

Given the existence of the "lemon problem" two main solutions are identified by the literature: the first way to solve it (a "market oriented" solution) is to devise a financing strategy which exactly signals to the market the firm type avoiding extra costs generated by imperfect information. The second way (an "intermediated" solution) is the improvement in the quality of financial intermediaries, whose role is that of reducing information asymmetries between lender and borrower (Figure 1.1)

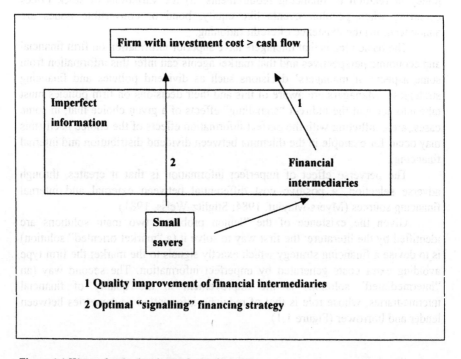

Figure 1.1 Ways of reducing imperfect information

In the first case, working on the assumption that an issue on the financial market is a signal of the firm's expected performance, many authors have examined the potential information revealed by it. This has progressively led to outline the existence of a signalling order in firms' different financing policies (Brennan-Kraus, 1987; Noe, 1988; Constantinides-Grundy, 1989; Stein, 1992; Santarelli, 1991). According to these authors, leverage increasing issues are generally viewed as a positive signal because debtholders seem to monitor investors more closely than shareholders and also because less free cash flow reduces the possibility for managers to pursue non profit rent-seeking activities (Jensen-Meckling, 1976; Ross, 1977; Harris-Raviv, 1991; Short 1994). Consequently, the signalling order of financing strategies, ranking from the stronger to the weaker signal, seems to be approximately the following: debt or equity buy-back, straight bond issue, convertible bond or bond-plus-equity-warrant issue, equity issue[6]. The crucial condition that mimicking costs outweigh mimicking benefits is needed for signalling strategies to be "value revealing signalling equilibria". For firm financing policies this means that, for instance, i) costs of financial distress must be higher than benefits from asset overpricing for a bad firm choosing a signal which is superior to its quality, and that ii) underpricing costs must be higher than gains for a good firm choosing a signal which is inferior to its quality[7].

Conditions for the existence of a signalling equilibrium are, however, quite restrictive and several financing strategies are likely to create pooling equilibria if mimicking costs are not relevant. These theoretical findings provide us with some normative suggestions on *how financial systems may play a major role in the reduction of the asymmetric information problem* and in the creation of an institutional framework that may help firms to find their optimal signalling strategy avoiding adverse selection effects.

The hypotheses on which these models are built clearly indicate that: i) bond rating; ii) the existence of derivatives that insure against non-diversifiable risk, and iii) the existence of an enforceable system of penalties in case of bankruptcy[8] are all measures that reinforce the system of costs and incentives that make a signalling equilibrium feasible. With respect to this point, it is interesting to note that relevant regulatory differences on penalties for the bankrupt exist among different financial systems. In particular, on one side of the spectrum we have the United States and France where priority is given to continued operation and managers' cost of financial distress are reduced by a high probability of avoiding liquidation and continuing their activity; on the other side we have Germany, the United Kingdom and Italy where liquidation is the main outcome of insolvency and managers' cost of financial distress are increased by liability to several civil an criminal penalties (see Table 1.10). These differences, once taken into account, may generate very different outcomes in theoretical signalling models.

Another important normative suggestion tends towards reshaping of the features of optimal financial intermediaries (FI) for supporting innovation.

The literature helps us in providing a series of FI features which also are rational justifications for their existence. Bhattacharya-Thakor (1992) highlight that the two main positive activities of FI are those of brokerage and of Quality Asset Transformation (QAT): the first one consisting mainly in the ability of FI to interpret signals and to exploit cross-sectional and temporal reusability of information; the second one being represented by the capacity of modifying term to maturity, divisibility, liquidity and credit risk of managed assets.

Boyd and Prescott (1986) stress how a group of entrepreneurs with poor quality projects may decide to invest in monitoring other investor projects. The consequence of this decision is that good and bad entrepreneurs specialise in the activity in which they have a comparative advantage (monitoring and entrepreneurial activity respectively) and the quality of aggregate investment increases; Diamond (1984) emphasises the QAT role of FI, in that it provides

19

depositors with a riskless claim while lending to risky investors; Leland and Pyle (1977), Diamond (1984) and Ramakrishnan-Thakor (1984) underscore that a bank can communicate information about a borrower more efficiently than can the borrowers individually among themselves, reducing the problem of free riding in monitoring activity and reducing costs of ex ante or ex post informational asymmetries between financiers and the entrepreneur. Prescott (1986) shows how endogenously formed coalitions of intermediaries may help reducing the "lemon" problem by creating the right incentive to support those with good projects and discourage those with bad ones. Moore (1987) emphasises the long-term nature of the relationship between lenders and borrowers, showing that it helps to build a reputation and to mitigate informational distortions. Restrictive conditions on the feasibility of signalling equilibria in market issues and their scarce empirical weight as a firm's financing choice seem to suggest, together with the emphasis on the importance of long term relationship between financiers and investors, that "intermediated systems" avoid "short termism" and have a comparative advantage on "market oriented systems".

Separate analyses of the capacity of financial markets and FIs in supporting investment and innovation, though, do not allow direct comparisons of the two systems and cannot provide direct answers on their relative efficiency. More recent papers have tried to do so.

Allen-Gale (1995) argue that the choice between a "market oriented system" and an "intermediated system" involves a trade-off between cross-sectional risk sharing (in which the "market oriented" system is relatively more specialised) and intertemporal risk sharing (in which the "intermediated system" is relatively more specialised). Given these broad distinctive features, the relative capacity of the two systems in supporting investment and innovation will depend on: i) the amount and ii) the price of investment and innovation financing provided; iii) the relative capacity of evaluating entrepreneurs and of selecting good projects; iv) the relative capacity of monitoring innovating firms' behaviour to avoid waste of resources: v) the relative effectiveness in spreading information about firm prospects and research activity in order to create technological spillovers.

In "marked oriented" systems, mergers and acquisitions are a channel for an informal market of internal funds. Enhancing the provision of internal funds is an implicit advantage in presence of imperfect information as it implies a reduction in the proportion between external and internal financing sources for innovating firms and, therefore, a reduction in financing costs. The relative weight of market issues and the existence of a significant residual between individual firm internal financing and total financing (see descriptive statistics in Table 1.6-1.7) in "market oriented systems" seems to suggest that this advantage does exist. Furthermore, the main function of the market for corporate control is that of management disciplining. This should offset "free-riding" inefficiencies *à la Diamond* in systems where dispersed shareholding reduces shareholders incentives in monitoring innovating firms' activities.

In "intermediated systems" concentrated shareholdings and bank-firm participation are assumed to provide more incentives for monitoring, even though Stiglitz (1993) emphasises the simple argument that relevant agency costs are induced by bank-firm participation ("the bank may have an incentive to lend the firm funds to tide it over a short run shortage of funds").

With regard to the ability of spreading technological information and fostering technological spillovers, Dewatripoint-Maskin (1995) argue that centralised lenders have a higher relative ability in gathering information concerning their borrowers. Bhattacharya-Chiesa (1995) analyse the issue from a different perspective showing that it is the financial agreement structure, irrespective of the financial system in which it is determined, that may or may not support technological knowledge sharing. The two authors show that, in an environment where information is not verifiable so that interim knowledge cannot be licenced for a fee, an interim knowledge sharing commitment by innovating firms is time inconsistent even though it should be ex ante efficient. In this framework multilateral financing (one bank lending to multiple firms competing with each other) may be the appropriate commitment mechanism for promoting interim knowledge sharing, as it occurs in this case since it is in the lender's interest. The model does not ignore, though, that multilateral financing implies a trade-off between the described advantage and the free-rider problem generated by disclosure of property knowledge to a borrower's competitor.

Other direct comparisons in the relative capacity of the two systems to provide means for innovation financing are implicitly presented in papers analysing borrowers' choices between bank loans and direct debt financing on the market. Chan et al. (1990) suggest that, in the presence of unestablished management skills, venture capital is an option to be preferred both to bank loans and bond financing. According to other authors, bond financing (bank loans) should be preferred in case of good (bad) prospects for future profits (Rajan, 1992), low (high) credit risk (Berlin-Mester, 1992), established (unestablished) credit reputation (Diamond, 1990), severe (not severe) intrafirm incentive problems (Wilson, 1992).

Most of these considerations, together with the lack of reputation of the banking system, should explain why direct market financing, as a percentage of total sources in investment financing, is so much higher in fastly developing countries (between 20 percent and 30 percent in Thailand, Korea and Taiwan (Stiglitz, 1995)) than in industrialised countries (not higher than 5 percent in France, Germany, Japan, the UK and the US).

21

In order to check whether general considerations on the effectiveness of financial systems in supporting physical investment do apply to innovation and R&D investment, it is necessary to focus on the specificity of the latter type of investment. A main feature of innovation is the production of scientific knowledge which is generally a non excludable, non rivalrous public good, though it can be made excludable when patented. R&D and innovating returns usually occur with considerably longer lags compared with physical investment returns so that the delicate problem of interim stages of the investment process arises. In these stages immaterial intermediate research output can be hardly marketed (unless knowledge is publicly verifiable and then licenced for a fee) but can be appropriated by competitors if some form of disclosure occurs. This is why the traditional pecking order in signalling financing strategies may not hold. While for physical investment a convertible or bond plus equity warrant issue is a stronger signal than an equity issue and may be an optimal strategy for a good firm in order to avoid adverse selection and issue underpricing, for R&D investment the signalling benefit may be outweighted by costs of diclosing knowledge to competitors (Bhattacharya-Ritter, 1983)[9]. The other side of the problem is that, while interim knowledge disclosure has private costs, it also has social benefits as it generates positive spillovers increasing the innovating capacity of the system. In addition, given the ex ante uncertainty on the outcome of the race, an interim knowledge sharing commitment may be ex ante efficient, increasing R&D incentives for all competitors (Bhattacharya-Chiesa, 1995).

Differences in market structure between high-tech sectors and traditional sectors also need to be taken into account when analysing optimal financing schemes for innovation. A crucial feature is that while in traditional sectors with horizontal product differentiation new entries only reduce market share, in high-tech sectors with "vertical product differentiation" à la Shaked-Sutton new entries may eliminate some of the incumbents from the market when certain conditions on the quality of products and on the distribution of income are met. A higher risk of exit has obvious consequences in terms of a more prudent leverage structure.

Innovating races also generate particular incentive problems in intrafirm agreements. It is much easier to design efficient incentive schemes for a joint venture lasting until the final production stage, than for a research joint venture which stops at earlier stages before the realisation of output profits. How to avoid knowledge free riding when RJV members are lone racers at the final stage and how to compensate intermediate results when profits have still not materialised? A suggested solution is that of imposing large licencing fees for winners at the final stage if they received information at the earlier stage (Bhattacharya-Glazer-Sappington, 1991). Another distinguishing feature is that the informational asymmetry between financiers and R&D investors may be

22

more relevant than that between financiers and traditional investors given that the more complex technicalities of an R&D investment are more difficult to be fully understood by a financier. It is in the light of this that the optimal FI for innovation must then develop a financial and technological monitoring capacity more effectively than the traditional banking system does. This is particularly true when the FI has to ascertain the potential capacity of small innovators lacking collateral. The direction taken by "equity oriented" systems to solve the issue has been that of developing "venture capital" financial supply; while the direction taken by "bank oriented" systems has been that of reinforcing the long-term-type relationship between borrowers and banking lenders (Becchetti, 1995).

The greater success of "industrial venture capital" in supporting the most innovative phases of the product cycle (seed and start-up) shows that venture capital funds generated by spin-off from industries have an informational advantage over "bank venture capital funds" in terms of technological monitoring capacity and are then more competitive in financing innovation (Cavallo, 1995) when banks are not able to bridge their informational disadvantage in technological knowledge.

This probably shows that the exact nature of the informational asymmetry in innovation financing is given by market sector knowledge and by technological and scientific knowledge needed to evaluate the potential success of an innovation. "Bank oriented" and "equity oriented" systems will be effective in innovation financing to the extent to which they will be able to bridge this specific informational gap.

What seems to emerge from this survey of micro-theoretical literature is a clear need for a more direct comparative approach, directly focused on the issue of finance and innovation. This approach should be able to tackle some important issues: why have different countries generated different financial systems? Which FI are more effective in reducing "lemon problems"? How are existing national financing systems adapting spontaneously to face the challenge of financing high-risk innovating projects? Does an optimal "finance-innovation" system exist; and how does the idea of optimal organisational form depend on country fundamentals?

Some authors (Becchetti, 1995b) tried to provide a synthetic way to define the interaction between finance and innovation, considering the three "archetypal" forms of institutional interaction (German, Anglosaxon, Japanese). The idea is based on the presentation of a "technological area" in which many atomistic financial and innovating units exist and on the analysis of the dynamics of horizontal and vertical integration processes which represent these units' optimal response to the basic problems of interaction between entrepreneurial and financial risk (see Figure 2.2).

23

Real sector   **Financial sector**

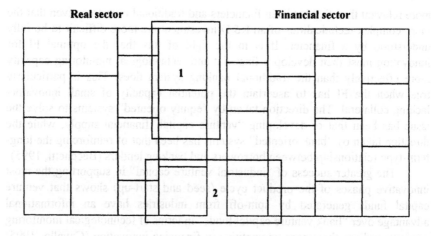

1. Vertical integration
2. Horizontal integration

Figure 1.2 Technological district structure

     The simplest version of the technological area assumes the existence of only two units: the first one is made by a venture capital unit financing risky and high-tech investments (unit F); the second one is made by a small innovating unit that has developed a project for a product or a process innovation and needs gradual financial support for the different phases of the technological cycle (unit I).

     In the model, the technology function of the system is defined as $T = f(a_F, a_I) f_1 > 0, f_2 > 0$. where the development of new product or process technologies relies on the effort of each unit and additional effort has the effect of increasing each unit ability to cope with technological innovation (a_F and a_I). In the model the profit functions (or the two agents' payoffs in the technological game) for the financier and the innovator are respectively: $V_I = g_I(T, a_I) g_{I1} > 0, g_{I2} > 0$ and $V_F = g_F = (T, a_F) g_{F1} > 0, g_{F2} > 0$ or $V_I = g_I(f(a_F, a_I), a_I)$ and $V_F = g_F = (f(a_F, a_I), a_F)$.

     In this kind of approach the "fundamentals" of each country (intended as country social and legal norms that affect internal and external transaction costs between and within units) may in fact determine the prevalence of the atomistic form (in the Anglo-Saxon case), of the horizontally integrated form (in the German case) and of the vertically integrated form (in the Japanese case). Among the legal norms the most important to be considered are for example legal "constraints" like antitrust legislation, rules on the separateness between the banking and the industrial systems, rules on reserve requirements of different intermediaries and on insider trading.

A further reflection on the basic problem may suggest two additional sources of the coordination failure problem, consistently with the approach of the existing literature (Tyebee-Vickery, 1988): i) the "small ticket problem", that is, the unwillingness of the financial unit to provide the innovating one with small amount financing, which is needed in the first phase of the innovating product cycle. The financial unit incurs fixed costs of project evaluation that require both financial and technical skills. Therefore, it can reach the break-even point only for an amount of financing larger than that required by the innovative firm in the first stage; ii) the "equity dilution syndrome", that is, the resistance of the innovating firm to the dilution of its capital and to the reduction of decisional power to the advantage of the financing unit. In this case, the lack of confidence between the two counterparts may lead to paradoxical results, such as agreements where the innovating unit is ready to provide the financial units with "preference shares", without decision power, but with a positive dividend differential in order not to lose its full control over the enterprise.

To fully analyse these two issues, the original model is successively extended to "N" financial and "M" real units. As a result, positive effects arising from Marshallian externalities in the technological area are offset by negative effects of competition for the "loser" (intended as the unit that is negatively affected by increased market competitiveness). In these cases, "weak spillovers" and "weak strategic complementarities" are likely to occur. Other extensions of the basic model can be considered, allowing for: i) creation and destruction of units; ii) partial opening to the market of international technology; ii) complete opening to the market of international technology. The main normative result that is likely to occur in this extension of the model is that, contrary to what happens in the initial two-unit model, a policy intervention may not easily achieve Pareto improvements as problems of losers' compensation occur.

A first solution to the problem is the endogenisation of the choice of the organizational form by firms that can choose between three options: atomistic form, horizontal integration, vertical integration. Every unit is now considered to be a firm whose production function has a managerial input and a labour input measured in terms of efficiency units. Net gains for managers and workers in switching from one form to another are presented and it is shown how historical forms of technological district organisation may have been influenced by country fundamentals, where the Japanese preference for integration with respect to Western countries may have been induced by: i) differences in legal constraints fixed by national laws on antitrust and bank-industry separateness; ii) higher

25

worker loyalty to a firm and a lower extent of rent-sharing in wage determination.

A second solution to the problem is the "thickening" of the TD through "spin-off" (the voluntary separation of workers from the original firm to create a new innovating unit) or the creation of a "captive unit" which autonomously develops innovative projects and whose capital is shared by parent companies. In this second solution the policy maker may play a role designing a system of fiscal incentives that may affect the process of creation of new units from a quantitative and from a qualitative point of view.

The informational problem between the two units is shown to have two consequences: a number of financing agreements lower than ought to be and an inefficient management of the agreements concluded[10].

Another model which may provide a useful benchmark for a comparative institutional microtheoretical approach to the relationship between finance, investments and innovation is that of Aighion-Tirole (1993). In this model the original "coordination failure" approach, based on two units (financier and innovator), is enlarged to three participants and a more detailed analysis of the interaction between research and development at industrial level is provided. In the model, the three units are: a Research Unit (RU) which has the innovating skills but no cash; a Customer (C) (alternatively a manufacturer, a user or a supplier of a complementary product) which may put its monetary and contractible or nonmonetary and noncontractible investment in the venture; and a cofinancer (F) which steps in if the amount of financing needed exceeds the financial capacity of the Customer. The "technology function" of the general model is in this case represented by a linear rule where the probability of achieving innovation is positively related to the efforts of the two basic units (RU and C). The model provides interesting insights into the coordination inefficiencies, addressing the crucial issue of property rights sharing among units: assuming that no cofinancing from a third unit is needed, property rights on the innovation are bargained ex ante between the two counterparts and the inputs of the process are: i) bargaining power ex ante and; ii) marginal efficiency of the two units' efforts in determining the innovation (the marginal effort of the customer may be more important if the innovative process requires a large amount of capital infrastructure, while the marginal effort of the research unit may be more important when such structure is not needed). The intermediate output of the bargaining process is the allocation of property rights which in turn determines the expected value of innovation affecting incentives of both units.

The inefficiency arises in the model when the distribution of the marginal efficiency of unit efforts is asymmetric with respect to their ex ante bargaining power. If, in other terms, the role of the Research Unit is determinant for the innovation but the ex ante bargaining power is entirely in the Customer's hands, the property rights may be allocated inefficiently because, if the Customer has the property rights, the incentives of the Research Unit are reduced[11].

The two authors also show that, if cofinancing is needed, another inefficiency may be added in that the cofinancier requires a stake in the expected profits and the equity dilution has the effect of furthermore reducing Research Unit incentives.

The interpretation of the model, in the light of the general framework described in this paper, is the following: a *weak cash constraint* of the Research Unit (the Customer's financial capacity is sufficient to cover Resarch Unit's investment expenditures) may reduce incentives to innovate for sectors where the owner of the capital infrastructure has more bargaining power than the innovator; a *strong cash constraint* (both Customer and Cofinancier are needed to finance the investment) may further reduce the incentive to innovate because of equity dilution.

What the two models presented in this section seem to suggest, from a normative point of view, is that a first decisive step toward the improvement of the relationship between investors and financiers may be: i) the creation of missing markets and ii) the thickening of existing ones. Point i) may be achieved through the development of a market of derivative products for innovation. Point ii) may be achieved through increased participation in the "technological district". This may be achieved by increasing the amount and the types of technology financing, thereby creating the necessary conditions for business venturing diffusion. Necessary prerequisites for this are the diffusion of closed-end investment funds and pension funds which are venture capitalists' main source of funds. Market thickening has also to be achieved, on the technological side, with fiscal incentives that can promote "spin-off" or creation of "captive units" by large innovative firms.

The increased number of participants in the market may help to reduce informational asymmetries that are the root of the interaction problem between financial and entrepreneurial risk. This general policy suggestion has the important peculiarity of being neutral with respect to the choice of the "archetypal form" of organisation.

4. The micro-empirical approach: comparative results and methodological problems

A major task of the "imperfect information" based empirical analysis on finance, investment and innovation is to demonstrate the existence of the positive cost differential between internal and external financing and to analyse whether the suggested solutions reduce such differential.

Some recent empirical analyses provide interesting results for costs' evaluation of informational asymmetries between financiers and investors. They may then provide a benchmark for the comparative performance of national financing systems in supporting investments and innovation: the two main tests surveyed here are the analyses of: i) liquidity constraints on firms' investments and; ii) average announcement effects of issues on firm market value. The first test aims at measuring the incidence of liquidity measures on firm investment plans and at demonstrating that (in the presence of cash constraints) the access to external finance is rationed or relatively more costly, and therefore negatively affects investment perspectives.

In this respect three main paths are followed for empirical estimation: i) direct estimation of an investment equation derived from first order conditions of a stochastic firm profit maximization. In such an equation the significance of cash flow in explaining investment is considered as a signal of the presence of financial costraints, while Tobin's q is used as a control regressor, (Srini-Vasan, 1986; Fazzari-Hubbard-Petersen, 1987; Gertler-Hubbard, 1988, for US firms; Devereux-Schiantarelli, 1989, for UK firms; Becchetti, 1994; Hoshi-Kashyap-Scharfstein, 1992; Hayashi-Inoue, 1988 for Japanese firms); ii) estimation of a Euler equation obtained combining two different first order conditions in the firm profit maximisation (with respect to investment and with respect to capital stock) to avoid the presence of Tobin's q as a regressor. Neoclassical irrelevance of finance in affecting investment implies a specification of the Euler equation where cash-flow is negative or not significant. Rejection of this specification with positive and significant effect of cash-flow on investment is interpreted as presence of financial constraints (Withed, 1992 and Bond-Meghir, 1994); iii) estimation of an investment equation as in method i) where Tobin's q is proxied by a VAR forecast of firm profit perspectives (Gilchrist-Himmelberg, 1995)[12].

In this field, some preliminary comparative considerations may be drawn: i) small firms appear to be more financially constrained both in Italy and in the UK; ii) Japanese firms seem to have, with respect to US, UK and Italian firms, a relatively more equal distribution of agency costs across different groups classified according to size, age and other relevant split variables (see results in chapter 3); iii) high-tech firms are less cash constrained than firms belonging to the traditional sector in some countries (Japan) but not in others (Italy) (see results in chapters 3 and 4).

Point i) is "structurally" justified by the observation that a project risk is run in financing small firms while only firm risk is run in financing large firms. It is also justified by the fact that large firms may have access to intragroup lending reducing their dependence on cash flow; point iii) shows that innovating firms are nonetheless constrained. It cannot be interpreted in the sense that innovative firms have less financing problems. It is in fact likely that high-tech firms require more independence from cash flows in investment plans than those firms belonging to traditional sectors, given that the time horizon of their investment is also longer. In this perspective the Italian case shows that, if neither long term relationship between financiers and investors (Japan), nor FI specialised in high-tech investment financing exist (UK), high-tech investors experience a cost differential between external and internal financing sources as compared with traditional investors.

These preliminary results may then suggest that: i) highly integrated systems (like the Japanese one) provide better resources to solve informational asymmetries between firms and that among less integrated systems (the US, the UK and Italy) (see also chapter six of this book); ii) imperfect information has more evident negative effects on those firms for which market information is scarce (newly quoted firms) (Devereaux-Schiantarelli, 1989; Fazzari-Hubbard-Petersen, 1987); iii) imperfect information may lead firms to operate a costly signalling strategy (as a high dividend policy).

In the evaluation of the results from the above mentioned empirical contributions, a question may be raised: do methodological problems, occurring in panel data methods usually chosen for these analyses, pose serious limits to the conclusions reached?

In this respect, the first problem to be considered is the presence of endogeneity among regressors. Given that cash flow and investment are probably simultaneously determined, liquidity proxies can be considered neither strictly nor weakly exogenous, and an instrumental variable estimation should be carried out. Endogeneity seems to affect some conclusions more than others. In fact, while it is very easy to reverse the causality assumption when we relate firms in less favourable financial conditions with relatively higher cash constraints, it is quite difficult to do the same when we relate cash constraints with firm size and firm "age" on the stock market. In this perspective, the positive relation between firm age and costs of external finance seems to be the strongest empirical support in favour of the imperfect information rationale.

From an econometric point of view the endogeneity problem imposes the adoption of more sophisticated techniques than a simple regression in levels. The Hoshi et al. (1988) objection that the dimension of bias might be the same in different subsamples cannot be applied to the endogeneity problem. This is because the bias may indeed vary across different subsamples and because, even if it does not, it can lead to the formulation of an erroneous conclusion on the relevance of liquidity constraints for groups whose coefficients are weakly significant[13]. In this respect, the approach followed by Devereaux-Schiantarelli (1989) to overcome this shortcoming seems more correct; that is, an estimate of the model in first differences with a dynamic specification using a GMM estimator and adopting as instruments the levels of the dependent and independent variables included in the equation.

Another serious threat to the validity of empirical tests on firm financial constraints based on dynamic specifications has been recently posed by Pesaran-Smith (1992). The two authors observe that fixed and random effects produce unbiased estimates only when regressors are strictly exogenous and when coefficients differ randomly and independently from the regressors between groups. If this does not occur the correct procedure should be the one of providing mean group estimators. The problem with this procedure is that it can be applied to "data fields" only, (panel with large T and large N). With the small T panel data available for micro-empirical tests on firm financial constraints, the possibility of using mean group estimators is precluded.

To overcome all these difficulties, the procedure to follow seems, therefore, to be that of testing the robustness of the results with respect to the different techniques adopted, comparing both static and dynamic specification and verifying if longitudinal estimates (when N is large) confirm coefficient differences between groups. An even better procedure would be that of checking results obtained from balance sheet panel data with direct tests of informational asymmetries which can be obtained by analysing qualitative firm responses on the issue. An approach of this kind will be followed in the fourth chapter dealing with an empirical analysis of informational asymmetries on a sample of about 4,000 Italian firms.

The second relevant field of empirical tests on imperfect information in corporate finance is that of the announcement effects of firm issues. For this second test as well, it is possible to draw some preliminary comparative conclusions on the basis of recent literature contributions. With regard to the US, empirical results seem to confirm the existence of a "signalling order" for firm financial issues : i) equity reaction to the announcement of convertible bond offering is around -1.5% (Dann-Mikkelson, 1994; Eckbo, 1986); ii) equity reaction to the announcement of stock offering, calculated with the same methodology, is around -3.5% (Asquith-Mullins, 1986; Masulis-Korvar, 1986; Mikkelson-Partch, 1986). With regard to Japan, some recent results (Kato-Schalleim, 1994) go in the opposite direction contradicting Myers-Majluf's conclusions and showing that announcement effects of equity issues may even generate positive changes in the issuers market value[14]. Is this another consequence of the "short-termist" hypothesis and of the Japanese system's better capacity of bridging the informational gap between investors and financiers?

Several methodological problems do not allow us to give a definite answer: the first problem is that equity effects mature at different times: at the announcement date and at the issue date. At the announcement date agents receive the "revealed" signal about firm financial conditions and react to it, but signal and reaction are not complete, given that full information about issue details will be known only on the date of issue.

In fact, high abnormal common stock returns before and after the announcement date may be justified by the same signalling models in the presence, respectively, of insider trading and of multiple announcements.

A rigorous control must be exerted on the presence of other important firm events occurring at the time of the announcement and at the date of issue. Moreover, the empirical analysis must be able to discriminate between the downward sloped demand rationale (Loderer et al., 1991) and the imperfect information rationale (Stein, 1992). In this respect, an estimate of equity changes connected with the announcement date and not with the date of issue seems more advisable.

In the light of all these considerations, a test of ex post cumulative abnormal common stock returns may circumvent insider trading, multiple announcements and announcement/issue date problems and may result to be the best way to check if ex post common stock performance corresponds to firm quality revealed through the financing strategy adopted (this approach will be followed in chapter 5 to test the signalling model on a sample of bond-cum-equity-warrant issuers).

To sum up, the contributions given by the micro-empirical sub-branch seem to show that *equity and bank oriented financial systems have different performances when measured through liquidity constraint and announcement effect tests*. Both tests need improved accuracy to solve some important methodological problems. In this perspective it is important to develop comparative empirical studies aimed at directly comparing intragroup results between different countries, once reasonably uniform data collection methods and estimating procedures are established[15].

5. The macro-theoretical and the macro-empirical approaches

Within macro-theoretical and macro-empirical approaches we consider models that, even though being microfounded, place particular emphasis on the aggregate consequences of agency costs in the relationship between financiers and investors.

On the macro-theoretical side, a seminal contribution by Bernanke-Gertler (1987) presents a "market oriented" model where coalitions of internal and external financiers are endogenously determined. In this model conditions establishing the optimality of intermediated finance in Diamond (1984) are reversed because auditing results are public information and external lenders can

31

commit themselves in advance to sharing auditing costs. The equilibrium level of investment profitability and interest rate in the model is a function of auditing costs, hazard rate and of the marginal cost of becoming an internal financier. In such a model, changes in interest rates and in per capita saving may generate business cycle fluctuation affecting the ratio between inside and outside finance, and, then, bankruptcy costs via changes in the hazard rate. An important insight of the model is that the "informational paradox" of financial systems is represented in a new original way. If information is expensive its costs can never be completely eliminated as gains from information gathering (gains from becoming an "informed trader" in the Grossman-Stiglitz (1980) model and gains from becoming an internal financier in the Bernanke-Gertler (1987) model decrease when gathering information is less costly.

If the interaction between agents with more and less information may then create robust fluctuations and financial crises with serious real effects in "market oriented" systems, in times of business cycle fluctuations the fragility of "intermediated systems" has been clearly evidenced by the "credit view" literature. In "intermediated" systems with: i) weak substitutability of bonds with bank debt as external financing; ii) real or nominal price rigidities; and iii) scarce autonomy of commercial banks from the Central bank; credit crunches in times of restrictive monetary policies have strong real effects (Kashyap-Lamont-Stein, 1993). These crunches are likely to have asymmetric effects on firms when informational asymmetries are a negative function of firm size and age (Gertler-Gilchrist, 1993).

Credit view models then implicitly suggest what may be the positive effects from the integration of "market oriented" and "intermediated" systems, if we consider that a development of financial markets might increase substitutability between bank debt and other forms of external financing for firms and might increase the capacity of banks to issue reserve-free liabilities.

All these models focus on the cyclical effects of the relationship between finance and innovation without directly referring to the growth issue.

Other contributions follow the endogenous growth approach that replaces the exogenous technological progress with a self-sustaining growth relying on Marshallian externalities or on non decreasing returns in the accumulated production factor. With endogenous growth, financial intermediation may be shown to have not only level but also growth effects. In the King-Levine (1992) model, for example, FI have four crucial roles: i) pooling funds, ii) evaluating entrepreneurs, iii) diversifying risk and iv) rating expected profits from innovative activities. In this way they not only affect the level of saving, but also the rate of growth. In the Saint Paul model (1992), the existence of strategic complementarity between financial markets and technology (both are instruments that can be used for diversification) allows entrepreneurs to spread risk through financial diversification and to choose riskier and more profitable technologies. Without financial markets entrepreneurs can limit risk only by choosing less specialised and less productive technologies.

On the macro-empirical side, tests on the asymmetric effects of restrictive monetary policies under the credit view hypothesis showed that firms with more financial constraints seem to be more affected by credit crunches (Gertler-Gilchrist, 1993). The problem, however, is that the division between financially constrained and unconstrained firms is exogenously determined by using the dimensional variable and is not estimated in the sample.

The first attempts to test for the correlation between growth and finance come from Goldsmith (1969), McKinnon (1973) and Shaw (1973), who find a positive correlation between the rate of growth and the degree of financial intermediation. These early contributions leave two questions unsolved: the causality direction of the relationship and the effects of financial development on efficiency or, merely, on the rate of investment. Here too, the endogeneity problem makes it difficult to establish whether the contemporaneous correlation between financial and real variables has to be interpreted as a positive role played by FI in stimulating investment and growth or, according to the real business cycle explanation (Long-Plosser, 1983), as the financial system's endogenous response which "catches up" on the development of the real sector of the economy.

The other main problem of this literature is that it considers the role of financial institutions as largely passive treating them generally as perfect competitors. But financial markets are actually imperfectly competitive and ridden with agency costs, as Stiglitz (1995) clearly points out, focusing on the public good features of information and monitoring and providing several examples of externalities, moral hazard and adverse selection existing in these markets. Given these considerations, the relevant issue in the relationship between finance and growth is whether financial repression and directed market credit may reduce market failures increasing growth (even if at the price of a reduction of the total amount of credit available) or whether this result is simply obtained through financial deepening and reliance on market mechanisms.

The rationale for not considering financial repression always a negative phenomenon is that (in a perfectly competitive framework) low interest rates may reduce savings and inhibit economic growth, but in an imperfectly competitive environment with information costs, they may reduce adverse selection and moral hazard effects, thereby improving the quality of borrowers.

Directed credit may, on the other hand, allocate more resources to high-tech sectors where social returns of the projects, which include knowledge accumulation, are higher than private returns. This will lead, in these sectors, to a decrease of underinvestment resulting from unregulated financial markets. The problem with government intervention, however, lies in the fact that regulatory standards are based on subjective assessments of crucial variables (such as risks and premiums), while market pricing mechanisms provide a more "objective" assessment of them.

Even though government intervention may be beneficial in redressing market failure affecting the relationship between finance and growth, it always involves the risk of misjudgement and also corruption.

Several empirical papers have tried to test the relative validity of these different rationales in order to identify the aggregate relationship between finance and growth. Recent works like those of King-Levine (1993) and of Roubini-Sala-y-Martin (1991) apply causality tests to the relationship using several controls related to fiscal policy, monetary policy and human capital variables. The indicators of financial development used are quite aggregated (ratio of credit to GDP, ratio of deposit bank domestic assets to the sum of deposit bank and Central Bank domestic assets, real interest rate as a measure of financial distortion) and cannot point out the different contributions of financial intermediaries to growth. The macro approach to the interaction between finance and innovation proposed by Jovanovic (1993) provides evidence, from the aggregate point of view, of the effects of finance on the real sector.

This approach follows the Greenwood-Jovanovic (1990) assumption that "the greater the amount of intermediation, the greater the efficiency with which the capital stock is allocated". Financial intermediaries have, with respect to normal lenders, the advantage of possessing more general information about general business conditions and are, consequently, better judges of the profitability of investment proposals.

Overall, the Jovanovic approach, while providing a clear-cut ranking of countries where finance and technological developments seem to be strongly correlated, suffers from the obvious shortcoming of not being adequately microfounded. It has, nonetheless, the usefulness of an "aerial view" that shows the main features of the phenomenon and stimulates a more detailed lower scale analysis which would bring into focus the complex risk analysis and asymmetric information consequences of the individual relation between a financier and an innovator.

A further interesting response to this objection and to the above mentioned one (the objection of input elasticity sectorial invariance) is that of estimating sectorial TFP to check if financial development has relevant effects on sectorial innovation. Jovanovic performs this kind of analysis using sectorial TFP data from a cross-country productivity study by Wolff (1993) and Costello (1993). This analysis shows the existence of a positive relationship in almost all sectors. The limit of all these macro empirical results seems to be that they merely demonstrate, in a very general way, the link between the two sectors, without

34

solving at all the difficult task of defining a good proxy to measure the degree of country financial development.

6. Conclusions and normative suggestions

The chapter provides a critical evaluation of the literature on finance, investment and innovation and suggests insights for a new comparative research method for evaluating the comparative performance of financial systems in supporting innovation.

The survey on microtheoretical contributions describes the asymmetric information problem between investors and financiers and the role of financial intermediaries in reducing this asymmetry and shows that country specific features of financial systems for investment and innovation financing are nonneutral with respect to the solution of the problem.

Opinions on the relative effectiveness of the two "archetypal structures" of financial systems (the "market oriented" and the "intermediated") are mixed. Intermediaries may reduce monitor free-riding problems of individual lenders and may avoid "short termism" by creating long-term relationships with borrowers (but close integration between intermediaries and firms may generate severe agency costs). They may also guarantee the secrecy of information on interim values on high-tech project thereby increasing incentives for long term investment on innovation (Bhattacharya-Chiesa, 1995).

The effectiveness of "market oriented systems", on the other hand, may be understated. The market for corporate control, not only provides alternative forms of monitoring and control on managers' activities, but is also an important source of internal funds for managers. In addition, even though it is argued that multilateral banking may promote information sharing (and then technological spillovers) between firms, it seems that the diffusion of information and better opportunities for mergers and acquisitions are a comparative advantage of "market oriented" systems.

The microempirical survey analyses the results of liquidity constraints and average announcement effects of equity/bond issues as tests on the relative performance of national financial systems. These results seem to confirm that "bank oriented" systems have an informational comparative advantage over "equity oriented" systems. The survey also stresses which methodological problems have to be solved in order to improve the quality of comparative analyses.

The survey on aggregate empirical papers shows that these types of contributions do not seem to solve interpretational ambiguities related to the endogeneity problem and to the direction of the causality links between finance and innovation, or the monetary and the real sector. With regard to the comparative evaluation of financial systems, it appears that both of them possess inherent causes of fragility ("market oriented" systems are more exposed to financial crises generated by the interaction of agents having different informational sets, while "intermediated systems" amplify the real effects of monetary restrictions through the "credit view"). An implicit suggestion of these models is that the integration of the two systems may partially solve at least the "credit view" problem.

As a conclusion, this survey points out three main paths among the less explored in the literature on finance, investment and innovation. These paths are represented by: i) theoretical analyses of informational asymmetries and coordination failures between investors and financiers in case of venture capital financing (the problem of informational asymmetries between investors and financiers in case of bank and stock market financing being widely explored by the existing literature); ii) comparative empirical analyses of financial constraints on firm investments (with the opportunity of comparing the relative efficiency of different country systems of innovation and investment financing); iii) direct tests on firm financial constraints based on qualitative data which may be used to check traditional results from traditional indirect tests on financial constraints (based on balance sheet data); iv) the effect of particular forms of market financing that may be of particular help for supporting innovation. The aim of the following chapters of this book is then that of proposing contributions in the four indicated directions.

Table 1.1a Summary features of corporate governance and industrial structure in selected OECD countries

	Italy	United States	Japan	Germany
Corporate governance				
Ownership and control patterns				
Ownership concentration	High	Low	Low	High
Separation ownership/control	Weak	Strong	Weak	Weak
Constraints on bank ownership	Strong	Strong	Weak	Very Weak
Dominant control model				
Cross-shareholdings	Large	Small	Large	Medium
Inter-group	Large	-	Small	Medium
Intra-group	Large	-	Large	Small
Corporate monitoring				
Board composition	Insider	Mixed	Insider	Insider
Large shareholders	Yes	No	Yes	Yes
Other stakeholders	No	No	Yes	Yes
Board power over management	High	Low	Medium	High
Independence of management	Low	High	Low	Low
Public disclosure requirements	Medium		Medium	Low
Role of financial intermediaries	Low	Low	High	High
Role of stock market	Low	High	Low	Low
Corporate financial patterns				
Self-finance	Medium	High	Low	Medium
Leverage	High	Low	High	Medium
Industrial structure				
Sectors of specialisation	Cap. Int.	R&D Int.	R&D Int.	Cap. Int.
	Labour Int.	Cap. Int.	Cap. Int.	R&D Int.
Average firm size	Small	Large	Small	Large
Diffusion of business groups	High	Low	High	Medium
Producer/supplier relationship				
Employer/employee relationship	Medium-term	Short-term	Long-term	Long-term
R&D intensity	Low	High	High	Medium
Internationalisation of firms	Low	High	Medium	Medium

Source: OECD Country Profiles: Italy (1995) and Germany (1995).

37

Table 1.1b Summary features of financial structure in selected OECD countries

	Italy	United States	France	UK	Japan	Germany
Banking system efficiency (spread between lending and deposit rates)	7.3	2	10	7	4.5	3.4
Banking system internationalisation (cross-border deposits from non residents/national deposits)	1.3	4	28.3	35	4	6
Stock market capitalisation (market value of listed domestic firms as percentage of GDP)	15	66	37	129	68	21
Foreign firm participation to stock exchange:	2	6.6	45	26	6	34
Market value of bonds listed by domestic private sector	4	215	117	182	159	767
Amount of new capital raised by domestic companies (billlion US dollars)	10	102	21	26	7	9
Legal restraints on banks' large credit exposure (maximum share of capital of individual borrower)	100	15	Informal	Informal	30	50
Legal and regulatory constraints on institutional shareholdings for:						

Table 1.1b (con't) Summary features of financial structure in selected OECD countries

a) commercial banks stock ownership	Prohibited prior to 1993	Prohibited or passive under FRB approval	---	May be discouraged on prudential grounds	up to 5%	No restrictions
b) mutual fund stock ownership	No more than 5%	Tax penalties if it exceeds 10%	--	Large stakes not allowed	--	No more than 5%
c) Life insurance companies stock ownership	Up to 5% of firm stock	Up to 2% securities and 20% equities	--	Self imposed limits stemming from fiduciary liquidity requirements	--	No more than 20% of firm's equities

Source: author working of OECD data.

39

Table 1.1c Summary features of state support to small-medium firm investment and innovation in selected OECD countries

France
- Programme for the promotion of the use of electronic components (PUCE). Services provided include: financial support, technical verification, special training for the execution of a project, market study to match expected performance with customer requirements, commercial launch of the final prototype. - Programme for the promotion of the use of advanced materials (PUMA). Services provided include: financial support, design of a new product, modernisation and improvement of an existing product, studies and projects related to the introduction of advanced materials. - Programme for the improvement of computer data management and circulation in the enterprise (LOGIC). Services provided include: financial support for liaison engineering in the industrial field and related studies. In 1992 direct aid totalled FF 90 million.

Germany
- Programme of management consultancy for small-medium firms. Services provided include: financial support for business start-up with a government share of 60 percent with a maximum of DM 3000; general business and innovation consultancies. In 1992 the programme funded 24,300 consultancies with an average subsidy level around 2,800 per consultation.

Italy
- Law 46/82 for Research and Innovation support. This law provides a soft grant covering from 35% to 70% of total investment costs. The rate is 40-50% lower than the market rate for small medium firms and 75% lower than the market rate for firms in the South. Law 1329/65 (Law Sabatini for small-medium firms). It provides soft loans for leasing or purchase of investment goods by small-medium firms up to a maximum of 3 billion liras. - Law 949/52 provides medium-long term soft loans refinancing of bank credit for small-medium firm innovative investments. - Italian intervention has very little focus on monitoring and evaluation of programme results and on advisory and consultancy services to investing firms. Selection of subsidy recipient is not always efficient and long delays occur between selection of recipients and effective provision of subsidies.

Japan
- Assistance for equipment organisation: MITI support to local governments providing loans for equipment modernisation. - Special tax deduction for electronic equipment purchases: 7 percent tax credit or 30 percent depreciation on advanced manufacturing equipment. - Vocational training: premiums collected from employers and employees support wage costs of SME employees on external vocational training courses.

United Kingdom
- Enterprise Initiative (EI) launched by the Department of Trade and Industry including a package of advice and guidance to firms with less than 500 employees. The services include: access to collaborative research projects, information about technological developments, links with local schools, universities and polytechnics. The program is continuously implemented according to feedback form periodical monitoring and evaluation initiatives. The program is delivered through the private sector and does not include the provision of state subsidies or the utilisation of public sector consultants.

Table 1.1c (con't) Summary features of state support to small-medium firm investment and innovation in selected OECD countries

United States
Several federal and state programmes to modernise manufacturing exist. Services provided include: technology assistance to small-medium sized entreprises, "incubators" to provide office and laboratory space for start-up companies below market rates; research parks (grouping of technology based companies to encourage university-private company relationship); seed capital (often in the form of grants for research and product development for projects in the early stages). Most relevant programs are Manufacturing Technology Center (MTC) programs (each of them costs approximately $6 million per year from Federal, State and industry source. Other relevant local program experiences have been: Ohio Technology Transfer Organisation (OTTO), Centre for Innovative Technology (CIT) in Virginia, the Technology Extension Service (TES) in Georgia, Industrial Technology Extension Service (ITES).

Source: OECD "Boosting businesses", 1995.

Table 1.2 Taxonomy of the literature on finance and innovation

Research sub-branch	Hypotheses and methodologies	Questions asked	Main contributions
Micro-theoretical	Imperfect information is the cause of the unequal distribution of agency costs among firms. Cost differential between internal and external finance and cash constraints reduce quality and quantity of project financed	i) Is there a cost differential between internal and external finance? ii) Which is the role of FI in the reduction of informational asymmetries? iii) How are different financial systems effective in reducing the informational problem? iv) Which form of national interaction between FI and innovating entrepreneurs is the optimal one?	Aighion-Tirole (1993), Allen-Gale (1995), Bhattacharya-Thakor (1995), Bhattacharya-Chiesa (1995), Boyd-Prescott (1986), Dewatripoint-Miskin (1995), Diamond (1984), Harris-Raviv (1991), Jensen-Meckling (1987), Leland-Pyle (1977), Myers-Mayluf (1984), Short (1994), Stiglitz-Weiss (1981)
Micro-empirical	i) Tests of investment sensitivity to cash-flow on panel data (techniques adopted: one way, two way, fixed effects, random effect, instrumental variable with GMM, mean group estimators) ii) estimation of equity price effects in connection with of the announcement date or of the issue date of firm straight bonds, convertible bonds or equity	i) Are long term investment plans constrained by liquidity? ii) How may the endogeneity problem in estimating the effects of liquidity on investment be solved? iii) Does equity price fall in connection with changes of new firm issues because of imperfect information of simply because of downward sloping equity demand? iv) Are high-tech firms more constrained than firms in traditional sectors? v) Are some national "finance-innovation" systems more effective than others in relaxing financial constraints?	Asquith-Mullins (1986), Asquith-Mullins (1991), Atella (1993), Atzeni (1993), Becchetti (1993), Dann-Mikkelson (1984), Devereaux-Schiantarelli (1989), Eckbo (1986), Fazzari-Hubbard-Petersen (1988), Gertler-Hubbard (1988), Hayashi-Inoue (1988) Hoshi-Kashyap-Sharfstein (1988), Hubbard-Kashyap (1992), Klemkosky-Maness, (1980), Loderer-Cooney- van Drunen (1991), Masulis-Korwar (1986), Mikkelson-Partch (1986)

Table 1.2 (con't) Taxonomy of the literature on finance and innovation

Macro-theoretical (microfounded but paying particular attention to aggregate effects)	Endogenous growth models. FI pool funds and select good investment	How do business cycle movements affect and how are they affected by the interaction between investors and financiers in "market oriented" and in "intermediated" systems? Do financial intermediaries affect the rate of growth? Which are the relative fragilities of the two systems eventually leading to financial crises?	Bencivenga-Smith (1991), Bernanke-Gertler (1987), Greenwood-Jovanovic (1990), King-Levine (1993), Kashyap-Lamont-Stein (1993), Roubini-Sala-y-Martin (1991 and 1992).
Macro-empirical	Correlation between growth and financial indicators on cross-country data (schooling and measures of fiscal, monetary and trade performance used as controls)	Are more financially constrained firms more affected by credit crunches? Is there a causality link between the degree of financial development and the rate of growth?	Atje-Jovanovic (1992), Jovanovic (1992), Gertler-Gilchrist (1993), Goldsmith (1969), Jappelli-Pagano (1992), King-Levine (1992), McKinnon (1973), Shaw (1973), Roubini-Sala-y-Martin (1991).

Table 1.3 Percentage of Business Enterprise R&D expenditures financed by government (1988-1993)

	Japan	Germany	US	France	UK	Italy
1988	1.5	11.4	31.3	20.8	17	18.9
1989	1.2	11	28	19.3	17.2	16.3
1990	1.3	10.7	25.6	19.8	16.7	19.3
1991	1.4	10	22.5	22.3	14.6	11.8
1992	1.1	9.8	20.8	18.3	13.8	9.9
1993	1.4	9.2	19.3	16.6	12.4	10.2

Source: OECD

Table 1.4 Percentage of Business Enterprise R&D expenditures financed abroad(1988-1993)

	Japan	Germany	US	France	UK	Italy
1988	0.1	2.1	0	9.2	12	6.6
1989	0.1	2.7	0	10.9	13.4	6.5
1990	0.1	2.7	0	11.1	15.5	7.3
1991	0.1	2.6	0	11.4	16	8.6
1992	0.1	2.7	0	12	15	5.4
1993	0.1	2.9	0	11.3	15.4	6

Source: OECD.

Table 1.5 Net financing of private physical investment by national flow of funds data (percentage on overall net financing) (1970-1985)

	UK	US	France	Germany	Japan
Retentions	107	90	62	73	65
Loans, deposits and short term securities	5	26	37	12	42
Trade credit	-2	-1	-1	-3	-10
Bonds	-2	12	1	-2	1
Shares	-4	-3	5	1	4

Source: Mayer (1985).

Table 1.6 OECD flow of funds from company accounts data: (a) France

	80-82	81-83	82-84	83-85	84-86	85-87	86-88	87-89	88-90	89-91	90-92
PHINV/TOTINV	0.64	0.58	0.56	0.57	0.55	0.52	0.44	0.42	0.43	0.49	0.58
IF/ PHINV	0.53	0.55	0.62	0.72	0.87	1.10	1.36	1.49	1.47	1.39	1.24
STD/PHINV	0.33	0.31	0.25	0.17	0.08	-0.08	-0.21	-0.34	-0.27	-0.18	-0.05
TR/PHINV	0.14	0.12	0.13	0.11	0.07	0.01	-0.07	-0.10	-0.07	0.01	0.04
LTD/PHINV	0.14	0.14	0.13	0.12	0.05	-0.02	-0.15	-0.16	-0.20	-0.21	-0.19
BOND/PHINV	0.01	0.02	0.01	0.01	0.01	0.02	0.00	0.00	-0.01	-0.01	-0.01
PHINV											
SHARES/PHINV	0.03	0.03	0.04	0.05	0.02	-0.08	-0.15	-0.19	-0.13	-0.17	-0.12
PHINV											
LTBA/PHINV	0.10	0.09	0.08	0.06	0.03	0.04	-0.01	0.03	-0.06	-0.03	-0.06
PHINV											

Variable legend for OECD statistics:
PHINV = Investment in tangible fixed assets + investment in intangible nonfinancial assets. TOTINV = PHINV + investment in financial assets. IF: Gross income finance (including depreciation and provisions). STD: increase in short term debt (increase in short term borrowing from banks, others, increase in trade credits received, increase in accounts payable). TR: increase in trade credits received. STBA: increase in short term borrowing from banks. LTD: increase in long term debt (issues of long term bonds, issues of shares, increase in long term borrowing from banks and from others). BOND: issues of long term bonds. SHARES: issues of shares.

1.6(b) United Kingdom

	81-92 Avg	81-83	82-84	83-85	84-86	85-87	86-88	87-89	88-90	89-91	90-92
PHINV/TOTINV	0.77	0.63	0.66	0.68	0.70	0.73	0.76	0.79	0.90	0.94	1.09
IF/ PHINV	0.77	1.02	0.93	0.97	0.88	0.86	0.72	0.63	0.57	0.55	0.59
STD/PHINV	0.15	-0.04	0.05	-0.02	0.05	0.05	0.21	0.29	0.31	0.29	0.18
TR/PHINV	0.00	0.00	0.00	0.00	0.00	0.00	0.00	0.00	0.00	0.00	0.00
STBA/PHINV	0.15	-0.03	0.00	0.18	0.21	0.17	0.05	0.11	0.23	0.26	0.31
LTD/PHINV	0.08	0.02	0.02	0.05	0.07	0.09	0.06	0.08	0.12	0.16	0.22
BOND/PHINV	-0.06	-0.03	-0.01	-0.47	-0.44	-0.38	0.13	0.13	0.24	0.30	0.51
SHARES/PHINV	0.03	-0.03	-0.02	-0.01	0.00	0.01	0.02	0.03	0.08	0.10	0.15
LTBA/PHINV	0.11	0.08	0.04	0.53	0.50	0.46	-0.08	-0.08	-0.19	-0.23	-0.44
PHINV											

1.6(c) Japan

	81-92 Avg	81-83	82-84	83-85	84-86	85-87	86-88	87-89	88-90	89-91	90-92
PHINV/TOTINV	0.77	0.49	0.58	0.62	0.68	0.62	0.57	0.51	0.60	0.73	0.98
TOTINV											
IF/ PHINV	0.90	0.89	0.88	0.86	0.93	1.05	1.08	0.96	0.83	0.76	0.78
STD/PHINV	0.18	0.07	0.09	0.08	0.10	0.04	0.04	0.04	0.08	0.06	0.53
PHINV											
TR/PHINV	0.15	0.04	0.04	0.02	0.05	0.02	0.03	0.01	0.05	0.00	0.48
STBA/PHINV	0.03	0.04	0.05	0.06	0.05	0.02	0.01	0.02	0.03	0.06	0.05
LTD/PHINV	-0.08	0.04	0.03	0.06	-0.03	-0.10	-0.12	0.01	0.10	0.18	-0.32
BOND/PHINV	0.06	0.01	0.01	0.02	-0.01	-0.03	-0.04	0.00	0.03	0.05	0.21
SHARES/PHINV	-0.01	0.01	0.02	0.03	0.01	-0.04	-0.04	-0.01	0.04	0.05	-0.06
LTBA/PHINV	-0.13	0.02	-0.01	0.01	-0.03	-0.03	-0.04	0.01	0.03	0.09	-0.47
PHINV											

1.6(d) Italy

	80-92 Avg	81-83	82-84	83-85	84-86	85-87	86-88	87-89	88-90	89-91	90-92
PHINV/TOTINV	0.59	0.55	0.54	0.55	0.59	0.60	0.61	0.60	0.59	0.58	0.60
IF/ PHINV	0.88	0.60	0.68	0.86	0.95	0.97	0.94	0.87	0.84	0.85	0.84
STD/TOTINV	0.08	0.17	0.14	0.07	0.03	0.02	0.05	0.10	0.12	0.10	0.11
TR/PHINV	0.04	0.10	0.08	0.05	0.02	0.01	0.03	0.05	0.06	0.05	0.05
STBA/PHINV	0.01	0.01	0.02	0.01	0.01	0.00	0.01	0.02	0.03	0.02	0.03
LTD/PHINV	0.04	0.23	0.18	0.07	0.03	0.01	0.01	0.03	0.05	0.05	0.05
BOND/TOTINV PHINV	0.01	0.04	0.03	0.01	0.00	0.00	0.00	0.00	0.00	0.00	0.00
SHARES/TOTINV	0.01	0.11	0.09	0.04	0.01	0.01	0.01	0.02	0.02	0.02	0.02
LTBA/TOTINV PHINV	0.03	0.08	0.06	0.02	0.01	0.00	0.00	0.02	0.03	0.03	0.03

1.6(e) United States

	79-92 Avg	79-81	80-82	81-83	82-84	83-85	84-86	85-87	86-88	87-89	88-90	89-91	90-92
PHINV/TOTINV	0.78	0.72	0.78	0.78	0.79	0.78	0.77	0.76	0.73	0.76	0.77	0.82	0.82
IF/ PHINV	0.99	0.78	0.80	0.87	0.90	0.92	0.91	0.98	1.00	1.01	1.01	1.05	1.21
STD/PHINV PHINV	0.07	0.12	0.09	0.06	0.06	0.05	0.05	0.01	0.00	0.00	0.00	0.22	0.17
TR/PHINV	0.00	0.06	0.04	0.02	0.02	0.02	0.02	0.00	0.00	0.00	-0.01	-0.02	-0.06
STBA/PHINV	0.05	0.03	0.04	0.03	0.03	0.01	0.01	0.00	0.00	0.00	0.00	0.18	0.19
LTD/PHINV	-0.06	0.10	0.10	0.07	0.05	0.03	0.04	0.01	0.00	-0.01	-0.01	-0.27	-0.38
BOND/PHINV	-0.03	0.05	0.06	0.04	0.05	0.04	0.05	0.02	0.00	-0.01	-0.01	-0.14	-0.22
SHARES/PHINV	-0.02	0.02	0.02	0.01	-0.01	-0.03	-0.04	-0.01	0.00	0.00	0.00	-0.04	-0.08

1.6(f) Germany

	78-80 Avg	79-81	80-82	81-83	82-84	83-85	84-86	85-87	86-88	87-89	88-90	89-91	90-92
PHIS INV. ON TOT INV.	0.74	0.75	0.83	0.79	0.76	0.71	0.75	0.79	0.79	0.74	0.70	0.67	0.67
AUTOF./FISIC. INV.	1.01	0.83	0.91	1.06	1.18	1.17	1.18	1.15	1.08	0.95	0.90	0.93	0.95
STD/PHIS INV.	-0.01	0.17	0.09	-0.06	-0.18	-0.17	-0.18	-0.15	-0.08	0.05	0.10	0.07	0.05

Table 1.7a Sector disaggregated indicators of internal and external finance by company flow of funds data (UK - average values 1986-1995)

	PHARM	AER	CHMMT	CHMSP	ELETR	TOTMK
ATPN2/TNFA	1.70	0.59	0.68	0.84	0.83	0.62
ATPN2/ INP	1.72	0.69	0.93	1.09	0.96	0.86
ATPN2/ INP+I	1.65	0.63	0.75	0.64	0.65	0.53
Equity/ TFA*(1-ATPN2/TNFA)	-0.05	0.06	0.12	0.11	0.03	0.06
Loan/ TFA*(1-ATPN2/TNFA)	0.10	0.06	0.08	0.01	0	0.05
Others/ TFA*(1-ATPN2/TNFA)	-0.76	0.30	0.12	0.05	0.15	0.28

Source: author's working of Datastream data.

Variable legend for Datastream statistics

TNFA: fixed asset purchased including asset purchased by subsidiaries. ATPN2: PTPG - company published charge for taxation net of tax inflows caused by claims and overpayments. INP = investments purchased. INP+I = investments plus intangible purchased. Equity/---: equity issued for cash plus equity issued for acquisition as a percentage of total financial sources times the percentage of the relevant measure of investment (TNFA, NFA, NFA+I, INP,INP+I) uncovered by internal finance. Loan/---: loans issued minus loans repaid during the year as a percentage of total financial sources times the percentage of the relevant measure of investment (TNFA, NFA, NFA+I,INP,INP+I) uncovered by internal finance.

Others/---: percentage of the relevant measure of investment (TNFA, NFA, NFA+I) uncovered by internal finance, equity or loans. It includes other forms of financial sources (total financial sources - equity - loans) such as long term provisions and other deferred liabilities.

PHARM--: Aggregate flow of funds for the Pharmaceutical sector for companies listed in the domestic market. AER--: Aggregate flow of funds for the Engineering-Aerospace sector companies listed in the domestic market. CHMMT--: Aggregate flow of funds for the Chemicals-technological materials sector for companies listed in the domestic market. CHMSP--: Aggregate flow of funds for the Chemicals-special ... sector for companies listed in the domestic market. ELETR--: Aggregate flow of funds for the Electronic Equipment sector for companies listed in the domestic market. TOTMK--: Aggregate flow of funds for all the companies listed in the domestic market.

Table 1.7b Sector disaggregated indicators of internal and external finance by company flow of funds data (France - average values 1986-1995)

	TOTMK	PHARM	AER	ELETR
	0.47	0.80	0.60	0.50
ATPN2/ INP	0.74	0.85	18.57	0.50
ATPN2/ INP+I	0.68	0.77	5.35	0.50
Equity/ TFA*(1-ATPN2/TNFA)	0.08	0.02	0.00	0.07
Loan/ TFA*(1-ATPN2/TNFA)	0.08	0.02	0.04	0.02
Others/ TFA*(1-ATPN2/TNFA)	0.31	0.15	0.33	0.39
RES/ TFA*(1-ATPN2/TNFA)	0.06	0.02	0.04	0.02

Table 1.7c Sector disaggregated indicators of internal and external finance by company flow of funds data (USA- average values 1986-1995)

	TOTMK	PHARM	ELETR	CHMSP	CHMMT	AERSP
ATPN2[a]/TNFA	0.30	0.94	0.18	0.11	0.46	0.51
Equity/ TFA*(1-ATPN2/TNFA)	-0.04	-0.09	0.01	-0.23	-0.02	-0.04
Loan/ TFA*(1-ATPN2/TNFA)	0.01	0.02	-0.04	-0.39	-0.04	0.16
Others/ TFA*(1-ATPN2/TNFA)	0.73	0.09	0.63	2.08	0.73	0.37

a: does not include associates' profits.

Table 1.7d Sector disaggregated indicators of internal and external finance by company flow of funds data (Japan - average values 1986-1994)

	TOTMK	PHARM	ELETR	CHMSP	CHMMT
RET EARN/TOTINV	0.13	0.35	0.43	0.18	0.19
PTPR/TOTINV	0.63	1.63	1.76	0.73	0.69
STL/(PTPR-TOTINV)*(1-PTPR/TOTINV)	0.04	--	0.42	--	--
LTL/(PTPR-TOTINV)*(1-PTPR/TOTINV)	0.02	--	0.20	--	--
TTL/(PTPR-TOTINV)*(1-PTPR/TOTINV)	0.68	0.33	0.67	0.55	0.33

Table 1.8 US Firms engaged in biotechnology research with equity warrants listed (1992)

Allou Health and Beauty	Centocor
Bamberger Polymers	Interneuron
Epigen	Lidak Pharmaceuticals
Alpha 1 Biomedicals	Nova Pharmaceuticals
American Biomed Inc	SciClone
Chemex Pharmaceuticals	Somanetics
Cortex Pharmaceuticals	Technology Research
Cybernetics Products	Vital Living Products
Deprenyl USA	ENVIR
Enazon	Fountaint Pharmaceuticals
Applied Microbiology	Genetics Institute
Bio-Dyne Corp	Genzyme
Biogen	Immunex
Medarex	Staodyn
Protein Polymere Technologies	VIMRx Pharmaceuticals
Senetek	International Murex
Bradley Pharmaceutical	

Source: Investors Bulletin Warrants Survey, 14 May 1992.

Table 1.9 Japanese firms engaged in biotechnology research with equity warrant listed (1980-1992)

Firm	Size of research staff	Kind of research	Estimated bio-tech related sales as a % of the total sales in the year 2000
Ebara (Engineering)	10	Research on waste-water treatment equipment; use of activated sludge	11-30%
Sumitomo Heavy Ind.	10	Production of vitamins for drug and fertiliser additives through bioreactor and mass culture	less than 5%
Sharp	several	Development of molecular chips using Longmuir-Blodgett film; development of biosensor by immobilising technique	less than 5%
Toshiba	20-30	Development of equipment using monoclonal antibodies; development of light emitting devices	6-10%
NGK Insulators	25	Development of bioreactors, fermenters and refining devices for use in food production and waste-water treatment	6-10%

Table 1.9 (con't) Japanese firms engaged in biotechnology research with equity warrant listed (1980-1992)

Nissin Electric	several	Research into bioelectronics including biosensors	less than 5%
Mitsubishi Petrochemical	4	Development of fermenters and refining devices and facilities for biotech-related research	6-10%
Mitsubishi Electric	-	Research on production of cellulase and sweeteners through genetic engineering: alcohol production through biomass conversion	less than 5%
Fujitsu	20	Bio-architecture, molecule design, protein engineering	less than 5%
Yashima Chem	5	Development of vaccines by bacteria culture	51-70%
Kubota	10	Breeding of lactic acid bacteria for silage through protoplast cell fusion	
Olympus OPt.	-	Development of agents for HTLV-III antibody inspection by peptide synthesis; development of reagents for immunopathology	11-30%
Asahi Chemical	200	Development of tumour necrosis	
Sankei Chemical	-	Electric cell fusion processor	
Sumitomo Corp.	15	Research into pharmaceuticals, diagnostics, microbial insecticide	less than 5%

Table 1.9 (con't) Japanese warrant issuers from the estimating sample involved in bio-tech research (1980-1992)

Firm	Staff size	Kind of research	Estimated bio-tech related sales as a percentage of the total sales in the year 2000
Mitsui		Development of hybrid rice	
Sanyo-Kokusako Pulp	26	Research on production of yeast extracts through fermentation and fungi breeding; research on sweeteners	6-10%
Dai-ichi		Breeding of disease resistant flower-seedlings	
Showa Hakko	2	Research into microbial insecticide and mushrooms	more than 71%
Asahi Glass	30	Development of monoclonal antibodies by cell fusion; cell culture of carcinoembryonic antigens	less than 5%
Osaka Gas		Use of immobilised fungi in waste-water treatment and to improve activated sludge	less than 5%
Dowa Mining	10	Extraction of enzymes from Froxidans Thiobacilli for use in mining	less than 5%
Sumitomo Metal Industries		Chemical production and waste-water treatment using fungi and fermentation technology	less than 5%

Table 1.9 (con't) Japanese warrant issuers from the estimating sample involved in bio-tech research (1980-1992)

Kobe Steel	25	Waste-water treatment and production of hydrogen and methane gas through bioreactor	6-10%
Sankyo	40	Research on production of biologically active compounds through genetic engineering	11-30%
Dainippon Pharm.	26	Research on production of biologically active compounds through genetic engineering; research on cytokinin	11-30%
Ajinomoto		Development and production of anti-cancer agents and amino acid through genetic engineering	31-50%
Takeda Chemical	65	Research on production of vaccines and biologically active compounds through genetic engineering	11-30%
Showa Denko	50	Production of amino acid and enzymes by genetic engineering	6-10%
Sumitomo Chemical	70	Production of monoclonal antibodies	less than 5%
Sekisui Chemical	15	Production of monoclonal antibodies	6-10%
Kao	100	Research on microbial pesticide	11-30%

Source: Nippon Keizai Shimbun (1980-1992)

Table 1.10 Summary features of bankruptcy regulation in selected OECD countries

France
- With the 1985 Act the general philosophy has switched from the punishment of bankrupt debtors to the reorganisation of failing business at the earliest date in order to prevent bankruptcy ("accord amiable" or friendly agreement). - The Act considers the possibility of continuation of the business by the debtor but only if there are no potential purchasers for the business. In this case creditors are encouraged to write-off part of their claims against the debtor. - The 1985 Act has eliminated a previous statutory presumption so that a creditor initiating bankruptcy proceeding must now prove manager negligence.

Italy
- The individual bankrupt is "dispossessed" of his present and future assets except those necessary to the bankrupt's own and his family's sustenance. - The individual bankrupt is subject to a number of disabilitites such as: loss of political rights either as a voter or as a candidate for no more than 5 years; ii) prohibition of several professions such as all firm mangerial activities, brokerage activities, law professions, etc. for no more than 5 years. - For limited liability companies, bankruptcy does not extend to members even though normal rights of members are considerably restricted. - Some manager's bankrupt acts (in limited liability companies), that have per se no criminal connotation may acquire it retroactively, after the declaration of bankruptcy (in i.e. accounting book not kept in order, etc.). - More serious acts classified as "bancarotta fraudolenta" (removal, concealment or dissipation of assets) entail imprisonment from 3 to 10 years. -Most of the bankruptcy law deals with rules for distribution of assets among creditors. No special focus on reorganisation of activities. The only exception is for firms with at least 300 employees (Amministrazione straordinaria di grandi imprese in crisi) which explicitly focuses on reorganisation and continuation of activity

United Kingdom
- A 1986 law severely restricted conditions for directors of companies going bankrupt. These restrictions were aimed at avoiding the "Phoenix syndrome" according to which directors of a company would allow it to become insolvent and then set up a new company to rise out of the ashes of the old one as a too frequent occurrence. - the 1986 law imposes personal liability on directors for "wrongful trading". Wrongful trading does not require any fraudulent intent. It is enough that the director fails to take every step to minimise potential losses of the company before bankruptcy or that he is involved in trading activities when he knows that there is no reasonable prospect to avoid bankruptcy. Very few cases of wrongful trading reached Court but the impact of these provisions as a deterrent has been strong. - the Court may impose a "disqualification order" preventing an individual from being director or advisor of a company for up to 15 years. - the 1986 law introduced a procedure for voluntary arrangement between the debtor and the creditor but the empirical relevance of these arrangements remains small (rescue outcomes allow for less than 1 percent of all company insolvencies).

Table 1.10 (con't) Summary features of bankruptcy regulation in selected OECD countries

United States

- The most influential and controversial part of the US bankruptcy law is the statute known as Chapter 11, enacted in 1978 and amended after a reform in 1994.
- Between 1978 and 1994 Chapter 11 granted the debtor and the creditors the flexibility to work out a plan of reorganisation that could meet the interest of all parties. Under most circumstances the management of the financially troubled company remains with the debtor as a "debtor in possession". In the first 120 days the debtor has the exclusive right to propose a plan of reorganisation. Creditors are organised in Committees whose primary function is that of negotiating a plan of reorganisation.
- Given that management, under 1978 Chapter 11, no longer needs to fear being summarily displaced, US business is less reluctant to seek for timely relief under the Bankruptcy Code. A Chapter 11 case may be initiated voluntarily by the debtor or by petitioning creditors holding a least US$5,000 in the aggregate of non-contingent undisputed unsecured claims against the debtor.
- The debtor in possession continues the business of the debtor, enjoys the protection of automatic stay and exerts most of the powers of the trustee.
- The debtor in possession may obtain credit or the postpetition financing (called DIP loan) he may need to carry operations during the pendency of his loan. Financial institutions usually compete to make DIP loans, being then secured by a lien of the highest priority.
- A debtor in possession may obtain unsecured credit or incur unsecured debt in the ordinary course of his business as an administrative expense of the estate.
- 1994 Chapter 11 reform tried to avoid the previous excessive use of chapter 11 itself to solve a myriad social and economic issues such as mass tort liability, environmental disasters, seriously underfunded pension plans and labour strikes. The new provisions of the 1994 Act try to shift leverage to creditors. It is too early to evaluate the effects of the reform.

Germany

- Domestic bankruptcy law envisages liquidation as the main outcome of insolvency. Debtor is liable to civil and criminal penalties in case of delay in filing a petition for bankruptcy procedure.
 - A manager is personally liable to civil and criminal penalties if he does not file for bankruptcy within three weeks after his company is unable to repay debt.
- The likelihood that a reorganisation agreeement be reached is reduced by the fact that secured creditors have to assert their right outside the bankruptcy proceedings.
- The possibility of reaching an agreement through a "voluntary" composition procedure avoiding liquidation is highly reduced by the request that creditors be paid at least 35 percent of their claims. This condition, in practice, denies access to reorganisation for a majority of insolvent firms.

Source: "Establishing financial discipline: experience with bankruptcy legislation in central and Eastern European countries", OECD Economic Studies, 25,1995, and "Corporate bankruptcy and reorganisation procedures in OECD and Central and Eastern European countries", OECD, 1994.

Notes

*Paper prepared for the CNR Strategic Project 92.4716 st 74 "Technological Change and Industrial Development: policies for international technological co-operation". Working unit ISPE No.3, co-ordinator Professor Bagella. Even though the paper is fruit of a common work, sections 1 and 5 may be attributed to M.Bagella, while the remaining sections to L.Becchetti. The authors thank P.Aghion, S.Bhattacharya and S.Nickell for useful comments and suggestions.

[1] Banks often possess a relevant stake of company shares because they add the management of portfolios of individual savers to their own participation. Their proximity to firms mitigates informational asymmetries and generates "lender of last resort" advantages while it is not possible to say that it reduces the cost of external financing. Interest rates on bank loans are generally expensive because of monitoring costs and reserve requirement costs implicitly charged on them (Edwards-Fisher, 1993).

[2] Historical reasons have contributed to the existing organisation of the relationship between the financial and real sector in Japan (government regulations imposing interest rate ceilings and the impossibility of raising money abroad during the 1970's). Many firms are part of groups (keiretsu) in which banks play an important role (Takagi, 1993).The Japanese system, with respect to the UK system presents: i) higher bank-firm participation; ii) lower reliance on internal sources and higher reliance on bank loans to finance investments: iii) a group of stable shareholders including financial and non financial corporations compared with the dispersed ownership structure of the UK (Edwards-Fisher, 1993; Takagi, 1993; Hodder-Tschoegl, 1993).

[3] For these countries it is not possible to disaggregate net profits from equity issues and the weight of internally financed investments is clearly overstated.

[4] While the Modigliani-Miller theorem remains a benchmark for theoretical analysis in the same way as a "frictionless" model in physics, the imperfect information approach has more "external consistency" and may explain why certain behaviours are determined as a response of the system to the existence of frictions. An idea of how many frictions exist in financial markets (monitoring and information as public goods, externalities in intermediaries bankruptcy, etc.) may be provided by Stiglitz in his survey (1993).

[5] The principal objection to this (Mayer, 1992) is that looking at firm publicly revealed figures is the easiest way to improve information on firm perspectives. The response to this objection is that accounting statistics may be easily manipulated. They regard in fact past performance more than future firm perspectives and do not provide better information than "revealed preferences" represented by managers financing and dividend policies.

[6] An optimal financing strategy for innovating firms may be that of bond plus equity warrant issues. BW issues are optimal for firms whose research activity approaches the achievement of results that can be manufactured and marketed. For these types of firms, a BW issue is preferred to convertible bond issues because of its more time flexible financing profile that avoids excessive increases in leverage at the issue date. If firm research results are not positive, the equity price falls below the exercise price and warrants are not exercised. In this case the firm finds itself with lower leverage than in the case it had chosen a convertible issue.

At the same time the warrant is a signal that subordinates firm future leverage reductions to future positive results and is then implicitly a bet of the firm itself on these results. This interpretation of equity warrants may explain why warrant financing strategy is so widespread among firms engaged in biotechnology research (see Tab 1.8 and 1.9). The history of the 1980's in Japan, though, shows that the weak point of this strategy is given by the assumption that the equity price fully reflects the advancement of firm research and future firm market perspectives. The main problem is in fact that the nondiversifiable risk component may drive the equity price far below the warrant exercise price at the exercise deadline in spite of a good firm performance. The fall of the Nikkei index in the last part of the 1980's caused the failure of many high-tech Japanese firm financing strategies because of this reason (see chapter 5).

[7] A problem for this literature is that only some and not all the possible financing strategies are considered within the same model. The consequence is that such models provide partial perspectives of firm optimal financing strategy in an high-tech sector. For example, Stein (1992) compares debt, equity and convertibles, Santarelli (1991) venture capital and debt.

[8] Haugen and Senbet (1988) argue that bankruptcy costs, generally overstated in the literature, should be bounded below by the lowest between: i) costs through formal reorganisation involving the court system; ii) transaction costs of informal reorganisation. What really matters, though, in signalling models of financing strategies are individual manager's bankruptcy costs. These costs are particularly high for managers-owners of small-medium firms with nontransferable skills. In certain financial systems these costs are increased by temporary loss of civil and economic rights (voting rights and entrepreneurial rights). In addition to it, a fundamental component of these costs is that, in a world of imperfect information, bankruptcy is likely to reveal negative information about the manager-entrepreneur.

[9] In first rudimentary nonstochastic R&D contest models where an R&D race could be won with certainty after a certain number of research steps (i.e. experiments) were carried out, the issue of disclosure costs was completely ignored, while in more reasonable stochastic frameworks knowledge disclosure generated by a market financing strategy may increase the probability of "leapfrogging" from competitors.

[10] This idea finds important confirmation in literature: Holmstrom-Milgrom (1985) show that when financial units charge informational fixed costs to the innovative unit, the latter has no more interest in obtaining venture capital financing for low risk projects. As a result, informational problems may cause adverse selection and venture capital rationing. Myerson-Satterthwaite (1985) show how market thickening may reduce informational asymmetries avoiding contract failures and positively affecting real activity.

[11] What is often likely to happen is that the financier has many other financial investment alternatives which often stochastically dominate innovation financing, while the innovative entrepreneurs only possess a nonmonetary intellectual asset represented by their innovative project which cannot be converted in alternative opportunities. The imbalance between outside options for the two counterparts generates an inefficient number of financed ventures where innovator conditions are often unfavorable. The only situation in which this inefficiency may be avoided is when the financer has an extra interest in financing the venture, because this one

represents a human capital investment that reduces sunken costs preventing his access to the innovative sector.

[12] The two authors use a two equation system of profit to capital and sales to capital ratios and set at three years the VAR lenght.

[13] The need for instruments and for some dynamic in the specification of the equation suggests the adoption of programs which can easily allow for GMM and lagged variables, like DPD (Arellano-Bond, 1991) and, more recently, TSP 4.3.

[14] A theoretical rationale for this empirical finding is provided by the Cooney-Kalay (1993) version of the Myers-Mayluf model allowing for the existence of negative NPV projects. The two authors demonstrate that, if several negative NPV projects in the "no issue-no invest" region exist, the "issue and invest" decision may result to be good news for new shareholders. This model might explain why equity issue announcement effects are anticyclical (Ercoli, 1995).

[15] Additional methodological problems occur because of different accounting procedures. For instance, Japanese firms appear more indebted than UK firms. This is because, due to differences in accounting conventions, land and securities in Japan are registered in the balance at their original value and assets of associated companies are not consolidated. Moreover, intercountry differences in leverage may vary significantly, reflecting the effect of bearish or bullish stock exchange behaviour (Hodder-Tschoegl, 1993).

Another problem is that many items (mainly all those related to technology measures) are not available and also that a different proxy for liquidity has to be found. For this reason, among many others, it is not entirely correct to make direct comparisons of coefficient magnitudes between countries, while some comparative insights may be provided confronting intra-country subgroup estimates when homogeneous split criteria are adopted.

References

Aaker, D. and Jacobson, R. (1993), "Myopic management behaviour with efficient but imperfect financial markets: a comparison of informational asymmetries in the US and Japan", *Journal of Accounting and Economics*, 16, 383-404.

Adams, W.J. and Yellen, J.L. (1976), "Commodity bundling and the burden of monopoly", *Quarterly Journal of Economics*, pp. 475-498.

Aghion, P. and Tirole, J.J. (1993), "On the management of the innovation", paper presented to the World Bank Conference "How do National Policies Affect Long Run Growth", Estoril, January.

Allen, F., and Gale, D. (1995), "A welfare comparison of intermediaries and financial markets in Germany and the US", *European Economic Review*, 39, 179-209.

Arellano, M. and Bond, S. (1991), Some tests of specifications for panel data: Monte Carlo evidence and an application to employment equations", *Review of Economic Studies*, 58, pp. 277-297.

Asquith, P. and Mullins, D. (1986), "Equity issues and offering dilution", *Journal of Financial Economics*, 15, 61-89.

Asquith, P. and Mullins, D. (1991), "Convertible debt: corporate call policy and voluntary conversion", *Journal of Finance*, 46, pp. 1273-1289.

Bagella, M. (1994), "A model of the interaction between derivative finance products and technology investment: empirical evidence from UK and USA data", mimeo.

Bagella, M. and Tivegna, M. (1993), "Modelling German and Italian interest rate convergence", Paper presented to the International Seminar on "Financial Integration and Monetary Stability", *CEIS Working Paper*.

Bagella, M. and Becchetti, L. (1995), "The buy-out/property right choice in film financing: credit rationing, adverse selection and the Bayesian dilemma", *Journal of Cultural Economics*, 279-304.

Becchetti, L. (1994), "Finance, investment and innovation: an empirical analysis of the Italian case", *Sviluppo Economico*.

Becchetti, L. (1995a), "Finance, investment and innovation: a theoretical and empirical comparative analysis", *Empirica*, 22, 167-184.

Becchetti, L. (1995b), "Financing nonneutralities in technological venturing: three coordination inefficiencies", paper presented at the 1995 Conference of the Royal Economic Society, Canterbury, in (M.Bagella) (eds.) *Finance, Investment and Innovation: Theory and Empirical Analyses*, Avebury, forth.

Becchetti, L. (1996),"The effect of bond plus equity warrant issues on stock volatility: an empirical analysis with conditional and unconditional volatility measures", *Applied Financial Economics*, August.

Becchetti, L. Caggese A. (1995), "Effects of index option introduction on stock index volatility: a procedure for empirical testing based on SSC-GARCH models", *CEIS Working Paper* n. 48.

Bencivenga, V.R., Smith, B.D. (1991), "Financial intermediation and endogenous growth", *Review of Economic Studies* 58, 195-209.

Berlin, M. and Mester, L. (1992), "Debt convenants and renegotiation", *Journal of Financial Intermediation*, 2, 95-133.

Bernanke, B.S. Gertler, M. (1987), "Financial fragility and economic performance", *NBER, Working Paper n. 2318*.

Besanko, D. and Thakor, A.V.(1993) "Collateral and rationing: sorting equilibria in mopolistic and competitive credit markets", *International Economic Review*, 28, pp. 671-689.

Bester, H. (1985), "Screening vs. rationing in credit markets with imperfect information", *American Economic Review*, 75, pp.850-855.

Bhattacharya, S and Thakor, A.V.(1993), "Contemporary banking theory", *Journal of Financial Intermediation, 3, 2-50*.

Bhattacharya, S. and Chiesa, G. (1995), "Proprietary information, financial intermediation and research incentives", *Journal of Financial Intermediation*, 4, pp.328-357.

Binmore, K., Rubinstein, A. and Wolinsky, A. (1986), The Nash bargaining solution in economic modelling", *Rand Journal of Economics*, 17, (2), pp. 176-188.

Blanchard, O.J., Rhee C. and Summers,L. (1993), "The Stock Market, Profit and Investment", *Quarterly Journal of Economics* 108.

Boyd, J. and Prescott, E. (1986), "Financial intermediaries coalitions", *Journal of Economic Theory* 38, pp. 211-232.

Brennan, M. and Kraus, A. (1987), "Efficient financing under asymmetric information", *Journal of Finance* 42, pp. 1225-1243

Brigham, E. (1966), "An analysis of convertible debentures: theory and some empirical evidence", *Journal of Finance*, 21, pp. 35-54.

Calomiris, C. and Hubbard, G. (1988), "Firm heterogeneity, internal finance, and credit rationing" *Economic Journal* 100, pp. 90-104.

Cavallo, L. (1996), "Venture Capital and Innovation", in M.Bagella (ed.) *Finance, investment and innovation: theory and empirical analysis*, Avebury, forth.

Chan, Y., Siegel, D. and Thakor, A.V. (1990), "Learning corporate control and performance requirements in Venture Capital contracts", *International Economic Review*, 31, 365-381.

Chirinko, R.S. (1987), "Tobin's q and financial policy", *Journal of Monetary Economics* 19.

Chirinko, R.S. (1993), "Business fixed investment spending", *Journal of Economic Literature* 31.

Chirinko, R.S. and Schaller, H. (1995), "Why does liquidity matter in investment equations?", *Journal of Money Credit and Banking*, 27, pp. 537-548.

Cooper, R. and John, A. (1988), "Coordinating coordination failures in keynesian models", *Quarterly Journal of Economics* 103, pp. 441-464.

Corbett, J. (1987), "International perspectives on financing: evidence from Japan", *Oxford Review of Economic Policy*, 3(4), 30-55.

Cosh, A.D., Hughes, A. and Singh, A. (1990), "Analytical and policy issues in the UK economy", in A.D. Cosh, A. Hughes and A. Singh, J. Carty and J. Plender, *Takeover and Short-Termism in the UK*, London: Institute of Public Policy Research.

Costantinides, G. and Grundy, B. (1989), "Optimal investment stock with repurchase and financing as signals", *Review of Financial Studies*, pp. 445-465.

Costello, D. (1993), "A cross-country comparison of productivity growth", *Journal of Political Economy* 101, 207-222.

Dann, L. and Mikkelson, W. (1984), "Convertible debt issuance, capital structure change and financing related information", *Journal of Financial Economics* 13, 157-186.

De Long, J.B., Shleifer, A., Summers, L.H. and Waldmann, R.J. (1990), "Noise trader risk in financial markets", *Journal of Political Economy*, 98, 703-738.

Devereaux, M. and Schiantarelli, F. (1989), "Investment, financial factors, and cash flow: evidence from UK panel data", *NBER Working Paper 3116*, 1989.

Dewatripont, M. And Maskin, E. (1995), "Credit and efficiency in centralised versus decentralised markets", *Review of Economic Studies*, forth.

Diamond, D.W. (1991), "Monitoring and reputation: the choice between bank loans and directly placed debt", *Journal of Political Economy*, 99, 689-691.

Easterbrook., F.H. (1986), "Two agency-cost explanations of dividends", *American Economic Review*. Vol. 74. N.4.

Edwards, J. and Fisher,K. (1993), "Banks, finance and investment in Germany", Cambridge University Press.

Ercoli, R. (1995), "Effetto annuncio delle emissioni in borsa: un'analisi empirica delle imprese italiane", mimeo.

Fama, E. (1980), "Banking in the theory of finance", *Journal of Monetary Economics* 6, pp. 39-57.

Fama, E. (1985), "What's different about banks?", *Journal of Monetary Economics* 15, pp. 29-40.

Fazzari, S.M., Hubbard, G.R. and Petersen, B.C. (1988), "Financing constraints and corporate investment" *Broking Papers on Economic Activity*, pp. 141-195.

French, K. and Roll, R. (1986), "Stock return variances: the arrival of information and the reaction of the traders", *Journal of Financial Economics*, 17, pp. 5-26.

Fudenberg, D. and Tirole, J. (1992), *Game Theory*, MIT Press.

Gale, D., and Hellwig, M. (1985), "Incentive compatible debt contracts: the one-period problem", *Review of Economic Studies*, 52, pp. 647-663.

Gertler, M. and Gilchrist, S. (1993), "The role of credit market imperfections in the monetary transmission mechanism: arguments and evidence", Federal Reserve Board, *Finance and Economics Discussion Series*, N.5.

Greenwald, B.C. and Stiglitz, J.E. (1993), "Financial market imperfections and business cycles", *The Quarterly Journal of Economics* 91, pp. 77-114.

Greenwood, J. and Jovanovic, B. (1990), "Financial development, growth and the distrtibution of income", *Journal of Political Economy* 88, pp. 1076-1107.

Grossman, S. and Stiglitz, J.E. (1980), "On the impossibility of informationally efficient markets", *American Economic Review*, 70, pp.393-608.

Harris, M. and Raviv, A. (1991), "The theory of capital structure", *Journal of Finance* 46, pp. 297-355.

Haugen, R. And Senbet, L. (1988), "Bankruptcy and agency costs: their significance to thetheory of optimal capital structure", *Journal of Financial and Qualitative Analysis*, 23, pp.27-38.

Hodder, J.E. and Tshoegl, A.E. (1985), "Some aspects of japanese corporate finance", *Journal of Financial Quantitative Analysis*, 20(2), 173-91.

Holmstrom, B. (1989), "Agency costs and innovation", *Journal of Economic Behaviour and Organization*, 2.

Holmstrom, B. and Milgrom, P. (1987), "Aggregation and linearity in the provision of intertemporal incentives", *Econometrica*, 55, 303-328.

Hoshi, T., Kashyap, A. and Scharfstein, D. (1992), "Corporate structure, liquidity and investment: evidence from japanese industrial groups", *Quarterly Journal of Economics* 90, 33-61.

Hubbard G.R. and Kashyap A.K. (1992) "Internal net-worth and the investment process: an application to us agriculture", *Journal of Political Economy*, 506-534.

Jaffe, D. and Russel, T. (1976), "Imperfect information, uncertainty, and credit rationing", *Quarterly Journal of Economics*, pp. 651-666.

Jensen, M.C. and Meckling, W.H. (1976), "Theory of the firm: managerial behaviour, agency costs and ownership structure", *Journal of Financial Economics*, 3, 305-360.

Jovanovic, B. (1983), "Innovation technology and finance: a cross-country analysis", *CNR Strategic Project*, mimeo.

Kashyap, A.K., Lamont, O.A. and Stein, J.C. (1993), "Credit conditions and the cyclical behaviour of inventories", Federal Reserve Bank of Chicago, WP n.7.

King, R.G. and Levine, R. (1993), "Finance, entrepreneurship and growth: theory and evidence", paper presented to the World Bank Conference "How do national policies affect long run growth", Estoril, January.

King, R.G. and Levine, R. (1992), "Finance and growth: Schumpeter might be right", *The Quarterly Journal of Economics*, August.

Leland, H. Pyle, D. (1977), "Informational asymmetries, financial structure and financial intermediation", *Journal of Finance*, 32.

Mayer, C. (1985), "New issues in corporate finance", *European Economic Review*.

Mayer, C. (1990), "Financial systems, corporate finance and economic development", (ed. Chicago IL; University of Chicago Press).

Masulis, R. and Korwar, A. (1986), "Seasoned equity offerings: an empirical investigation", *Journal of Financial Economics* 15, pp. 91-118.

Meyer, R.J. Kuh, E. (1957), *The investment decision: an empirical study*, Harvard University Press.

Mikkelson, W. and Partch, M. (1986), "Valuation effects of security offerings and the issuance process", *Journal of Financial Economics* 15, pp. 31-60.

Modigliani, F. and Miller, M. (1958), "The cost of capital, corporation finance and the theory of investment", *American Economic Review* 48, pp. 261-97.

Myers, S.C. and Majluf, N.S. (1984), "Corporate financing decisions when firms have investment information that investment do not", *Journal of Financial Economics* 13, pp. 187-221.

Myerson, R. and Satterthwaite, M. (1985), "efficient mechanisms for bilateral trading", *Journal of Economic Theory*, 28.

Nelson, R. (1993), *National innovation systems*. Oxford University Press. New York.

Pagano, M. (1993), "Financial markets and growth: an overview", *European Economic Review* 37, pp. 613-622.

Panes, N. (1989) "A tax stimulus for corporate venturing a catalyst for British enterprise", *Bow Paper*, Bow Publication.

Rajan, R. (1992), "The choice between informed and arm's-length debt", *Journal of Finance*, 47, 1367-1400

Ramakrishnan, R.T.S. and Thakor, A.V. (1991), "Information reliability and a theory of financial intermediation", *Review of Economic Studies*, 51, pp.415-432.

Ramsey, J.B. Lian, C.P. (1993), "An exploratory analysis of the growth rates of economic and financial data", *Ricerche Economiche* 47, pp. 31-64.

Rosman A.J., O'Neill, H.M. (1993), "Comparing the information acquisition strategies of venture capital and commercial lenders: a computer based experiment", *Journal of Business Venturing*, 8.

Ross, S. (1977), "The determination of financial structure: the incentive signalling approach", *Bell Journal of Economics*, 8, pp.23-40.

Saint-Paul, G. (1992), "Technological choice, financial markets and economic development", *European Economic Review*, 36, pp. 763-781.

Sakakibara, K. and Westney, D.E. (1985), "Comparative study of the training. Careers and organization of the engineers in the computer industry in the United States and in Japan", *Hitotsoubashi Journal of Commerce and Management*, 20 (1).

Schumpeter, J.A. (1911), *The theory of economic development*, Cambridge MA, Harvard University Press.

Shapiro, C. and Stiglitz, J.E. (1984), "Equilibrium unemployment as a worker-discipline device", *American Economic Review*, 74 June.

Stein, J.C. (1992), "Convertible bonds as backdoor equity financing", *Journal of Financial Economics*, Vol. 32, n.1.

Stiglitz, J.E. (1993), "The role of the state in financial markets", Proceedings of the World Bank Annual Conference on Development Economics, 19-56.

Stiglitz, J. and Weiss, A. (1981), "Credit rationing in markets with imperfect information", *American Economic Review* 71, pp. 912-927.

Sutton, J. (1986), "Non-cooperative bargaining theory: an introduction", *Review of Economic Studies*, 53 (5), pp. 709-724.

Takagi, S. (1993), "Japanese capital markets"", Blackwell, Oxford.

Whited. T.M. (1992), "Debt, liquidity constraints, and corporate investment: evidence from panel data", *The Journal of Finance*, Vol. XLVII. n.4, September.

Williamson, D. (1986), "Costly monitoring, financial intermediation, and equilibrium credit rationing", *Journal of Monetary Economics* 18, pp. 159-79.

Wilson, P. (1992), "Public ownership, delegated project selection and corporate financing policy", Working paper, School of Business, Indiana University.

Wolff, E. (1993), "Productivity growth and capital intensity on the sector and industry level: specialization among oecd countries, 1970-1988", mimeo, New York University.

2   Equity dilution, small ticket problem and coordination inefficiency in venture capital financing of innovation

Leonardo Becchetti

1. Introduction

Coordination failure models were originally developed within a neoKeynesian theoretical framework in order to microfound Keynes theoretical intuitions on underemployment equilibria or, more generally, non-market clearing equilibria (Cooper-John, 1988; Bryant, 1983). According to this approach, Keynesian results were brought about by dilemmas arising in "thin markets" and explained within a game theoretical framework.

The argument developed in this section is that coordination failure can be a valid approach not only to explain fluctuations, but also to provide a microfounded explanation of the longer term determinants of the behaviour of economic variables such as technological growth. The coordination failure approach is applied to the problem of venture capital financing in order to show that the conflict arising between two maximising agents (the venture capitalist and the innovator) on the division of property rights on future innovation may reduce incentives to innovate.

The section is structured as follows. In the first section, a short introductory description of the venture capital phenomenon i) outlines the tendency of "real" and "financial" innovating units to agglomerate in restricted geographical areas in order to exploit the externalities provided by a "technological district"; ii) documents the relative shift of venture capital activity from support to innovation to other financial activities (management buy-in and buy-out, etc).

Two intuitive explanations often quoted in literature to explain point ii) are those termed as "equity dilution syndrome" and "small ticket problem". The model presented in the second section shortly explains these two intuitive concepts and formalises them within the perspective of a coordination failure dilemma arising in venture capital financing of innovation. The same model has two different representations that are consistent with each other: the first "encompassing" representation is general and allows analyses of the links between the dilemma of financing technological innovation through venture capital and the coordination failure theory; the second "encompassed" representation provides more details on the issue and tries to explain it by investigating the link between ex ante bargaining on property rights and incentives to innovate.

The "encompassing" representation indicates how positive spillovers may arise in a game between an innovating unit (real unit) and a venture capitalist unit (financial unit). This happens when both unit payoffs are positively affected by the other player's effort with the consequence that a symmetric cooperative equilibria cannot be attained.

The "encompassed" representation, readapting an Aghion-Tirole (1993) approach to the issue, gives a property right incentive explanation to the dilemma. The probability of innovating is a function of the innovator and the financer efforts which, in turn, are positively affected by the share of property rights on future innovation. A reduction of the innovator share, which may be determined by the bargaining process, causes an effort disincentive justifying the "equity dilution syndrome" described in venture capital literature and reducing the expected value of innovation.

The "encompassed" representation shows that a coordination failure inefficiency may occur when the asymmetry between relative bargaining power and the relative contribution to innovation determines a division of property rights that is individually and socially suboptimal *for a given incentive structure*. This happens because an inefficient sharing rule caused by imperfect information reduces the dimension of the profit "cake". Further analysis, though, shows that, even in a context of perfect information on relative contributions to the venture, the asymmetry between relative bargaining powers and relative contributions exists and has potential negative effects on social optimality. This is because the unit that enjoys the asymmetry has an individual convenience in maintaining this advantage, exerting all her bargaining power because, to her, a larger share of a smaller cake is in any case bigger than a smaller share of a larger cake. In this case the bargaining outcome is individually optimal for the financier, but socially suboptimal, *given the existing incentive structure.*

The results obtained in the two-unit model are slightly modified when fixed information costs of the financer are considered. The fixed information costs of the financer are calculated as a percentage of the exploitable rent from the venture, net of the outside opportunity given by external pure financial operation. If the financed project has a small revenue, fixed costs and opportunity costs may be so high to make it unprofitable for the venture capitalist to finance the innovative project. This result is partly different from what asserted in the "small ticket" problem because the fact that expected revenues from the innovation cannot cover fixed information costs is not linked to the dimension of the initial venture capitalist investment.

The second part of the section presents an extension of the model considering the presence of multiple real and financial agents. The analysis of the issue with the "encompassing" model provides interesting insights because it fixes formal conditions for the profitability of a technological district. Unit agglomeration has the positive effect of adding more public knowledge to the technology function, increasing the overall probability of innovation and the negative effect of increasing the level of competition among units of the same type modifying unit exploitable rents and outside options in the bargaining process. An interesting normative consideration is that, if the innovator has the higher relative contribution in the innovation, while the financial unit has the higher relative bargaining power, the second level coordination inefficiency described in the two-unit model occurs and an increase in the number of financial units may restore the social optimum for the given incentive structure. This is consistent with innovation policies adopted in several countries which support, with tax relief and other instruments, the creation of venture capitalist specialised in financing risky ventures[1].

2. Main trends in UK venture capital

At the beginning of the 1980s venture capital market explosion occurred according two fundamental creative processes. The first is the constitution of "captive funds" funded by clearing banks, merchant banks and pension funds as autonomous units being part of a larger financial institution. The second process is the generation of independent venture capital funds according to a spin-off process fostered by self-employment decisions of managers abandoning their previous positions in larger organisations.

With regard to the sources of venture capital units funding, the situation of the 1980s shows that in the UK a large share is constituted by pension funds and investment funds (EVCA, 1985-1992). A comparison with the rest of the world shows how this funding source structure is quite similar to the US one and markedly different from those in the rest of Europe and in South East Asian countries (Bygrave-Timmonds, 1992).

It is important to underline that venture capital activity includes, but is not confined to, new technology financing. It is possible to observe that a decreasing share of funds is addressed by venture capital units to start-up, while a larger increasing share is directed towards management buy-out and management buy-in operations (EVCA, 1985-1992). It is nonetheless difficult to individuate exactly the share of financing devoted to technological innovation, given that this last one does not necessarily coincide with start-up financing.

Another indication of the evolution of the venture capital activity in the UK is the analysis of funds' destinations by the industrial sector. This clearly shows the existence of a crisis of innovation financing with a trend in decreasing shares, both in the percentage of invested sums and in the number of companies financed for high-tech sectors such as electronics, computers and biotechnology (EVCA, 1988-1992).

Another relevant phenomenon in the UK venture capital market is that of the geographic concentration in restricted areas of the activity of both real and financing units which operate in innovative sectors. It is well known that, at world level, innovations are developed in restricted areas where Marshallian externalities can be beneficial to technological growth. Well known cases are the electronic industry in the US where both innovating firms and the financial units that may provide new capital for them are concentrated in two main regions such as California and Massachussets. A similar case happens in the UK: there is a main area in the South-East where most innovating firms, venture capital units (BVCA members) and the total of BVCA invested capital are concentrated. This region includes some smaller technological district like the Cambridge University Science Park, the Silicon Corridor and the Silicon Glen in Fife.

The theoretical model presented in the paper will try to show in a simple way the plausible reasons for a decline in venture capital in supporting innovation, and will outline the crucial problems of this form of external financing.

3. The "encompassing" representation of the coordination failure model of the technological venture

The simplest version of the "encompassing model" which analyses the problem of finance and technological innovation assumes the existence of only two units operating in a segment of a technological sector: the first is represented by a venture capital unit, financing risky and high technology investment (unit F); the second is represented by a small, cash constrained, innovating unit that has developed a project for a product or a process innovation and needs gradual financial support for the different phases of the technological cycle (unit I). We

70

know from previous descriptive analysis that venture capital firms are divided primarily into captive and independent funds. In this version of the model only independent funds are taken into account for simplicity.

In the simplest two unit model there is a technology or "common knowledge" function:

$$T = f(a_F, a_I) f_1 > 0, f_2 > 0 \tag{1}$$

describing the fact that the development of product or process new technologies relies on the effort of each unit (a_F and a_I). The peculiar abilities required in this case are: i) for the financial unit, the capacity of evaluating technical validity, manufacturing viability and marketability of a project, together with a good "financing technology" for risky projects (which may include availability of assets for long term coverage against interest and exchange rate risks); ii) for the innovating unit, the capacity of creating, manufacturing and selling new technologies.

In the model a differentiable technology function is adopted as substitutability between the two inputs is assumed. This hypothesis implies that there is a continuum of solutions for the innovating firms between a fully self-financed project and a project entirely financed by the venture capital unit.

In the model the profit functions for the two units are:

$$\pi_F = \pi(T, a_F) \quad \pi_1, \pi_2 > 0 \quad \pi_{11}, \pi_{22} < 0 \tag{2}$$

$$\pi_I = \pi(T, a_I) \quad \pi_1, \pi_2 > 0 \quad \pi_{11}, \pi_{22} < 0 \tag{3}$$

This means that, for both units, profit is a function of the capacity of the small integrated system to develope technology (T) and of one's own individual effort (a_i). The profit of the innovating unit depends on the possibility of developing its project and then on the financial support of the venture capital unit. The profit of the financing unit is linked to the overall technology of the system as the solvability of the innovating firm is linked to the success of its product and then, ultimately, to its ability in terms of technological and manufacturing capacity.

Adopting a game theoretical approach, the profit functions may be considered as the two agents payoff in the game:

$$.V_F = p(f(a_F, a_I), a_F) \tag{4}$$
$$.V_I = p(f(a_F, a_I), a_I) \tag{5}$$

Following the theoretical framework introduced by Cooper-John (1988) we can define for this simple game a set of Symmetric Nash Equilibria (SNE) for the player i:

$$S = \left\{ a \in [0, A] \middle| Vi_1 (a_i, a_j) = 0 \right\} \quad where \quad Vi_1 = \frac{\partial Vi}{\partial a_i} \tag{6}$$

where SNE is defined as a situation where there is no profitable deviation from equilibrium for player i ($Vi_1 = 0$)

And the set of Nash Cooperative Equilibria (SCE) for the player i intended as the set of actions that represents the local solution to the joint profit maximisation problem of the two agents:

$$S = \left\{ a \in [0, A] \middle| Vi_1 (a_i, a_j) + Vi_2 (a_i, a_j) = 0 Vi_{11} (a_i, a_j) + 2Vi_{22} (a_i, a_j) < 0 \right\} \tag{7}$$

This last definition contains first order and second order conditions ensuring that the game solution will be a "cooperative maximum". An additional term to the first order condition ($Vi_2 = 0$) is added in this case to the SNE previously described.

With regard to our model, we may verify, on the base of the formal definitions presented, if positive spillovers exist in the two unit game. If we rewrite the payoff function in a general way:

$$V_i (a_i, a_j) = \left[f(a_i, a_j), a_i \right] \tag{8}$$

and consider the definition of positive spillover we can see that the game presents positive spillovers as:

$$\frac{\partial Vi(.)}{\partial a_i} = \pi_1 f_2 > 0 \tag{9}$$

because an increase in the second player's ability positively affects the technology function of the integrated two-unit system and then exerts a positive effect on the first player payoff[2].

The encompassing model of the venture capital financing to innovation allows for the possibility of positive spillovers and suboptimal equilibria. An important question now arises: what are the causes of these suboptimal outcomes?

According to descriptive venture capital literature they are the "equity dilution" problem and the "small ticket" problem (Gladstone, 1988; Bygrave-Timmons, 1985).

With regard to the first, the manager of the small innovating firm is reluctant to release part of the control on his firm in exchange for a long term financing coming through participation in the profits and in the decision process of the project. Using the terminology of the model, the innovating unit has reduced incentives to exert its effort in the coordinated action and then only partially disposes of the advantage of an improved financial funding to the project. This may lead it to prefer short term indebtedness to the loss of complete control on the project.

With regard to the second, we observe that the venture capital firm faces the high fixed costs of acquiring all relevant technical information for the evaluation of the project of the innovating firm. These fixed costs can be recovered only with the return from the investment of great sums and this is in contrast with the "small ticket" investment required by the innovating unit in the first phase of the cycle of the innovating product. The financing unit increasing its effort and its ability might then develop a portfolio diversification that allows it to run eventual short term losses in exchange for the opportunity of providing capital and getting profits from the following stages of the product cycle.

In the following paragraph it will be shown in which way these two problems may affect the optimal solution of the innovating game with a more detailed formal specification which is defined as the "encompassed version" of the model described above and readapts an Aghion-Tirole approach (1993).

3.1 The "encompassed" representation of the model with undivided property rights

The "encompassed model" provides a more detailed rationale of the coordination failure phenomenon, describing it as a result of a bargaining process and analysing the "common knowledge" function through its effects on the probability of innovation.

Following an Aghion-Tirole (1993) intuition we may define the expected value of the innovating project of the real unit as $E(V) = p(a_I, a_F)V$ where $p(.)$ is a probability function which depends on the two units' effort. What we termed before as "common knowledge" of the technology function is reinterpreted now as the probability of innovation, given the plausible strict positive correlation between the technological capacity of the system and its effect on the probability of achieving the innovation. For this reason we postulate that $T(a_I, a_F) = p(a_I, a_F) = q(a_I) + v(a_F)$ with a separable technology function.

In this version of the model each side tries to maximise its utility contracting ex ante the property rights on the innovation. The inputs of the bargaining process are i) the marginal efficiency of the two agents in the innovative process (the immaterial input of the real unit or the technological and financial support of the financial unit may be relatively more important)[3] and ii) the ex ante bargaining power.

As an example, the utilities of the two counterparts will be generally equal respectively to:

$$U_F = p(a_I(q_I), a_F(q_F))q_F V - c_F(a_F) \qquad (10)$$

for the financial unit and to:

$$U_F = p(a_I(q_I), a_F(q_F))q_I V - c_I(a_I) \qquad (11)$$

for the innovating unit where q_F and q_I are respectively the property right shares of the financier and of the innovator and V the expected value of the innovation.

Two other novelties presented in equations (10-11) with respect to the "encompassing" version of the model need to be emphasised. The effort of the two units is a function of the reward expected from the innovation and the profit function is now described as an utility function. This is more correct because, in the eventuality of complete attribution of property rights to the financier, the innovating unit becomes a dependent worker whose utility is equal to the wage given by the "employer" net of the disutility of effort.

The intermediate output of the bargaining process will be the definition of property rights which will in turn influence each agent's incentives and the probability of obtaining the innovation.

The first result from the model shows that there is a coordination failure problem because a suboptimal equilibrium with positive spillovers may arise when there is a "drastic" division rule for property rights.

We define U_I' and U_F' as the two agents' utility when the real unit (I) has the property-rights and the financial unit behaves like a bank financier respectively equal to:

$$U_I' = p(a_I(q_I), a_F(0))V - c_I(a_I) \qquad (12)$$

and:

$$.U_I' = [1 - p_{BKR}(a_I(q_I), a_F(0))]rB - C_f(a_F, mc) \qquad (13)$$

where B is the amount of money lent by the bank financier, r is the interest rate and p_{BKR} is the probability of bankrupcy generically defined as a function of the expected value of the innovation.

We then define U_I'' and U_F'' the two utilities when the financial unit F has the property rights respectively equal to:

74

$$U_I^{'} = 0 \qquad\qquad (14)$$

and:

$$U_F^{'} = p(a_I(0), a_F(p_F))V - C_F(a_F, mc) \qquad (15)$$

the (14) means that the real unit exerts the minimal level of effort, normalised to zero for simplicity, when it looses property rights. In this case we may define the conditions for the occurrence of positive spillovers in the game in the following way.

PROPOSITION 1: (first inefficiency) a coordination failure from positive spillover between a financial and an innovating unit occurs when: i) a disutility due to the loss of property rights exists for both units with $U_{I'} < U_I$ and $U_{F'} > U_F$; ii) the financial unit obtains full property rights; iii) the financial unit payoff would be improved if the real unit disincentive could be avoided:

$$[U_F^{'} | a_I(U_I^{'})] > [U_F^{'} | a_I(U_I^{'})] \qquad (16)$$

In this case, the first level of inefficiency described in the "encompassing" version of the model occurs and the positive spillover condition occurs because $U_F / a_I > 0$. The SCE is not attained because the utility of the financial unit might be improved should the disincentive problem of the real unit be solved[4].

The drastic property right example of the encompassed model presented in this section seems to show that there is no role for policy in reducing inefficiency unless the incentive structure of the game is changed. In the model with bargaining and property right sharing, it will be shown that ad hoc policies may reduce coordination inefficiencies bridging the gap between private optimum and social optimum.

3.2 The encompassed representation of the model with shared property rights and bargaining

The formalisation of a bargaining rule in the game and the removal of the hypothesis of a "drastic" division of property rights provides additional insights into the coordination failure issue.

A first obvious general rule may be obtained by defining the optimal sharing rule from the social point of view, as the maximisation of the expected value of innovation. We may then rewrite the "common knowledge" function as $p = a_I(q_I) + (1-q_I)a_F$. Looking for the highest probability of innovation and deriving with respect to the real unit share, we obtain a maximum of the probability function at the point where:

$$a_i'(q_i) - a_F'(q_i) = 0 \qquad (17)$$

From the social point of view, the real unit share must be increased until the marginal contribution to innovation given by an increase of the real unit effort equalises the marginal cost of a reduction of the financial unit contribution given by the decrease of its effort.

Given that we assume that property right shares are determined in a bargaining process, what are the effects of bargaining on the optimal social sharing rule?

In order to analyse this point we introduce here a bargaining procedure based on the well known "perfect equilibrium" approach to bilateral monopoly bargaining (Rubinstein, 1982; Binmore et al., 1986; Sutton, 1986). The innovation is the share that has to be split into two parts in a game with alternating offers ending when one player's proposal is accepted by the other player. The players' bargaining strength depends on their "relative impatience" represented by the ratio of their respective discount rates r_j/r_i. In this first simple version of the model there is no outside option for the two counterparts (there are no other players in the same technological segment) and the imperfect information on the opponent quality makes uncertain the definition of relative contribution to the technological venture. The consequence is that bargaining on relative shares is not weighted for the expected value of innovation. When the value of innovation is normalised to one then the Nash maximand of the game is then equal to:

$$\Omega = q_i^\beta (1 - q_i) \qquad (18)$$

with $\beta = r_F/r_I$. The first order condition with respect to q_I gives the following result:

$$\frac{\partial \lg \Omega}{\partial \lg q} = \frac{\beta}{q_i} - \frac{1}{1 - q_i} = 0 \qquad (19)$$

with $q = \beta/1-\beta$

The introduction of the bargaining procedure in the model allows us to give a new, richer interpretation of the (17). Given that the probability or "common technology" function must now be expressed as:

$$p = a_i(q_i(\beta)) + 1 - (q_i(\beta))a_F \qquad (20)$$

we have that:

$$\frac{\partial p}{\partial \beta} = \frac{\partial p}{\partial p} \frac{\partial p}{\partial \beta} = \left[a_i^{'}(q_i) - a_i^{'}(q_i) \right] (\frac{1}{1+\beta^2}) \tag{21}$$

Social optimality is achieved in the same way as in (17) when the marginal revenues in terms of contribution to innovation given by an increase of the real unit effort equalises the marginal cost of a reduction of the financial unit contribution given by the decrease of its effort.

3.3 A parametric example of the encompassed model with shared property rights

A parametric example may better illustrate the above considerations. Without great loss of generality we assume that in the probability or "common knowledge" function, the property share incentive has a linear and multiplicative effect on effort $(q'(a_I)>0, q''(a_I) = 0)$ and that unit efforts are expressed in terms of relative contribution to the venture with $a_I + a_F = 1$.

The probability function is now equal to $p = q_I a_I + (1-q_I) a_F$. When $q_I = a_I$ then $p = 2(a_I)^2 + 1 - 2 a_I = X$. If instead, an imbalance exists between relative property rights and relative contributions to the technological venture and if, for instance, the financial unit relative bargaining strength exceeds its relative contribution ($q_I = a_I - \epsilon$), the probability outcome will be $p = 2(a_I)^2 + 1 - 2 a_I + [\epsilon(1-2a_I)]$. The term which is now added to X will be negative only if $a_I > 1/2$. We must remember that i) the previously adopted bargaining procedure gives a share to the real unit so that $q_I = \beta/(1-\beta)$; ii) the imbalance between relative property rights and relative contributions $q_I < a_I$ reflects the imbalance between relative bargaining strength and relative contributions given that $\beta/(1-\beta) < a_I$ can be rewritten as $\beta < a_I/1 - a_I$.

In this case, the asymmetry between relative bargaining powers and relative contributions to innovation is not always negative in social terms as it raises (respectively lowers) the probability of innovating when it is in favour of the unit which has the relatively higher (lower) contribution to innovation.

Provided that social nonoptimal equilibria may be achieved (but are not necessarily achieved) with the bargaining strength-contribution asymmetry and that the incentive problem obviously creates a coordination failure-positive spillover problem, we should verify if the second level of inefficiency is realised. This happens when a unit, even being informed on relative contributions and calculating the consequences of its bargaining power on the expected value of innovation has still an individual incentive to achieve a social suboptimal equilibria. This occurs when a larger share of a smaller cake is better for her than a smaller share of a larger one (see Figure 2.1).

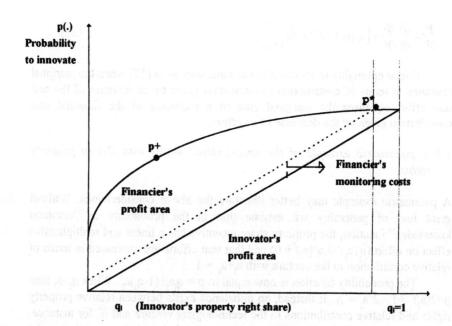

Figure 2.1 The incentive-property right dilemma in venture capital financing

Legend:

Let $p(.)$ be the probability of finding a technological innovation whose market value is normalised to 1.

If $p(.)$ is concave and only depends on the innovator effort and if all the bargaining strength is in the hands of the financier the property right share equilibrium is at p^+ (which is also the private optimum of the financier), a point which is socially inferior to p^*(the social optimum constrained to the zero profit condition of the financier). The solutions of the bargaining may be found at any point on the arch between p^+ and p^*. But any point different from p^* turns out to be socially inefficient.

Using a previous example, we know that the probability of innovating when $q_I = a_I - \varepsilon$ is equal to:

$$p = X + \varepsilon(1 - 2a_1)$$ (22)

where $X = 2(a_1)^2 + 1 - 2a_1$ stands for the probability of the case with no bargaining asymmetry. We suppose that the asymmetric information bargaining inefficiency occurs and that $a_1 > 1/2$. In this context, if the payoff of the financial unit with $q_i = a_1$ is $U_F = XV(1-q_i)$ with an increase of the financial unit bargaining power $(q_i = a_1 - \varepsilon)$ it becomes:

$$p = [X + \varepsilon(1 - 2a_1)]V + (1 - a_1 + \varepsilon)$$ (23)

We may then define the following proposition:

Proposition 3: (third inefficiency). In a context of perfect information over relative contributions to innovation, provided that the ratio between relative bargaining powers and relative contributions to the innovation is in favour of the financial unit and that this unit is perfectly informed on the relative contributions, it pays it to exert more bargaining power than what would be socially optimum if: $XV\varepsilon + \varepsilon$ (1-2a₁)V(1-a₁+ε) 0 which is the same as [X + (1-2a₁)(1-a₁+ε)] 0. In this case the division of property rights is socially inefficient.

3.4 The encompassing representation of the model with multiple financial and real agents: the conditions for the generation of a district

The simple two agent game analysed above has the advantage of deriving the three kinds of inefficiencies of venture capital financing of a technological venture. Nonetheless, a better approximation to reality may be represented in a more complex model where, in the market segment of the technological product, more than one financial and real unit exist and where the original coordination failure problem is mixed with market dynamics that can affect the bargaining terms of the problem. We represent the technological district (TD) in the model as an area where, according to the description for British markets provided in previous paragraphs, "N" financing units and "M" innovating units exist. In the modified version of the game, new effects are added to the simple version problem and what happens is mainly that a positive effect for the overall system due to Marshallian externality is offset by a negative effect due to the Schumpeterian phenomenon of "creative destruction" that underlines the presence of "losers" in the innovating process.

The presence of many units modifies the "common knowledge" function of the encompassing model in the following way:

$$T = f(a_F a_I, N, M) \quad f_1, f_2, f_3, f_4 > 0 \; f_{12} > 0$$

$$F = 1, .., N \tag{24}$$

$$I = 1, .., M$$

where T has constant returns in (a_F, a_I) and increasing returns in (a_F, a_I, N, M), positive externalities stemming from the number of participants to the TD are added to the previously analysed interaction between the fundamental units of the district. The increase in the number of participants has the effect of increasing the production of technology which is a quasi-public good and that part of technological and financial knowledge which is "appropriable" by all the members of the TD.

The payoffs for the different kind of players will be respectively:

$$.V_F = p\left[f(a_F, a_I, N, M)a_F, a_{-F}, N, M\right] \tag{25}$$

and:

$$.V_I = p\left[f(a_I, a_F, N, M)a_I, a_{-I}, N, M\right] \tag{26}$$

where a_{-F} and a_{-I} represent respectively the incidence of other financial (real) units on the payoff function of a financial (real) unit. To control the existence of positive spillovers in the model we must consider that in the model the two relevant equations for partial spillovers are for financing units:

$$\frac{\partial V_F}{\partial a_I} = \pi_1 f_2 > 0 \tag{27}$$

$$\frac{\partial V_F}{\partial a_{-F}} = \pi_1 f_1 - \pi_3 \leq \; \geq 0 \tag{28}$$

and for innovating units:

$$\frac{\partial V_I}{\partial a_F} = \pi_1 f_2 > 0 \tag{29}$$

$$\frac{\partial V_I}{\partial a_{-I}} = \pi_1 f_1 - \pi_3 \leq \; \geq 0 \tag{30}$$

the uncertainty on the sign of the derivative in (28) and (30) depends on the presence of two effects. The improved strategy of one firm has, on one side, a negative effect on another firm belonging to the same sector, because, ceteris paribus, it reduces its profit margins. But, on the other side, it has a positive effect because it positively affects the technology function.

3.5 The encompassed model with many real and financial agents

In the encompassed model the introduction of multiple units changes the probability function into:

$$T(a_I, a_F, M, N) = p(a_I) + v(a_F) + d(M, N) \qquad (31)$$

where d(M,N) represents the positive external knowledge contribution added to the probability of achieving innovation given by the existence of Marshallian externalities in a multiple unit district.

We maintain the imperfect information assumption that units are imperfectly informed on their relative strength, since they cannot exactly know the "counterpart type". Nonetheless, they are aware that the presence of multiple units has a double effect. It increases the external knowledge and the probability of innovation, but it reduces the expected profits from innovation[5]. New arguments are consequently introduced in the expected value of the innovation that will now be EV = p(N,M,..)V(M,..) where p'(M) and p'(N) are positive reflecting the positive external knowledge effect and V'(M) is negative reflecting the negative market competitiveness effect.

The existence of multiple units produces an additional change in the model because the outside option for the units, represented by the possibility of reaching an agreement with another unit is now strictly positive. The Nash maximand is now:

$$\Omega = (q_I p(M, N, ..) V(M, ..) A_I)^{\beta} \left\{ [p(M, N, ..) - q_I V(M, ..)] - A_F \right\} \qquad (32)$$

where A_I and A_F represent the outside option for the innovator and for the financier respectively and may be written as:

$$A_I = p_{OI} q_I p(M, N, ..) \qquad (33)$$

and:

$$A_I = \max \left\{ p_{OF} p(M, N, ..) V(M, ..)(1 - q_I), F \right\} \qquad (34)$$

81

where $p_{OI}=f(M/N)$ is the probability of finding another partner for the innovating unit which is decreasing in the M/N ratio ($f_1<0$) and $p_{OF}=g(M/N)$ is the probability of finding another partner for the financial unit which is increasing in the M/N ratio $g_1>0$. The financier's outside option has another important factor F which represents financing investment opportunities alternative to innovation financing (more purely financial operations such as buy-in and buy-out financing).

The first order condition from the logarithmic transform of the Nash maximand gives the following expression:

$$\frac{\beta}{q_1 V(M,..)-A_1}\left[V(M,..)-f\left(\frac{M}{N}\right)V(M,..)\right]=\frac{V(M,..)-g(\frac{M}{N})V(M,..)}{V(M,..)(1-q_1)-A_F} \qquad (35)$$

Comparative statics on (35) shows that an increase in the N/M ratio has an unambiguously negative effect on the innovating unit share, while an increase of the N units has three effects: it reduces real unit outside option, it increases the common knowledge and the probability of innovation and it reduces expected profits from innovation itself.

This result provides relevant normative insights. The conditions stated by the model with multiple agents for the occurrence of the coordination failure inefficiency are quite likely to be met in the empirical venture capital reality. In fact, the financier is very likely to have higher relative bargaining power and lower relative time impatience than the innovator running the technological race. Moreover, the alternative financing opportunities of the financier increase his outside option, further reducing the innovator's property right share resulting from the bargaining procedure. What often occurs is that the property right share obtained by the innovator seriously underevaluates his marginal contribution to the innovation, reducing the expected value of innovation and thereby leading to a nonoptimal social outcome. The model explains why innovation policies in several countries are aimed at creating more financial units in the district (BES experience in UK, R&D partnerships in US and the SOFICA (Société Financière Cinematographiques) in France (Panes 1988; Florida-Kenney, 1988; Bygrave-Shulman, 1988), meanwhile providing tax relief for venture capital financing. In this way outside options of financing units are reduced and those of real units increased, thus redressing the bargaining strength unbalance and reducing social inefficiency.

This explains also the above documented phenomenon of the decline in financing innovation by venture capital units. When outside financing opportunities are favourable and information costs reduce the profit margin of financing innovation, a large part of the financial unit may choose less risky investment opportunities, reducing their support for innovation.

3.6 The effect of financier information costs in the encompassed model with multiple agents

The important issue underlined by the "small ticket" problem is that the venture capitalist incurs relevant informational costs in the evaluation of the innovative project[6]. It is then reasonable to assume in our model that informational costs for the financier do matter in the bargaining procedure and in the determination of final property rights.

Starting from the simple two-unit "encompassed" model we may calculate informational costs as a percentage of the financier profits from innovation. In this case the Nash maximand becomes:

$$\Omega = q_I^\beta (1 - q_I - c_F) \tag{36}$$

where c_f represents the information costs as a share in the financier's net exploitable rent. It is trivial to show that in this case the first order condition from the (35) gives $q_I = (1-c_f)/(1+\beta)$. This means that the informational cost, as a reduction of the net exploitable rent of the financier reduces innovator share. This generates three potential negative effects: i) if a relative bargaining/relative contribution asymmetry in favour of the financier does exist, it is worsened by informational costs and social efficiency is further reduced; ii) if the situation is such that: $\beta/(1+\beta)=a_1$ but $\beta(1-c_f)/(1+\beta)<a_1$ the presence of financier information costs generates a social inefficiency that would not have existed otherwise; iii) if there is an outside option for the financier and it is larger than the exploitable rent from the venture capital agreement net of information costs, the financing units prefer alternative investments to venture capital investment. In the perspective of a model with multiple agents, then a reduction of the financier's information costs may then lead to more financial units in the venture capital bargaining process, reducing the asymmetry when this is not in favour of the innovators.

4. Conclusions

The empirical evidence on the relationship between finance and innovation shows that for small and new innovating firms asymmetric information may impose severe agency costs on equity and bond financing (Fazzari-Hubbard-Petersen, 1988; Devereux-Schiantarelli, 1989) making it more advantageous to resort to a form of venture capital financing where a financing partner with some technological skills relaxes the innovator cash constraint in exchange for a participation in future profits from innovation.

Such a form of innovation financing, though, has recently declined, with the tendency of venture capital units to prefer pure financial investments to the provision of technology financing in favour of small innovative firms. The model presented in the paper provides a formal framework capable of explaining all these phenomena and connecting these explanations to the rationales often quoted in literature. The possibility for the innovating unit to be financed while maintaining full property rights on the venture is precluded by the "small ticket" problem of the financier (its informational costs prevent him from obtaining profits when the innovator has full property rights). On the other side, the division of property rights between the two units causes an "equity dilution" effect reducing incentives to innovate and the expected value of innovation. A further insight of the model is that it shows, by adopting a coordination failure approach, that in the game between one financier and one innovator two levels of coordination inefficiency may occur. This is because, when property right shares are bargained ex ante, an imbalance between relative bargaining strengths and relative contributions to the venture generates an inefficient division of property rights with a divergence between private and social optimum. The model also indicates as a normative prescription that such inefficiencies may partially be solved by an increase in the number of financiers, which explains why these policies are starting to be adopted in some industrial countries.

84

Notes

[1] BES experience in UK, R&D partnerships in US and the SOFICA (Societe Financiere Cinematographiques) in France (Panes 1988; Florida-Kenney, 1988; Bygrave-Shulman 1988).

[2] The following results, according to Cooper-John (1988), also apply to our game: i) strategic complementarity is a necessary condition for the existence of multiple SNE; ii) if the game exhibits positive spillovers the ability level, implementable with more effort, is inefficient; iii) if there are multiple SNE and global spillovers, SNE can be Pareto ranked and equilibria with higher level of effort (and consequently ability) are preferred; iv) strategic complementarity is a necessary condition for the presence of a multiplier in the game. The proof of the above mentioned statement may be found in Cooper-John. The demonstration of the second one simply comes from the definition of SCE and positive spillover as $V_2 > 0$ immediately removes the first order condition for a Symmetric Cooperative Equilibrium.

[3] To provide an example it may be considered that in some high-tech sector, like the development of software technology, the immaterial contribution of the innovative unit is much more important and less financial support is needed, while the discovery of a new drug in the pharmaceutical sectors requires far higher capital structure and financial support.

[4] The game implies the existence of a trade-off between entrepreneurial and financial risks where the solution of the coordination dilemma coincides with the improvement of the trade-off itself. In fact, before the venture capital agreement is reached, the real unit has full property rights on future innovation and a cash constraint which involves a relevant degree of financial risk. The agreement solves the cash constraint and the ensuing reduction of the financial risk is achieved against an increase of the entrepreneurial risk given by the property dilution disincentive effect on the real unit which is the one bearing the immaterial and intellectual effort costs.

[5] This happens in basic versions of vertical and horizontal oligopolistic competition. With vertical competition (Shaked-Sutton, 1983) an innovation from a competitor may reduce a firm market share or even drive it out of the market. With the traditional Hotelling horizontal competition (D'Aspremont et al., 1979) any new entry can only reduce market share.

[6] According to the institutional IMI experience (an Italian public venture capital financier) when a project is going to be financed two types of evaluation are performed: a financial one on the balance sheet of the innovator (requiring accountability skills) and a technological one (requiring engineering and economic skills) on the technical feasibility of the project and on its market feasibility.

85

References

Aghion, P. and Tirole, J.J. (1993), "On the management of the innovation", paper presented to the World Bank Conference "How do National Policies Affect Long Run Growth". Estoril, January.

Becchetti, L. (1994), "Finance, investment and innovation: a theoretical and empirical comparative analysis", paper presented to the 1994 Conference of the EEA, Maastricht.

Becchetti, L. (1994), "Finanza, investimenti e innovazione: un'analisi empirica del caso italiano". *Sviluppo Economico*.

Binmore, K., Rubinstein, A. and Wolinsky, A. (1986), "The Nash Bargaining Solution in Economic Modeling", *Rand Journal of Economics*, 17, (2): 176-188.

Bravard, N.W. and Frigstad, B.D. (1983), *Venture Capital Proposal Package*, Oasis Press.

Bryant, J. (1983), "A Simple Rational Expectations Keynes-Type Model", *Quarterly Journal of Economics*, 98, 525-528.

Bygrave, D.W. and Timmons, J.A. (1992), *Venture Capital at the Crossroads*, Harvard Business School Press, Boston.

Bygrave, D.W. and Timmons, J.A. (1985), "An Empirical Model for the Flows of Venture Capital", in J.A. Hornaday et. al. eds., *Frontiers of Entrepreneurial Research*, Wellesley MA, Centre for Entrepreneurial Studies.

Bygrave, D.W. and Shulman, J. (1988), "Capital Gains Tax: Bane of Boon for Venture Capital?" in B.A. Kirchhoff et al. eds., *Frontiers of Entrepreneurship Research*, Wellesley MA, Centre for Entrepreneurial Studies.

BVCA (British Venture Capital Association) (1985-92), *Report on Investment Activity*, London, British Venture Capital Association.

Cary, L. (1989), *The Venture Capital Report: Guide to Venture Capital in the UK*, London: Pitman, 4th edn.

Cooper, R. and John, A. (1988), "Coordinating Coordination Failures in Keynesian Models". *Quarterly Journal of Economics* 103, 441-464.

Devereaux, M. and Schiantarelli, F. (1989), "Investment, Financial Factors, and Cash Flow: evidence from UK Panel Data", *NBER Working Paper* 3116.

Fazzari, S.M., Hubbard, G.R. and Petersen, B.C., (1988) "Financing Constraints and Corporate Investments", *Brooking Papers on Economic Activities*, 141-195.

Florida, R. and Kenney, M. (1988), "Venture Capital and High Technology Entrepreneurship", *Journal of Business Venturing*, 3.

Fudenberg, D. and Tirole, J. (1992), *Game Theory*, MIT Press.

Gladstone, D. (1988), *Venture Capital Investing*, Prentice Hall.

Henderson, J.W. (1988), *Obtaining Venture Financing: A Guide for Entrepreneurs*, Lexington Books.

Rubinstein, A. (1982), "Perfect Equilibrium in a Bargaining Model", *Econometrica*, 50 (1), 97-109.

Santarelli, E. (1991), "Asset Specificity, R&D Financing and the Signalling Properties of Firm's Financial Structure", *Economics of Innovation and New technology*, 1.

Sutton, J. (1986), "Non-Cooperative Bargaining Theory: an Introduction". *Review of Economic Studies*, 53 (5), 709-724.

Tyebjee, T. and Vickery, L. (1988), "Venture Capital in Western Europe" *Journal of Venturing*, 15.

3   Venture capital and innovation in Europe

Laura Cavallo[*]

1. Introduction

The development of a venture capital market is a necessary condition for the growth of the economy. This is a truth that is now universally acknowledged and which is confirmed by experience in many countries. Many other countries are currently engaged in promoting programmes devoted to the stimulation of investment in new companies operating in the high technology sector.

Some interesting questions arise on the matter: what are the most effective of these initiatives, in which direction is it best to move and, most importantly, is the same programme of development equally effective in different countries? Is the creation of new systems of investment sufficient to guarantee the functionality of new initiatives and to produce positive economic effects?

The questions and the problems that we meet in analysing the financing of venture capital are inter-related, and therefore it is unrealistic to hope that any one possible solution could give an exhaustive answer to the problem. We need to select certain key aims and to identify the best way to achieve them. The solution generally proves to be country-specific, since each country is characterised by its own structure and by psychological and cultural traditions which are difficult to model.

Take for instance the case of Italy. The development of a market economy in Italy has long been hindered by a deep-rooted culture of bonds and grants. Lately, the picture has profoundly changed, as evidenced, for example, by the SIM law, the Antiriciclaggio law, the Antitrust law, the law against insider trading, the beginning of privatisation, the law that enables banks to embark on business ventures and the approval of the much-needed law on closed-end funds.

On paper, all the conditions exist for the improved working of the financial system and for the relaunch of economic development. In fact, the system has experienced difficulty in starting up: there are still some legal obstacles that must be eliminated and there's more work to be done to remove cultural setbacks.

In this study, it is appropriate to begin with a brief picture of the conditions of venture capital supply and demand in Italy. Once the characteristics of the market have been outlined, we have tried to define the subjects of this study, namely venture capital and technological innovation.

We have also studied the relationship between innovation and its financial requirements. The uncertainty on the results of innovation and about the time before they take effect are affected by the nature of the required financing. Financial risks and economic risks are strongly correlated.

The innovative activities, moreover, produce financial requirements that it is difficult to quantify, because it is not easy to separate the single innovations from the overall conduct of the firm. We have therefore analysed the characteristics of venture capital, which is by definition the finance directed towards new firms with strong potential for growth. These firms are also very risky as they are subject to a high probability of failure. In any case, the venture capitalist is an investor who is willing to risk, and who usually possesses specific competences that enable him to follow and to monitor at close quarters the innovative activity, thereby giving material as well as financial support.

A venture capitalist must study the optimal level of involvement with the firm that he is financing. Over-involvement by the venture capitalist can cause excessive reduction in the authority of the manager undertaking the project and can result in a lack of incentive on the part of the manager to minimise costs and to look after the interests of other shareholders - the well known principal-agent problem.

It is also important to determine the stage of development of the firm, since this will greatly affect the need for capital and the degree of investment risk involved. For example, a closed-end fund diversifies its portfolio among instruments in firms at an early stage of development, which are riskier but have high probability of gain, and in firms in expansion.

We then focus our attention on the sources of venture capital: we note that a large proportion of such funds come from banks. Banks are a typical source of venture capital in most countries; in Italy, they have been able to exploit the potential offered by the new banking laws, under which banks are permitted to purchase firms' equity. Given that Italy does not possess a proper venture capital sector at the moment and that such a sector will take time to build up, and also that the stock market is not able to handle a large amount of risk capital from foreign or private Italian companies, banks are currently a very important source of such capital to new firms.

However, empirical results show that, although most venture capital funding comes from banks, there is no correlation between bank financing and early-stage financing, i.e. finance to new and young firms, which is of most interest to us. Presumably banks, which are by nature risk-averse, prefer to diversify their own portfolio and to offset the financing of the riskier firms by financing other firms also, which are at a more advanced stage of development and which are therefore safer.

By means of an analysis of panel data on sixteen European countries, I have tried to find a relationship between venture capital raised by different types of investor and the distribution of investment, with the aim of identifying ways by which the high-technology sector can attract investment funds. The financial potential of the bank sector and of institutional investors is not to be underestimated. But in order to extract the maximum advantage from this potential, it is necessary to overcome the risk aversion of such investors. The closed-end fund could be used as an instrument to channel these investors towards new firms and towards technological innovation by offering them the safety of an efficient portfolio diversification. The international experience has shown the efficacy of such investment in favouring the growth of small and medium-sized firms. The necessary laws now exist, together with many other legislative measures which seem to herald a promising future. It is possible that the only problem that remains is the excessive strictness and lack of co-ordination of the different actions. As Marco Vitale, President of AIFI, says, "the problem is in passing from a bureaucratic culture to a market culture".

2. Obstacles to the introduction of risk capital in Italian firms: conditions surrounding the issue of new shares

The capitalist system in Italy is of the "family" type, i.e. strongly linked to the firm owner or to his family.

This characteristic is one of the main reasons why the Italian system is incapable of ensuring growth other than through profits re-investment. The existing shareholders have always seen the issue of new shares on the market as a threat to their control over the firm rather than an opportunity to develop and eventually qualitatively to improve the firm structure. More recently we seem to be approaching a more mature stage of capitalism, where a modest increase in the recourse to the market can be seen, even though it is not sufficient, at the moment, to produce a radical change in the choice faced by firms.

To the above scant willingness of firms to finance themselves by means of venture capital funds, we need to add the difficulty met by firms in finding these funds. The poor performance of the stock market in Italy, the scantiness of the market, the over-large ratio of return to risk on Treasury bonds, have all contributed to decrease the savers' interest in firms. Firms investing in technological innovation, which are the subject of the present analysis, find it rather difficult to finance their activities, given the high level of risk involved. The recent legislative moves constitute the basis for renewing the system and for increasing the overall supply of risk capital.

3. The qualitative and quantitative characteristics of the financial needs of innovation

3.1 Definitions of innovation

Before analysing the sources of finance for innovation, we need to analyse the activity of innovation itself and the financial needs arising out of it.

It is important that the innovating industry be able to "isolate" the innovation, so as to establish the qualitative and quantitative dynamics of the specific financial needs of innovation and to identify specific risks and returns that the innovation can offer. The possibility of "isolating" the innovation is no doubt very important to the innovating industry, which is as much interested in determining the qualitative and quantitative dynamics of the specific financial need as in the relative contribution to financial re-balancing that the object of innovation can offer. Identification of innovation is also important for a potential overseas financier, who will certainly be interested in verifying the capacity of the innovation to generate adequate profits and in examining the possibilities it offers in terms of risk and return.

Project financing is useful as long as it is possible to identify and to evaluate, by means of adequate objective criteria, flows and sources of finance generated by investment internal to the firm. If these criteria are missing, we move from a situation where we study the financing of innovation to a situation in which we study the financing of the firm itself.

A survey carried out by the IMI on innovative activity in manufacturing firms (Pezzoli, 1984) confirmed that the overall approach to firms' financing has an impact on the development of innovation. The analysis demonstrates that, save for very rare cases, the more innovative firm has better financial controls and higher levels of self-investment.

This does not imply that it is possible to continue to finance well-defined innovatory projects by means of destination funding, even though it is easier to generate such funds from public sources, as it has so far been the case, than from private investors.

92

3.2 Determination of financial need

It is not easy to quantify the financial needs of technological innovation, because it is very difficult to separate innovation from the general functioning of the firm as a whole.

This is demonstrated by the fact that, in spite of the existence of a large amount of literature on other aspects of technological innovation, very little of it is devoted to the analysis of innovation financing. However, it is possible to find incidental references to the subject within studies of other aspects of the process of innovation.

Existing relationships between technology and firms have to be analysed before we can study the financial aspects of innovation. First of all, we can divide firms that produce technological innovation into three types (Paci, 1979; Munari, 1979):

- newly established firms
- established firms that intend to introduce a product innovation
- established firms that intend to introduce a process innovation.

Each of the above types can be inserted into a general model that can predict volume and dynamics of innovation financial requirements and therefore suggest appropriate methods of financing. For established firms that intend to introduce a new product, a life-cycle model will be appropriate, with the different phases of the product life cycle characterised by different magnitudes of funding need and associated levels of risk. It is possible to see how different forms of venture capital intervention can respond to the different combinations of risk and funding requirement.

It is also important to distinguish between big and small firms. Size-related discrimination between firms is implicit in the categorisation of firms according to their relationship with their technology. It is obvious that a small firm would not be able to fund its innovatory activity itself and would probably purchase rights to other firms' innovations.

In any case, the distinction between big and small firms is highly significant in that the difficulty that small firms often face in finding sources of finance can form an obstacle to innovation and reduce the range of opportunities available to them. In addition, small firms will face more difficulties than big firms in planning a strategy for innovation and in costing the expected risks and returns of the project.

3.3 Typical risks associated with innovation

Returns from investment in innovation are subject to a high level of uncertainty and are not easily predicted from past experience in the process of innovation. Classical investment analysis methods are not always suitable tools with which to measure project risk; forecasts about the cash flows and their associated probabilities are at best approximate. Additionally, financial limitations themselves can increase the risk of the innovatory activity: financial risk has a strong positive correlation with economic risk. This last can depend on:

- technological risk, i.e. the possibility that innovation may not lead to useful results
- temporal risk, i.e. the possibility that the innovation may be ahead of time, so that the system is yet not mature enough to exploit it, or that the innovation is already obsolete by the time that it is completed
- market risk, i.e. the possibility that the invention may be insufficiently competitive in the market.

4. Venture capital

4.1 Identification of venture capital activity

Venture capital is finance directed towards the innovating firm rather than towards the individual project.

The literature on venture capital has provided different definitions of the aims and characteristics of venture capital. Generally, venture capital is defined as finance targeting either new or very young firms, which undertake innovation in the broad sense of the word and which have a strong potential for growth (Sandro Sandri, 1988). Firms which are in receipt of venture capital typically have a high probability of failure.

Venture capital investment usually takes the form of a minority participation in the company's share capital or of a subscription to convertible bonds, for a medium to long period of time, in a small or medium-size company, together with the contribution of professional expertise that will be useful to the development of the targeted firm.

Even if venture capital takes the form of equity participation, it still remains a form of intervention, because the investing firm can withdraw its finance, even in the initial phase of such investment. If the company is quoted on the stock exchange, shares can be sold to the public or to other companies that may wish to take over the firm. The investing firm generally derives its profit from capital gains, which are realised when the price of discontinuing participation is higher than the cost of purchase. Periodic remuneration such as dividends can be expected only on rare occasions when the investing company participates indirectly by means of convertible debt or options.

Since the definition of venture capital is not unique, it may be useful to select those characteristics that all definitions have in common in order to correctly identify the venture capitalist. Homogeneous definitions can be supplied by the main associations operating within the sector.

The main agent in Europe is the European Venture Capital Association (EVCA), established in Brussels in 1983 and aimed stimulating and co-ordinating the development of venture capital at European level. Our empirical analysis, which is presented in a later section of this paper, relies on EVCA data. EVCA definitions are essential in order to interpret the data correctly. Given that venture capital is an important means of innovation finance in Europe, the EVCA was set up with the active support of the EC[1].

EVCA defines venture capitalists as agents:

- whose main activity consists of the provision of finance by means of a participation in the capital of firms which are in the early stages of their lifecycle and which demonstrate a significant potential for growth in areas involving new products or services or new technology

- whose main objective is the achievement of sufficient capital gains in the medium to long-term to offset the high level of risk

- who invest principally in unquoted securities or securities which are accepted in other regulated markets

- who can provide active management support to administer their investments

- who can provide active management support to the recipients of their investment.

The last point is particularly important as it underlines the level of internal involvement of the venture capitalist, who may feel able to provide advice and support in addition to capital investment. However, unlike similar interventions which are designed to provide support for development and which may have a predominantly public character, the only objective of venture capitalists is the realisation of significant capital gains. These must be sufficient to compensate not only for the cost of the invested capital and the operating costs of the support provided for the investment, but also for the high risk and for any losses resulting from unsuccessful investment.

4.2 Distribution of the stages of investment

The venture capitalist can choose between several methods of financing. The venture capitalist's portfolio strategy will usually dictate the criterion that is selected. The criteria most often used for selecting the type of financing agreement are as follows:

1. Volume of investment: generally the venture capitalist would prefer to concentrate his portfolio rather than to diversify into a large number of investments. It also must be remembered that increased diversification results in increased costs. On the other hand, the phenomenon of several venture capitalists investing in a single company has also been observed. In the US, for example, the average innovating company figured in the portfolios of ten venture capital companies.

2. Technology and the sector of the market: venture capitalists prefer to invest in sectors of which they have previous experience, so that they can more easily value the company and control the development of their investment. Venture capitalists are most likely to invest in manufacturing companies and in innovation products.

3. Stage of development: each stage of development of a company is associated with a different level of investment capital need and connected investment risk. A firm can be described as being either in an early stage of development, or in the growth stage, or in some other stage (such as being the subject of a leveraged buy-out). Such classification can help the venture capitalist to predict the sequence of future requirements for finance and to decide on a suitable investment strategy. The possible kinds of finance are:

Seed financing: the financing of an idea which is still at experimental stage. Such financing requires limited resources but entails a very high level of risk. This stage involves product development, but rarely includes product marketing.

Start-up: the financing of the development and initial marketing of the product. Such finance is usually directed at new or very young companies, usually less than one year old. Such companies may have insufficient information on the commercial value of their product due to limited distribution and marketing opportunities. At this stage these companies must redefine their organisational structure and management as well as their marketing strategy, to improve product targeting. Investment in this phase is characterised by high resource requirements as well as high levels of risk.

First-stage financing: financing of the initial phases of expansion of innovation. The activity is already well underway, but the full commercial value of the product is yet to be established. It is generally at this stage that finance is first received from venture capitalists. At this stage, the financial requirement is high, but is offset by a lower level of risk than at the previous stages.

Expansion financing: this can be of two kinds.
- Second stage finance, when the product's profitability is known, but the company is still in its growth stage and has yet to show profits.
- Later stage financing, which includes third-stage finance and bridging finance. Third stage finance is required to consolidate development while the company is still growing and has begun to yield profits or has reached its break-even point. Funds are used to generate further expansion, to improve the product, or to launch new products and to increase market share. Risks are moderate at this stage, but the need for finance is still high. Bridging finance is the finance that is made available to a company to carry it through the transition from being privately owned to being publicly quoted.

Financing at other stages
- leverage/management buy-out financing: for various reasons, the business can be subjected to a change of management or ownership. Institutional investors may favour a change in management but lack the necessary finance. The most frequently used methods of raising such finance are:
  - management buy-out: this enables current management and investors to acquire an existing product line or business.
  - management buy-in: in this case, the financing aims at enabling a manager or group of managers from outside the company to buy-in to the company with the support of venture capital investors.
  - Leveraged buy-out: the purchase of the majority of shares in the company by using internal financial means. A new group takes control of the company using funds originating from within the company itself. Venture capital intervention serves not only to organise the operation, but also to supply the new managers or entrepreneurs with financial and professional support.
  - Turn-around financing: financing aimed at companies experiencing financial difficulties, with the purpose of providing not only capital but also professional expertise to re-establish financial viability.

97

4.3 Preliminary considerations in the choice of Optimal Portfolio Strategy according to the stage of financial intervention

To summarise the previous section, four stages of intervention can be distinguished: financing at the initial stage of development, expansion financing, leveraged buy-out and re-balancing operations. Venture capital most often operates during the first and second stages; indeed, venture capital is strictly defined as being financial intervention at the early phases of development, because it is only at these stages that it can be clearly distinguished from more traditional financing. In fact, traditional finance is not usually able to support innovation in the early stages, as the risks involved are excessive under standard loan valuations.

The first stage and the leveraged buy-out represent extreme cases when ranked by level of risk, so that venture capital intervention at each of these stages can meet portfolio diversification requirements. Venture capital funding, in the strict sense, is directed to a company which does not yet possess sufficient collateral to guarantee financing from other sources. The company may not yet have a market, nor a developed product, nor sufficiently experienced personnel. The risk is that the company will never be able to develop a level of activity that is sufficient for the investor to profit from the investment.

A leveraged buy-out defines the acquisition of a firm that is financed by minimum recourse to risk capital and maximum recourse to credit. This permits the exploitation of the debt potential of the company subject to the take-over in order to obtain the necessary financing. This differs from the usual acquisitions in terms of reduced requirement on the part of the predator company. The objective of this latter is simply to obtain the highest level of credit concession compatible with the repayment capability of the target company. The cash flow from the company's ordinary operation should allow to repay the financing obtained. In such a case, market, production and management risk do not exist; the sole risk is financial risk and this is represented by the eventuality that the value of the company and the cash flows generated are insufficient to repay the debt incurred. At the early stages of development, the amount of risk is certainly higher, particularly if the investment is directed towards innovation. As a result, the capital gains which can be expected from intervening at this stage will also be correspondingly high.

The choice between specialisation of investment, which increases the likelihood of high returns, and diversification, reduce risk, is based on several factors (Norton and Tenenbaum, 1933).

We need to examine first the investor's access to sources of professional expertise: if he has proven experience in the firm's sphere of activity, the probability of failure is greatly reduced and specialisation would be the best course.

We also need to examine the environment within which venture capital operates. In the US, we see increased competition in equity investment between venture capital and business and investment banks, brokers and leveraged buy-out funds (Sandri, 1988). The increased competition has resulted in the reduction of the mobility of portfolio funds, leading to increased diversification, to a greater tendency towards leveraged buy-outs, and resulting in a change in the basic definition of venture capital. That is why we must first attempt to distinguish between the activities of merchant banks and those of venture capitalists. We have already said that venture capital, strictly speaking, applies to firms at early stages of their development. Merchant banks generally operate at the expansion and growth stages, when their activity is characterised by reduced levels of risk , and target their financing at more mature companies. They also prefer to invest in companies whose activities are strategic/financial rather than technological.

In Europe, start-up finance, being the riskiest form of venture capital finance, is the most difficult to organise, and accounts for 10-11% of all venture capital investment, on average. In the US, it accounts for 30% of all venture capital investment.

The following table emphasises the typical distribution of investment by closed-end funds in the US. The highest figures are shared by early stage (40.9%) and expansion (40.7%) investment. The data also shows that early stage investment is characterised by high risk (61.9 % failure) but high prospects of gain (50% of the successful investments generated profits of 400% or more); expansion investment, in spite of the prospect of relatively lower gain, offered greater security (23.8% failure).

Table 3.1 Distribution by stage of closed end fund quotas (US 1992)

	A	B	C
Early stage	40.9%	61.9%	50.0%
Expansion	40.7%	23.8%	38.3%
LBO/acquisition	10.2%	11.9%	6.7%
Other	8.2%	2.4%	5.0%

4.4 Sources of finance and their portfolio choices

Motivations driving participants in European venture capital will obviously differ from financier to financier. The public operator will naturally be more interested in matters concerning public interest such as the creation of new employment, support for regional development plans, promotion of incentives to research and the application of new technology.

On the other hand, financial institutions such as banks, insurance companies and investment funds mainly see venture capital as a highly remunerative type of investment that is capable of compensating the profit loss resulting from falling interest rates, due to the increasingly prevalent phenomenon of banking disintermediation and to the success of other sources of finance.

Investment funds, which have access to large sums of capital and which prefer a higher degree of diversification, are potentially an important source of venture capital. However, the portfolio approach which informs the investment decisions of these institutions forces them to seek out low risk investments, which are generally short-term in duration. This is undoubtedly an obstacle to the development of this source of capital.

In some European countries, the closed-end funds have been developed; this constitutes what is potentially a very promising instrument for venture capital activity, overcoming as it does the limit of open-end funds (investors cannot withdraw their funds and claim redemption of their quotas at any time prior to the terminal date of the investment).

"Corporate venture capital", that is the venture capital coming from the big industrial groups, follows an investment strategy that is less strongly linked to the achievement of certain short-term profitability. In fact, such firms tend to share companies which specialise in the development of new or technologically oriented activities, aiming at combining the respective advantages of large and small dimension with the objective of continuously supporting research and development: small firms have often demonstrated greater efficiency, producing better results with lower costs. Private investors, who have substantial personal funds, have an important role too: unlike institutions, private individuals have personal interests which can over-ride purely economic considerations; they are willing to run greater risks and to be satisfied with lower profits.

5. Survey of the sources and destinations of venture capital in Europe

Venture capital activity in Europe has shown remarkable growth over the last ten years. Nowadays, this sector covers over 500 industries and comprises some 2,400 professional or specialist investors.

5.1 Sources of investment funds

Banks are generally the main protagonists in the area (Figure 3.1) of venture capital, accounting for over a third of newly generated funding. Pension funds' and insurance companies' investment also has a key role in the growth of venture capital: in 1992 we can see a reduction of the pension fund contribution and a growth of investment capital by means of realised capital gains.

A significant proportion, between 9 and 10%, of funds flowing into the European market comes from overseas investors. As the table shows, the volume of funds generated by banks has been maintained over time at a higher level than the volume of funds generated by other sources. The data clearly show that the banking sector is a potential source of venture capital, even though it has not played a significant role in the financing of innovation so far.

Table 3.2 Venture capital investment in Europe 1987-92

	1987	1988	1989	1990	1991	1992
Cumulative funds raised to date	13,632,998	17,116,512	22,929,189	28,385,903	33,025,832	38,471,495
Venture capital raised by type of investor						
Corporate finance	477,686 (16.1%)	290,112 (8.3%)	421,350 (7.2%)	233,733 (5.1%)	214,892 (5.1%)	249,382 (5.9%)
Private individuals	134,171 (4.5%)	173,937 (5.0%)	125,935 (2.2%)	168,741 (3.7%)	196,866 (4.7%)	146,589 (3.5%)
Government agencies	112,014 (3.8%)	169,847 (4.9%)	299,543 (5.2%)	125,493 (2.7%)	66,729 (1.6%)	391,822 (9.3%)
Banks	1,044,184 (35.3%)	1,080,351 (31.0%)	1,788,194 (30.8%)	1,799,818 (39.3%)	1,517,132 (36.2%)	1,491,066 (35.4%)
Pension funds	560,859 (19.0%)	756,319 (21.7%)	765,663 (13.2%)	735,041 (16.1%)	611,354 (14.6%)	544,077 (12.9%)
Insurance companies	360,641 (12.2%)	408,651 (11.7%)	811,817 (14.0%)	698,156 (15.2%)	472,483 (11.3%)	389,890 (9.3%)
Academic institutions	16,845 (0.6%)	4,316 (0.2%)	4,029 (0.1%)	19,031 (0.4%)	12,345 (0.3%)	198 (0.0%)
Other sectors	146,206 (4.9%)	341,607 (9.8%)	1,176,143 (20.2%)	307,171 (6.7%)	374,911 (9.0%)	312,309 (7.4%)
Realised capital gains available for reinvestment	105,610 (3.6%)	258,374 (7.4%)	420,004 (7.2%)	491,396 (10.7%)	721,089 (17.2%)	688,441 (16.3%)
Tot.new funds for venture capital	2,958,216 (100%)	3,483,514 (100%)	5,812,677 (100%)	4,578,580 (100%)	4,187,801 (100%)	4,213,775 (100%)

Source: EVCA Yearbook.

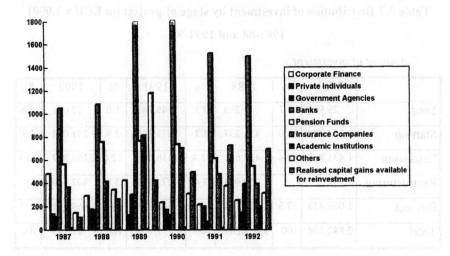

Figure 3.1 Sources of venture capital funds in Europe

5.2 Distribution of investment by stage

Data related to the volume and number of investments are differentiated according to the stage at which the investment was made. These show that there has been a major decrease in so-called "seed capital" or start-up financing, i.e. in the early stages of experimentation or introduction of a new product, in favour of investment in more mature projects at a later stage of development. This risk aversion which guides the investors' choices could strangle innovation, which is essential to national economic growth but which is risky to the individual investor. This is one of the problems that could be at least partly solved by the introduction of closed end funds. By diversifying investment, such funds allow high levels of repayment even in early-stage investment without increasing the risk of an individual investor's portfolio.

Table 3.3 Distribution of investment by stage of project (in ECU x 1,000)
1987-88 and 1991-92

Amount of investment

	1987	%	1988	%	1991	%	1992	%
Seed	29,982	1.1	9,238	0.3	45,942	1.0	27,001	0.6
Start-up	313,828	11.0	423,237	2.3	273,165	5.9	251,014	5.3
Expansion	1,431,862	50.4	1,427,681	41.4	2,436,048	52.6	2,150,937	45.8
Restructuring	/	/	259,904	7.4	272,863	5.9	402,650	8.6
Buy-out	1,066,436	37.5	1,331,144	38.6	1,603,883	34.6	1,869,641	39.8
Total	2,842,108	100	3,451,204	100	4,631,900	100	4,701,243	100

Number of investments

	1991	%	1992	%
Seed	255	3.7	133	2.2
Start-up	976	14.1	797	12.9
Expansion	3,906	56.6	3,527	56.9
Restructuring	478	6.9	631	10.2
Buy-out	1,292	18.7	1,109	17.9
Total	6,907	100	6,197	100

Source: EVCA Yearbook, 1993.

6. Progress of the law relating to innovation and the participation of banks in the management of firms

The new Consolidation Act relating to banks, which follows the Second Community Directive CEE 89/646 relating to the co-ordination of the activity of credit corporations, represents an important development in the relationship between banks and businesses. The law allows the possibility of operations similar to those of the German "Universal Banks", permitting credit corporations to intervene directly in firms' operations, while permitting firms to hold shares in the banks. This could constitute an important step towards favouring the influx of risk capital towards business. The bank sector is a major source of venture capital; given the unlikely prospect that a flourishing venture capital sector will be established within the foreseeable future in Italy, either by Italian or foreign agencies, we should not neglect the potential that the banks represent as a source of finance for innovation.

The results achieved the merchant banks, which are designed to participate in the management of their client firms, have not been as good as it might be expected when compared with the performance of their peers elsewhere. One of the reasons for the poor performance of Italian merchant banks could be the small size of Italian firms, which makes the cost of monitoring investment too high. The well-known problem of asymmetric information (Stiglitz and Weiss, 1981) reduces the efficiency of the relationship between banks and firms, resulting in market imperfections (Akerlof, 1970) and problems such as moral hazard and adverse selection. A closer examination of themes in the literature on this subject points out the fact that the only instrument that the bank has to protect itself from risks and to reduce informational asymmetry is to gain some degree of control over the firms to which they grant funds. This control can be gained by a more sustained and comprehensive monitoring of the firm's financial statements and of its operations. It is easy to understand the advantages enjoyed by merchant banks in countries where the average firm size is large, since controlling a small number of big firms is less difficult than monitoring a large number of small ones.

The interest shown by financial institutions in merchant banking activity, with the exception of Mediobanca, has dropped. The aggregate figures shown in the table below show the relatively low levels of equity investments by Special Credit Institutes (ICS).

Table 3.4 Equity held by ICS (100,000,000 mlira)

1980	1985	1986	1987	1988	1989	1990	1991	1992	1993	1994
790	2,775	3,450	3,682	4,529	5,247	6,516	6,183	5,076	4,907	4,903*

* interim data for the month of February.

Bank of Italy, Annual Report, 1993.

6.1 The 1993 Banking Law: an incentive to venture capital from banks?

In Italy the implementation of the Second EC directive on bank co-ordination in Italy has occurred at a time of great change in finance and credit markets, owing

to a considerable legislative innovation which has come about in recent years[2].
The new law on banking has eliminated many of the mandates and limitations
shown above. Credit institutions can now freely assume control of firms:
provided that certain limits are not exceeded, there is no longer any need for
external authorisation. Such control can be acquired directly, without the need for
intermediation by merchant banks. Some limitations still exist and particular care
has been taken to limit the acquisition of control over firms which are in financial
difficulty. However, thanks to the elimination of past constraints, one can hope
that the involvement of banks in business will grow and that they will come
closer to the model of the "Universal bank".

The distinction between banks and ICS has been eliminated and the future
field of bank operation can range from the short term to the medium and long
term. The understandable fear that opening up the possibility of participation by
banks in the capital of non-financial firms will produce a new version of a mixed
bank, resulting in a breakdown of the system similar to what occurred in the past,
does not seem to hold under deeper scrutiny. The participation by banks was not
the cause of the crisis nor the result of a reasoned strategy; it was instead the
inevitable consequence of a downward spiral provoked by the policy of
centralisation of the finance interaction between "mixed" banks and large firms,
and by the ensuing difficulty for the latter to find resources in the property
market. (Portrain, 1992).

In any event, banks have the advantage, compared with risk capital
holders, of already being in possession of information about firms they are to
become involved with, and also of being able to gain information about firms
with which they had no previous dealings. As economic financiers, banks must
constantly monitor the companies they finance; therefore, the bank has an inside
knowledge of the firm's financial health even prior to participating in the firm's
operations and is in a good position for a constructive intervention in decision
making.

A recent survey (Becchetti, 1994) examines the financial systems that
favour technological innovation by comparing the German system, where the
universal bank prevails, with the British system, which prefers to use specialised
banks. Analysis shows that the German system is more capable of sustaining
firms of all sizes in their investment programmes than is the British system. This
result raises the hope that such a system will work in Italy as well. In order to
obtain the right result, it is necessary to prevent the bank from gaining complete
control over the firm and to guarantee the rights of minority shareholders. It is
interesting to note that the German system allows small shareholders to vote by
proxy; their representative can also ensure that the votes thus cast carry some
importance (Ristuccia, 1994).

Nevertheless, it can be seen that even negative effects can eventually have positive results. A firm having a representation on the board of directors of a bank will certainly have competitive advantage over rival firms, if they happen to be clients of the same bank, from its access to confidential information about them, and presumably it will also benefit from the availability of cheaper credit (Bagella and Paganetto, 1994). This effect on competition between firms can have a distorting effect on resource allocation, but can also favour the growth of firm size, leading eventually to the growth of industrial groups, with a correspondingly high market power. This is a desired result, since the family character of most Italian firms is an obstacle to international competitiveness, as it has already been pointed out: the firms' growth means economic growth. If the different interests could be balanced so as to favour competition, the banking system could become more competitive and venture abroad would have a higher probability of success.

6.2 The role of closed-end funds

Closed-end funds, even though they operate in a different legal and structural framework, are broadly homogeneous across the markets in which they are present and have developed very similar operative characteristics. Typically, a closed-end fund concerns itself with the collection of savings, which are invested in a portfolio mainly composed of non-quoted firms with a good probability of success, issuing a bond of medium to long-term maturity in return. The implication is that fund subscribers do not have the right to an early redemption of their share, as with open-ended investments. The money is tied up for a fixed number of years: this allows the fund to invest in non-quoted companies and to seek for longer-term investments. At the expiration, the fund is liquidated and the proceeds are divided among the subscribers. If no expiry is foreseen the investors' assets can be guaranteed by the quotation of the fund on the stock exchange or on another market.

The British experience shows that the closed-end fund performs a primary role in the venture capital sector, if it is used in a way that is consistent with the sector within which it operates. In the US and in most major European countries, closed-end funds are managed mainly by merchant banks or venture-capital firms. In France, the "fonds commun de placement a risques" have permitted the relaunch of national venture capital initiatives (Velo, 1990). Profits from venture capital investment flow principally from the share premia that are realised when the investment matures, so that the investment is kept frozen for quite a long time. Interim proceeds tend to be low, because client firms are still at an early phase of development or are otherwise unable to yield early returns on invested capital.

It is for this reason that the "patient money" provided by the closed-end fund represents an excellent solution to the need for long-term investment, while investors for their part are encouraged either by the limitation of the risk to which they are exposed or by the prospect of very high yield. Moreover, the small investor can find that this is an easy solution to the problem of having to directly manage his funds.

Client firms also look with favour on closed-end funds, since they manage their portfolio without the objective of achieving control over the firms' operations. Unlike merchant banks and venture capital companies, they do not supply professional expertise to help the firm's growth. In this way, they attract the interest of firms which are reluctant to accept the intervention of new investors and which avoid resorting to venture capital so as to retain full control over their own management. However, and this is an aspect of closed-end funds that we have already discussed, they generally do not invest at the early stage of the firm's life, unlike venture capital companies, nor at the expansionary or reorganisational phase, unlike merchant banks. They invest when the firm is likely to be successful and risk is low; for this reason, they show little interest in management-level intervention.

Recently, the above limitation has been overcome in the US with the introduction of the venture capital closed-end fund, which combines the two functions.

From the above considerations, it is easy to see why closed-end funds have had a difficult start-up in Italy, even though the legal basis for their introduction was approved in 1993. They cannot rely on the activity of an intermediary such as a merchant bank or a venture capital company because these are not yet well developed in this country. But these very reasons underline the importance of introducing such funds into Italy, so that they can in turn sustain the development of other intermediaries specialising in the investment of risk capital.

Moreover, if it is true that closed-end funds are added to a stockmarket where they do not yet exist, they could contribute to stimulate the development of the exchange; their presence is a pre-condition for the development of the second and third market.

7. The current relationship between venture capital funds and the stage at which investment occurs in European countries: an empirical analysis

7.1 The hypothesis

The following analysis is designed to demonstrate the correlation between the financing agent and the phase of development at which intervention occurs, with the aim of determining which investors favour early-stage financing. As we have already seen, financing at early stages of the firm's development and particularly start-up financing is highly risky, even though it represents venture capital in the strict sense of the term and is the most typical kind of financing for high technology. We therefore use the variable *starseed* to proxy investment in high technology, our objective being the identification of the agents which may be most important in generating finance for innovation.

7.2 Structure of the sample

We use the model to analyse data from 16 European countries. For each of them, we study the performance of 14 variables over a period of six years between 1987 and 1993.

The analysis is incomplete in the sense that some of the data are missing, in particular, 1987 and 1988 data for Finland and 1988 data for both Ireland and Norway.

We have chosen to use percentage data rather than absolute values; this choice has been dictated by data non-homogeneity because of the discrepancy between the annual flow of funds and the total venture capital investment.

The first nine variables represent the contributions to the total investment by the different types of agents, while the other five represent the percentage of investment made at each phase of development. The source of the data is the EVCA Yearbook.

The sample has been narrowed down in order to reduce distortions due to missing data. The variables are:

Venture capital raised by type of investor   *Distribution stage*

Corpor = Corporate finance	Seed
Privat = Private individuals	Start-up
GovAg = Government Agencies	Expansio = espansion
Bank = Bank	Replace = Replacement capital
Penf = Pension funds	Buy-out
Insuran = Insurance Companies	Starseed=startup+seed
Academic Institutions	
Others	
Capital g = capital gains	
Invist=Bank+penf+insuran	

The two variables *invist* and *starseed* result from the aggregation of other variables. Starseed represents the total percentage of investment target at the early stage; invist represents the global investment coming from institutional investors.

7.3 Graphic and economic analysis

We have drawn scattered diagrams in order to have a first and immediate view of the relations between sources and destination of investments. Each diagram evidences the relation between two variables; each point represents a country in a certain year. Interpolating the data through a regression line, we can observe that only one variable, corporate finance, seems to significantly contribute in financing innovation. We can see a positive relation between investments coming from industrial groups and those directed towards the initial stages, in particular to the start-up. On the other hand, there is a negative relation between investments of industrial groups and funds directed towards the growth stages, in particular the replacement capital.

Empirical evidence supports the importance of corporate venture capital in financing innovation. As it has already been emphasised, small companies have often proved to be more flexible and more efficient than big ones. They usually obtain better results with lower costs. This evidence leads most large groups to allocate single projects to small and highly qualified companies rather than creating their own department of study and research. A solution which besides higher costs, would not have the necessary elasticity, both in terms of physical and human capitals, to undertake several innovating projects.

Personal venture capital, that is the investment provided by private investors, does not seem to play a significant role in financing innovation. Even if private investors are very averse to risk, expecially when compared with professional institutions, this empirical result is not very obvious. Despite of their risk aversion, private investors have always significantly contributed to risky investments, moved by interests that are not stricly economic, such as speculation or other personal interests.

A positive even if not very significant relation can be observed between private investments and expansion financing. It tell us that private investors prefer to direct their investment to more safer companies, which have already reached a growing stage.

Institutional investors, such as banks, insurance companies, pension funds, do not seem to contribute in financing innovation. This empirical result was easy to foresee, given the strong risk aversion which characterises this type of investor.

7.4 Analysis of parameters which influence early stage financing

The next step of the analysis consists in testing the statistical significance of the relationship, that we have seen to be more relevant, between corporate venture capital and start-up stage financing.

In order to isolate the country effect, a dummy has been inserted for each of the countries considered in the sample. A dummy for each year isolates the temporal effects, to evidence if data are affected by particular economic events occurred in the sample period.

The method used is the ordinary least squares (OLS). We relate start-up, the dependent variable, to the different sources of finance. As evidenced by the graphic analysis, the only variable whose coefficient is statistically significant is corporate finance. Excluding variables whose coefficients are not consistently different from 0, and therefore do not contribute to explain the behaviour of the dependent variable, the functional form of the model which seems better to approximate the dependent variable starseed is:

$$\text{starseed} = \alpha_0 - \alpha_1 \text{capitalg} - \alpha_2 \text{insuran} + \alpha_3 \text{corporate} + \alpha_4 \text{denm} + \alpha_5 \text{finl} + \\ + \alpha_6 \text{spai} + \alpha_7 1988 - \alpha_8 1992$$

Dependent variable: starseed

Variable	Coeff. (β)	t stat.	R^2	0.59
$c=b_0$	0.15	5.57	correct R^2	0.55
capitalg	-0.15	-2.09	F stat.	14.44
insuran	-0.32	-2.34		
corporate	0.38	5.99		
denm	0.22	4.39		
finl	0.14	2.41		
spai	0.17	3.56		
a1988	0.09	2.87		
a1992	-0.08	-2.40		

The analysis of the residuals showed a strong distortion of the values relating to Austria in 1987. By a more accurate examination of the original data we observed that in 1987, the entire amount of available funds was attributed to the start-up and came from the bank sector: this totally contradicts the expectations and negatively affects the relationship between dependent variables and corporate finance.

A dummy was then inserted in order to reduce this effect, with the result of a significant increase in the value of the R^2, the percentage of the dependent variable explained by the model. The value of the same index corrected to take into account the effects of the number of variables, and the sufficiently elevated value of the statistic F, demonstrate that the explanatory variables are not redundant and that R^2 is not affected by the number of variables.

The coefficients of the variables capital gain and insurance company are quite significant and have a negative sign. This is evidence of the existence of a negative relation between these sources of finance and the financing of innovation.

Omitting these two variables we obtain:

$$\text{starseed} = \beta_0 + \beta_1 \text{ corporate} + \beta_2 \text{ aus} + \beta_3 \text{ denm} + \beta_4 \text{ finl} + \beta_5 \text{ spai} + \beta_6 \text{ 1988} - \beta_7 1992$$

Table 3.6 Dependent variable: starseed

Variabile	coeff.(β)	t stat.	R^2	0.57
$c = b_0$	0.09	4.85	correct R^2	0.53
corporate	0.40	6.28	F stat.	15.68
aus	0.12	2.04		
denm	0.18	3.70		
finl	0.17	2.74		
spai	0.20	4.13		
a1988	0.09	2.81		
a1992	-0.08	-2.52		

In the model so modified we can observe an increase of the weight of the corporate finance and of its level of significance. A slight increase of the F statistic is noted, therefore the elimination of the two variables has not excessively influenced the significance of the model.

We used the method of White's least squares to reject the hypothesis of presence of heteroskedasticity. Estimating the relationship between industrial groups and financing of expansion we obtain the following functional form:

$$\text{expansion} = \gamma_0 - \gamma_1 \text{ corporate} - \gamma_2 \text{ govag} - \gamma_3 \text{ insuran} - \gamma_4 \text{ denm} - \gamma_5 \text{ gb} + \gamma_6 \text{ nor} + \gamma_7 \text{port} + \gamma_8 \text{ } 1987$$

Table 3.7 Dependent variable: expansion

variabile	coeff	t stat
c	0.65	26.09
corporate	-0.39	-5.50
govag	-0.30	-3.92
insuran	-0.40	-2.60
denm	-0.13	-2.43
GB	-0.24	-4.47
nor	0.3	4.97
port	0.15	2.70
a1987	0.15	3.81

Even if coefficients are quite small, this model is evidence of the existence of a negative relation between investment coming from industrial groups and the financing of expansion. As we have pointed out many times, the espansion is for its nature a quite safe investment and the big industrial groups prefer to face higher risk levels in order to realise higher returns. Insurance companies are instead tipically averse to risk, and it was more logical to expect a positive rather than a negative coefficient for this variable.

8. Conclusions

The analysis conducted provides evidence that corporate finance plays a relevant role in financing innovation. The rapid technological progress makes it necessary to operate on more research fronts. It is more convenient for the firm to entrust different projects to small, high qualified firms rather than substain high costs of structure.

Smaller firms are concerned with specific niches of the market, and have means and competence more adequate to single projects. Moreover they usually have an efficient distribution system, which allows them to work on large volumes. This guarantees shorter times of development and amortisation of research projects. Big industrial groups have objectives that differ completely from the institutional investors' aims. They can be considered as a risk-neutral investor, because they are willing to accept higher risk not only to make larger profits, but also to keep active in a constantly changing world.

That is why it is logical to foresee that the relationship between these groups and innovation financing will get stronger rather than come to an end. It would be useful to intervene in order to favour it.

An historical example of intervention is that of the 3M. In the 1950s, this company encouraged its employees to leave and become entrepreneurs, almost totally financing their initial investment, giving them stock options to facilitate them to reach the 51%, and guaranteeing them, in the case of a failure, the possibility of going back to the company (Paolo Colonna, 1987).

Stock options could contribute to the financing of innovation. The issue of stock options can in fact be a solution to the principal agent problem between entrepreneur and venture capitalist when they share a project, and particularly when the latter owns the majority of the shares.

This position could in fact be an incentive for the entrepreneur not to adopt all the necessary measures to control costs and to protect the interests of other possible shareholders (Chua and Woodward, 1993).

In Italy, some important measures in favour of small and medium firms have recently been introduced. They mainly consist of soft loans and grants offered to these firms or to financial intermediates wishing to purchase shares.

Such measures do not concern the role of corporate finance. Industrial groups are subject to the tax on capital gains, from which only shares held for more than fifteen years are exempted and which are, for that reason, not included in the venture capital finalities.

The analysis has shown that private investors and financial istitutions do not have a significant role in financing innovation. However, we know that the banking sector represents the main source of financing in Europe, and the

115

pension funds in the US. It is then important to intervene in order to direct this huge economic potential towards innovative firms and high technology projects.

Closed-end funds probably represent the easiest way to converge the resources of institutional investors towards innovative sectors. Closed funds are tied up for a given period (usually five years) guaranteeing the stability of financing. In addition, the specific competence which characterises venture capital companies, enables them to correctly value the innovative investment and to follow their development until disinvestment These funds provide then a certain financial stability to innovative firms, and grant investors the safety of an efficient portfolio diversification.

The international experience, in particular in the US, has proved the efficacy of such investment in financing innovation. Closed-end funds could therefore represent a valid support to the new banking law, directing risk capital not only towards already mature firms, but also towards innovative and growing companies, which present higher financial needs and face more difficulties in attracting resources.

Notes

*Paper prepared for the CNR Strategic Project 92.4716 st 74 "Technological Change and Industrial Development: policies for international technological co-operation". Working unit ISPE No.3, co-ordinator Professor Bagella. The author thanks M. Bagella, L. Becchetti, B. Maturi, C. Noli, U. Moorthy, G. De Nuccio and D. Archibugi.

[1] The main objectives of the Association are the following:
- to promote venture capital in Europe,
- to represent venture capital organisations at European and world level and complement the existing national venture capital oragnizations;
- to develop and stimulate investment in venture capital throughout the various markets and members of the association;
- to circulate information to members and to the outside world;
- to stimulate and maintain contacts within the membership;
- to contribute to the management development of investors;
- to study and provide the Commission of the European Communities with proposals for possible legal or tax provision changes in order to develop venture capital in Europe;
- to maintain ethical and professional standards.
Every year EVCA publishes a Yearbook titled: *Venture Capital in Europe* which collects data and information on the venture capital activities in various countries.

[2] Among the main legislative innovations, remember: the Amato law, n.218 of 1990, which, introducing Polifunctional Bank Groups, established the foundation for a substancial change in public banks; the Antitrust law, n.287, 1990; law n.1 1991 about SIM, the discipline of insider trading, the "Antiriciclaggio" law, n. 197, 1991.

117

References

A.I.F.I. (Associazione Italiana delle Finanziarie d'Investimento nel capitale di rischio) (1987), "Venture Capital, Capitale di rischio per lo sviluppo", ed. *Il sole 24 Ore.*

A.I.F.I. (1993), "Capitale di rischio per lo sviluppo, un quadro internazionale", ed. *Il sole 24 Ore.*

Akerlof, G (1970), "The Market for Lemons: Qualitative Uncertainty and the Market Mechanism", in: *Quarterly Journal of Economics.*

Bagella, M. and Paganetto, L. (1994) "La Banca Universale e l'Economia Italiana: Punti di Forza e Punti di Debolezza".

Bagella, M. and Becchetti, L. (1994),"Finance, Investment and innovation: a review of the literature and a proposal for a comparative approach", working paper CNR.

Becchetti, L. (1994), "Finance Investment and Innovation: a Theoretical and empirical comparative analysis", CNR, mimeo.

Bollani L., Tibiletti L. (1993), "Sulla valutazione della performance dei fondi comuni d'investimento: un metodo di segmentazione multicriteriale" in: *Rivista Milanese di Economia*, April-June.

Brophy, D.J. (1981), "Venture Capital Investment", in: Bahson College Entrepreneurship Research Conference Proceedings, ed. The Center for Entrepreneurial Studies of Babson College, Wellesley, Mass.

Chua J.H. and Woodward R.S. (1993), "Splitting the Firm Between the Entrepreneur and the Venture Capitalist With the Help of Stock Options", in: *Journal of Business Venturing*, vol. 8, n.1, Jan.

Colonna, P. (1987), "Ricerca e innovazione: proposte per una nuova politica fiscale", Eurovenca in atti del convegno Dec. Rome.

Confindustria, (1989),"Strumenti per il rafforzamento del capitale di rischio", a cura del Gruppo San Paolo, Collana Europa Finanza, Oct.

Cotta Ramusino, P. (1987), "L'innovazione nei sistemi finanziari: il Venture Capital".

Dessy, A. Gervasoni, A. (1989) "Le piccole medie imprese ed il capitale di rischio".

Donovan, P. (1994), "Closed-end Mutual Funds in the United States of America", in "Funds and Portfolio Management Institutions", Preda Stefano.

Dubini, P. (1988),"Il Venture Capital: confronto Italia-Stati Uniti" in *Economia & Management*, Sept.

Forestieri, G. (1985) "Le società di Venture Capital: formule istituzionali e organizzative e politiche di gestione", in *Il finanziamento all'innovazione nelle imprese industriali*, Isa Marchini.

Gladstone, D.(1988), "Venture Capital Investing", Prentice Hall.

Imperatori, G. (1992), "I fondi chiusi: un nuovo intermediario a supporto delle piccole e medie imprese" in *Il Merchant Banking Oggi*, Edibank.

Kay, William (1992) "Il Merchant Banking Oggi", Edibank.

Kensinger, J.W. and Martin, J.D. (1990), "Project Financing for Research and Development" in *Research in Finance*, vol. 8.

Lumbau, D. (1990), "Il disegno di legge n. 3118 sui fondi mobiliari chiusi: la via italiana al venture capital" in *Banca, borsa e titoli di credito*, sept.oct.

Mantovani, G. M. (1993) "Un NASDAQ europeo per le società di Venture capital" in *Rivista milanese di economia*, Jan-March.

Norton, E. and Tenenbaum, B.H. (1993), "Specialization versus diversification as a venture capital investment strategy", in *Journal of Business Venturing*, 8.

Porteri, A. (1992), "Despecializzazione del sistema bancario e introduzione della "Banca universale in Italia", in *Notiziario Economico della banca S.Paolo di Brescia*.

Ristuccia, C.A. (1994), "Il rapporto tra banca e industria, regole istituzionali e trasferimento delle informazioni", in *Bancaria*, n. 1.

Sandri, S. (1988), "Il Venture Capital: analisi dell'esperienza statunitense e prospettive per l'Italia", in *Banca, Impresa Socieà* n. 1.

Savino, M. (1992), "Le partecipazioni degli Istituti di Credito Speciale: aspetti normativi e tendenze evolutive", in F. Cesarini: *La gestione degli ICS tra riforme e mercato*.

Stiglitz, Weiss (1981),"Credit Rationing in Markets with imperfect Information", in *American Economic Review*.

Velo, D. (1990), "Il finanziamento di rischio delle imprese minori: il ruolo dei fondi chiusi" in *Osservatorio economico, cassa di risparmio di Torino*.

4 The optimal financing strategy of Japanese high-tech firms: the role of warrants

Michele Bagella and Leonardo Becchetti

1. Introduction

The present paper analyses, theoretically and empirically, the economic effects of a bond cum equity warrant (BW) financing strategy.

After a short survey of the literature on equity issue signalling effects (section 2), we present a model that is a refinement and an extension of the Stein (1992) approach (sections 3.1 and 3.2). The aim of the model is to show that, when costs of financial distress are relevant, a bond cum warrant issue (BW) is an intermediate signal for firms having good but risky projects. In this respect, it is shown that a BW issue is preferred as an intermediate signal i) to convertible bonds (CB) for their higher time flexibility and ii) to straight equity issues for the absence of adverse selection costs.

The signalling model is then analysed under two different extensions: i) the presence of bond rating that partially eliminates imperfect information on firm financial conditions (section 3.3) and ii) the existence of stock market fluctuations . In these sections is then shown that, under the presence of bond rating, "medium firms" may avoid the adverse selection effects of a "pooling equilibrium" with "bad firms". This occurs only if they reinforce their signal by choosing a bond cum "knock-out warrant" (equity warrant with a put option) issue. Another result is that, with the presence of stock market fluctuations, bond cum warrant issues may be an inefficient signal when a bearish market is expected. This happens because the expected value of firm equity at the warrant exercise deadline depends not only on the expected value of the project, but also on exposition to nondiversifiable risk.

In fact, although warrant issuers have rational expectations, they tend to err systematically as they cannot revise their decision on the warrant exercise price in all periods following the issue and preceding the exercise deadline. Rational shareholders anticipate this and tend to overreact to index changes (when a drop of the index occurs, for instance, they anticipate the increased probability of failure of warrant conversion and the increased firm leverage).

In the empirical side of the chapter some descriptive and econometric evidence on the "signalling" effect is provided (section 4.1) with, an empirical test on Japanese BW, convertible bond (CB) and straight bond (SB) issues between 1984 and 1987. The test shows that: i) firms in traditional sectors with less risky investments, consistently with firm types defined in our model, prefer SB to CB and BW, while firms in high-tech sectors prefer BW to SB and also to CB; ii) the ranking of the average abnormal common stock returns at the issue date indicates that BW together with CB causes a more negative price reaction than SB; iii) the after issue performance of BW issuers and CB issuers is dramatically inferior to that of SB issuers in terms of cumulative average abnormal returns confirming ex post the correspondence between firm type and the signal given to the market; iv) electrical companies who traditionally choose SB financing are strongly penalised when they choose "weaker" signals like BW or CB.

2. The "signalling effect" of issuing warrants: state of the art

The Modigliani-Miller approach to corporate finance is incapable of explaining many empirical facts in corporate finance such as the limited significance of taxation in the choice of financing patterns, the inflexibility of dividend policy in relation to financing requirements, variation in stock prices occurring when peculiar events like new equity issues or takeovers are announced.

The imperfect information approach to corporate finance tries to provide consistent explanations for these facts.

A basic reference for the imperfect information literature is represented by the Myers-Majluf (1984) "story" saying that, when managers have superior information on firm perspectives, financial agents are unable to distinguish firm projects, and adverse selection is then associated with new equity issues, as high-quality firms are associated with low quality ones. This model, and those that followed, seems to suggest the existence of a financing order where agency costs create a differential between internal and external finance (Mayer, 1990) and where internally generated funds are always preferred to debt and debt is preferred to equity. Firms then experience a trade-off between costs of emitting low quality signals with external finance and costs of reducing dividend payments (a negative signal in itself) to reduce external finance requirements.

Recent literature contributions show that, within this theoretical framework, convertibles may play an important role for high-tech firms in reducing agency costs and in conveying the right information on firm perspectives to the market (Brennan-Kraus, 1987; Noe, 1988; Constantinides-Grundy, 1989 and Stein, 1992)[1].

The contribution of Stein is a model where convertibles are an intermediate signal used by "medium firms" to distinguish them from "good firms" issuing bonds and "bad firms" issuing equities. The approach is supported by three pieces of relevant empirical evidence based on stock exchange statistics, case studies and surveys on manager attitude towards the issue.

In the first it is shown that the unweighed average of the two-day announcement impact of convertible bond offering on the market shows that equity reaction is around -1.5% (Dann-Mikkelson, 1984; Eckbo, 1986; Mikkelson-Partch, 1986) while the equity reaction to common stock offering calculated with the same procedure is substantially more negative (-3.5) (Asquith-Mullins, 1986; Masulis-Korwar, 1986; Mikkelson-Partch, 1986)[2].

In the second, the MCI case study, is described a highly leveraged firm, with good but still uncertain market perspectives, which chooses, as an optimal financing strategy, to raise external funds through convertibles or debt plus warrants issues given that the costs of issuing bonds in term of financial distress are too high.

In the third, it is described how surveys on convertible finance by Pilcher (1955), Brigham (1966) and Hoffmeister (1977) show that managers consider convertibles far more for their capacity of "raising common equity on a delayed action basis" than for their capacity of "sweetening" senior leverage. All these facts have encouraged us to follow this theoretical path to explain several interesting empirical facts which occurred in financial markets in the 1980s

3. The "signalling model" assumptions

The model presented in this section aims at assessing the role of warrants in financing strategies of high-tech firms and at providing a rationale for the often observed empirical evidence of the preference of innovating firms (and in particular of small and new high-tech firms) for debt plus equity warrant financing issues. This evidence is provided both by economic literature (Ferri-Kremer-Oberhelman, 1986; Essig, 1991) and by financial investors information services (Investor Bulletin - Warrants Survey, 1992).

The model is a refinement of the Stein approach with three important extensions: i) it focuses on debt plus warrant issues and not on convertible issues trying to provide a rationale for the often more likely substitution of the second type of issues with the first type; ii) it keeps into consideration the negative incentive effects of property right dilution on innovative effort; iii) it considers extensions such as the effects of stock index fluctuations, bond rating and effects on shareholders expectations of the irreversibility in the warrant exercise price decision.

The model is in three periods and assumes the existence of three types of firms (good, medium, and bad firms).

The three types of firms present the following features: good firms are those having projects for which the relevant research activity has been almost completely carried out before t_0. Their innovation manufactured and marketed will give an output of X_{ht} with certainty. Medium firms are a bit behind good firms but have a good research project. Their research activity is carried out in t_0 and requires an investment of K (K<I). If unsuccesful it will in any case contribute to firm technological knowledge giving and intermediate output X_m = K. If successful, it will allow medium firms to invest in a "blockbuster" innovation giving an X_{ht} output with probability $p(e(\pi))$ or just to obtain an imitative product with output X_I with probability $[1-p(e(\pi))]$, where p(.) depends on the research effort (e(.)) which is, in turn, a monotonic function of the innovator share of property rights on future returns from innovation (π).

Bad firms have worse projects than medium firms. Their possibility of obtaining a "blockbuster" innovation (X_{ht}) is only $q(e(\pi))$ where $1>p(.)>q(.)$ and the probability of obtaining an imitating innovation is $[1-q(e(\pi))]$. Another feature of bad firms is the higher volatility of their expected research outcome. Bad firms in fact are assumed to have, in the period t_2, a probability z of definitively renouncing to their perspective of creating an innovative product $q(e(\pi)) = 0$ and a probability 1-z of improving their research activity and becoming a medium firm with probability $p(e(\pi))$ of achieving X_{ht}. The main difference between good and bad firms is that good firms are more advanced in their research activity and would like to signal it to the market to pay lower agency costs on their external financing sources[3].

Other crucial assumptions of the model are that: i) in t_0 firm types are private knowledge of firm managers; ii) the values of various projects are such that $X_{ht}>I>X_I$ and; iii) firm types are revealed in t_2; iv) agents are risk neutral.

Firms have six choices in their financing strategies: i) debt; ii) debt cum warrants (with conversion deadline in t_2); iii) convertible bonds (with conversion deadline in t_2); iv) equity; v) short term bond in t_0 plus short term equity in t_2: vi) "venture capital" finance[4]. Each financing strategy gives rise to a certain degree of equity dilution. We assume for simplicity that ex ante property rights are undivided. We can simply analyse ex post property rights according to the different financing strategies and observe that $\pi_B=1$ in case of bond financing, $\pi_E<1$ in case of equity financing, $\pi_{BW}<1$ in case of bond cum warrant financing, $\pi_{CV}<1$ in case of convertible financing, and $\pi_{VC}<1$ in case of venture capital financing.

The dinstinguishing feature of venture capital finance is that it has the advantage over equity finance of reducing bankruptcy risks with a different kind of agency cost disadvantage. In venture capital finance, the informational asymmetry is transferred from market investors to only one "specialised" shareholder represented by the venture capitalist. The venture capitalist is not just a financing partner sharing the risk of the venture with his partner, as he also brings his peculiar skills into the venture. When a venture capital agreement is concluded, the probability of a "blockbuster" innovation becomes $p(e(\pi_{VC})$, $E(\pi_{(1-CV)})$ where E is the complementary effort of the venture capitalist as a function of his share in the venture (Becchetti, 1994).

Therefore, we may define a "perfect" venture capital agreement as one where there is no asymmetry between the bargaining strength of the two agents (venture capitalist and innovator) and their relative capacity to contribute to the development of innovation so that the bargained share exactly reflects relative contributions and the dilution disincentive of the innovator is exactly compensated by the additional effort brought by the venture capitalist. In all other cases, the venture capital agreement will have a certain degree of imperfection and the imperfect information on relative partner contributions, combined with bargaining asymmetry, will generate effort disincentive costs on the expected value of the innovation.

In the above described model a signalling equilibrium exists if: i) the firms maximize the difference between the price received for the security issued and the true, full information value of the security, with the constraint of raising the amount K needed for the investment; ii) the markets for securities are competitive and investors have rational expectations; iii) the "net claim issued under each financing strategy is priced under the supposition that it has been made by the firm type with characteristics that would cause the net claim to have the lowest true full information value, and that supposition is correct" (Brennan-Kraus, 1987).

3.1 The signalling model equilibrium

The equilibrium of the model rests on the following assumptions.
A1 (*Asymmetric information*) Firm type is positive information in t_0 and is revealed in t_2.
A2 (*Hierarchy of investments and profits*) $X_h>I>K>X_1$

A3 (*Relevance of financial distress costs*) $c>(I-X_1)$.

A4 (*Interest payments irrelevance*) Interest payments on issued bonds, Ir, are small and not higher than $I-[(1-p(e(\pi_{BW})))(I-X_1)+(1-q(e(\pi_E)))X_1-q_1]/3$

A5 (*High probability of medium firm innovation*) The probability of high outcome on the medium firm project is high enough to ensure that $p(e(\pi_B))>X_1(1-K)/K(X_h-X_1)$.

A6 (*Positive issue transaction costs*) $I=I_0+tc$ where tc is a small positive transaction cost.

A7 Agents are risk neutral

Given all the above stated assumptions we want to demonstrate the following proposition (E1):

E1) If assumptions A1-A7 are respected the following occurs:

ia) good firms issue debt with face value I and invest or ib) conclude a venture capital agreement if it imposes lower costs than interests paid on bonds and invest;

iia) bad firms issue an amount of equity representing $I/[q(e(\pi_E))X_{ht}+(1-q(e(\pi_E))X_l]$ of total firm equity and invest or iib) conclude a venture capital agreement if it imposes lower dilution costs than those imposed by the equity issue;

iiib) medium firms issue bonds plus equity warrants where bonds have a face value K (with $X_l\ K\ I$), warrants exercise price is equal to the face value of the bond and warrants represent $I/[p(e(\pi_{BW}))X_h+(1-p(e(\pi_{BW}))X_l]$ of firm equity, or iiib) conclude a venture capital agreement if it imposes lower dilution costs than those imposed by the WB issue.

The model has a signalling equilibrium in three financing strategies. The choice of each strategy exactly reveals only one type of firms, with the exception of the venture capital choice. The role of venture capital finance in the model is that of providing an alternative solution to the information costs of external finance, transferring agency problems from dispersed market investors to a single "specialised financier". If costs of information with this financier are lower than those occurring with the preferred form of external finance (respectively debt for a good firm, debt plus equity warrant for a medium firm and equity for a bad firm), then the venture capital solution is adopted and preferred to any other market financing choice.

More formally, we term C_{vc} as the sum of lump sum transfer costs and dilution costs that may arise when the venture capitalist either is imperfectly informed over relative contributions to innovation or, is perfectly informed but there is an unbalance between bargaining strengths and relative contributions to the innovation of the two counterparts[5]. In this case: i) a venture capital agreement will be preferred to bonds by good firms if $C_{vc}<rI$; ii) will be preferred to a bond plus equity warrant issue by medium firms if

$C_{VC}<p(Ed_{BW})+c(1-p)$; iii) will be preferred to an equity issue by bad firms if $C_{VC}<q(Ed_E)+c(1-q)$, where synthetically Ed_{BW} and Ed_E are respectively equity dilution costs arising from the WB issue and from the equity issue.

Another distinguishing feature is that warrants are always preferred to convertibles in this model. According to Cox (1988), an emission of a bond plus equity warrants is equivalent to an emission of a convertible where the warrant striking price is equal to bond value. In this case, when a warrant is exercised, the price necessary to extinguish the bond is paid and a new share is issued. The result is the same of the conversion of a bond into an equity obtained when the conversion option of a convertible is exercised. The two period horizon of the investment makes a WB issue more convenient than a convertible issue as no interest payments on bonds are required[6].

To demonstrate E1 we need to demonstrate that incentive compatibility constraints are satisfied by the equilibrium solution. This is equivalent to show that there is no profitable deviation from the signalling equilibrium for the three types of firms. Two are the intuitive arguments of the demonstration: i) "superior" firms do not mimick "inferior" firms not to incur in underpricing costs and ii) "inferior" firms do not mimick "superior" firms because costs of financial distress are higher than gains from asset overpricing. These arguments can be illustrated in the six following propositions.

P1) *A good firm does not mimic a bad firm.* A good firm is certain that it will obtain a net present value for its project that is higher than the investment it needs to finance it (I). Why should it prefer bond financing to equity financing? An abstract comparison of these two financing forms shows that bonds have the relative disadvantage of higher bankruptcy risks and due interest payments before redemption. They have, though, the relative advantage of avoiding dilution on property rights and security underpricing due to adverse selection. But the good firms are certain about the results of their projects. The relevant effects of issuing equity instead of bonds are two additional costs and a small relative advantage.

Because of the dilution cost the probability of achieving the innovation is reduced $(e(\pi_E)<e(1))$. Because of the underpricing due to adverse selection, investors mistake a good firm for a bad firm if it opts for a straight equity issue to cover the full investment cost I. The no mimicking conditions hold as their equity dilution costs are higher than interest payment costs[7].

P2) *A good firm does not mimic a medium firm.* The reasoning is similar to the one followed at point A1. With no costs of financial distress, the emission of debt plus warrants bears both the equity dilution cost (the debt will be converted in equity when investors will realise that the firm is a good one and $e(_E)<e(1)$) and the underpricing cost (the ratio at which warrant is converted implies underpricing). The good firm will not choose convertibles in that they

127

provide analogous results of a debt plus warrant emission with extra interest payments.

P3) *A medium firm does not mimic a bad firm.* According to the signalling equilibrium described above, the medium firm will choose the BW issue. This happens because in t_2 firm types are revealed and warrant holders know that, if the firm is a medium one, they will be entitled to the promise share of property rights on the future innovation times the expected value of the project for a medium firm. Given that the equity value after conversion is higher than the striking price, this strategy is successful and is preferred to the convertible one as it avoids extra interest payments. Consequently, a medium firm has no incentive in mimicking a bad one because it knows that its security will be underpriced. Rational investors know, in fact, that good firms have no interest in issuing equity.

P4) *A medium firm does not mimic a good firm.* If a medium firm mimics a good firm it issues debt for a face value I whose true net claim value is actually lower than I as a probability 1-p this firm will obtain an output $X_1 < I$. This will generate for it a net gain form overpricing this security. These gains will be nonetheless lower than costs of mimicking wich are those of financial distress in case the innovation is not achieved (1-p(.))c. An important additional condition for P4 is that additional mimicking costs due to interest payments on straight bonds compensate additional mimicking gains. These gains are given by the net reduction in dilution cost that a straight bond strategy ensures with respect to a bond plus equity warrant strategy.

P5) *A bad firm does not mimic a good firm.* The reason is similar to that shown in P4.

Bad firms issuing debt with a face value I will have net gains from bond overpricing. The real value of issued bonds is in fact lower than I given that with probability 1-p they will obtain an output X_1. Costs of mimicking caused by probability of financial distress are nonetheless higher than bond overpricing gains and, as a consequence, the mimicking behaviour is not rational. An important additional condition for P5 is that additional mimicking costs, given by interest payments on straight bonds, compensate additional mimicking gains given by the net reduction in dilution costs that a straight bond strategy ensures with respect to an equity strategy.

P6) *A bad firm does not mimic a medium firm.* With probability z it will be known in t_2 that a bad firm has a low project value. In this case, if it mimics a medium firm with a debt plus warrant issue, there is a possibility that the warrant will have in t_2 a conversion value lower than K. Warrants will not be exercised and firms will not be able to service their original debt. Such a mimicking strategy is characterised by a cost of financial distress equal to zc.

128

The gains from mimicking will be instead those of security overpricing. The real value of the bond issued is:

$$(1-z)K + zX_1 \qquad\qquad (1)$$

with an overpricing of $z(K-X_1)$

But $c > I - X_1 > K - X_1$ and this behaviour is not rational. What happens if the bad firm uses convertibles? Here, for an equal cost of mimicking the overpricing advantage will be higher. The conclusion does not change as $zc > z(I-X_1)$.

A final step in the demostration of the equilibrium is to explain why medium firms could not use a short term bonds in t_0 plus an equity issue in t_2.

Stein proposes the same question in its model where only convertibles and not bond plus warrants are allowed. If the asymmetric information disappears in t_2, why medium firms do not issue short term debt in t_0 and equity in t_2? This strategy also satisfies conditions for a signalling equilibrium. The answer to this objection can be given by Stein only by changing the basic features; the author in fact assumes that managers are always one-step ahead of investors and that, even in t_2, the informational advantage is maintained. This is simply not needed if we replace debt plus warrants with convertibles because *a debt plus warrants issue (D+W) is just the same as the short term debt plus deferred equity issue (STB+E)* which the author tries to rule out with his additional assumption. Furthermore, given the assumption A6 on the existence of small but positive issue transaction costs, the (D+W) strategy is better than the (STB+E) strategy, given that transaction costs are paid only once.

3.2 Signalling equilibrium with a relaxation of the financial distress cost hypothesis

The main weakness of the signalling model described above is its reliance on financial distress costs that need to be higher than the difference between the amount invested and the low outcome of the project ($c > I - X_1$). The dependence of equilibrium results from costs of financial distress is crucial and is consistent with the hypothesis that debt issuance implies lower agency costs than equity issuance only if debtors incur in relevant bankrupcy costs. This is often true if debtors are firm owners as in the model, but is less likely to be true in limited liability models where there are managers with limited stake in the enterprise. In this case managers have the incentive to undertake risky projects. These projects are riskier than those debtholders would like to undertake when manager bankrupcy costs are lower than those of debtholders and when such costs are limited to the manager's equity participation in the firm (Jensen-Meckling, 1976).

129

Without changes in the theoretical structure of the model we want to show that its qualitative results may still be confirmed when assumption A3 is relaxed. This occurs if we introduce into the model two typical features of contemporary financial markets not considered in the basic version.

The first of these features is the answer to the following reasonable objection: can firms with fewer investment perspectives (medium and bad firms in the model) obtain overpricing gains by issuing bonds when "perfect" rating companies with informational economies of scale can reduce informational asymmetries for the rest of the market? If we consider that straight bond emissions are rated there should not be anymore overpricing opportunities for bad and medium firms that mimic good firms.

The second feature is the possibility of more complex warrants emissions where, beyond the original call option, other "taylormade" characteristics are added in the emission (basket warrants, covered warrants, knock-out warrants).

The extended version of the model then includes three new elements: i) relaxation of the financial distress cost assumption; ii) straight bond rating; iii) opportunity of "taylormade" warrant emissions. This modifies the signalling equilibrium and gives place to proposition E2, which implies the following changes on A1-A7 assumptions:

A1' (asymmetric information for non bond issuers) Firm types for straight bond issuers are revealed at t_0 while firm types of equity and warrant issuers are revealed in t_2.

A3' (relaxation of financial distress costs) $c+p(.)((X_h-X_l)*I/(p(.)X_h-(1-p(.))X_l)$ $(1-X_l)$ c where $p(.)=p(e(\pi_{BW}))$

PROPOSITION E2) If assumptions A1'-A2-A3'-A4-A5-A6-A7 hold the following occurs:

a) good firms issue debt with face value I and invest or ib) conclude a venture capital agreement if it imposes lower costs than interests paid on bonds rI and invest.

iia) bad firms issue an amount of equity representing $I/[q(e(\pi_E)X_h+(1-q(e(\pi_E))X_l]$ of firm equity and invest, or iib) conclude a venture capital agreement if it imposes lower dilution costs than those imposed by the equity issue.

iiia) medium firms issue bonds plus "knock-out" warrants, with a put option that allows warrant holders to sell to the firm its shares at the price $p(.)X_h+(1-p)(.)X_l$. The put option can be exercised if the share price at the expiration date is less than K. The bonds have a face value K (with X_l K I), the warrants exercise price is equal to bond face value and warrants represent $I/[p(e(\pi_{BW})X_h+(1-p)(e(\pi_{BW}))X_l]$ of firm equity, or iiib) conclude a venture capital agreement if it imposes lower dilution costs than those imposed by the BW issue.

In this case, neither bad nor medium firms have any interest in mimicking good firms. This happened in the basic model because costs of financial distress were assumed higher than gains from overpricing the security (the condition c>(I-K) was the same both for medium and bad firms). In the modified version of the model it is not known if financial distress costs are higher than I-K but it is known that, due to the ability of rating agencies, it is not possible to gain from overpricing a security when bonds are issued.

It remains unconvenient for good firms to issue equity or bond plus equity warrants given that this would lead to security underpricing.

Bad firms do not mimic medium firms because costs of mimicking are higher than benefits. Benefits from mimicking are benefits from equity overpricing (see P6) and are equal to z(I-K), but costs from mimicking are now generated by the put option incorporated in the "knock-out warrant". Given firms' probability to degenerate into the low outcome project, these costs will be:

$$zc + z\{[p(e(\pi_{BW}))X_n + (1 - p(e(\pi_{BW})))X_l] - X_l\} * \frac{I}{(p(e(\pi_{BW}))X_{hl} + (1 - p)(e(\pi_{BW})))X_l} \qquad (2)$$

or:

$$zc + z[p(e(\pi_{BW}))(X_n - X_l)] * \frac{I}{(p(e(\pi_{BW}))X_n + (1 - p)(e(\pi_{BW})))X_l} \qquad (3)$$

the amount added to previous financial distress costs is represented by firm losses incurred when warrant holders exercise their put option. These losses are relevant if we consider that, by A2, $X_h > I > K > X_l$.

The conclusion from the modified version of the model is the following: in a situation where "perfect" rating eliminates informational asymmetries in case of straight bond issues, but not in case of equity issues (rating is directly on the bond and only indirectly on the firm), a signalling equilibrium is still possible and medium firms can avoid "adverse selection" problems if they reinforce their "warrant signal" with a put option.

3.3 Model extensions: the divergence between the financial and real economy with bearish stock markets

An important problem to be considered in the economic analysis of firm issues is the potential effect of stock index fluctuations. This section will show that a bearish stock exchange market may prevent any kind of signalling equilibrium.

We reasonably suppose that the value of a share is influenced by two different components: the first reflects the intrinsic value of firm project plans, the second the influence of nondiversifiable market risk on firm share. In such a case, a medium firm expects the price of its shares (Ps) in t_2 to be, after firm types are revealed[8]:

$$E_{t_0}\left[Ps_{t_2}\right] = p(.)X_n + (1 - p(.))X_1 + \beta_{t_2} E_{t_0}\left[I_{t_2} - I_{t_0}\right]$$

$$\beta_{t_2} > \beta_{t_0}$$

(4)

where I is the stock index and the firm expectation of the stock share price, $E_{t0}[Ps_{t2}]$, reflects the project value plus the nondiversifiable risk component, $_{t2}E_{t0}[I_{t2}-I_{t2}]$, expressed through the elasticity that links the share to index changes. This means that: i) either the revealed information is not perfect in t_2 and investors are nonetheless influenced by general stock market conditions; ii) or that, even if information about firm projects is perfect, speculators' activity drives share value away from the parity with firm investment perspectives. Moreover, the difference t_2-t_0 is nonnegative and represents the increment of nondiversifiable risk due to WB issue. The increase is justified by the fact that firms are "locked-in" in the choice of the warrant exercise price. Therefore, even if they are rational, they do incur in systematic errors in their forecast of $[I_{t2}-I_{t0}]$. Shareholders are aware of it and overreact to index changes knowing that they may determine changes in firm leverage (for example a sharp fall of the index may lead the deadline share price below the exercise price, inducing warrant holders not to exercise their call option with negative effects on firm leverage).

If the stock index is expected to decline and the medium firm has the following expectation on it:

$$E_{t_0}\left[I_{t_2} - I_{t_0}\right] \geq -\frac{(I - K)}{\beta_{t_2}}$$

(5)

the bond plus warrant issue is not an efficient signal anymore and there is no possibility of being distinguished from the bad firm. Such a firm will find itself in front of two costly alternatives: an underpriced stock issue or a bond issue with high risk of financial distress[9].

Changeable stock market conditions also negatively affect bad firms, while good firms are unaffected. When it comes to issuing equity, bad firms have to consider that, given the bearish stock market expectations, they will have to concede to new shareholders an amount of stock corresponding to the following share of total firm equity:

$$\frac{I}{\left[q(.)X_h + (1-q(.))X_1\right] + \beta_{t_2}E_{t_0}\left[I_{t_2} - I_{t_0}\right]} \qquad (6)$$

They will then be forced to accept a higher dilution to obtain the financial amount needed and this will, in turn, have a negative effect on their incentives for innovation.

Bearish stock markets then have two negative effects on innovative firms: they transform the previous signalling equilibrium into a pooling equilibrium creating an adverse selection problem between medium and bad firms. They in fact expose medium firms to issue underpricing with resulting property dilution and reduced incentives for innovation.

The events reported in Table 4.1 seem to show that Japanese firms did not anticipate this effect. Between 1992 and 1993 in fact, share prices of several BW issues fell far below the exercise price driven by a bearish japanese stock market. Consequently, almost no warrants were exercised to pay back the debt issued, worsening financial conditions and leading to new debt emissions.

4. The empirical test on firm signalling strategies: previous literature results

Recent empirical tests on the effects of firm financing strategies on underlying assets seemed to confirm the Myers-Majluf "lemon" hypothesis showing that equity issues always lead to a decline in the price of the underlying common stock. This opinion has been recently contrasted by Cooney-Kalay (1993) who show that, modifying only one of Myers-Majluf assumptions (they postulate the existence of potential firm projects with negative NPVs), increases in common stock price after equity issues could not be ruled out.

A first confirmation of the Cooney-Kalay theoretical hypothesis comes from Kato-Schalleim (1992) who document positive announcement effects of equity issues for Japanese firms in the 1980s.

Two important issues related to these empirical studies concern the interpretation of the results and the choice between issue date and announcement date.

About the first point, apart from the imperfect information rationale, there are at least two other explanations for equity price changes after new issues: price pressure and wealth redistribution (Cooney-Kalay, 1993). The price pressure hypothesis simply states that the demand for a security is downward sloped and that a decrease in price must correspond to an increase in the quantity supplied (Loderer-Cooney-Van Drunen, 1991). The wealth redistribution hypothesis states that the decrease in equity price is caused by a transfer of wealth to bondholders. Empirical tests seem, though, to reject this hypothesis because in correspondence of new issues there seems to be a positive, and not a negative, relationship between equity and bond price (Kalay-Shimrat, 1987).

The choice between issue date and announcement date is also strategical in order to discriminate between the three hypotheses. According to Dann-Mikkelson the "price pressure" effect should be anticipated by agents at the announcement date and no price pressure should then arise at the issue date. Moreover, when bonds are issued only partial information is provided at the announcement date and some addditional information about bond yield, issue amount, coupon rate and maturity may be disclosed at the issue date only.

4.1 The empirical test on firm signalling strategies: results

The insights from the theoretical model presented in the previous paragraph suggest that "medium firms" choose a bond cum equity warrant issue, or alternatively a convertible issue if certain assumptions are respected. These two financing strategies are equivalent in terms of signal and the choice between them depends on the desired investment schedule and on the leverage variability. The model also shows that "good" firms choose straight bond issues because this signal dominates the two previous ones since an increase in leverage is considered a positive signal by the market.

It is important to remember that the model considers as "good" firms those which expect with certainty high returns from their investments and "medium" firms those which have an high probability of a good investment outcome and a low probability of a bad investment outcome. It seems then that the features of "medium" firms with riskier investment are more similar to those of high-tech firms, whose investment perspectives are linked to the success of ongoing research. Conversely, the features of "good" firms are more similar to those of firms in traditional sectors or firms less engaged in innovative investment.

The empirical analysis presented in this section tests these theoretical conclusions investigating for the presence of abnormal common stock returns in correspondence of the issue date on the Japanese market.

Our sample considers the following public issues: 102 bond plus equity warrant issues (BW); 83 straight bond issues (SB) and 103 convertible bond issues (CB).

These issues have been drawn from all public issues occurring in Japan between 1982 and 1989 registered by the *Japan Economic Journal*. The choice of the sample depends on the availability of a sufficiently large dataset on daily equity prices. Only those firms for which no other important news emerged on the issue date have been selected.

A first important information from this empirical investigation is the sectorial split of Japanese public issues in the 1980s compared with the sectorial split of the sample. From the analysis of financing strategy choices of Japanese firms between 1983 and 1987 some interesting points seem to emerge (Table 4.2): i) firms in high-tech sectors with riskier investment prefer CB or BW issues consistently with "medium firm" behaviour described in the model (SB represents only 11% of Chemicals' issue, 9% of Mechanical Enginering's issues and 16% of Electronics' issues); ii) firms in traditional sectors with less risky investment prefer SB consistently with "good firm" behaviour in the model (SB represents 71% of Electrical companies' issues; 57% of Metal manufacturing's issues and 56% of Financials' issues); iii) BW choice dominates CB in every sector (with the exception of financial firms) confirming the relative advantage of BW over convertibles in term of minimisation of leverage variability and higher investment flexibility.

For the calculation of abnormal stock returns we follow the Dann-Mikkelson approach. We consider equity prices 200 days before and after the issue date. We then calculate theoretical returns regressing log equity price returns over index returns using Fowler-Rorke (1983) method for the whole time length excluding 60 days around the issue date. Abnormal returns are then computed in term of residuals between observed returns and theoretical returns.

We then present results of the average abnormal returns and the distribution of returns for the subsample relative to the three different types of issues at the issue date.

These results confirm the expected hierarchy for financing sources according to the theoretical model even if they are statistically not very significant.

The average abnormal stock return at the issue date is positive for SB issues (0.17%), while average abnormal stock returns at the issue date for CB and BW are negative (respectively -.08% and -.22%) and are quite similar confirming that these last two financing strategies provide the same kind of signal (Table 4.3). An interesting ex post confirmation that SB, CB and BW financing strategies may identify firms with good and medium perspectives is given by the inspection of cumulative average prediction errors before and after the issue date. It is impressive to note how the firm hierarchy changes after the issue. Before it, BW and CB issuers present higher positive cumulative average prediction errors than SB issuers; after it BW and CB issuers experience a sharp decline while SB issuers maintain their position (see Figure 4.1).

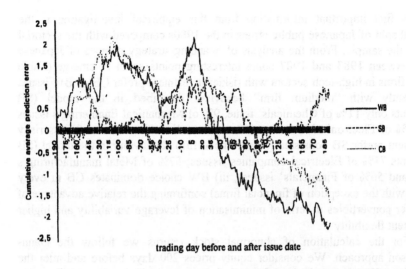

Figure 4.1 Effects of SB, CB and WB issues on cumulative average prediction error

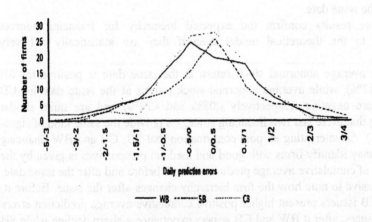

Figure 4.2 Abnormal common stock return distributions for different financing strategies at the issue date

If we observe with more detail the distribution of these abnormal returns for the three subsamples we note that the hierarchy is respected for positive abnormal returns, while in the low tail of the distribution (more negative abnormal returns) SB causes more negative responses than CB (Figures 4.2 and 4.3).

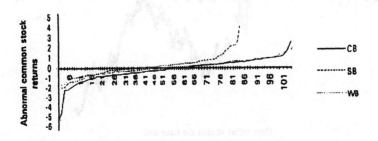

Firms included in the sample

Figure 4.3 Distribution of abnormal common stock returns across firms for CB, SB and WB issues

An indirect confirmation of the imperfect information rationale in equity price changes at the issue date is given by the behaviour of Electricals. Electricals prefer as a financing strategy SB to BW and CB (71% against 21% and 8% respectively) and this result also appears consistent with the model presented in section 3.2. A plausible explanation is that Electrical companies have relatively less risky investments and, consequently, lower expected failure costs allow these firms to reap gains from emitting strong signals (exactly as in the model where good firms have projects whose outcome is certainly higher than investment costs).

It is interesting to see how the market reacts when Electrical companies choose BW and CB. In spite of the reduced number of observations, it seems that warrant or convertible emmissions from such firms are regarded as a particularly bad signal (Figure 4.4).

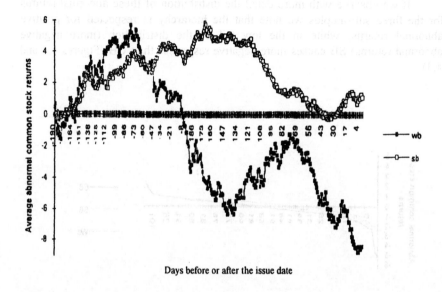

Days before or after the issue date

Figure 4.4 Average abnormal common stock returns for electrical companies choosing WB or SB financing strategy

An explanation could be that these firms are strongly penalised because they use a signal which is lower than the average sectorial signal. This hypothesis seem to be confirmed by the inspection of abnormal common stock returns that diverge dramatically after the issue date.

5. Conclusions

The theoretical and empirical analysis of bond cum equity warrant financing strategies developed in this paper leads to some interesting conclusions. From a theoretical point of view, the signalling model presented shows that a BW issue is an optimal intermediate signalling strategy for high-tech firms undertaking risky investments. As an intermediate signal BW are preferred to convertibles when an investment is multistage because they allow firms to have a more flexible financing strategy with a lower leverage variance.

In spite of these advantages, the BW signalling strategy presents some problems if low costs of financial distress do not discourage bad firms from mimicking medium firms and if a decline in the stock market index occurs. The

138

first kind of problem may be solved in the model if firms decide to reinforce their signal, accompanying their bond issue with "knock-out warrant" (warrants incorporating a put option together with the traditional call option). The second problem explains why exposition to nondiversifiable risk condemned some firms, even in the presence of good investing opportunities, to the failure of their warrant conversion. Both phenomena are explained in an extension of the signalling model presented in the paper, with the further conclusion that the same bond cum warrant issue has the effect of increasing firm exposition to nondiversifiable risk. This happens because shareholders know that a firm's choice of exercise price cannot be revised until the deadline conversion date. They then anticipate, in case of market index falls during the conversion period, the failure of a firm's financing strategy and the increase in its future leverage.

The empirical part of the section directly tests the validity of the signalling model and finds four results providing partial support to it: i) firms in traditional sectors, presumably more similar to the "good" firms in the model, and having investment with certain positive expected outcome prefer SB to CB and BW, while firms in high-tech sectors presumably more similar to "medium" firms in the model having expected investment outcomes with probability of being larger or smaller than investment costs, prefer BW to SB and CB; ii) the average abnormal common stock return after SB issues is slightly higher than after BW and CB and substantially coincident for these last two financing strategies; iii) Electrical companies who traditionally choose SB financing are strongly penalised when they choose "weaker" signals like BW or CB; iv) cumulative average abnormal stock returns confirm ex post the information revealed at the issue date over future firm perspectives: BW and CB experience a higher decrease in cumulative average abnormal stock returns than SB.

The main conclusion of the section is that a BW financing strategy is widely adopted by high-tech firms that have good intermediate research results and want to subordinate their opportunity to delay a following investment stage in order to obtain further positive results in research activities. This instrument often has the advantage of reducing the underlying asset volatility but is sensitive to nondiversifiable risk and to adverse selection issuing costs, as several warrant financing strategy failures that occurred in the 1990s have recently shown. The solution for the adverse selection problem is the reinforcement of the signal through the introduction of put options in issued warrants. In addition, the exposition to nondiversifiable risk should be reduced if firms are given the opportunity of hedging against it by purchasing stock index futures when a market where these derivatives are traded does exist.

Table 4.1 Warrant issuers affected by bullish stock market

Warrant issuer	Event announced	Date
Nippon Steel	30 billion yen of straight bonds issue to compensate for non exercised warrants	10-11-93
Toshiba	straight bond issue and bank loans to compensate for non exercised warrants	10-11-93
Kanebo	only 23.6% convertibles (incorporating a put option) issued in 1991 exercised before the expiring date	27-09-93
Sekisui Plastic	$100 million cash reserves are used to redeem bonds whose accompanying warrant has not been exercised	08-03-93
Kawasaki	60 billion Yen straight bonds to compensate for non exercised warrants (ex. price 441 - last share price 300)	22-03-93
Keio Teito	60 billions Yen needed to buy back bonds issued with non exercised warrants	22-03-93
Mitsubishi Rayon	150 billion Yen cash reserves are used to redeem bonds with non exercised warrants (ex. price 844 - last share price 300)	15-02-93
Honda	35-40 billion Yen estimated to redeem bonds with non exercised warrants	15-02-93
Suzuki	40.4 billion Yen bonds with non exercised warrants to be redeemed in June	25-01-93
Oki elect.	43 billion Yen of bond with non exercised warrants to be redeemed (ex. price 1,118 - last share price 300)	23-11-92
Asahi Chemical	40 billion Yen cash reserves and 22 billion Yen bank loans to buy back bond with non exercised warrants	11-09-92

Table 4.1 (con't) Warrant issuers affected by bullish stock market

Nippon Oil	94 billion Yen cash reserves to buy back bonds with non exercised warrants	11-09-92
Nissan Motor	$500 million dollar needed to redeem bonds with non exercised warrants	08-01-92
Mitsubishi Material	600 billion Yen borrowed to redeem bonds with warrants exercised only for 10% of total amount	07-18-92
Nippon Steel	100 billion Yen needed to redeem bonds with non exercised warrants	10-11-92
Sumitomo Metal	60 billion Yen needed to redeem bonds with non exercised warrants	07-07-92
Nisshin	17.7 billion Yen cash reserves to buy back bonds with non exercised warrants	06-07-92
Sankyo	8 billion Yen to buy back bonds with non exercised warrants	06-02-92
Fuji Foto	$400 million needed to buy back bonds with non exercised warrants (ex. price 2,857 - actual share price 2,700)	15-02-92
Keio Teito	$300 million needed to buy back bonds with non exercised warrants (ex. price 1,383 - actual share price 750)	15-02-92

Table 4.2 Private issues in Japan between 1983-1987

Sectors	% of issue type			% of total sector issue		
	SB	BW	CB	SB	BW	CB
Chemical Pharmaceutical	2.91	17.44	4.76	10.81	81.08	8.10
Mechanical Engineering	0.72	4.60	3.17	9.09	72.72	18.18
Electronics	3.64	8.01	19.04	16.12	45.16	38.70
Electricals	25.54	5.81	6.34	71.42	20.40	8.16
Construction	1.45	16.27	10.11	5.40	75.67	18.91
Motors	5.83	5.23	1.00	44.40	50	5.55
Metal manuf.	11.67	5.81	3.17	57.14	35.71	7.14
Financials	27.00	6.97	26.98	56.06	18.18	25.75
Transports Telecom.	8.02	4.65	4.76	50.00	36.36	13.63
Property	7.29	12.20	3.17	30.30	63.63	6.06
Others	5.80	12.60	17.40	25.00	50.00	25.00

Table 4.3 Common stock daily average prediction error in correspondence of SB (straight bond) issues CB (convertible bond) issues and WB (bond plus equity warrant issues)

Trading day	Average prediction error		
	WB	SB	CB
-50	-0.05777	-0.07983	-0.18472
-40	0.219665	0.126116	-0.0481
-30	-0.09663	-0.08534	-0.03448
-20	0.011321	-0.0046	0.066689
-19	-0.04732	0.136885	-0.08772
-18	0.008486	0.133335	-0.04839
-17	0.062504	0.071297	0.14073
-16	0.089368	0.010238	0.137603
-15	-0.09167	-0.05765	0.135494
-14	0.20034	-0.06134	0039154
-13	-0.01919	0.113905	0.097091
-12	0.022116	0.019612	0.150903
-11	0.106685	-0.14414	-0.02313
-10	-0.06898	-0.02248	-0.07427
-9	0.011298	-0.01019	0.004833
-8	0.197305	-0.28489	0.006115
-7	0.112038	-0.09082	0.151992
-6	0.007096	0.098898	-0.04345
-5	-0.07061	0.149631	-0.11338
-4	0.130945	0.018443	-0.0706
-3	-0.02241	0.118285	-0.01052
-2	0.166597	0.070303	-0.10833
-1	0.19654	0.141044	0.14044
0	-0.22808	0.173901	-0.08715
1	0.104536	-0.13681	0.093257
2	0.104508	-0.12548	-0.08578
3	-0.06808	0.107004	-0.13272

Table 4.3 (con't) Common stock daily average prediction error in correspondence of SB (straight bond) issues CB (convertible bond) issues and WB (bond plus equity warrant issues)

Trading day	Average prediction error		
	WB	SB	CB
4	0.089301	0.138096	-0.04544
5	0.056742	-0.07246	-0.07504
6	0.035231	0.086767	0.01053
7	0.144416	0.02417	0.059228
8	-0.12316	0.021363	-0.14655
9	-0.16346	0.078862	-0.15098
10	0.004936	0.013594	-0.03924
11	-0.01615	-0.10007	0.005599
12	-0.01309	-0.17849	0.070739
13	0.021902	-0.06654	-0.0601
14	-0.16204	0.014022	0.044049
15	-0.15016	0.039952	0.039339
16	-0.20737	0.076207	-0.15458
17	-0.08026	0.017504	-0.11497
18	0.12906	-0.05069	-0.06917
19	-0.0976	0.006349	0.019528
20	-0.0142	0.074032	-0.05955
30	-0.17546	-0.10595	-0.23758
40	-0.17192	0.032359	-0.00269
50	0.065923	0.013204	-0.14395

Notes

[1] Brennan-Kraus (1987) find that under particular conditions two financing strategies like junior convertible bond issues and equity issues combined with debt retirement are "value revealing signalling equilibria". For these authors the role of convertibles is particularly important when ex-post risk shifting is concerned or when it is difficult to evaluate asset risk. Constantinides-Grundy (1989) assume that, in order to reinforce the signal, convertible issue should be accompanied by "stock repurchase", but the problem is that "stock repurchase" obviously reduces external financing sources collection and no satisfying empirical evidence is found for it.

[2] This is an important empirical support to the signalling effects of convertibles even though some authors simply give a "negative inclined demand explanation" to the issue (Loderer, Coney, Van Drunen, 1991).

[3] The efficiency of financing strategies as a signal for firms to avoid asymmetric information costs has been recently questioned by Mayer (1992). The argument is that such a signal is inefficient given that it merely duplicates information which is available on public balance sheet data. This is not true for two main reasons. Balance sheet data i) are not a good signal because a problem of accounts "counterfeiting" may always invalidate their information; ii) provide information about the past and not about the future perspectives of a firm.

[4] Venture capital finance is defined in the paper as an agreement where the venture capitalist provides monetary (and, to a lower extent, non monetary) support to the innovator in exchange of a participation to the returns of the innovating project.

[5] It is possible to demonstrate that, in presence of heterogeneous investors (as it is the case of the model), the optimal mechanism design devised by the venture capital financier will be represented by a {q,w} contract where q is the share of property rights obtained by the investor and w is a (usually negative) lump sum transfer from the innovator to the financier. In particular if the financier optimises, the IR constraint of the lowest quality investor is satisfied with equality (Becchetti, 1995). C_{vc} will then be the sum of transfer and property dilution costs. It is then clear that the maximising solution of the venture capital financier then imposes high costs on investors. Lower costs are imposed in bargaining solutions.

[6] Another reason why a BW issue may be preferred to a convertible issue is because it reduces leverage variance. This second point may be explained with a simple example. We assume that all firm types have in t_0 a D/E leverage position and that the base research investment K =x and the development and marketing investment I-K=x as well.

Suppose that small and new high-tech firms run the risk of going bankrupt if the leverage gets too high ($(D+x+\varepsilon)/E$) is their bankruptcy treshold) and of losing control over the venture if leverage gets too low because of equity dilution ($(x+\varepsilon)/(E+x+\varepsilon)$) is their equity dilution treshold). Therefore, a departure in both directions from the leverage in t_0 negatively affects firm future perspectives.

It is then easy to see that, for a medium firm, the expected level of leverage in t_2 will be:

$$E_{t_2}[LV|BW] = p(\frac{D+x}{E}) + (1-p)(\frac{D}{E+x})$$ (1)

145

in case of bond plus equity warrant issue (BW) and:

$$E_{t_1}[LV|CNV] = p(\frac{D+2x}{E}) + (1-p)(\frac{D}{E+2x}) \qquad (2)$$

in case of convertible issue where the convertible issue hits both bankruptcy and equity dilution threshold while the BW issue does not.

[7] It can be objected that also the straight bond can be underpriced if the market believes that also medium and bad firms can issue it. But this is not a rational belief given that medium and bad firms have no advantage in mimicking good firms (respectively propositions A4 and A5). The validity of proposition A1 therefore rests on the validity of propositions A4 and A5.

[8] This does not contradict the rational expectation hypothesis as, with RE $E_{t1}[I_{t1}-I_{t0}] = 0$ but $E_{t2}[I_{t2}-I_{t0}] \neq 0$ if $I_{t1}=I_{t0} + \varepsilon$.

[9] The firm may be provided with the opportunity of hedging against the risk if a market on stock index futures exists. But the insurance does have a cost and if this cost is again higher than I-K, a signalling equilibrium cannot still be reached.

146

References

Adams, W.J. and Yellen, J.L. (1976), "Commodity bundling and the burden of monopoly", *Quarterly Journal of Economics*, 475-498.

Asquith, P. and Mullins, D. (1986), "Equity issues and offering dilution", *Journal of Financial Economics* 15.

Asquith, P. and Mullins, D. (1991), "Convertible debt: corporate call policy and voluntary conversion", *Journal of Finance* 46.

Becchetti, L. (1995), "Venture capital financing with heterogeneous innovators: an optimal mechanism design", mimeo.

Brennan, M. and Kraus, A. (1987), "Efficient financing under asymmetric information", *Journal of Finance* 42.

Brigham, E. (1966), "An analysis of convertible debentures: theory and some empirical evidence", *Journal of Finance*, 21.

Cooney J.W. and Kalay, A. (1993), "Positive information form equity issue announcements", *Journal of Financial Economics*, 33, 149-172.

Costantinides, G. and Grundy, B. (1989), "Optimal investment stock with repurchase and financing as signals", *Review of Financial Studies*, 2.

Cox, J.C. and Rubinstein, M. (1985), *Option Markets*, Prentice Hall, Englewood Cliffs, New Jersey.

Cuthberson, K., Hall. S.G. and Taylor, M.P. (1992), *Applied Econometric techniques*, Philip Allan, Hemel Hempstead.

Dann, L. and Mikkelson, W. (1984), "Convertible debt issuance, capital structure change and financing related information", *Journal of Financial Economics* 13.

Eckbo, B. (1986), "Valuation effects of corporate debt offerings", *Journal of Financial Economics*, 15.

Essig, S. (1991), "Convertible securities and capital structure determinants", Ph.D. dissertation Graduate School of Business, University of Chicago, IL).

Fazzari, S.M., Hubbard, G.R. and Petersen, B.C. (1988), "Financing Constraints and Corporate Investments", *Brooking Papers on Economic Activities*.

Ferri, M., J. Kremer, and Oberhelman, H. (1986), An analysis of models for pricing corporate warrants, *Advances in Futures and Option Research* 1A.

Fowler, D.J. and Rorke, C.H. (1983), "Risk measurement when shares are subject to infrequent trading:Comment", *Journal of Financial Economics*, 12.

French, K. and Roll, R. (1986), "Stock return variances: the arrival of information and the reaction of the traders", *Journal of Financial Economics*, 17.

Green, R. (1984), "Investment incentives, debt and warrants", *Journal of Financial Economics* 13, March.

Hirshcleifer, J. and Riley, J.G. (1992), *The analytics of uncertainty and information*, Cambridge University Press.

Hoffmeister, J.R. (1977), "Use of convertible debt in the early 1970s: a revaluation of corporate motives", *Quarterly Review of Economics and Business*, 17.

Holmstrom, B. (1989), "Agency costs and innovation", *Journal of Economic Behaviour and Organization*, 2.

Hull, J.C. (1993), *Options, Futures and Other Derivative Securities*, Prentice Hall, Englewood Cliffs, NY.

Kalay, A. and Shimrat, A. (1987), "Firm value and seasoned equity issues: price pressure, wealth redistribution, or negative information", *Journal of Financial Economics*, 19, 109-126.

Kato, K. and Schallheim, J.S. (1992), "Public and private placements of seasoned equity issues in Japan", Unpublished working paper David Eccles School of Business, University of Utah, Salt Lake City, UT.

Klemkosky, R.C. and Maness, T.S (1980), "The impact of options on the underlying securities", *Journal of Portfolio Management*, Winter.

Loderer, C.F., Cooney, J.W. and van Drunen, L.D. (1991) "The price elasticity of demand for common stock", *Journal of Finance*, 46.

Long, M. and Sefcik, S. (1990), "Participation financing: a comparison of the characteristics of convertible debts and straight bonds issued in conjunction with warrants", *Financial Management* 19 (3).

Masulis, R. and Korwar, A. (1986), "Seasoned equity offerings: an empirical investigation", *Journal of Financial Economics* 15.

Mayer, C. (1990), "Financial systems, corporate finance and economic development", (Chicago IL; University of Chicago Press).

Mikkelson, W. and Partch, M. (1986), "Valuation effects of security offerings and the issuance process", *Journal of Financial Economics*, 15.

Myers, S.C. and Majluf, M.S. (1984), "Corporate Financing Decisions When Firms Have Investment Information That Investments Do Not", *Journal of Financial Economics* Vol. 13.

Phelps, K., Moore, W. and Roenfeldt, R. (1991), "Equity valuation effects of warrant-debt financing", *Journal of Financial Research* 14.

Pilcher, C.J. (1955), "Raising capital with convertible securities, Michigan business studies no", 21/2 (University of Michigan, Ann Arbor, MI).

Santarelli, E. (1991), "Asset Specificity, R&D FInancing and the Signalling Properties of Firm's Financial Structure", *Economics of Innovation and New technology*, 1.

Scholes, M. and Williams, J. (1977), "Estimating betas from nonsynchronous data", *Journal of Financial Economics*, 5.

Skinner, D.J. (1989), "Option market and stock return volatility", *Journal of Financial Economics*, Vol. 23.

Stein, J.C. (1992), "Convertible bonds as backdoor equity financing", *Journal of Financial Economics*, Vol. 32, n. 1.

Trennepohl, G.L. and Dukes, W.P. (1979), "CBOE options and stock volatility", *Review of Business and Economic Research*, Vol. 14.

Whiteside, M.M, Dukes, W.P. and Dunne, P.M. (1983), "Short term impact of option trading on the underlying securities", *Journal of Financial Research*, 6.

5   Effects of options introduction on stock price volatility: an empirical testing on high-tech firm equities based on SSC-GARCH models

Andrea Caggese

1. Introduction

The introduction of futures and options markets is usually considered a move toward market completeness that introduces additional information and reduces transaction costs. Moreover an increase in speculation activity caused by the introduction of new agents into the market lowers the aggregate risk aversion, thereby strengthening arbitrage forces that lead to the stabilisation of prices (Stein, 1987).

Some theoretical papers (Dantine, 1978; Turnovsky, 1983) emphasised the stabilising effect of futures market speculation. The fact, though, that during financial crises (such as the stock market crash in October 1987) higher volatility of spot prices was accompanied by a dramatic increase in trading activity in derivatives led regulatory authorities to suspect that future markets might have a destabilising effect on prices. This has been reflected for example in SEC concerns (Skinner, 1989), and in the decision of the Japanese regulatory authorities to reduce trading hours, increase margin and commission charges and reduce daily price limits (Robinson 1993). A rationale for it is the pyramiding (market euphoria) and depyramiding (market panic) phenomenon caused by destabilising speculation, that can be increased by derivative margin trading (Seguin, 1990).

The theoretical arguments for the effects of derivatives introduction on market volatility have not, then, been able so far to solve the issue in univocal direction: changes in the composition of traders are factors that can produce changes in market volatility, but the introduction of derivatives generates in fact several possible fluxes from different kinds of traders with movements from bond-stock portfolio hedgers to i) static derivative hedgers and to ii) dynamic derivative hedgers; from non traders to iii) noise traders (non-rational speculators), iv) good speculators (rational speculators) and to v) insiders (speculators with private information). Given the complexity of these fluxes, it is almost impossible to disentangle from all these passages the net effect on overall market stability.

From the empirical point of view, recent attempts to analyse the effects of derivatives introduction are generally based, for a sample of individual firm stocks, on the estimation of the mean group unconditional standard deviation, corrected for market standard deviation before and after the introduction of derivative trading (Skinner, 1989; French-Roll, 1986; Trennepohl-Duke, 1979; Witheside-Dukes-Dunne, 1983; Klemkosky-Maness, 1980; Edwars, 1988; Stoll-Whaley, 1987).

A few other works are based on the estimation of models taking into account the phenomenon of volatility persistence (Robinson, 1993; Lee-Ohk, 1992; Baldauf-Santoni, 1991; Antoniou-Holmes, 1992). These contributions consider in fact that stock returns distribution is typically non-stationary (Baldauf-Santoni, 1991) and shows both skewness and excess kurtosis (Bollerslev-Chou-Kroner, 1992). Time-varying persistence in conditional variance is justified by shock induced changes in the composition of market traders. Strong unpredictable stock returns shift traders from a static medium-term return strategy to a speculative short term trading strategy, and this has the effect of creating persistence in changes in price volatility. Particularly interesting is the approach made by Engle-Ng (1993). His contribution provides a technique for estimating the "news impact curve", the curve that relates volatility response to past shock magnitude, and allows for asymmetries in conditional second moment reaction to negative and positive shocks. Becchetti-Caggese (1995) applied this method for the analysis of changes in market volatility after stock index option introduction, with a specification (sign and size conditional GARCH) that detects more precisely changes in the "news impact curve" shape, and with the introduction of a "sign persistence" variable, that signals the effect of a sequence of shocks (unpredictable returns) of the same sign on conditional volatility.

This study intends to apply this methodology to test the effects of derivatives introduction on stock price volatility of individual firms' equities. In particular the inspection of significant changes between the behaviour of price volatility ex ante and ex post derivative introduction allows us to test:

152

i) the destabilising effect of the "pyramiding/depyramiding" phenomenon, through the analysis of the "sign persistence" coefficient before and after option introduction;

ii) the effects of option introduction on stock-price volatility: we analyse changes in volatility levels (intercept's breaks) as well as changes in news impact curve shape (changes in the "law" of market reaction to shocks).

This procedure is applied to 22 industrial firm equities of five European countries, which have experienced the introduction of stock options at different times from 1978 to 1992.

The chapter is divided into four sections. In the first section a brief survey of recent theories about speculation and asset-price variability is presented, focusing on the role of information distribution among different market participants in determining price volatility. In the second section the conditional volatility models used for the empirical analysis are described. In the third section the procedure used for the estimation of firms' abnormal returns is illustrated: we include as regressors of stock returns all significant lagged values of the dependent variable, day-of-the-week effects and present and lagged returns of the stock index.

In the fourth section the results of the estimates are presented. We found a predominant positive sign persistence coefficient before option introduction. In almost every case the coefficient is eliminated ex post. This confirms the positive effect of option introduction on market efficiency. Option trading seems to reduce the pyramiding/depyramiding phenomenon instead of worsening it. A plausible explanation of it is that volatility reaction to shocks is weaker by substitution of "stock-bond portfolio hedging" with "static derivative hedging". For example the "depyramiding effect" caused by a negative shock on the market is dampened because automatic stop-loss rules are replaced by hedged positions. On the other hand we didn't find evidence of a univocal positive or negative effect of option introduction on price volatility. Firms with the same effect, though, appear very homogeneous by industrial sector and by conditional volatility behaviour. The majority of firms with an increase in price volatility present an "inverted leverage" effect (conditional volatility is more sensitive to past positive than past negative shocks). These results suggest that market characteristics, especially the informative structure, could influence market reaction to option introduction. An explanation for this could be that, in some sectors, there is a significant presence of insider information, in the form of private news that is expected to raise firms' market value when released to the public. Option introduction gives more profitable speculation opportunities to small traders, allowing them to take high-risk leveraged positions, but together with small "informed" traders (insider traders), uninformed "irrational" traders (noise traders) enter the market, so that spot traders are unable to discern if option trading reflects new information or irrational behaviour. The destabilising effect of this is consistent with the theoretical model of Stein (1987), where a change in the informational content of prices when more speculators with different information enter the market can, on certain assumptions (the new information is not perfectly observed), lower the informational content of prices and increase market volatility.

2. Information, speculation and asset-price volatility

The impossibility of market equilibrium with perfect information has been proved by Grossman and Stiglitz (1980): in a market with costly information the effort spent in obtaining such information has to be balanced in equilibrium by the return from transactions made with uninformed traders. If the equilibrium price exactly reflects market information nobody can use it against others. The result is an "equilibrium degree of disequilibrium" that implies the coexistence of informed (rational) and uninformed (both rational and noise) traders.

Black and Tons (1992), using a theoretical framework similar to Grossman-Stiglitz', show that the simultaneous presence of rational informed and uninformed traders generates more volatility than the presence of all informed or all uninformed traders. This is because, when the uninformed are aware of the presence of the informed, they try to extract information from price movements, but in this way they amplify the destabilising effect of shocks generated by noise traders.

Another model in which uninformed "near rational" traders generate instability has been theorised by Wang (1993), where rational informed traders are "maximisers", while uninformed traders follow an adaptive rule that amplifies the effects of exogenous shocks in a market.

In both models an increase in market information could reduce volatility. This could be the case of future markets introduction. These markets make additional costless information available to rational uninformed and adaptive traders, so that they can change their behaviour into rational maximisers.

The key to the problem is the informational structure of the market. If we assume homogeneous information, then rational traders can be informed (if they make efforts to obtain information) or uninformed. On the contrary, the information can be heterogeneous among different traders. Stein (1987) makes a particular hypothesis: there is a category of traders with access to different information with respect to traders already present in the market. They have a chance of using it in speculative trading only after a futures market is introduced (secondary traders), because they have inadequate resources to take risky positions in the spot market. Stein shows that, when secondary traders observe a noisy signal from a different source of information, their presence causes a reduction in the informational content of prices. This negative externality caused by the option market introduction could be sufficiently strong to counteract the stabilising effect of the risk-sharing property of secondary markets, raising price volatility.

3. Empirical models for estimating financial series volatility

Empirical contributions to the issue of the effects of derivatives introduction on market volatility presented by academics may be divided into two subgroups. The first subgroup uses filtered or unfiltered unconditional second order moments (Skinner, 1989; French-Roll, 1986; Trennepohl-Duke, 1979; Witheside-Dukes-Dunne, 1983; Klemkosky-Maness, 1980; Edwars, 1988; Stoll-Whaley, 1987), while the second takes into account the seminal paper of Engle (1982) and tries to model explicitly the phenomenon of volatility clustering with time-varying second-order moments (Robinson, 1993; Lee-Ohk, 1992; Baldauf-Santoni, 1991, Antoniou-Holmes, 1992).

The reason why the second group approach should be preferred is that simple standard deviation measures of changes in volatility through a fixed or a moving window before and after the introduction of derivatives are not appropriate as stock returns usually exhibit nonnormal unconditional sampling distributions especially in the form of excess kurtosis (Bollerslev-Chou-Kroner, 1992).

For these reasons, although unconditional changes in individual stock variances before and after the introduction of derivatives are correctly weighted for changes in market variances and for the volumes traded, they do not take into account the important phenomenon of variance persistence.

The new approach which explicitly models variance has been introduced by the Engle (1982) ARCH model. In this model the residual of an appropriate regression where stock returns are the dependent variable is a discrete time stochastic process $\{\varepsilon_t\}$. The process is composed by the product of two variables: z_t which is i.i.d and σ_t which is a time varying, positive and measurable function of the information set in time t-1.

A basic ARCH(q) model of stock returns will then be equal to:

$$Rt = a_0 + \Sigma_i a_i x_{it} + \varepsilon_t \tag{1}$$
$$\varepsilon_t | I_{t-1} \sim N(0, h_t)$$
$$h_t - b_0 + \sum_j b_j \varepsilon_{t-j}^2 \tag{2}$$
$$j=1,...,q$$

155

where R_t are stock index returns x_{it} all exogenous variables (i.e. lagged stock returns, weekday dummies, interest rate term structure) and the conditional variance of the residual of the first equation is dependent on lagged shocks. Important conditions are $b_0 > 0$ and $b_j > 0$ to ensure positive conditional variance and $\Sigma_j b_j < 1$ to have stationary conditional variance.

After Engle's contribution, several other implementations of the original model have been made: the first modification that tried to model persistence of the shocks on conditional second moments is the simple GARCH (1,1) proposed by Bollerslev (1986). In the model, the conditional variance equation of the original ARCH was modified by the introduction of a lagged dependent variable as a regressor whose coefficient described the law of decay of individual shocks persistence on the dependent variable itself. In fact, simple algebraic manipulation shows that a GARCH (p,q) model is an infinite order ARCH process with a rational lag structure (Bollerslev, 1986; Bera-Higgins, 1993).

The analysis of the moments of a GARCH process demonstrate that it is unconditionally homoskedastic, serially uncorrelated, has constant zero mean and excess kurtosis. An important feature of GARCH is that it provides an explanation for the nonnormality in the distribution of residuals from the stock return equation. In this respect, the test of kurtosis on GARCH residuals, standardised for the conditional variance, should then assess whether all excess kurtosis of original data, or only part of it, can be explained by the model. Another interesting feature of the GARCH model is that it can be demonstrated that it is the discrete equivalent of a diffusion process, which is a quite frequently adopted way of theoretically modelling a speculative asset behaviour.

These features make GARCH structure capable of capturing most time series non-linear dynamics, and quite attractive for the description of the "stylised facts" of financial time series.

The modelling of shock effects on conditional variance has been further refined after several authors observed a negative correlation between current returns and future volatility (Christie, 1982). This led to the formulation of asymmetrically centred models such as the EGARCH (Nelson, 1990), which is capable of taking into account different impacts of shocks on conditional second order moments according to the size and to the sign (bad or good news) of the shock. Similar models that are able to capture variations of shock impact according to size and sign are the Sign Switching GARCH (Fornari-Mele, 1994), the GJR (Glosten, Jagannathan and Runkle, 1989), and the AGARCH (Engle, 1990).

The most recent contribution of Engle-Ng (1993) provides a fundamental unified approach to studies in the field through the analysis of the "news impact curve" (henceforth NIC) which illustrates the crucial relationship between past return shocks and conditional variance for all different specifications adopted in modelling variance clustering. The NIC provides an immediate graphical evaluation of the hypothesis on the conditional variance behaviour implied by the model, while the evaluation of the different models is achieved by Engle-Ng through a series of tests the most important of which are: i) the Sign Bias Test; ii) the Negative Size Bias Test; iii) the Positive Size Bias Test; iv) the excess kurtosis test and v) the Pagan-Sabau (PS) Test.

Becchetti-Caggese (1995), following Engle-Ng, developed a "Sign and Size conditional GARCH" that exactly detects changes in volatility behaviour after structural breaks. It performs better than other conditional volatility models when the asymmetry in volatility reactions to different sign shocks is very strong (high leverage or inverted leverage effects).

For the present analysis of conditional volatility changes after option introduction we have estimated eight different models. The first 3 models are symmetrically centred: ARCH, GARCH and Sign Switching GARCH. In these models a 0/1 dummy signals the presence of an intercept break in volatility after option introduction. In GARCH and Sign Switching GARCH we introduce a Pr coefficient that represents the effect of shock sign persistence on conditional volatility.

The next two models, G.J.R. and Sign-Size Conditional GARCH, are centred (lower volatility H_t correspond to $\varepsilon_{t-1} = 0$), but allow asymmetric reaction of volatility to positive and negative shocks. In particular the SSC-Garch model identifies ex-post changes in the sensitivity to past positive and negative shocks (slope and leverage effect of NIC). While the first three models detect an increase or reduction in volatility after option introduction, the other two distinguish if the change is in conditional (law of reaction to past shocks) or unconditional (constant) volatility.

The last three models are asymmetric and centred at ε_{t-1} (0 (AGARCH, NAGARCH, VGARCH).

These are the specifications of the eight models:

The first simple model estimated is an ARCH(5) specification. The ARCH includes as additional variables: i) a dummy testing the existence of structural breaks after the introduction of options (D_{IO}) which takes value 0 before and value 1 after the day options started being traded on the relevant national market; ii) a trend dummy, that is present in all eight models.

The second model is a GARCH with "sign persistence". The GARCH (1.1) we propose is the following:

$$R_t = a_0 + \sum_j a_i a_{it} + \varepsilon_t \tag{3}$$

$$\varepsilon t | I_{t-1} \sim N(0, h_t)$$

$$h_t = b_0 + b_1\varepsilon^2_{t-1} + b_2 h_{t-1} + b_3 D_{IO} + b_4 \text{Pr} + b_5 D_{IO}\text{Pr} + b_6 Trnd \qquad (4)$$

where a negative and significant value for b_3 indicates a reduction of market volatility after the introduction of index option. The variable Pr is the dummy which tests the existence of additional "sign persistence" effects on conditional volatility. This dummy is such that $\text{Pr}_t = 0$ if $sign[\varepsilon_{t-1}] \neq sign[\varepsilon_{t-2}]$ and $\text{Pr}_t = n$ where n is the number of consecutive past shocks which have the same sign as ε_{t-1}. "Trnd" is the trend variable.

The third model proposed is a sign-switching GARCH model (SGARCH, Mele-Fornari, 1994). This is the simplest way to take into account the problem of the asymmetric reaction to shocks of different sign. The conditional variance in the second equation is modelled as:

$$h_t = b_0 + b_1\varepsilon^2_{t-1} + b_2 h_{t-1} + b_3 D_{IO} + b_4 D^+ + b_5 \text{Pr} + b_6 D_{IO}\text{Pr} + b_7 Trnd \qquad (5)$$

where D^+ is a dummy variable which is equal to 1 when the lagged shock is positive and equal to -1 when the lagged shock is negative.

The fourth model proposed is a GJR (Glosten-Jagannathan-Runkle, 1989). Conditional variance is given by:

$$h = b_0 + b_1 h_{t-1} + b_2\varepsilon^2_{t-1} + b_3 S^-_{t-1}\varepsilon^2_{t-1} + b_4 D_{IO}\varepsilon^2_{t-1} + b_5 D_{IO}S^-_{t-1}\varepsilon^2_{t-1} + b_6 Trnd$$
$$(6)$$

where S^-_{t-1} is a dummy that takes value 1 if the t-1 shock is negative and zero otherwise. This model captures asymmetry having a steeper slope for negative than for positive ε_{t-1}. A significant and positive b_3 would indicate the existence of a "leverage effect" with higher impact of negative shocks and a significant and positive b_5 would indicate that changes in the "leverage effect" have occurred after the introduction of index options.

The fifth model is a sign and size conditional ARCH model (SSC-GARCH) where the second equation is given by:

$$h_t = b_0 + b_1 h_{t-1} + b_2 S^-_{t-1}\varepsilon^2_{t-1} + b_3 S^+_{t-1}\varepsilon^2_{t-1} + b_4 S^-_{t-1} +$$
$$b_5 D_{IO}S^-_{t-1} + b_6 D_{IO}S^+_{t-1}\varepsilon^2_{t-1} + b_7 D_{IO}S^-_{t-1}\varepsilon^2_{t-1} + b_8 Trnd \qquad (7)$$

where two other dummies are introduced to take into account the size effect of positive sign shocks (S^+_{t-1}, which takes value 1 if the t-1 shock is positive and zero otherwise) and the size effect of negative sign shocks (S^-_{t-1}, which takes value 1 if the t-1 shock is negative and zero otherwise).

The sixth model proposed is a two stage non-linear asymmetric ARCH (NAGARCH). In the traditional NAGARCH model conditional variance is specified as (Engle-Ng, 1993):

$$h_t = b_0 + b_1 h_{t-1}^2 + b_2(\varepsilon_{t-1} + b_3\sqrt{h_{t-1}})^2 \tag{8}$$

and presents a symmetric news impact curve, centred at $\varepsilon_{t-1} = (-b_3)\sqrt{h_{t-1}}$. We estimated a NAGARCH model whose second equation is given by:

$$h_t = \omega_0 + \omega_1 h_{t-1}^2 + \omega_2\varepsilon_{t-1}^2 + \omega_3\varepsilon_{t-1}\sqrt{h_{t-1}} + \omega_4 D_{IO}\varepsilon_{t-1}^2 + \omega_5 D_{IO}\varepsilon_{t-1}\sqrt{h_t} + \omega_6 Trnd \tag{9}$$

In absence of significant changes in the equation after the introduction of index options we expect that $\omega_4 = \omega_5 = 0$. The estimated equation is in fact just a reparametrisation of the original GARCH model where $=b_0+b_2$, $b_1= \omega_1 - \omega_2 /2$, $b_2=\omega_2$ and $b_3= \omega_3/2\omega_2$.

The seventh model is an asymmetric ARCH. In the traditional AGARCH model conditional variance is given by:

$$h_t = b_0 + b_1(\varepsilon_{t-1} + b_2)^2 + b_3 h_{t-1} \tag{10}$$

The "news impact curve" is centred at positive ε_{t-1} and is then capable of capturing the asymmetric reaction to shocks of different sign. We estimate an AGARCH model where the second equation is given by:

$$h_t = \omega_0 + \omega_1\varepsilon_{t-1}^2 + \omega_2 h_{t-1} + \omega_3\varepsilon_{t-1} + \omega_4 D_{IO}h_{t-1} + \omega_5 D_{IO}\varepsilon_{t-1} + \omega_6 Trnd \tag{11}$$

If we assume no structural breaks then $\omega_4=\omega_5=0$. The original parameters of the AGARCH are given by the following combination of the reparametrised equations where $b_1=\omega_1$, $b_3=\omega_2$, and $b_3=\omega_3/2\omega_1$ and the intercept is:

$$b_0 = \omega_0 - \omega_1(\omega_2/2\omega_1)^2$$

The eighth model proposed is a VGARCH. In the traditional VGARCH model the conditional variance is modelled as:

$$h_t = b_0 + b_1 h_{t-1} + b_2(\varepsilon_{t-1}/\sqrt{h_{t-1}} + b_3)^2 \tag{12}$$

We estimate a VGARCH model where the second equation is given by:

$$h = \omega_0 + \omega_1 h_{-1} + \omega_2 \varepsilon - \sqrt{} \ h_{-1} + \omega_3 \varepsilon - \sqrt{} \ \sqrt{h_{-1}} + \omega_4 Dio\varepsilon - \sqrt{} \ h_{-1} + \omega_5 Dio\varepsilon - \sqrt{} \ \sqrt{h_{-1}} + \omega_6 Tind$$

(13)

where $\omega_4/2\omega_5$ tests for changes in the conditional volatility equation after the introduction of index options. The original parameters of the VGARCH are obtained by the following combination of the original parameters where $b_1=\omega_1$, $b_2=\omega_2$, and $b_3=\omega_3/2\omega_3$ and the intercept is $b_0 = \omega_0 - \omega_1(\omega_3/2\omega_2)^2$.

4. The empirical procedure for the estimate of the "best base equation"

In order to detect the necessity of using models where nonlinearity is modelled through a conditional variance, we present six different tests on stock return residuals (abnormal returns) based on the general model of stock return behaviour:

$$R_t = \alpha_0 + \sum_j \beta_j DW_j + \sum_j \gamma_i R_t - i + \sum_j \delta_i RInd_{t-1}$$

(14)

R_t is the one-day difference between logs of stock return for the equity, $RInd_{t-i}$ are the same differences for the relative stock market (all significant present and lagged values are included), DW_j are five dummies for "day of the week" effects.

Kurtosis and skewness tests are performed on the residuals obtained from the estimation of the base equations. Further tests which evaluate the appropriateness of using more sophisticated techniques to estimate conditional volatility are the bias tests proposed by Engle-Ng (1993) with the following specification for the error term:

$$\varepsilon_t = a_0 + \sum_i a_i \varepsilon_{t-i} + e_t$$

(15)

On the basis of this equation Sign Bias, Negative Size Bias and Positive Size Bias tests are carried out. The regressions for these three tests are respectively the following:

$$h_t = a + bD^+_{t-1} + e_t$$

(16)

$$h_t = a + bD^-_{t-1}\varepsilon_{t-1} + e_t$$

(17)

$$h_t = a + bD^+_{t-1}\varepsilon_{t-1} + e_t$$

(18)

where D^-_{t-1} is a dummy which takes value 1 when the residual of the stock return equation in the previous period is negative and value 0 when it is positive. D^+_{t-1} is just equal to $1-D^-_{t-1}$. When the T-ratio on the coefficient b is significant in one of the three equations, this indicates the necessity of using a conditional volatility specification.

The three biases will be again tested on the filtered unpredictable stock returns, calculated according to the following formula $v_t = u_t / \sqrt{h_t}$, where H_t is the conditional volatility estimated in the GARCH models. Then v^2_t is regressed on D^-_{t-1}, $D^-_{t-1}u_t$, and $D^+_{t-1}u_t$ to test for the presence of the three biases after the normalisation of the residuals (in this case a significant b coefficient indicates a misspecification in the "news impact curve"). An additional test that may be carried out is the Pagan-Sabau (PS) test. In this case what has to be done is a regression of the log of stock returns rate of change squared on an intercept and on the conditional variance estimated in the GARCH model:

$$R_t = a + bh_t + \varepsilon_t \qquad (19)$$

Under the null hypothesis of GARCH capturing most of data nonlinearity the intercept must be equal to zero and the slope is expected to be equal to one. The presence of these biases indicates the need for a specification able to consider a different impact of past shocks on conditional variance according to size and bias of the past shock, such as GJR or SSC-GARCH models.

5. Estimation results

We selected our sample of equities in five European countries where stock-option markets exist: France, Germany, Switzerland, Netherlands, United Kingdom. For each market we selected industrial firms with traded options, for a total of 22 firms: 7 from Germany, 5 from France, 4 from the U.K., 3 from Switzerland and 3 from the Netherlands. 19 firms belong to high-tech sectors, two others to the food-production sector, and one firm to the transport sector (Eurotunnel).

Table 5.1 provides additional information about firms selected for the estimation. The sample is diversified in terms of countries, industrial sectors, and option introduction dates. This allows us to analyse results at different levels, and to avoid spurious structural or business-cycle effects on price volatility. The sample is in fact nonsynchronous and ranges from approximately five years before to three years after option introduction.

The base equations (14), estimated for each firm, have some common elements (Table 5.2). Lagged values of the dependent variable are not very significant. The only exception is Eurotunnel, which presents a highly significant elasticity (.20). The presence of return autocorrelation signals imperfect market information about the firm's perspectives. This is not surprising for a young firm that doesn't have a steady reputation in the market. On the other hand, one-day returns of stock indexes are very significant, and values of firms' beta are near to 1 for the majority of firms. The consequence is relatively high R^2 values for the base equations, with almost all values between 0.40-0.70. Two exceptions are Eurotunnel, with a weak correlation with the market, and BMW, with a non significant beta coefficient. Kurtosis and skewness tests (Tables 5.4-5.25) show that distributions are stationary but not normal variates. The existence of excess kurtosis is present in 19 equities out of 22; this confirms the "stylised fact" of financial time series presenting thick tails, first observed by Mandelbrot (1963,a,b, 1970). Bias tests performed on best equation residuals (Tables 5.4-5.25) in all cases show significant values for positive and negative size bias tests, and, in some cases, for sign bias tests too, justifying the necessity of using conditional volatility models.

In tables 5.4-5.25 results of model estimates with residual diagnostics are reported. For all firms the presence of conditional volatility is confirmed. In particular we found that: i) the log-likelihood is greater in conditional volatility models than in base equation; ii) the excess kurtosis of normalised residuals is reduced for all firms except Eurotunnel and Hoechst, as well as sign-size bias tests significance; iii) the best models seem to be the asymmetric and centred Sign Switching GARCH and SSC-GARCH. They perform better in terms of log-likelihood for 11 firms. Garch performs better for 5 firms, while for the other six firms asymmetric un-centred models are slightly better (NAGARCH in three cases, AGARCH in two, VGARCH in one).

Another interesting result is the predominance of a negative volatility trend, found in 14 cases out of 22 (only 3 equities have a positive trend, while the other 5 cases present no clear tendency). This finding supports the thesis that progressive integration and increased efficiency of financial markets have a stabilising effect on firm risk. Another result that supports this view is the ex post reduction of sign persistence effects: 11 firms present, before option introduction, a significant and positive sign persistence coefficient (the sign persistence of abnormal returns increases volatility), against only 5 cases of negative coefficient. In 8 of these firms we find an ex post reduction that completely eliminates the persistence effect; in the other 3 cases the ex post variation is negative but non significant. This seems to confirm the hypothesis that option markets improve market efficiency and reduce the pyramiding/depyramiding problem instead of worsening it.

On the other hand, we found that option introduction doesn't have a univocal effect on volatility magnitude. The intercept break in conditional variance after option introduction is strong and significant for all the firms except Peugeot, Volkswagen and British Petroleum, but is positive in 11 cases and negative in the other 8.

This result is not surprising, given that neither past empirical studies nor theoretical models have solved the issue in a univocal direction. According to Stein's (1987) model the influence of derivative markets on volatility can be positive or negative depending on informational levels of new secondary market traders. In general if firm sector characteristics, expecially the informational structure (the degree of heterogeneity of information among different traders), influence market reactions to derivatives introduction, we expect to find some common elements among the firms of the same subgroup with positive/negative ex post changes in volatility.

The ex post behaviour of conditional volatility for the two subgroups is compared in Table 5.3, from which we can draw some interesting considerations: i) there exists a positive correlation between intercept break and NIC slope. This means that an increase in overall volatility (positive intercept break) is mainly explained by an increase in conditional volatility (increase in NIC's slope), and vice versa; ii) equities from the same sector have similar reactions to option introduction. Sectors with an increase in volatility are Chemicals (3 firms out of 4), Food Production (2 out of 2), Oil Production (2 out of 3); with a reduction are Electronics (3 out of 4) and Pharmaceuticals (2 out of 2). Only the Vehicles sector does not present a clear tendency (2 reductions, 1 increase, 2 without effect); iii) firms with a reduction in volatility (negative intercept break) present, after option introduction, higher sensitivity of volatility to negative shocks, with only two exceptions: Ciba-Geigy (no curve) and Peugeot (symmetric curve). Other authors observed this phenomenon (Christie, 1982), which has been called "leverage effect" given that a plausible explanation of it says that negative shocks increase firm debt-equity ratio thereby increasing firm risk and its future volatility. Conversely, the majority of firms with an increase in ex-post volatility present an unusual "inverted leveraged" shape of NIC (6 firms, against 3 firms with leverage effect. For 4 firms, Basf, Elf, Michelin, Unilever, there is an inversion in the slope of the N.I.C., that is leveraged ex ante option introduction). For these firms the stronger market reaction to past positive shocks is responsible for greater volatility. This findings support the thesis that the informative structure of a sector influences the relationship between option introduction, trader behaviour and firm specific risk. Moreover it is consistent with Stein's theory about the destabilising effect of secondary traders' different information. In this case the "new information" could be insider information about news that is expected to raise the firm's market value. This new information is "biased", because option trading conveys to the market not only insiders with good information but also noise traders (an alternative way of seeing it is to suppose that secondary traders can only observe a noisy signal of the new information), and can destabilise the market lowering the informational content of prices for already existing traders.

6. Conclusions

The chapter adopts a methodology for the analysis of structural breaks on stock price volatility, based on eight different models of conditional volatility. They are applied to 22 equities of industrial firms listed in five European markets (France, Germany, UK, Netherlands, Switzerland) to test option introduction effects on firm specific risk.

The adopted methodology tries to amend two main shortcomings of previous analyses on structural breaks induced by the introduction of derivatives: i) the adoption of measures of unconditional volatility such as the simple standard deviation; ii) the limitation of the analysis to shifts in the intercept when measures of conditional volatility are considered.

The models used in this paper allow us to test for the intercept break, the shifts in the "news impact curve" slope and shape, and the change in the sign persistence coefficient (the relationship between persistence of abnormal returns sign and conditional volatility) after the introduction of options for any single firm.

The criteria used to verify the usefulness of conditional volatility models are: the capacity of these models to eliminate positive-sign, positive-size and negative-size biases (Engle-Ng tests); the capacity of the estimated variance to mimick the actual residual variance (P-S test); iv) the capacity of the conditional volatility model to eliminate part or all of the excess kurtosis contained in the data.

The conditional volatility analysis shows some important results: i) trend in volatility: in 14 cases out of 22 we find a negative trend in volatility, against 3 cases of positive trend (the other 5 cases are without a clear tendency). These findings support the thesis that the progressive integration and the increase in efficiency of financial markets have a stabilising tendency, at least for firm specific risks (a different result is obtained for the market non-diversifiable risk; Becchetti-Caggese, 1995). Another result that supports this thesis is the ex post reduction of sign persistence effects: 11 firms present before option introduction a significant and positive sign persistence effect (the persistence of shock sign increases volatility), against only 5 cases of a negative value; for these firms in 8 cases we find an ex post reduction that completely eliminates the persistence effect; in the other 3 cases the ex-post variation is negative but non-significant. This result argues against the thesis of a destabilising effect of derivative trading through the strengthening of the pyramiding/depyramiding phenomenon; ii) the analysis doesn't find evidence of a univocal positive or negative effect of option introduction on spot price volatility. The main contribution of this study is the identification of some important features of firms with the same option introduction effects. These are very homogeneous by industrial sector and by conditional volatility behaviour. The majority of firms with an increase in price volatility after option introduction presents an unusual inverted leverage effect (volatility is more sensitive to past positive than past negative shocks). These results suggest that market characteristics, especially the informative structure, could be an important determinant of option trading effects on prices volatility. An explanation of this could be the possibility, for small traders with private information on news that are expected to raise firms' market value (insider traders), to speculate taking risky positions in derivative markets. This new information is "biased", because option trading conveys in the market not only insiders with good information, but also noise traders (an alternative way of seeing it is to suppose that secondary traders can only observe a noisy signal of the new information), that can destabilise the market lowering the informational content of prices for already existing traders. This effect can counteract the stabilising effect of the risk sharing property of secondary markets, raising price volatility.

Table 5.1 Sample of equities on which the option introduction effect is measured

Equity	Country	Sector	Market Share*	Opt. Introd. Date
Elf Aquitaine	France	Oil Integrated	5.28%	08/10/78
Total	France	Oil Integrated	3.48%	21/10/90
Peugeot	France	Vehicles	1.94%	10/09/87
Michelin	France	Vehicles-comp.	1.10%	22/01/88
Eurotunnel	France	Transport	0.59%	09/05/89
Siemens	Germany	Electronic	7.07%	26/1/90
Daimler Benz	Germany	Vehicles	6.25%	26/01/90
Bayer	Germany	Chemical	3.85%	26/01/90
Hoechst	Germany	Chemical	2.96%	26/01/90
Basf	Germany	Chemical	2.76%	26/01/90
Bmw	Germany	Vehicles	1.93%	26/01/90
Volkswagen	Germany	Vehicles	1.88%	26/01/90
Unilever	Netherlands	Food Production	7.25%	04/04/78
Akzo Nobel	Netherlands	Chemical	1.92%	26/06/78
Getronics	Netherlands	Electronic	0.19%	07/02/92
Nestle'	Switzerland	Food Production	12.11%	08/06/93
Roche	Switzerland	Pharmaceutical	4.82%	19/05/88
Ciba Geigy	Switzerland	Pharmaceutical	0.92%	20/02/92
British Petroleum	U.K.	Oil Integrated	2.60%	21/04/78
Cable & Wireless	U.K.	Telecommunication	1.25%	13/12/88
General Electric	U.K.	Electronic	1.23%	21/04/78
Amstrad	U.K.	Electronic	0.03%	23/04/87

*At 26 June 1995.

Table 5.2: Best equations

Table 5.2.1 France

Elf-Aquitaine

$R_t =$	$+.06R_{t-1}$	$+.04R_{t-4}$	$+1.03Rind_t$	$-.15Rind_{t-1}$
	(3.05)	(2.43)	(35.7)	(-4.3)

Eurotunnel

$R_t =$	$+.20R_{t-1}$	$+.69Rind_t$	$+.14E-2Fri$
	(5.98)	(8.36)	(1.74)

Michelin

$R_t =$	$+.03R_{t-1}$	$-.05R_{t-2}$	$-.06R_{t-4}$	$+1.34Rind_t$	$-.10E-2Thru$
	(2.01)	(-3.56)	(-3.91)	(41.4)	(-2.89)

Peugeot

$R_t =$	$+.07R_{t-1}$	$+1.34Rind_t$	$-.17Rind_{t-1}$	$+0.6Rind_{t-6}$	$-.57E-3Thru$
	(3.65)	(46.3)	(-4.3)	(2.32)	(-1.8)

Total

$R_t=$	$+.08R_{t-1}$	$+.78Rind_t$	$-.19Rind_{t-1}$	$+0.7Rind_{t-6}$	$+.78E-3Thru$
	(4.03)	(27.4)	(-5.7)	(2.56)	(2.46)

R_t = Log returns of stock prices

$Rind_t$= Log returns of Stock Market Index

Mon. Tue. Wed. Thu. Fri. = day-of-the-week dummies

Table 5.2.2 Germany

Bmw

$$Rt = \quad -.02R_{t-3} \quad +.03R_{t-9} \quad +.10E\text{-}2Rind_t$$
$$\quad\quad (-1.07) \quad\quad (1.66) \quad\quad (.03)$$

Basf

$$Rt = \quad +.85Rind_t \quad +.05Rind_{t-1} \quad -.39E\text{-}3Fri$$
$$\quad\quad (60.1) \quad\quad (3.65) \quad\quad (-2.22)$$

Siemens

$$Rt = \quad -.11R_{t-1} \quad +.03R_{t-2} \quad +.03R_{t-5} \quad +.92Rind_t \quad +.21Rind_{t-1} \quad -.80E\text{-}3Fri$$
$$\quad\quad (-5.88) \quad\quad (2.94) \quad\quad (3.21) \quad\quad (74.4) \quad\quad (9.4) \quad\quad (-5.2)$$

Hoechst

$$Rt = \quad -.03R_{t-5} \quad -.036R_{t-8} \quad +.83Rind_t \quad +.06Rind_{t-1}$$
$$\quad\quad (-2.5) \quad\quad (-2.6) \quad\quad (54.9) \quad\quad (4.06)$$

Volkswagen

$$Rt = \quad -.04R_{t-1} \quad +.03R_{t-9} \quad +1.15Rind_t \quad -.17Rind_{t-1}$$
$$\quad\quad (-2.04) \quad\quad (2.3) \quad\quad (58.1) \quad\quad (5.79)$$

Mercedes

$$Rt = \quad +.02R_{t-6} \quad +.02R_{t-8} \quad +1.14Rind_t \quad +.09Rind_{t-1} \quad +.39E\text{-}3Mon$$
$$\quad\quad (2.28) \quad\quad (2.16) \quad\quad (74) \quad\quad (6.36) \quad\quad (2.06)$$

Bayer

$$Rt = \quad -.06R_{t-1} \quad -.02R_{t-4} \quad +.02R_{t-5} \quad .87Rind_t \quad .13Rind_{t-1}$$
$$\quad\quad (-3.32) \quad\quad (-2.04) \quad\quad (2.23) \quad\quad (59.9) \quad\quad (5.8)$$

Rt = Log returns of stock prices

Rindt= Log returns of Stock Market Index Index

Mon. Tue. Wed. Thu. Fri. = day-of-the-week dummies

Table 5.2.3 Switzerland

Ciba Geigy

$$R_t = +.07R_{t-1} \quad +.05R_{t-2} \quad +.03R_{t-9} \quad 1.17Rind_t \quad -.18Rind_{t-1}$$

(3.3)   (3.8)   (2.04)   (49)   (-4.99)

Nestle

$$R_t = -.03R_{t-8} \quad 1.00Rind_t$$

(-1.9)   (48.6)

Roche

$$R_t = -.17R_{t-1} \quad -.03R_{t-5} \quad +.03R_{t-7} \quad .98Rind_t \quad +.37Rind_{t-1}$$

(-8.55)   (-2.41)   (2.25)   (39.5)   (11.7)

Rt = Log returns of stock prices

Rindt= Log returns of Stock Market Index Index

Mon. Tue. Wed. Thu. Fri. = day-of-the-week dummies

Table 5.2.4 The Netherlands

Akzo

$R_t=$	$+.06R_{t-1}$	$-.03R_{t-4}$	$+1.42Rind_t$	$-.18Rind_{t-1}$
	(2.84)	(-2.07)	(40.1)	(-3.7)

Unilever

$R_t=$	$+.09R_{t-1}$	$+.95Rind_t$	$-.09Rind_{t-1}$	$+.41E\text{-}3Mon$
	(4.23)	(49.1)	(-3.16)	(2.53)

Getronics

$R_t=$	$-.09R_{t-6}$	$-.05R_{t-8}$	$+.89Rind_t$	$+.24Rind_{t-1}$	$-.99E\text{-}3Mon$
	(-4.68)	(-2.5)	(19.5)	(5.5)	(-2.4)

Rt = Log returns of stock prices

Rus = Log returns of Dow Jones Composite 65 Index

Rindt= Log returns of Stock Market Index

Mon. Tue. Wed. Thu. Fri. = day-of-the-week dummies

Table 5.2.5 United Kingdom

Amstrad

$Rt = .68E\text{-}3$	$.06R_{t-1}$	$+1.23Rind_t$	$-.15Rind_{t-1}$	$-.21E\text{-}2Tue$
(2.31)	(3.1)	(18.46)	(-2.2)	(-3.33)

British Petroleum

$Rt =$	$+.04R_{t-1}$	$+.2R_{t-8}$	$+.93Rind_t$	$-.08Rind_{t-1}$	$-.48E\text{-}3Mon$ $+.62E\text{-}3Thur$
	(2.03)	(1.77)	(40.9)	(-2.8)	(-1.74) (2.03)

Cable

$Rt =$	$+.06R_{t-1}$	$-.04R_{t-5}$	$-.03R_{t-6}$	$+1.37Rind_t$ $-.20Rind_{t-1}$
	(2.8)	(-2.85)	(--2.09)	(37.3) (-4.2)

General Electric

$Rt = .43E\text{-}3$	$-.16R_{t-1}$	$-.04R_{t-2}$	$-.05R_{t-6}$	$+1.16Rind_t$ $-.79E\text{-}3Thru$
(2.83)	(-10.6)	(-2.7)	(-3.6)	(48) (-2.3)

Rt = Log returns of stock prices

Rus = Log returns of Dow Jones Composite 65 Index

Rindt= Log returns of Stock Market Index

Mon. Tue. Wed. Thu. Fri. = day-of-the-week dummies

Table 5.3 Ex post behaviour of conditional volatility

Equity	Sector	Ex-post intercept chang	Ex post shape of N.I.C.	Ex post change in NIC slope
Hoechst	Chemical	****Positive	Inverted Leverage	+
Basf	Chemical	***Positive	Inverted Leverage	none
Bayer	Chemical	***Positive	Inverted Leverage	+
Cable	Telecomm.	***Positive	Leverage	+
Getronics	Electronic	***Positive	Leverage	+
Unilever	Food Prd.	***Positive	Inverted Leverage	+
Nestle'	Food Prd.	**Positive	Leverage.	none
Eurotunnel	Transport	**Positive	Symmetric	+
Michelin	Vehicles	**Positive	Inverted leverage	+
Total	Oil Int.	*Positive	No curve	-
Elf Aquitaine	Oil Int.	*Positive	Inverted leverage	-
Roche	Pharm.	****Negative	Leverage	-
Ciba Geigy	Pharm.	***Negative	No curve	-
Bmw	Vehicles	***Negative	Leverage	-
Daimler Benz	Vehicles	***Negative	Leverage	+
Akzo Nobel	Chemical	***Negative	Leverage	none
Amstrad	Electronic	***Negative	Leverage	none
Siemens	Electronic	**Negative	Leverage	-
General Electric	Electronic	**Negative	Leverage	-
Volkswagen	Vehicles	No effect	Leverage	none
Peugeot	Vehicles	No effect	Symmetric	+
British Petroleum	Oil Int.	No effect	Leverage	+

*	T-stat	1,5 - 2
**	T-stat	2 - 3
***	T-stat	3 - 8
****	T-stat	8 - UP

Table 5.4: Elf Aquitaine-1926 obs. - Sample Period: 04/01/82 - 08/10/90 -Option introd.

date: 8/10/878

D_{IO} = Option contract introduction dummy   Ssw = Sign switching dummy

Pr = Sign persistence variable   Trnd = Linear trend

ARCH (5)

Ht=+.41E-4	+.23E-5D_{IO}	+.20ε^2_{t-1}	+.05ε^2_{t-2}	+.01ε^2_{t-4}	+.11ε^2_{t-5}	-.13E-7Trnd
(21.8)	(1.1)	(7.6)	(3.8)	(1.3)	(7.0)	(-8.7)

GARCH (1.1)

Ht=+.11E-4	+.11E-5D_{IO}	+.71H_{t-1}	+.11ε^2_{t-1}	-.39E-8Trnd	+.78E-6Pr	-.43E-6D_{IO}Pr
(7.1)	(1.5)	(22.6)	(8.0)	(-6.7)	(1.7)	(-.7)

Sign Switching GARCH (1.1)

Ht =+.10E-4	+.99E-6D_{IO}	+.71H_{t-1}	+.11ε^2_{t-1}	-.37E-8Trnd	+.11E-5pr	-.58E-6D_{IO}Pr
(7.4)	(1.3)	(24.8)	(7.7)	(-6.2)	(2.4)	(-.9)
	+.36E-5Ssw					
	(6.7)					

SSC-GARCH (1.1)

Ht =+.49E-4	+.14H_{t-1}	+.16$S^+_{t-1}\varepsilon^2_{t-1}$	+.39$S^-_{t-1}\varepsilon^2_{t-1}$	-.15E-4S^-_{t-1}	-.15E-7Trnd
(12.6)	(2.9)	(3.9)	(6.6)	(-7.1)	(-8.7)
	+.12E-4$D_{IO}S^-_{t-1}$	+.68E-2$D_{IO}S^+_{t-1}\varepsilon^2_{t-1}$	-.27$D_{IO}S^-_{t-1}\varepsilon^2_{t-1}$		
	(4.5)	(.1)	(-3.4)		

GJR

Ht =+.34E-4	+.26H_{t-1}	+.21ε^2_{t-1}	+.57E-2$D_{IO}\varepsilon^2_{t-1}$	-.01$S^-_{t-1}\varepsilon^2_{t-1}$	-.09$D_{IO}S^-_{t-1}\varepsilon^2_{t-1}$	-.98E-8Trnd
(8.9)	(4.0)	(4.9)	(.0)	(-.2)	(-1.0)	(-7.0)

173

VGARCH (1.1)

$Ht = +.31E\text{-}4 \quad +.28H_{t-1} \quad +.80E\text{-}5\varepsilon_{t-1}/h_{t-1} \quad +.43E\text{-}5\varepsilon_{t-1}/\sqrt{h_{t-1}} \quad -.23E\text{-}5D_{IO}\varepsilon_{t-1}/h_{t-1}$

$\quad\quad (7.3) \quad\quad\quad (4.3) \quad\quad\quad\quad (2.3) \quad\quad\quad\quad\quad (.9) \quad\quad\quad\quad\quad (-.6)$

$\quad\quad\quad\quad -.64E\text{-}5D_{IO}\varepsilon_{t-1}/\sqrt{h_{t-1}} \quad -.84E\text{-}8Trnd$

$\quad\quad\quad\quad\quad\quad\quad (-1.1) \quad\quad\quad\quad\quad (-5.3)$

NAGARCH (1.1)

$Ht = +.31E\text{-}4 \quad +.31H_{t-1} \quad +.40\varepsilon^2_{t-1} \quad -26.2\varepsilon_{t-1}/\sqrt{h_{t-1}} \quad -80.7D_{IO}\varepsilon_{t-1}/\sqrt{h_{t-1}} \quad -.88E\text{-}8Trnd$

$\quad (7.0) \quad\quad (4.1) \quad\quad (4.4) \quad\quad (-2.7) \quad\quad\quad (-4.1) \quad\quad\quad\quad (-5.9)$

AGARCH

$Ht = +.30E\text{-}4 \quad +.27H_{t-1} \quad +.12\varepsilon^2_{t-1} \quad +.04D_{IO}\varepsilon^2_{t-1} \quad +.11E\text{-}2\varepsilon_{t-1} \quad -.10E\text{-}2D_{IO}\varepsilon_{t-1} \quad -.81E\text{-}8Trnd$

$\quad (7.4) \quad\quad (4.3) \quad\quad (2.0) \quad\quad (.4) \quad\quad\quad (1.9) \quad\quad\quad (-1.1) \quad\quad\quad (-5.1)$

Residual Statistics

	Best. eq.	Arch(5)	Garch(1,1)	SSwGarch	SSC-Garch	GJR	VGarch	NaGarch	AGarch
R^2	.36	.35	.35	.35	.35	.35	.35	.35	.35
Log Likelihood	8262	8372	8368	8380	8373	8365	8362	8362	8365
Kurtosis	6	6.1	6.1	6.1	6.1	6.1	6.1	6.1	6.1
Skewness	0.48	0.47	0.46	0.46	0.46	0.46	0.46	0.46	0.46
Kurtosis (standardised)		4.3	4.6	4.0	4.0	4.4	4.3	4.4	4.3
Skewness (standardised)		0.48	0.46	0.42	0.38	0.41	0.43	0.42	0.44
Positive sign bias test	-.22	1.7	1.7	.5	-.3	1.6	1.6	2.0	1.6
Negative size bias test	-3.6	-.5	-1.1	-1.1	.4	-.6	-.5	-.8	-.4
Positive size bias test	6.3	-.6	.5	.7	-.0	-.8	-.4	-.6	-.5
Pagan-Sabau intercept		+.20E-4	+.13E-4	+.14E-4	+.31E-4	+.18E-4	+.10E-4	+.20E-4	+.79E-5
(std. error)		+.61E-5	+.70E-5	+.70E-5	+.58E-5	+.64E-5	+.72E-5	+.66E-5	+.72E-5
Pagan-Sabau coefficient		+1.03	+1.20	+1.20	+.78	+1.10	+1.29	+1.04	+1.36
(std error)		+.11	+.14	+.14	+.10	+.12	+.14	+.12	+.14

D_{IO} = Option contract introduction dummy   Ssw = Sign switching dummy

Pr = Sign persistence variable   Trnd = Linear trend

ARCH (5)

$Ht=+.58E-5$	$+.21E-4D_{IO}$	$+.37\varepsilon^2_{t-1}$	$+.09\varepsilon^2_{t-2}$	$+.05\varepsilon^2_{t-3}$	$+.19\varepsilon^2_{t-5}$	$+.80E-7Trnd$
(3.7)	(2.8)	(5.1)	(2.5)	(1.7)	(5.8)	(8.9)

GARCH(1.1) not estimated because of collinearity problems

Sign Switching GARCH (1.1) not estimated because of collinearity problems

SSC-GARCH (1.1)

$Ht=+.20E-4$	$+.42H_{t-1}$	$+.24S^+_{t-1}\varepsilon^2_{t-1}$	$+.06S^-_{t-1}\varepsilon^2_{t-1}$	$-.20E-4S^-_{t-1}$	$+.39E-7Trnd$
(5.7)	(5.5)	(2.2)	(.9)	(-6.2)	(3.6)
	$+.46E-4D_{IO}S^-_{t-1}$	$-.06D_{IO}S^-_{t-1}\varepsilon^2_{t-1}$	$+.22D_{IO}S^-_{t-1}\varepsilon^2_{t-1}$		
	(3.7)	(-.4)	(1.5)		

GJR

$Ht=+.91E-5$	$+.51H_{t-1}$	$+.26\varepsilon^2_{t-1}$	$-.07D_{IO}\varepsilon^2_{t-1}$	$-.28S^-_{t-1}\varepsilon^2_{t-1}$	$+.50D_{IO}S^-_{t-1}\varepsilon^2_{t-1}$	$+.39E-7Trnd$
(3.1)	(4.8)	(2.4)	(-.5)	(-2.0)	(2.3)	(2.7)

VGARCH (1.1)

$Ht=+.87E-5$	$+.74H_{t-1}$	$+.18E-4\varepsilon_{t-1}/h_{t-1}$	$-.31E-4\varepsilon_{t-1}/\sqrt{h_{t-1}}$	$+.11E-4D_{IO}\varepsilon_{t-1}/h_{t-1}$
(2.5)	(7.7)	(3.6)	(-3.8)	(.5)
	$+.28E-4D_{IO}\varepsilon_{t-1}/\sqrt{h_{t-1}}$		$+.24E-7Trnd$	
	(1.1)		(2.0)	

175

NAGARCH (1.1)

$$H_t = +.11E\text{-}4 \quad +.43H_{t\text{-}1} \quad -.17\varepsilon^2_{t\text{-}1} \quad 42.7\varepsilon_{t\text{-}1}/\sqrt{h_{t\text{-}1}} \quad -62.3D_{IO}\varepsilon_{t\text{-}1}/\sqrt{h_{t\text{-}1}} \quad +.54E\text{-}7Trnd$$

| (4.3) | (5.4) | (-.6) | (1.0) | (-1.3) | (4.3) |

AGARCH

$$H_t = +.16E\text{-}4 \quad +.45H_{t\text{-}1} \quad +.35\varepsilon^2_{t\text{-}1} \quad -.25D_{IO}\varepsilon^2_{t\text{-}1} \quad -.27E\text{-}2\varepsilon_{t\text{-}1} \quad +.69E\text{-}2D_{IO}\varepsilon_{t\text{-}1} \quad +.27E\text{-}7Trnd$$

| (4.2) | (4.4) | (2.7) | (-1.3) | (-1.9) | (2.9) | (2.0) |

Residual Statistics

	Best. eq.	Arch(5)	SSC-Garch	GJR	VGarch	NaGarch	AGarch
R^2	.13	.08	.10	.11	.10	.11	.11
Log Likelihood	2341	2425	2454	2436	2432	2426	2431
Kurtosis	3.8	3.5	3.8	3.8	3.8	3.6	3.8
Skewness	0.02	0.03	0.07	0.06	0.08	0.06	0.07
Kurtosis (standardised)		6.3	3.9	4.8	4.7	4.5	4.4
Skewness (standardised)		0.50	0.38	0.50	0.56	0.50	0.51
Positive sign bias test	.5	1.2	.0	1.3	1.6	.9	1.6
Negative size bias test	-7.1	-.0	-.2	-.4	-1.1	-1	-.9
Positive size bias test	4.2	-1.0	-.1	-.7	-.4	.2	-.9
Pagan-Sabau intercept		+.42E-4	+.11E-4	+.32E-4	+.95E-5	+.89E-5	+.14E-4
(std. error)		+.12E-4	+.13E-4	+.12E-4	+.14E-4	+.15E-4	+.14E-4
Pagan-Sabau coefficient		+.59	+.99	+.77	+.99	+1.03	+.97
(std error)		+.07	+.09	+.08	+.10	+.11	+.10

Table 5.6: Michelin-2101 obs.-Sample Period: 04/01/83-22/01/91-Option introd.
date: 22/01/88

D_{IO} = Option contract introduction dummy   Ssw = Sign switching dummy
Pr = Sign persistence variable   Trnd = Linear trend

ARCH (5)

$Ht = +.40E-4$	$+.10E-4D_{IO}$	$+.24\varepsilon^2_{t-1}$	$+.09\varepsilon^2_{t-2}$	$+.10\varepsilon^2_{t-3}$	$-.13E-7Trnd$
(22.8)	(2.9)	(9.9)	(4.5)	(5.2)	(-5.0)

GARCH (1.1)

$Ht = +.26E-4$	$+.67E-5D_{IO}$	$+.40H_{t-1}$	$+.25\varepsilon^2_{t-1}$	$-.82E-8Trnd$	$-.13E-5Pr$	$+.31E-6D_{IO}Pr$
(10.6)	(2.9)	(9.2)	(11.3)	(-5.0)	(-1.8)	(.3)

Sign Switching GARCH (1.1)

$Ht = +.26E-4$	$+.67E-5D_{IO}$	$+.40H_{t-1}$	$+.25\varepsilon^2_{t-1}$	$-.83E-8Trnd$	$-.13E-5Pr$	$++.30E-6_{IO}Pr$
(10.6)	(2.8)	(9.2)	(11.2)	(-4.9)	(-1.8)	(.3)
	$-.77E-7Ssw$					
	(-.1)					

SSC-GARCH (1.1)

$Ht = +.34E-4$	$+.28H_{t-1}$	$+.93E-3S^+_{t-1}\varepsilon^2_{t-1}$	$+.25S^-_{t-1}\varepsilon^2_{t-1}$	$+.11E-5S^-_{t-1}$		$-.10E-7Trnd$
(9.5)	(4.6)	(.0)	(6.2)	(.5)		(-5.6)
/	$+.30E-5D_{IO}S^-_{t-1}$	$+.44D_{IO}S^-_{t-1}\varepsilon^2_{t-1}$	$+.10D_{IO}S^-_{t-1}\varepsilon^2_{t-1}$			
	(.9)	(5.4)	(1.2)			

GJR

$Ht = +.34E-4$	$+.30H_{t-1}$	$-.10E-3\varepsilon^2_{t-1}$	$+.41D_{IO}\varepsilon^2_{t-1}$	$+.25S^-_{t-1}\varepsilon^2_{t-1}$	$-.29D_{IO}S^-_{t-1}\varepsilon^2_{t-1}$	$-.88E-8Trnd$
(9.7)	(4.8)	(-.4)	(5.4)	(6.2)	(-2.7)	(-6.4)

VGARCH (1,1)

$$H_t = +.17E\text{-}4 \quad +.55H_{t-1} \quad +.18E\text{-}5\varepsilon_{t-1}/h_{t-1} \quad +.89E\text{-}5\varepsilon_{t-1}/\sqrt{h_{t-1}} \quad +.10E\text{-}4D_{IO}\varepsilon_{t-1}/h_{t-1}$$

$$(5.3) \qquad (9.9) \qquad (1.0) \qquad (2.2) \qquad (2.4)$$

$$-.69E\text{-}6D_{IO}\varepsilon_{t-1}/\sqrt{h_{t-1}} \qquad -.60E\text{-}8\text{Trnd}$$

$$(-.1) \qquad (-3.5)$$

NAGARCH (1.1)

$$H_t = +.27E\text{-}4 \quad +.41H_{t-1} \quad +.45\varepsilon^2_{t-1} \quad -49.3\varepsilon_{t-1}/\sqrt{h_{t-1}} \quad 67.2D_{IO}\varepsilon_{t-1}/\sqrt{h_{t-1}} \quad -.76E\text{-}8\text{Trnd}$$

$$(6.9) \quad (5.3) \quad (2.3) \quad (-1.6) \quad (2.1) \quad (-5.5)$$

AGARCH

$$H_t = +.23E\text{-}4 \quad +.39H_{t-1} \quad -.02\varepsilon^2_{t-1} \quad +.28D_{IO}\varepsilon^2_{t-1} \quad +.22E\text{-}2\varepsilon_{t-1} \quad -.67E\text{-}3D_{IO}\varepsilon_{t-1} \quad -.62E\text{-}8\text{Trnd}$$

$$(7.1) \quad (6.5) \quad (-.6) \quad (2.9) \quad (4.1) \quad (-.6) \quad (-3.8)$$

Residual Statistics

	Best. eq.	Arch(5)	Garch(1.1)	SSwGarch	SSC-Garc	GJR	VGarch	NaGarch	AGarch
R^2	.45	.45	.45	.45	.45	.45	.45	.45	.45
Log Likelihood	7377	7463	7469	7469	7482	7481	7471	7481	7480
Kurtosis	7.7	7.9	7.9	7.9	7.8	7.8	7.8	7.8	7.8
Skewness	-0.04	-0.06	-0.06	-0.06	-0.04	-0.04	-0.04	-0.05	-0.04
Kurtosis (standardised)		5.1	5.3	5.3	4.8	4.9	5.7	5.6	5.4
Skewness (standardised)		0.19	0.20	0.20	0.28	0.28	0.25	0.34	0.28
Positive sign bias test	1.4	.1	.1	.1	-.1	-.5	-.5	-.4	-.4
Negative size bias test	-8.4	-.6	-.6	-.6	-.3	.1	-1.0	-.3	-.6
Positive size bias test	3.3	-.7	-.7	-.7	.2	.3	.0	-.2	-.3
Pagan-Sabau intercept		+.55E-4	+.56E-4	+.56E-4	+.53E-4	+.54E-4	+.35E-4	+.72E-4	+.42E-4
(std. error)		+.84E-5	+.84E-5	+.84E-5	+.81E-5	+.79E-5	+.11E-4	+.66E-5	+.88E-5
Pagan-Sabau coefficient		+.73	+.71	+.71	+.79	+.76	+1.17	+.41	+1.02
(std error)		+.11	+.11	+.11	+.11	+.10	+.20	+.06	+.13

D_{IO} = Option contract introduction dummy   Ssw = Sign switching dummy

Pr = Sign persistence variable   Trnd = Linear trend

ARCH (5)

$Ht = +.35E{-}4$ $-.66E{-}5D_{IO}$ $+.18\varepsilon^2_{t-1}$ $+.07\varepsilon^2_{t-2}$ $+.03\varepsilon^2_{t-3}$ $+.09\varepsilon^2_{t-4}$ $+.04\varepsilon^2_{t-5}$

(16.1)   (-2.3)   (8.2)   (4.5)   (2.0)   (7.8)   (3.0)

$-.71E{-}8Trnd$

(-3.2)

GARCH (1.1)

$Ht = +.56E{-}5$ $+.29E{-}6D_{IO}$ $+.77H_{t-1}$ $+.12\varepsilon^2_{t-1}$ $-.16E{-}8Trnd$ $+.14E{-}5Pr$ $-.15E{-}5D_{IO}Pr$

(5.9)   (.3)   (32.5)   (8.8)   (-3.0)   (3.4)   (-2.7)

Sign Switching GARCH (1.1)

$Ht = +.59E{-}5$ $+.18E{-}6D_{IO}$ $+.76H_{t-1}$ $+.12\varepsilon^2_{t-1}$ $-.16E{-}8Trnd$ $+.14E{-}5Pr$ $+-.14E{-}5_{IO}Pr$

(6.0)   (.2)   (31.4)   (8.8)   (-3.1)   (3.3)   (-2.3)

$+.28E{-}6Ssw$

(.5)

SSC-GARCH (1.1)

$Ht = +.15E{-}4$ $+.59H_{t-1}$ $+.12S^+_{t-1}\varepsilon^2_{t-1}$ $+.18S^-_{t-1}\varepsilon^2_{t-1}$ $-.15E{-}6S^-_{t-1}$ $-.45E{-}8Trnd$

(3.6)   (9.9)   (3.8)   (3.8)   (-.0)   (-2.4)

$-.27E{-}5D_{IO}S^-_{t-1}$ $+.14D_{IO}S^+_{t-1}\varepsilon^2_{t-1}$ $+.04D_{IO}S^-_{t-1}\varepsilon^2_{t-1}$

(-1.0)   (2.1)   (.6)

GJR

$Ht = +.16E{-}4$ $+.59H_{t-1}$ $+.12\varepsilon^2_{t-1}$ $+.16D_{IO}\varepsilon^2_{t-1}$ $+.06S^-_{t-1}\varepsilon^2_{t-1}$ $-.14D_{IO}S^-_{t-1}\varepsilon^2_{t-1}$ $-.57E{-}8Trnd$

(4.1)   (9.5)   (3.9)   (2.4)   (1.1)   (-1.4)   (-3.6)

VGARCH (1.1)

$$H_t = +.14E\text{-}4 \quad +.66H_{t-1} \quad +.88E\text{-}5\varepsilon_{t-1}/h_{t-1} \quad -.63E\text{-}5\varepsilon_{t-1}/\sqrt{h_{t-1}} \quad +.34E\text{-}5D_{IO}\varepsilon_{t-1}/h_{t-1}$$

$$(3.5) \qquad (10.2) \qquad\qquad (3.6) \qquad\qquad (-1.3) \qquad\qquad (1.0)$$

$$-.64E\text{-}5D_{IO}\varepsilon_{t-1}/\sqrt{h_{t-1}} \qquad -.40E\text{-}8Trnd$$

$$(-1.0) \qquad\qquad\qquad (-2.1)$$

NAGARCH (1.1)

$$H_t = +.87E\text{-}5 \quad +.74H_{t-1} \quad +.44\varepsilon^2_{t-1} \quad -43.3\varepsilon_{t-1}/\sqrt{h_{t-1}} \quad -15.1D_{IO}\varepsilon_{t-1}/\sqrt{h_{t-1}} \quad -.34E\text{-}8Trnd$$

$$(2.3) \qquad (12.3) \qquad (2.7) \qquad (-1.9) \qquad\qquad (-.3) \qquad\qquad (-2.2)$$

AGARCH

$$H_t = +.17E\text{-}4 \quad +.57H_{t-1} \quad +.16\varepsilon^2_{t-1} \quad +.26D_{IO}\varepsilon^2_{t-1} \quad -.24E\text{-}3\varepsilon_{t-1} \quad -.14E\text{-}2\,D_{IO}\varepsilon_{t-1} \quad -.51E\text{-}8\,Trnd$$

$$(4.2) \qquad (8.9) \qquad (3.15) \qquad (2.2) \qquad (-.36) \qquad (-1.4) \qquad (-2.7)$$

Residual Statistics

	Best. eq.	Arch(5)	Garch(1.1)	SSwGarch	SSC-Garch	GJR	VGarch	NaGarch	AGarch
R^2	.49	.49	.49	.49	.49	.49	.49	.49	.49
Log Likelihood	8190	8302	8312	8312	8312	8310	8308	8318	8309
Kurtosis	3.1	3.2	3.2	3.2	3.1	3.1	3.1	3.1	3.1
Skewness	0.53	0.54	0.55	0.55	0.53	0.53	0.53	0.53	0.53
Kurtosis (standardised)		2.3	2.3	2.3	2.5	2.6	2.6	2.3	2.6
Skewness (standardised)		0.34	0.34	0.33	0.37	0.38	0.40	0.39	0.38
Positive sign bias test	.4	.4	.8	.6	-.0	.4	.5	.5	.3
Negative size bias test	-6.0	-.2	-1.2	-1.2	.1	-.0	-.5	-.5	-.2
Positive size bias test	6.1	-.6	.2	.2	-.1	-.3	-.2	-.1	-.4
Pagan-Sabau intercept		+.41E-4	+.38E-4	+.38E-4	+.25E-4	+.28E-4	+.34E-4	+.21E-4	+.27E-4
(std. error)		+.94E-5	+.99E-5	+.98E-5	+.10E-4	+.99E-5	+.10E-4	+.11E-4	+.91E-5
Pagan-Sabau coefficient		+.95	+1.01	+1.01	+1.33	+1.26	+1.13	+1.46	+1.26
(std error)		+.18	+.20	+.19	+.20	+.20	+.21	+.24	+.17

Table 5.8: Total - 2087 obs.-Sample Period: 23/09/85 - 21/09/93 - Option introd. date: 21/10/90

D_{IO} = Option contract introduction dummy   Ssw = Sign switching dummy

Pr = Sign persistence variable   Trnd = Linear trend

ARCH (5)

$Ht=+.43E-4$	$+.64E-5D_{IO}$	$+.11\epsilon^2_{t-1}$	$+.05\epsilon^2_{t-2}$	$+.04\epsilon^2_{t-3}$	$+.46E-2\epsilon^2_{t-4}$	$-.12E-7Trnd$
(15.7)	(2.0)	(5.6)	(3.1)	(2.5)	(.3)	(-4.6)

GARCH (1.1)

$Ht=+.42E-5$	$+.13E-5D_{IO}$	$+.83H_{t-1}$	$+.05\epsilon^2_{t-1}$	$-.12E-8Trnd$	$+.16E-5Pr$	$-.15E-5D_{IO}Pr$
(3.8)	(2.0)	(32.4)	(6.0)	(-2.4)	(3.5)	(-2.9)

Sign Switching GARCH (1.1)

$Ht=+.42E-5$	$+.14E-5D_{IO}$	$+.84H_{t-1}$	$+.05\epsilon^2_{t-1}$	$-.12E-8Trnd$	$+.16E-5Pr$	$-.15E-5D_{IO}Pr$
(3.7)	(2.1)	(32.2)	(5.9)	(-2.4)	(3.6)	(-2.9)
	$+.30E-6Ssw$					
	(.6)					

SSC-GARCH (1.1)

$Ht=+.28E-4$	$+.41H_{t-1}$	$+.13S^+_{t-1}\epsilon^2_{t-1}$	$+.17S^-_{t-1}\epsilon^2_{t-1}$	$-.77E-5S^+_{t-1}$	$-.67E-8Trnd$
(4.8)	(4.2)	(3.4)	(3.9)	(-3.3)	(-2.8)
	$+.10E-4D_{IO}S^-_{t-1}$	$-.08D_{IO}S^+_{t-1}\epsilon^2_{t-1}$	$-.12D_{IO}S^-_{t-1}\epsilon^2_{t-1}$		
	(3.2)	(-1.5)	(-2.3)		

GJR

$Ht=+.18E-4$	$+.48H_{t-1}$	$+.17\epsilon^2_{t-1}$	$-.11D_{IO}\epsilon^2_{t-1}$	$-.03S^-_{t-1}\epsilon^2_{t-1}$	$+.04D_{IO}S^-_{t-1}\epsilon^2_{t-1}$	$-.23E-8Trnd$
(3.4)	(4.7)	(4.1)	(-2.0)	(-.7)	(.6)	(-1.3)

VGARCH (1.1)

$$H_t = +.18E\text{-}4 \quad +.58H_{t-1} \quad +.11E\text{-}4\varepsilon_{t-1}/h_{t-1} \quad -.10E\text{-}4\varepsilon_{t-1}/\sqrt{h_{t-1}} \quad -.89E\text{-}5D_{IO}\varepsilon_{t-1}/h_{t-1}$$

$$(2.9) \qquad (5.5) \qquad (3.4) \qquad\qquad (-1.7) \qquad\qquad (-2.4)$$

$$+.91E\text{-}5D_{IO}\varepsilon_{t-1}/\sqrt{h_{t-1}} \qquad -.37E\text{-}8Trnd$$

$$(1.4) \qquad\qquad (-1.5)$$

NAGARCH (1.1)

$$H_t = +.14E\text{-}4 \quad +.57H_{t-1} \quad +.35\varepsilon^2_{t-1} \quad -29.7\varepsilon_{t-1}/\sqrt{h_{t-1}} \quad -15.7D_{IO}\varepsilon_{t-1}/\sqrt{h_{t-1}} \quad -.17E\text{-}8Trnd$$

$$(2.3) \qquad (4.7) \qquad (1.5) \qquad (-.9) \qquad\qquad (-.1) \qquad\qquad (-.9)$$

AGARCH

$$H_t = +.20E\text{-}4 \quad +.50H_{t-1} \quad +.23\varepsilon^2_{t-1} \quad -.16D_{IO}\varepsilon^2_{t-1} \quad -.10E\text{-}2\varepsilon_{t-1} \quad +.99E\text{-}3D_{IO}\varepsilon_{t-1} \quad -.35E\text{-}8Trnd$$

$$(3.4) \qquad (5.0) \qquad (3.3) \qquad (-1.8) \qquad (-1.2) \qquad (.9) \qquad (-1.5)$$

Residual Statistics

	Best. eq.	Arch(5)	Garch(1.1)	SSwGarch	SSC-Garch	GJR	VGarch	NaGarch	AGarch
R^2	.27	.27	.27	.27	.27	.27	.27	.27	.27
Log Likelihood	7548	7573	7582	7582	7588	7585	7586	7585	7586
Kurtosis	2.7	2.6	2.6	2.6	2.6	2.6	2.6	2.6	2.6
Skewness	0.19	0.18	0.18	0.18	0.18	0.18	0.18	0.18	0.18
Kurtosis (standardised)		2.5	2.3	2.3	2.3	2.4	2.4	2.4	2.4
Skewness (standardised)		0.08	0.15	0.15	0.05	0.05	0.04	0.05	0.05
Positive sign bias test	1.0	.6	.6	.5	.2	.9	.9	1.0	1.0
Negative size bias test	-3.2	.0	-.9	-.9	.1	-.1	-.1	-.0	-.0
Positive size bias test	3.4	-.1	1.4	1.5	-.0	-.3	-.1	-.1	-.3
Pagan-Sabau intercept		-.50E-5	-.94E-5	-.96E-5	+.69E-5	+.76E-5	+.93E-5	-.32E-5	+.15E-4
(std. error)		+.90E-5	+.92E-5	+.92E-5	+.81E-5	+.78E-5	+.78E-5	+.88E-5	+.70E-5
Pagan-Sabau coefficient		+1.50	+1.60	+1.61	+1.21	+1.19	+1.15	+1.46	+.99
(std error)		+.20	+.21	+.21	+.18	+.17	+.17	+.19	+.15

D_{IO} = Option contract introduction dummy   Ssw = Sign switching dummy

Pr = Sign persistence variable   Trnd = Linear trend

ARCH (5)

$Ht = +.13E-4$	$+.74E-5D_{IO}$	$+.26\varepsilon^2_{t-1}$	$+.10\varepsilon^2_{t-2}$	$+.07\varepsilon^2_{t-4}$	$+.01\varepsilon^2_{t-5}$	$-.67E-8Trnd$
(20.3)	(11.1)	(14.9)	(7.5)	(4.5)	(1.1)	(-11.3)

GARCH (1.1)

$Ht = +.78E-5$	$+.42E-5D_{IO}$	$+.42H_{t-1}$	$+.24\varepsilon^2_{t-1}$	$-.38E-8Trnd$	$+.96E-8Pr$	$-.84E-7D_{IO}Pr$
(10.6)	(8.0)	(12.5)	(15.0)	(-8.0)	(.0)	(-.4)

Sign Switching GARCH (1.1)

$Ht = +.78E-5$	$+.43E-5D_{IO}$	$+.42H_{t-1}$	$+.24\varepsilon^2_{t-1}$	$-.38E-8Trnd$	$-.15E-8Pr$	$-.72E-7D_{IO}Pr$
(10.4)	(8.1)	(11.8)	(15.0)	(-8.0)	(-.0)	(-.3)
	$-.37E-7Ssw$					
	(-.1)					

SSC-GARCH (1.1)

$Ht = +.67E-5$	$+.50H_{t-1}$	$+.14S^+_{t-1}\varepsilon^2_{t-1}$	$+.29S^-_{t-1}\varepsilon^2_{t-1}$	$-.18E-5S^-_{t-1}$	$-.17E-8Trnd$
(5.7)	(10.8)	(3.6)	(5.9)	(-2.6)	(-3.7)
	$+.25E-5D_{IO}S^-_{t-1}$	$+.24D_{IO}S^+_{t-1}\varepsilon^2_{t-1}$	$-.28D_{IO}S^-_{t-1}\varepsilon^2_{t-1}$		
	(3.6)	(4.5)	(-4.9)		

GJR

$Ht = +.55E-5$	$+.52H_{t-1}$	$+.16\varepsilon^2_{t-1}$	$+.22D_{I0}\varepsilon^2_{t-1}$	$+.04S^-_{t-1}\varepsilon^2_{t-1}$	$-.39D_{IO}S^-_{t-1}\varepsilon^2_{t-1}$	$-.10E-8Trnd$
(6.0)	(10.8)	(4.1)	(4.0)	(.8)	(-5.7)	(-2.9)

183

VGARCH (1.1)

$$H_t = +.43E\text{-}5 \quad +.63H_{t-1} \quad +.44E\text{-}5\varepsilon_{t-1}/h_{t-1} \quad -.22E\text{-}5\varepsilon_{t-1}/\sqrt{h_{t-1}} \quad -.38E\text{-}5D_{IO}\varepsilon_{t-1}/h_{t-1}$$

$$(3.8) \qquad (14.7) \qquad (4.0) \qquad\qquad (-1.3) \qquad\qquad\qquad (-3.5)$$

$$+.64E\text{-}5D_{IO}\varepsilon_{t-1}/\sqrt{h_{t-1}} \quad -.16E\text{-}8Trnd$$

$$(3.9) \qquad\qquad\qquad (-3.5)$$

NAGARCH (1.1)

$$H_t = +.46E\text{-}5 \quad +.59H_{t-1} \quad +.29\varepsilon^2_{t-1} \quad -26.3\varepsilon_{t-1}/\sqrt{h_{t-1}} \quad -140.0D_{IO}\varepsilon_{t-1}/\sqrt{h_{t-1}} \quad -.10E\text{-}8Trnd$$

$$(5.6) \qquad (13.7) \qquad (2.7) \qquad (-1.0) \qquad\qquad (-5.3) \qquad\qquad\qquad (-2.8)$$

AGARCH

$$H_t = +.34E\text{-}5 \quad +.54H_{t-1} \quad +.12\varepsilon^2_{t-1} \quad -.19D_{IO}\varepsilon^2_{t-1} \quad +.80E\text{-}3\varepsilon_{t-1} \quad +.12E\text{-}2D_{IO}\varepsilon_{t-1} \quad -.79E\text{-}9Trnd$$

$$(3.4) \qquad (12.4) \qquad (2.1) \qquad (-3.4) \qquad (2.4) \qquad (3.7) \qquad\qquad (-1.9)$$

Residual Statistics

	Best. eq.	Arch(5)	Garch(1.1)	SSwGarch	SSC-Garch	GJR	VGarch	NaGarch	AGarch
R^2	.60	.60	.60	.60	.60	.60	.60	.60	.60
Log Likelihood	9756	9860	9863	9863	9862	9859	9855	9846	9860
Kurtosis	7.3	7.3	7.3	7.3	7.3	7.3	7.3	7.3	7.3
Skewness	-0.62	-0.61	-0.61	-0.61	-0.61	-0.61	-0.61	-0.61	-0.61
Kurtosis (standardised)		6.1	6.2	6.2	6.1	6.1	6.4	6.5	6.3
Skewness (standardised)		-0.49	-0.46	-0.46	-0.40	-0.40	-0.50	-0.48	-0.51
Positive sign bias test	-.5	.0	.1	.1	.0	.2	-.6	.3	.1
Negative size bias test	-2.9	.7	.6	.6	-.0	-.1	.3	-.1	.1
Positive size bias test	5.2	-.0	-.0	-.0	-.0	-.1	.4	.6	.5
Pagan-Sabau intercept		+.27E-4	+.26E-4	+.26E-4	+.20E-4	+.18E-4	+.23E-4	+.23E-4	+.12E-4
(std. error)		+.32E-5	+.33E-5	+.33E-5	+.36E-5	+.38E-5	+.38E-5	+.41E-5	+.46E-5
Pagan-Sabau coefficient		+.61	+.65	+.64	+1.06	+1.24	+.87	+.93	.66
(std error)		+.15	+.16	+.16	+.19	+.22	+.21	+.24	+.28

Table 5.10: Bayer- 2348 obs. - Sample Period: 01/01/85 - 31/12/93 - Option introd.

date: 26/1/90

D_{IO} = Option contract introduction dummy   Ssw = Sign switching dummy

Pr = Sign persistence variable   Trnd = Linear trend

ARCH (5)

$H_t = +.13E-4$	$+.29E-5D_{IO}$	$+.31\varepsilon^2_{t-1}$	$+.06\varepsilon^2_{t-3}$	$+.10\varepsilon^2_{t-4}$	$+.05\varepsilon^2_{t-5}$	$-.59E-8Trnd$
(15.8)	(4.5)	(14.2)	(4.3)	(6.0)	(3.5)	(-9.0)

GARCH (1.1)

$H_t = +.55E-5$	$+.22E-5D_{IO}$	$+.56H_{t-1}$	$+.23\varepsilon^2_{t-1}$	$-.28E-8Trnd$	$+.75E-6Pr$	$-.81E-6D_{IO}Pr$
(9.4)	(5.8)	(21.7)	(15.4)	(-8.5)	(5.9)	(-5.4)

Sign Switching GARCH (1.1)

$H_t = +.47E-5$	$+.22E-5D_{IO}$	$+.61H_{t-1}$	$+.21\varepsilon^2_{t-1}$	$-.26E-8Trnd$	$+.63E-6Pr$	$-.61E-6D_{IO}Pr$
(10.1)	(6.3)	(28.9)	(15.8)	(-9.4)	(4.9)	(-4.2)
	$-.73E-6Ssw$					
	(-4.6)					

SSC-GARCH (1.1)

$H_t = +.18E-4$	$+.04H_{t-1}$	$+.28S^+_{t-1}\varepsilon^2_{t-1}$	$+.18S^-_{t-1}\varepsilon^2_{t-1}$	$-.62E-6S^-_{t-1}$	$-.68E-8Trnd$
(14.1)	(1.2)	(6.5)	(4.6)	(-.9)	(-11.7)
	$+.16E-5D_{IO}S^-_{t-1}$	$+.31D_{IO}S^+_{t-1}\varepsilon^2_{t-1}$	$-.57E-2D_{IO}S^-_{t-1}\varepsilon^2_{t-1}$		
	(2.2)	(5.1)	(-.08)		

GJR

$H_t = +.18E-4$	$+.03H_{t-1}$	$+.29\varepsilon^2_{t-1}$	$+.26D_{IO}\varepsilon^2_{t-1}$	$-.12S^-_{t-1}\varepsilon^2_{t-1}$	$-.22D_{IO}S^-_{t-1}\varepsilon^2_{t-1}$	$-.63E-8Trnd$
(17.3)	(1.0)	(7.1)	(4.6)	(-2.3)	(-2.6)	(-13.7)

VGARCH (1.1)

$$H_t = +.17\text{E-}4 \quad +.13H_{t-1} \quad +.60\text{E-}5\varepsilon_{t-1}/h_{t-1} \quad -.40\text{E-}5\varepsilon_{t-1}/\sqrt{h_{t-1}} \quad -.39\text{E-}5D_{IO}\varepsilon_{t-1}/h_{t-1}$$

$$(11.4) \qquad\quad (2.6) \qquad\qquad (4.7) \qquad\qquad\qquad (-2.2) \qquad\qquad\qquad (-2.9)$$

$$+.66\text{E-}5D_{IO}\varepsilon_{t-1}/\sqrt{h_{t-1}} \qquad -.69\text{E-}8\text{Trnd}$$

$$(3.5) \qquad\qquad\qquad\qquad (-10.5)$$

NAGARCH (1.1)

$$H_t = +.11\text{E-}4 \quad +.34H_{t-1} \quad +.44\varepsilon^2_{t-1} \quad -53.8\varepsilon_{t-1}/\sqrt{h_{t-1}} \quad -36.7D_{IO}\varepsilon_{t-1}/\sqrt{h_{t-1}} \quad -.40\text{E-}8\text{Trnd}$$

$$(7.4) \qquad\quad (5.4) \qquad\quad (8.0) \qquad\quad (-6.0) \qquad\qquad\qquad (-1.1) \qquad\qquad\qquad (-6.8)$$

AGARCH

$$H_t = +.16\text{E-}4 \quad +.09H_{t-1} \quad +.25\varepsilon^2_{t-1} \quad -.04D_{IO}\varepsilon^2_{t-1} \quad -.10\text{E-}3\varepsilon_{t-1} \quad +.11\text{E-}2D_{IO}\varepsilon_{t-1} \quad -.63\text{E-}8\text{Trnd}$$

$$(11.7) \qquad\quad (2.1) \qquad\quad (3.8) \qquad\quad (-.5) \qquad\qquad (-.2) \qquad\qquad (2.3) \qquad\qquad (-10.0)$$

Residual Statistics

	Best. eq.	Arch(5)	Garch(1.1)	SSwGarch	SSC-Garch	GJR	VGarch	NaGarch	AGarch
R^2	.61	.61	.61	.61	.61	.61	.61	.61	.61
Log Likelihood	9683	9848	9844	9848	9848	9846	9839	9849	9844
Kurtosis	7.4	7.6	7.7	7.7	7.9	7.9	7.8	7.8	7.8
Skewness	-0.26	-0.25	-0.26	-0.26	-0.27	-0.27	-0.27	-0.26	-0.26
Kurtosis (standardised)		6.3	6.5	6.4	5.5	5.4	5.9	5.9	5.9
Skewness (standardised)		-0.04	-0.04	-0.06	-0.00	-0.01	-0.06	-0.03	-0.06
Positive sign bias test	.17	-.9	-.0	.6	-.1	-.3	-.0	-.1	-.1
Negative size bias test	-5.5	.8	.4	.3	.0	.1	.4	.3	.8
Positive size bias test	6.19	.2	1.0	1.1	-.1	-.9	.7	.8	.6
Pagan-Sabau intercept		+.19E-4	+.16E-4	+.16E-4	+.16E-4	+.16E-4	+.15E-4	+.14E-4	+.16E-4
(std. error)		+.29E-5	+.30E-5	+.31E-5	+.33E-5	+.33E-5	+.32E-5	+.34E-5	+.33E-5
Pagan-Sabau coefficient		+1.21	+1.35	+1.39	+1.46	+1.42	+1.54	+1.61	+1.48
(std error)		+.12	+.13	+.13	+.16	+.16	+.15	+.18	+.16

Table 5.11: Bmw -2348 obs.-Sample Period: 01/01/85- 31/12/93 - Option introd.

date: 26/1/90

D_{IO} = Option contract introduction dummy   Ssw = Sign switching dummy

Pr = Sign persistence variable   Trnd = Linear trend

ARCH (5)

$Ht = +.27E-4$	$-.10E-4D_{IO}$	$+.19\varepsilon^2_{t-1}$	$+.12\varepsilon^2_{t-2}$	$+.12\varepsilon^2_{t-3}$	$+.08\varepsilon^2_{t-4}$	$+.08\varepsilon^2_{t-5}$
(9.2)	(-1.9)	(8.0)	(7.4)	(10.6)	(5.0)	(5.4)
	$+.11E-7Trnd$					
	(2.8)					

GARCH (1.1)

$Ht = +.37E-5$	$-.41E-5D_{IO}$	$+.83H_{t-1}$	$+.11\varepsilon^2_{t-1}$	$+.89E-9Trnd$	$+.14E-6Pr$	$+.36E-5D_{IO}Pr$
(5.4)	(-4.5)	(59.8)	(11.4)	(1.4)	(.8)	(3.7)

Sign Switching GARCH (1.1)

$Ht = +.38E-5$	$-.41E-5D_{IO}$	$+.83H_{t-1}$	$+.11\varepsilon^2_{t-1}$	$+.83E-9Trnd$	$+.10E-6Pr$	$+.37E-5D_{IO}Pr$
(5.4)	(-4.4)	(59.5)	(11.3)	(1.2)	(.6)	(3.7)
	$-.44E-6Ssw$					
	(-.5)					

SSC-GARCH (1.1)

$Ht = +.89E-5$	$+.73H_{t-1}$	$+.08S^+_{t-1}\varepsilon^2_{t-1}$	$+.12S^-_{t-1}\varepsilon^2_{t-1}$	$+.94E-6S^-_{t-1}$	$+.16E-8Trnd$
(2.2)	(15.1)	(1.9)	(2.9)	(.3)	(.5)
	$-.11E-4D_{IO}S^-_{t-1}$	$+.07D_{IO}S^+_{t-1}\varepsilon^2_{t-1}$	$+.19D_{IO}S^-_{t-1}\varepsilon^2_{t-1}$		
	(-2.5)	(.9)	(2.7)		

GJR

$Ht = +.98E-5$	$+.75H_{t-1}$	$+.07\varepsilon^2_{t-1}$	$+.09D_{IO}\varepsilon^2_{t-1}$	$+.05S^-_{t-1}\varepsilon^2_{t-1}$	$+.01D_{IO}S^-_{t-1}\varepsilon^2_{t-1}$	$-.18E-8Trnd$
(2.7)	(16.3)	(1.8)	(1.2)	(1.0)	(.1)	(-.8)

187

VGARCH (1.1)

$$H_t = +.17E-5 \quad +.81H_{t-1} \quad +.33E-5\varepsilon_{t-1}/h_{t-1} \quad +.83E-5\varepsilon_{t-1}/\sqrt{h_{t-1}} \quad +.33E-4D_{IO}\varepsilon_{t-1}/h_{t-1}$$

$$(.3) \qquad (19.5) \qquad (1.1) \qquad (1.3) \qquad (4.0)$$

$$-.32E-4D_{IO}\varepsilon_{t-1}/\sqrt{h_{t-1}} \quad +.86E-9Trnd$$

$$(-2.9) \qquad\qquad (.2)$$

NAGARCH (1.1)

$$H_t = +.88E-5 \quad +.78H_{t-1} \quad +.18\varepsilon^2_{t-1} \quad -8.5\varepsilon_{t-1}/\sqrt{h_{t-1}} \quad -21.8D_{IO}\varepsilon_{t-1}/\sqrt{h_{t-1}} \quad -.31E-8Trnd$$

$$(2.5) \qquad (17.2) \qquad (1.5) \qquad (-.6) \qquad (-1.2) \qquad (-1.2)$$

AGARCH

$$H_t = +.57E-5 \quad +.74H_{t-1} \quad +.05\varepsilon^2_{t-1} \quad +.19D_{IO}\varepsilon^2_{t-1} \quad +.12E-2\varepsilon_{t-1} \quad -.15E-2D_{IO}\varepsilon_{t-1} \quad +.56E-9Trnd$$

$$(1.2) \qquad (15.8) \qquad (1.1) \qquad (2.4) \qquad (1.5) \qquad (-1.3) \qquad (.1)$$

Residual Statistics

	Best. eq	Arch(5)	Garch(1.1)	SSwGarch	SSC-Garch	GJR	VGarch	NaGarch	AGarch
R^2	.17E-	.15E-2	.14E-2	.14E-2	.16E-2	.16E-2	.16E-2	.16E-2	.16E-2
Log Likelihood	7401	7569	7595	7595	7598	7596	7592	7587	7591
Kurtosis	4.7	4.7	4.7	4.7	4.7	4.7	4.7	4.7	4.7
Skewness	0.13	0.12	0.11	0.12	0.13	0.13	0.13	0.13	0.12
Kurtosis (standardised)		3.2	3.8	3.8	3.5	3.7	3.7	3.9	4.1
Skewness (standardised)		0.11	0.10	0.10	0.19	0.14	0.21	0.14	0.16
Positive sign bias test	.8	.6	.3	.5	-.2	.1	.5	.2	.2
Negative size bias test	-7.0	-.3	-.6	-.7	.4	.2	-.2	-.4	-.0
Positive size bias test	5.0	-.8	-.2	-.3	-.1	-.2	-.5	-.3	-.7
Pagan-Sabau intercept		+.25E-4	+.13E-4	+.13E-4	+.27E-4	+.22E-4	+.10E-4	-.45E-5	+.27E-4
(std. error)		+.67E-5	+.71E-5	+.71E-5	+.64E-5	+.65E-5	+.71E-5	+.80E-5	+.64E-5
Pagan-Sabau coefficient		+.68	+.82	+.82	+.65	+.71	+.86	+1.07	+.64
(std error)		+.05	+.06	+.06	+.05	+.05	+.06	+.07	+.05

Table 5.12: Daimler Benz-2348 obs.-Sample Period: 01/01/85-31/12/93-Opt. introd. date: 26/01/90

D_{IO} = Option contract introduction dummy Ssw = Sign switching dummy

Pr = Sign persistence variable $Trnd$ = Linear trend

ARCH (5)

$Ht = +.13E\text{-}4 \quad -.63E\text{-}5D_{IO} \quad +.27\varepsilon^2_{t-1} \quad +.13\varepsilon^2_{t-2} \quad +.05\varepsilon^2_{t-3} \quad +.01\varepsilon^2_{t-4} \quad +.72E\text{-}2\varepsilon^2_{t-5}$

$(15.6) \quad\quad (-6.1) \quad\quad (9.3) \quad\quad (6.4) \quad\quad (3.0) \quad\quad (.9) \quad\quad (.8)$

$-.11E\text{-}8Trnd$

(-1.8)

GARCH (1.1)

$Ht = +.60E\text{-}5 \quad -.25E\text{-}5D_{IO} \quad +.50H_{t-1} \quad +.26\varepsilon^2_{t-1} \quad -.48E\text{-}9Trnd \quad -.59E\text{-}7Pr \quad -.22E\text{-}6D_{IO}Pr$

$(8.1) \quad\quad (-3.9) \quad\quad (13.5) \quad\quad (10.2) \quad\quad (-1.5) \quad\quad (-.2) \quad\quad (-.8)$

Sign Switching GARCH (1.1)

$Ht = +.59E\text{-}5 \quad -.23E\text{-}5D_{IO} \quad +.51H_{t-1} \quad +.25\varepsilon^2_{t-1} \quad -.53E\text{-}9Trnd \quad -.82E\text{-}7Pr \quad +-.21E\text{-}6_{IO}Pr$

$(8.1) \quad\quad (-3.7) \quad\quad (13.7) \quad\quad (10.2) \quad\quad (-1.6) \quad\quad (-.3) \quad\quad (-.7)$

$-.17E\text{-}6Ssw$

$(-.9)$

SSC-GARCH (1.1)

$Ht = +.62E\text{-}5 \quad +.45H_{t-1} \quad +.32S^+_{t-1}\varepsilon^2_{t-1} \quad +.19S^-_{t-1}\varepsilon^2_{t-1} \quad +.16E\text{-}5S^-_{t-1} \quad -.14E\text{-}8Trnd$

$(4.5) \quad\quad (8.8) \quad\quad (6.5) \quad\quad (3.3) \quad\quad (1.6) \quad\quad (-2.3)$

$-.35E\text{-}5D_{IO}S^-_{t-1} \quad -.20D_{IO}S^+_{t-1}\varepsilon^2_{t-1} \quad +.42D_{IO}S^-_{t-1}\varepsilon^2_{t-1}$

$(-3.0) \quad\quad (-2.8) \quad\quad (3.8)$

GJR

$Ht = +.70E\text{-}5 \quad +.48H_{t-1} \quad +.30\varepsilon^2_{t-1} \quad -.15D_{IO}\varepsilon^2_{t-1} \quad -.08S^-_{t-1}\varepsilon^2_{t-1} \quad +.36D_{IO}S^-_{t-1}\varepsilon^2_{t-1} \quad -.22E\text{-}8Trnd$

$(4.8) \quad\quad (8.4) \quad\quad (6.5) \quad\quad (-2.2) \quad\quad (-1.2) \quad\quad (3.4) \quad\quad (-3.9)$

VGARCH (1.1)

$$H_t = +.23E\text{-}5 \quad +.66H_{t-1} \quad +.37E\text{-}5\varepsilon_{t-1}/h_{t-1} \quad +.24E\text{-}5\varepsilon_{t-1}/\sqrt{h_{t-1}} \quad -.14E\text{-}5D_{IO}\varepsilon_{t-1}/h_{t-1}$$

$$(1.6) \qquad (12.4) \qquad (3.0) \qquad (1.1) \qquad (-.9)$$

$$-.18E\text{-}5D_{IO}\varepsilon_{t-1}/\sqrt{h_{t-1}} \quad -.90E\text{-}9Trnd$$

$$(-.7) \qquad (-1.3)$$

NAGARCH (1.1)

$$H_t = +.44E\text{-}5 \quad +.59H_{t-1} \quad +.49\varepsilon^2_{t-1} \quad -47.6\varepsilon_{t-1}/\sqrt{h_{t-1}} \quad -46.9D_{IO}\varepsilon_{t-1}/\sqrt{h_{t-1}} \quad -.14E\text{-}8Trnd$$

$$(3.0) \qquad (9.8) \qquad (4.0) \qquad (-1.9) \qquad (-1.3) \qquad (-2.6)$$

AGARCH

$$H_t = +.31E\text{-}5 \quad +.55H_{t-1} \quad +.08\varepsilon^2_{t-1} \quad +.72E\text{-}2D_{IO}\varepsilon^2_{t-1} \quad +.16E\text{-}2\varepsilon_{t-1} \quad -.56E\text{-}3D_{IO}\varepsilon_{t-1} \quad -.10E\text{-}8Trnd$$

$$(2.3) \qquad (10.9) \qquad (1.4) \qquad (.0) \qquad (3.5) \qquad (-.9) \qquad (-1.7)$$

Residual Statistics

	Best. eq.	Arch(5)	Garch(1.1)	SSwGarch	SSC-Garch	GJR	VGarch	NaGarch	AGarch
R^2	.70	.70	.70	.70	.70	.70	.70	.70	.70
Log Likelihood	9542	9756	9770	9770	9758	9758	9775	9769	9774
Kurtosis	3.82	4.1	4.1	4.1	4.0	4.0	4.1	4.1	4.1
Skewness	0.42	0.40	0.40	0.41	0.41	0.41	0.41	0.41	0.41
Kurtosis (standardised)		2.7	2.5	2.5	2.7	2.6	2.6	2.8	2.6
Skewness (standardised)		0.29	0.27	0.28	0.35	0.32	0.31	0.29	0.26
Positive sign bias test	1.5	.9	.9	1.2	.9	1.0	1.0	.8	1.1
Negative size bias test	-8.0	-.1	-.2	-.3	.1	-.0	-.5	-.3	-.2
Positive size bias test	6.8	-.9	-.8	-.9	-.8	-.8	-.6	-.8	-.7
Pagan-Sabau intercept		+.18E-4	+.17E-4	+.17E-4	+.24E-4	+.22E-4	+.16E-4	+.20E-4	+.80E-5
(std. error)		+.55E-5	+.55E-5	+.55E-5	+.54E-5	+.54E-5	+.64E-5	+.59E-5	+.62E-5
Pagan-Sabau coefficient		+2.22	+2.28	+2.30	+1.85	+2.03	+2.45	+2.18	+1.94
(std error)		+.23	+.23	+.23	+.22	+.22	+.30	+.27	+.29

Table 5.13: Hoechst - 2348 obs. - Sample Period: 01/01/85 - 31/12/93 - Opt. introd.
date: 26/01/90

D_{IO} = Option contract introduction dummy   Ssw = Sign switching dummy

Pr = Sign persistence variable   Trnd = Linear trend

ARCH (5)

$Ht = +.20E\text{-}4 \quad +.12E\text{-}4D_{IO} \quad +.15\varepsilon^2_{t-1} \quad +.03\varepsilon^2_{t-2} \quad +.09\varepsilon^2_{t-3} \quad -.11E\text{-}7Trnd$

$(31.2) \qquad (19.9) \qquad (10.0) \qquad (2.7) \qquad (7.1) \qquad (-19.4)$

GARCH (1.1)

$Ht = +.11E\text{-}4 \quad +.79E\text{-}5D_{IO} \quad +.42H_{t-1} \quad +.15\varepsilon^2_{t-1} \quad -.64E\text{-}8Trnd \quad +.89E\text{-}6Pr \quad -.82E\text{-}6D_{IO}Pr$

$(8.6) \qquad (7.8) \qquad (7.9) \qquad (9.1) \qquad (-7.9) \qquad (4.3) \qquad (-3.2)$

Sign Switching GARCH (1.1)

$Ht = +.10E\text{-}4 \quad +.74E\text{-}5D_{IO} \quad +.45H_{t-1} \quad +.15\varepsilon^2_{t-1} \quad -.60E\text{-}8Trnd \quad +.88E\text{-}6Pr \quad -.86E\text{-}6D_{IO}Pr$

$(8.5) \qquad (7.8) \qquad (9.1) \qquad (9.1) \qquad (-7.9) \qquad (4.4) \qquad (-3.5)$

$-.48E\text{-}6Ssw$

(-2.6)

SSC-GARCH (1.1)

$Ht = +.70E\text{-}5 \quad +.59H_{t-1} \quad +.22S^+_{t-1}\varepsilon^2_{t-1} \quad -.43E\text{-}2S^-_{t-1}\varepsilon^2_{t-1} \quad -.61E\text{-}6S^-_{t-1} \quad -.25E\text{-}8Trnd$

$(3.9) \qquad (9.7) \qquad (6.3) \qquad (-.4) \qquad (-.8) \qquad (-3.8)$

$+.38E\text{-}5D_{IO}S^-_{t-1} \quad -.02D_{IO}S^+_{t-1}\varepsilon^2_{t-1} \quad +.11D_{IO}S^-_{t-1}\varepsilon^2_{t-1}$

$(4.5) \qquad (-.3) \qquad (2.9)$

GJR

$Ht = +.75E\text{-}5 \quad +.55H_{t-1} \quad +.20\varepsilon^2_{t-1} \quad -.01D_{IO}\varepsilon^2_{t-1} \quad -.20S^-_{t-1}\varepsilon^2_{t-1} \quad +.20D_{IO}S^-_{t-1}\varepsilon^2_{t-1} \quad -.18E\text{-}8Trnd$

$(5.2) \qquad (8.2) \qquad (6.2) \qquad (-.2) \qquad (-6.1) \qquad (2.9) \qquad (-3.9)$

VGARCH (1.1)

$$H_t = +.20E\text{-}4 \quad +.28H_{t-1} \quad +.11E\text{-}4\varepsilon_{t-1}/h_{t-1} \quad -.19E\text{-}4\varepsilon_{t-1}/\sqrt{h_{t-1}} \quad -.73E\text{-}5D_{IO}\varepsilon_{t-1}/h_{t-1}$$

$$(13.1) \qquad (5.3) \qquad\qquad (7.4) \qquad\qquad (-9.2) \qquad\qquad (-3.9)$$

$$+.16E\text{-}4D_{IO}\varepsilon_{t-1}/\sqrt{h_{t-1}} \qquad -.60E\text{-}8Trnd$$

$$(6.0) \qquad\qquad\qquad (-9.3)$$

NAGARCH (1,1)

$$H_t = +.44E\text{-}5 \quad +.72H_{t-1} \quad +.39\varepsilon^2_{t-1} \quad -74.2\varepsilon_{t-1}/\sqrt{h_{t-1}} \quad -2.1D_{IO}\varepsilon_{t-1}/\sqrt{h_{t-1}} \quad -.13E\text{-}8Trnd$$

$$(2.9) \qquad (10.1) \qquad (3.7) \qquad (-2.9) \qquad\qquad (-.0) \qquad\qquad (-2.9)$$

AGARCH

$$H_t = +.18E\text{-}4 \quad +.28H_{t-1} \quad +.50\varepsilon^2_{t-1} \quad -.25D_{IO}\varepsilon^2_{t-1} \quad -.34E\text{-}2\varepsilon_{t-1} \quad +.29E\text{-}2D_{IO}\varepsilon_{t-1} \quad -.51E\text{-}8Trnd$$

$$(11.7) \qquad (4.9) \qquad (6.8) \qquad (-2.4) \qquad (-7.8) \qquad (4.6) \qquad (-8.4)$$

Residual Statistics

	Best. eq.	Arch(5)	Garch(1.1)	SSwGarch	SSC-Garch	GJR	VGarch	NaGarch	AGarch
R^2	.56	.56	.56	.56	.56	.56	.56	.56	.56
Log Likelihood	9550	9619	9627	9628	9642	9619	9624	9611	9611
Kurtosis	7.2	7.2	7.1	7.1	7.1	7.1	7.1	7.1	7.1
Skewness	-0.42	-0.42	-0.42	-0.42	-0.41	-0.42	-0.42	-0.42	-0.41
Kurtosis (standardised)		7.2	7.1	6.9	6.9	8.6	7.0	8.3	7.4
Skewness (standardised)		-0.46	-0.48	-0.46	-0.42	-0.57	-0.40	-0.54	-0.46
Positive sign bias test	-.49	-.7	-.8	-.2	-.9	-.5	-.6	-.7	-.6
Negative size bias test	-1.3	1.7	1.6	1.5	.6	.9	1.4	1.4	1.4
Positive size bias test	3.8	.4	.6	.5	-.4	-.1	.2	.6	.3
Pagan-Sabau intercept		+.19E-4	+.19E-4	+.19E-4	+.14E-4	+.17E-4	+.30E-4	+.22E-4	+.28E-4
(std. error)		+.41E-5	+.43E-5	+.42E-5	+.43E-5	+.43E-5	+.30E-5	+.47E-5	+.32E-5
Pagan-Sabau coefficient		+1.10	+1.11	+1.08	+1.44	+1.24	+.42	+.94	+.54
(std error)		+.20	+.21	+.21	+.21	+.21	+.11	+.24	+.13

Table 5.14: Siemens - 2348 obs. - Sample Period: 01/01/85 - 31/12/93 - Option introd.

date: 26/1/90

D_{IO} = Option contract introduction dummy   Ssw = Sign switching dummy

Pr = Sign persistence variable   Trnd = Linear trend

ARCH (5)

$H_t = +.80E\text{-}5$ $-.33E\text{-}5D_{IO}$ $+.18\varepsilon^2_{t-1}$ $+.10\varepsilon^2_{t-2}$ $+.23\varepsilon^2_{t-3}$ $+.10\varepsilon^2_{t-4}$ $+.90E\text{-}2\varepsilon^2_{t-5}$

(15.8)   (-6.3)   (8.0)   (5.0)   (9.3)   (8.1)   (.7)

$-.14E\text{-}8Trnd$

(-4.7)

GARCH (1.1)

$H_t = +.18E\text{-}5$ $-.39E\text{-}6D_{IO}$ $+.71H_{t-1}$ $+.17\varepsilon^2_{t-1}$ $-.48E\text{-}9Trnd$ $+.36E\text{-}6Pr$ $-.37E\text{-}6D_{IO}Pr$

(6.8)   (-2.2)   (31.8)   (11.8)   (-5.1)   (2.7)   (-2.7)

Sign Switching GARCH (1.1)

$H_t = +.17E\text{-}5$ $-.33E\text{-}6D_{IO}$ $+.73H_{t-1}$ $+.16\varepsilon^2_{t-1}$ $-.46E\text{-}9Trnd$ $+.35E\text{-}6Pr$ $-.37E\text{-}6D_{IO}Pr$

(6.7)   (-1.9)   (34.5)   (11.7)   (-5.1)   (2.7)   (-2.8)

$-.78E\text{-}7Ssw$

(-1.4)

SSC-GARCH (1.1)

$H_t = +.21E\text{-}5$ $+.69H_{t-1}$ $+.18S^+_{t-1}\varepsilon^2_{t-1}$ $+.29S^-_{t-1}\varepsilon^2_{t-1}$ $-.32E\text{-}6S^-_{t-1}$ $-.69E\text{-}9Trnd$

(2.6)   (13.1)   (3.8)   (9.3)   (-.6)   (-2.1)

$+.55E\text{-}7D_{IO}S^-_{t-1}$ $-.10D_{IO}S^+_{t-1}\varepsilon^2_{t-1}$ $-.13D_{IO}S^-_{t-1}\varepsilon^2_{t-1}$

(.1)   (-1.6)   (-2.4)

GJR

$H_t = +.20E\text{-}5$ $+.69H_{t-1}$ $+.19\varepsilon^2_{t-1}$ $-.10D_{IO}\varepsilon^2_{t-1}$ $+.08S^-_{t-1}\varepsilon^2_{t-1}$ $-.04D_{IO}S^-_{t-1}\varepsilon^2_{t-1}$ $-.69E\text{-}9Trnd$

(2.8)   (13.8)   (4.1)   (-1.6)   (1.6)   (-.5)   (-2.2)

193

VGARCH (1.1)

$$H_t = +.69E\text{-}6 \quad +.85H_{t-1} \quad +.23E\text{-}5\varepsilon_{t-1}/h_{t-1} \quad -.43E\text{-}6\varepsilon_{t-1}/\sqrt{h_{t-1}} \quad -.22E\text{-}5D_{IO}\varepsilon_{t-1}/h_{t-1}$$

$$\quad (1.0) \qquad (16.2) \qquad\qquad (2.7) \qquad\qquad\qquad (-.2) \qquad\qquad\qquad (-2.4)$$

$$+.10E\text{-}5D_{IO}\varepsilon_{t-1}/\sqrt{h_{t-1}} \qquad -.36E\text{-}9Trnd$$

$$\qquad\qquad (.6) \qquad\qquad\qquad\qquad (-1.2)$$

NAGARCH (1.1)

$$H_t = +.11E\text{-}5 \quad +.76H_{t-1} \quad +.35\varepsilon^2_{t-1} \quad -32.9\varepsilon_{t-1}/\sqrt{h_{t-1}} \quad 16.3D_{IO}\varepsilon_{t-1}/\sqrt{h_{t-1}} \quad -.38E\text{-}9Trnd$$

$$\quad (1.5) \qquad (14.1) \qquad (4.6) \qquad (-1.6) \qquad\qquad (.2) \qquad\qquad (-1.2)$$

AGARCH

$$H_t = +.11E\text{-}5 \quad +.71H_{t-1} \quad +.08\varepsilon^2_{t-1} \quad +.01D_{IO}\varepsilon^2_{t-1} \quad +.85E\text{-}3\varepsilon_{t-1} \quad -.69E\text{-}3D_{IO}\varepsilon_{t-1} \quad -.35E\text{-}9Trnd$$

$$\quad (1.8) \qquad (12.8) \qquad (1.3) \qquad (.1) \qquad (2.2) \qquad (-1.5) \qquad (-1.1)$$

Residual Statistics

	Best. eq.	Arch(5)	Garch(1.1)	SSwGarch	SSC-Garch	GJR	VGarch	NaGarch	AGarch
R^2	.70	.70	.70	.70	.70	.70	.70	.70	.70
Log Likelihood	10050	10437	10436	10437	10442	10443	10443	10439	10449
Kurtosis	8.1	8.4	8.5	8.5	8.5	8.5	8.5	8.5	8.5
Skewness	-0.26	-0.28	-0.27	-0.27	-0.28	-0.28	-0.28	-0.28	-0.28
Kurtosis (standardised)		4.1	4.9	4.9	4.3	4.3	4.4	4.7	4.7
Skewness (standardised)		-0.15	-0.18	-0.18	-0.11	-0.13	-0.24	-0.13	-0.20
Positive sign bias test	-.1	.1	.2	.4	.2	.6	.4	.2	.4
Negative size bias test	-5.7	.1	-.1	-.3	.6	.4	-.6	.0	-.0
Positive size bias test	6.1	-.1	-.0	-.0	-.1	-.3	.4	-.2	-.1
Pagan-Sabau intercept		+.21E-4	+.16E-4	+.16E-4	+.21E-4	+.21E-4	+.19E-4	+.20E-4	+.13E-4
(std. error)		+.29E-5	+.31E-5	+.31E-5	+.28E-5	+.28E-5	+.33E-5	+.30E-5	+.33E-5
Pagan-Sabau coefficient		+1.43	+1.85	+1.88	+1.35	+1.34	+1.65	+1.47	+1.14
(std error)		+.15	+.18	+.18	+.13	+.13	+.21	+.17	+.20

194

Table 5.15: Volkswagen - 2348 obs.-Sample Period: 01/01/85-31/12/93 - Opt. introd.

date: 26/1/90

D_{IO} = Option contract introduction dummy   Ssw = Sign switching dummy

Pr = Sign persistence variable   Trnd = Linear trend

ARCH (5)

$Ht = +.22E-4$	$-.51E-5D_{IO}$	$+.18\varepsilon^2_{t-1}$	$+.03\varepsilon^2_{t-2}$	$+.02\varepsilon^2_{t-3}$	$+.06\varepsilon^2_{t-4}$	$+.15\varepsilon^2_{t-5}$
(21.4)	(-2.6)	(8.5)	(2.0)	(2.1)	(4.2)	(7.9)
	$-.38E-8Trnd$					
	(-3.2)					

GARCH (1.1)

$Ht = +.11E-5$	$-.42E-7D_{IO}$	$+.93H_{t-1}$	$+.04\varepsilon^2_{t-1}$	$-.35E-9Trnd$	$-.19E-6Pr$	$+.11E-6D_{IO}Pr$
(5.6)	(-.2)	(125.4)	(9.2)	(-3.8)	(-1.8)	(.8)

Sign Switching GARCH (1.1)

$Ht = +.11E-5$	$-.57E-7D_{IO}$	$+.93H_{t-1}$	$+.04\varepsilon^2_{t-1}$	$-.33E-9Trnd$	$-.19E-6Pr$	$++.12E-6_{IO}Pr$
(5.6)	(-.3)	(128.3)	(9.1)	(-3.7)	(-1.9)	(.9)
	$-.10E-6Ssw$					
	(-1.0)					

SSC-GARCH (1.1)

$Ht = +.43E-5$	$+.75H_{t-1}$	$+.12S^+_{t-1}\varepsilon^2_{t-1}$	$+.17S^-_{t-1}\varepsilon^2_{t-1}$	$+.73E-7S^-_{t-1}$	$-.10E-8Trnd$
(2.0)	(12.0)	(3.2)	(3.8)	(.0)	(-1.1)
	$-.24E-6D_{IO}S^-_{t-1}$	$+.40E-2D_{IO}S^+_{t-1}\varepsilon^2_{t-1}$	$-.07D_{IO}S^-_{t-1}\varepsilon^2_{t-1}$		
	(-.1)	(.0)	(-1.1)		

GJR

$Ht = +.41E-5$	$+.77H_{t-1}$	$+.10\varepsilon^2_{t-1}$	$+.01D_{IO}\varepsilon^2_{t-1}$	$+.07S^-_{t-1}\varepsilon^2_{t-1}$	$-.09D_{IO}S^-_{t-1}\varepsilon^2_{t-1}$	$-.10E-8Trnd$
(2.1)	(13.4)	(3.1)	(.2)	(1.2)	(-1.2)	(-1.4)

VGARCH (1.1)

$$H_t = +.84E\text{-}6 \quad +.83H_{t-1} \quad +.22E\text{-}5\varepsilon_{t-1}/h_{t-1} \quad +.48E\text{-}5\varepsilon_{t-1}/\sqrt{h_{t-1}} \quad -.41E\text{-}5D_{IO}\varepsilon_{t-1}/h_{t-1}$$

(.5) (21.1) (1.0) (1.3) (-1.9)

$$+.45E\text{-}5D_{IO}\varepsilon_{t-1}/\sqrt{h_{t-1}} \quad -.14E\text{-}8Trnd$$

(1.2) (-1.8)

NAGARCH (1.1)

$$H_t = +.57E\text{-}5 \quad +.71H_{t-1} \quad +.09\varepsilon^2_{t-1} \quad 9.0\varepsilon_{t-1}/\sqrt{h_{t-1}} \quad -2.3D_{IO}\varepsilon_{t-1}/\sqrt{h_{t-1}} \quad -.14E\text{-}8Trnd$$

(2.1) (9.1) (.9) (.5) (-.0) (-1.7)

AGARCH

$$H_t= +.32E\text{-}5 \quad +.74H_{t-1} \quad +.06\varepsilon^2_{t-1} \quad -.19D_{IO}\varepsilon^2_{t-1} \quad +.11E\text{-}2\varepsilon_{t-1} \quad +.13E\text{-}2D_{IO}\varepsilon_{t-1} \quad -.19E\text{-}8Trnd$$

(1.9) (19.8) (1.1) (-2.7) (2.0) (2.2) (-2.5)

Residual Statistics

	Best. eq.	Arch(5)	Garch(1.1)	SSwGarch	SSC-Garch	GJR	VGarch	NaGarch	AGarch
R^2	.59	.58	.59	.59	.59	.59	.59	.59	.59
Log Likelihood	8934	9065	9112	9112	9085	9089	9093	9080	9106
Kurtosis	5.5	5.8	5.8	5.8	5.7	5.7	5.7	5.8	5.8
Skewness	0.16	0.09	0.10	0.10	0.11	0.11	0.11	0.11	0.11
Kurtosis (standardised)		3.3	3.1	3.2	3.2	3.2	3.0	3.2	2.9
Skewness (standardised)		0.09	-0.08	-0.09	-0.04	-0.04	0.00	-0.04	0.00
Positive sign bias test	-.55	-.9	-.4	-.3	-.5	-.4	.0	-.2	.0
Negative size bias test	-3.5	.6	-1.2	-1.2	.3	.4	-.4	.1	.0
Positive size bias test	5.1	.4	1.5	1.5	.4	.4	.6	.0	-.0
Pagan-Sabau intercept		+.25E-4	+.21E-4	+.21E-4	+.24E-4	+.24E-4	+.17E-4	+.28E-4	+.13E-4
(std. error)		+.71E-5	+.76E-5	+.77E-5	+.70E-5	+.70E-5	+.93E-5	+.64E-5	+.79E-5
Pagan-Sabau coefficient		+1.50	+1.69	+1.71	+1.55	+1.54	+1.89	+1.40	+1.96
(std error)		+.18	+.21	+.21	+.18	+.17	+.28	+.15	+.22

Table 5.16:Ciba Geigy-1926 obs.- Sample Period: 01/01/87 - 31/12/93 - Opt.

introd.

date: 20/02/92

D_{IO} = Option contract introduction dummy   Ssw = Sign switching dummy

Pr = Sign persistence variable   Trnd = Linear trend

ARCH (5)

$Ht = +.18E\text{-}4 \quad -.98E\text{-}5D_{IO} \quad +.13\varepsilon^2_{t-1} \quad +.06\varepsilon^2_{t-2} \quad +.03\varepsilon^2_{t-3} \quad +.22E\text{-}2\varepsilon^2_{t-4} \quad -.62E\text{-}9Trnd$

(15.8)   (-6.7)   (6.1)   (2.9)   (1.8)   (.1)   (-.4)

GARCH (1.1)

$Ht = +.31E\text{-}5 \quad -.21E\text{-}5D_{IO} \quad +.78H_{t-1} \quad +.08\varepsilon^2_{t-1} \quad +.12E10Trnd \quad -.16E\text{-}6Pr \quad +.40E\text{-}6D_{IO}Pr$

(5.9)   (-4.4)   (28.4)   (7.6)   (.0)   (-1.0)   (1.4)

Sign Switching GARCH (1.1)

$Ht = +.37E\text{-}5 \quad -.24E\text{-}5D_{IO} \quad +.74H_{t-1} \quad +.10\varepsilon^2_{t-1} \quad -.86E10Trnd \quad -.23E\text{-}6Pr \quad +.79E\text{-}6_{IO}Pr$

(6.3)   (-4.9)   (26.5)   (7.5)   (-.2)   (-1.5)   (2.8)

$+.15E\text{-}5Ssw$

(5.8)

SSC-GARCH (1.1)

$Ht = +.10E\text{-}4 \quad +.55H_{t-1} \quad +.14S^+_{t-1}\varepsilon^2_{t-1} \quad +.22S^-_{t-1}\varepsilon^2_{t-1} \quad -.44E\text{-}5S^-_{t-1} \quad -.22E\text{-}8Trnd$

(4.5)   (6.4)   (4.4)   (5.1)   (-4.8)   (-1.8)

$+.90E\text{-}6D_{IO}S^-_{t-1} \quad -.21D_{IO}S^+_{t-1}\varepsilon^2_{t-1} \quad -.17D_{IO}S^-_{t-1}\varepsilon^2_{t-1}$

(.5)   (-3.7)   (-1.7)

GJR

$Ht = +.12E\text{-}4 \quad +.37H_{t-1} \quad +.17\varepsilon^2_{t-1} \quad -.20D_{IO}\varepsilon^2_{t-1} \quad +.01S^-_{t-1}\varepsilon^2_{t-1} \quad -.02D_{IO}S^-_{t-1}\varepsilon^2_{t-1} \quad -.38E\text{-}8Trnd$

(4.7)   (3.7)   (4.8)   (-2.9)   (.2)   (-.2)   (-3.1)

VGARCH (1.1)

$$H_t = +.98E\text{-}5 \quad +.54H_{t-1} \quad +.49E\text{-}5\varepsilon_{t-1}/h_{t-1} \quad -.33E\text{-}5\varepsilon_{t-1}/\sqrt{h_{t-1}} \quad -.50E\text{-}5D_{IO}\varepsilon_{t-1}/h_{t-1}$$

$$\quad (3.3) \quad\quad (5.2) \quad\quad\quad (3.7) \quad\quad\quad\quad (-1.5) \quad\quad\quad\quad (-2.9)$$

$$+.31E\text{-}5D_{IO}\varepsilon_{t-1}/\sqrt{h_{t-1}} \quad\quad -.30E\text{-}8Trnd$$

$$\quad\quad (1.0) \quad\quad\quad\quad (-2.1)$$

NAGARCH (1.1)

$$H_t = +.52E\text{-}5 \quad +.66H_{t-1} \quad +.34\varepsilon^2_{t-1} \quad -37.0\varepsilon_{t-1}/\sqrt{h_{t-1}} \quad -184.1D_{IO}\varepsilon_{t-1}/\sqrt{h_{t-1}} \quad -.12E\text{-}8Trnd$$

$$\quad (2.2) \quad\quad (7.3) \quad\quad (2.7) \quad\quad (-1.4) \quad\quad\quad (-.2) \quad\quad\quad (-1.1)$$

AGARCH

$$H_t = +.14E\text{-}4 \quad +.35H_{t-1} \quad +.23\varepsilon^2_{t-1} \quad -.18D_{IO}\varepsilon^2_{t-1} \quad -.64E\text{-}3\varepsilon_{t-1} \quad +.59E\text{-}5D_{IO}\varepsilon_{t-1} \quad -.41E\text{-}8Trnd$$

$$\quad (4.6) \quad\quad (3.2) \quad\quad (4.1) \quad\quad (-1.3) \quad\quad (-1.4) \quad\quad (.6) \quad\quad (-2.7)$$

Residual Statistics

	Best. eq.	Arch(5)	Garch(1.1)	SSwGarch	SSC-Garch	GJR	VGarch	NaGarch	AGarch
R^2	.57	.57	.57	.57	.57	.57	.57	.57	.57
Log Likelihood	7268	7354	7368	7379	7373	7358	7360	7367	7358
Kurtosis	4.6	5.0	4.9	5.0	5.1	5.1	5.1	5.0	5.2
Skewness	0.38	0.40	0.42	0.41	0.39	0.38	0.37	0.38	0.38
Kurtosis (standardised)		3.1	3.2	3.0	3.2	3.4	3.3	3.4	3.3
Skewness (standardised)		0.40	0.45	0.38	0.37	0.44	0.46	0.49	0.43
Positive sign bias test	2	2.0	2.0	.7	.1	2.1	2.4	2.4	2.2
Negative size bias test	-5.6	-.9	-1.6	-1.3	.0	-.8	-1.1	-1.1	-.9
Positive size bias test	4.8	-.8	-.0	-.0	-.3	-.9	-1.1	-1.1	-.9
Pagan-Sabau intercept		-.17E-4	-.14E-4	-.11E-4	-.26E-6	-.82E-5	-.37E-6	-.98E-5	-.32E-5
(std. error)		+.66E-5	+.64E-5	+.62E-5	+.55E-5	+.59E-5	+.60E-5	+.63E-5	+.56E-5
Pagan-Sabau coefficient		+1.24	+1.09	+1.93	+1.32	+1.75	+1.36	+1.84	+1.49
(std error)		+.29	+.28	+.26	+.22	+.25	+.25	+.27	+.23

Table 5.17: Nestle- 1565 obs. - Sample Period: 01/01/88 - 31/12/93 - Option introd.

date: 8/6/93

D_{IO} = Option contract introduction dummy   Ssw = Sign switching dummy

Pr = Sign persistence variable   Trnd = Linear trend

ARCH (5)

$Ht = +.55E-5$	$+.29E-5D_{IO}$	$+.31\varepsilon^2_{t-1}$	$+.05\varepsilon^2_{t-2}$	$+.11\varepsilon^2_{t-4}$	$+.06\varepsilon^2_{t-5}$	$-.17E-8Trnd$
(16.6)	(3.4)	(11.7)	(2.7)	(4.8)	(2.5)	(-5.0)

GARCH (1.1)

$Ht = +.18E-5$	$+.13E-5D_{IO}$	$+.64H_{t-1}$	$+.19\varepsilon^2_{t-1}$	$-.58E-9Trnd$	$-.47E-7Pr$	$-.26E-6D_{IO}Pr$
(8.3)	(2.1)	(20.9)	(10.2)	(-4.2)	(-.7)	(-.9)

Sign Switching GARCH (1.1)

$Ht = +.19E-5$	$+.13E-5D_{IO}$	$+.64H_{t-1}$	$+.19\varepsilon^2_{t-1}$	$-.58E-9Trnd$	$-.47E-7Pr$	$+-.24E-6_{IO}Pr$
(8.3)	(2.0)	(20.8)	(10.2)	(-4.1)	(-.7)	(-.8)
	$-.47E-8Ssw$					
	(-.0)					

SSC-GARCH (1.1)

$Ht = +.46E-5$	$+.33H_{t-1}$	$+.19S^+_{t-1}\varepsilon^2_{t-1}$	$+.39S^-_{t-1}\varepsilon^2_{t-1}$	$-.14E-5S^-_{t-1}$	$-.81E-9Trnd$
(5.8)	(4.8)	(5.1)	(8.3)	(-3.3)	(-2.1)
	$+.19E-5D_{IO}S^-_{t-1}$	$-.11D_{IO}S^+_{t-1}\varepsilon^2_{t-1}$	$+.19E-2D_{IO}S^-_{t-1}\varepsilon^2_{t-1}$		
	(1.7)	(-.9)	(.9)		

GJR

$Ht = +.31E-5$	$+.42H_{t-1}$	$+.24\varepsilon^2_{t-1}$	$-.14D_{IO}\varepsilon^2_{t-1}$	$+.05S^-_{t-1}\varepsilon^2_{t-1}$	$+.33D_{IO}S^-_{t-1}\varepsilon^2_{t-1}$	$-.52E-9Trnd$
(5.3)	(6.2)	(7.3)	(-1.1)	(1.1)	(1.4)	(-1.4)

VGARCH (1.1)

$H_t = +.19E-5 \quad +.53H_{t-1} \quad +.45E-6\varepsilon_{t-1}/h_{t-1} \quad +.26E-5\varepsilon_{t-1}/\sqrt{h_{t-1}} \quad +.13E-6D_{IO}\varepsilon_{t-1}/h_{t-1}$

$\quad\quad (3.1) \quad\quad\quad (7.5) \quad\quad\quad\quad (1.0) \quad\quad\quad\quad\quad\quad (3.3) \quad\quad\quad\quad\quad\quad (.0)$

$\quad\quad\quad\quad\quad +.18E-5D_{IO}\varepsilon_{t-1}/\sqrt{h_{t-1}} \quad\quad\quad -.79E-9Trnd$

$\quad\quad\quad\quad\quad\quad\quad (.6) \quad\quad\quad\quad\quad\quad\quad\quad (-2.0)$

NAGARCH (1.1)

$H_t = +.16E-5 \quad +.63H_{t-1} \quad +.75\varepsilon^2_{t-1} \quad -177.6\varepsilon_{t-1}/\sqrt{h_{t-1}} \quad -20.8D_{IO}\varepsilon_{t-1}/\sqrt{h_{t-1}} \quad -.38E-9Trnd$

$\quad\quad (2.4) \quad\quad (7.6) \quad\quad (6.4) \quad\quad\quad (-4.2) \quad\quad\quad\quad\quad (-.3) \quad\quad\quad\quad (-1.0)$

AGARCH

$H_t = +.35E-5 \quad +.30H_{t-1} \quad -.03\varepsilon^2_{t-1} \quad -.03D_{IO}\varepsilon^2_{t-1} \quad +.14E-2\varepsilon_{t-1} \quad +.90E-3D_{IO}\varepsilon_{t-1} \quad -.88E-9Trnd$

$\quad\quad (5.4) \quad\quad (3.8) \quad\quad (-.6) \quad\quad (-.1) \quad\quad (4.9) \quad\quad (.9) \quad\quad (-2.3)$

Residual Statistics

	Best. eq.	Arch(5)	Garch(1.1)	SSwGarch	SSC-Garch	GJR	VGarch	NaGarch	AGarch
R^2	.60	.60	.60	.60	.60	.60	.60	.60	.60
Log Likelihood	690	6950	6950	6950	6947	6947	6947	6952	6939
Kurtosis	4.28	4.4	4.4	4.4	4.3	4.3	4.3	4.3	4.3
Skewness	-0.2	-0.20	-0.20	-0.20	-0.20	-0.20	-0.20	-0.20	-0.20
Kurtosis (standardised)		3.4	3.9	3.9	3.4	3.5	3.3	3.3	3.6
Skewness (standardised)		-0.11	-0.20	-0.20	-0.12	-0.12	-0.14	-0.11	-0.22
Positive sign bias test	.76	1.0	1.0	.9	.0	1.1	1.1	.9	1.3
Negative size bias test	-3.8	-.3	-.8	-.8	.4	-.0	-.4	-.3	-.7
Positive size bias test	2.8	-1.0	-.3	-.3	-.1	-.7	-.8	-.6	-.7
Pagan-Sabau intercept		+.17E-4	+.16E-4	+.16E-4	+.17E-4	+.17E-4	+.13E-4	+.16E-4	+.11E-4
(std. error)		+.29E-5	+.33E-5	+.33E-5	+.29E-5	+.31E-5	+.48E-5	+.36E-5	+.58E-5
Pagan-Sabau coefficient		+.41	+.53	+.53	+.32	+.39	+.88	+.53	+1.13
(std error)		+.25	+.32	+.32	+.25	+.27	+.53	+.36	+.67

Table 5.18: Roche - 2346 obs. - Sample Period: 01/01/83 - 31/12/91 - Option introd.

date: 19/5/88

D_{IO} = Option contract introduction dummy   Ssw = Sign switching dummy
Pr = Sign persistence variable   Trnd = Linear trend

ARCH (5)

$Ht = +.99E\text{-}5 \quad -.14E\text{-}4D_{IO} \quad +.22\varepsilon^2_{t-1} \quad +.14\varepsilon^2_{t-2} \quad +.06\varepsilon^2_{t-3} \quad +.05\varepsilon^2_{t-4} \quad +.01\varepsilon^2_{t-5}$

$(14.5) \qquad (-16.3) \qquad (10.3) \qquad (10.0) \qquad (3.5) \qquad (3.5) \qquad (1.4)$

$+.59E\text{-}8Trnd$

(7.7)

GARCH (1.1)

$Ht = +.36E\text{-}5 \quad -.50E\text{-}5D_{IO} \quad +.63H_{t-1} \quad +.19\varepsilon^2_{t-1} \quad +.20E\text{-}8Trnd \quad -.22E\text{-}6Pr \quad +.11E\text{-}6D_{IO}Pr$

$(9.4) \qquad (-9.1) \qquad (27.3) \qquad (13.2) \qquad (5.8) \qquad (-2.9) \qquad (.8)$

Sign Switching GARCH (1.1)

$Ht = +.42E\text{-}5 \quad -.58E\text{-}5D_{IO} \quad +.58H_{t-1} \quad +.21\varepsilon^2_{t-1} \quad +.22E\text{-}8Trnd \quad -.17E\text{-}6Pr \quad +.15E\text{-}6_{IO}Pr$

$(9.9) \qquad (-9.0) \qquad (21.9) \qquad (12.9) \qquad (5.5) \qquad (-2.1) \qquad (1.0)$

$+.93E\text{-}6Ssw$

(4.2)

SSC-GARCH (1.1)

$Ht = +.32E\text{-}5 \quad +.58H_{t-1} \quad +.31S^+_{t-1}\varepsilon^2_{t-1} \quad +.19S^-_{t-1}\varepsilon^2_{t-1} \quad +.20E\text{-}5S^-_{t-1} \quad +.11E\text{-}8Trnd$

$(3.3) \qquad (15.4) \qquad (7.4) \qquad (6.3) \qquad (3.2) \qquad (1.9)$

$-.61E\text{-}5D_{IO}S^-_{t-1} \quad -.23D_{IO}S^+_{t-1}\varepsilon^2_{t-1} \quad +.06D_{IO}S^-_{t-1}\varepsilon^2_{t-1}$

$(-6.2) \qquad (-4.2) \qquad (1.0)$

GJR

$Ht = +.51E\text{-}5 \quad +.59H_{t-1} \quad +.34\varepsilon^2_{t-1} \quad -.21D_{IO}\varepsilon^2_{t-1} \quad -.12S^-_{t-1}\varepsilon^2_{t-1} \quad +.17D_{IO}S^-_{t-1}\varepsilon^2_{t-1} \quad -.10E\text{-}8Trnd$

$(5.4) \qquad (16.1) \qquad (8.3) \qquad (-3.7) \qquad (-2.5) \qquad (2.1) \qquad (-2.5)$

VGARCH (1.1)

$$H_t = +.83\text{E-}6 \quad +.72H_{t-1} \quad +.42\text{E-}5\varepsilon_{t-1}/h_{t-1} \quad +.28\text{E-}5\varepsilon_{t-1}/\sqrt{h_{t-1}} \quad -.24\text{E-}6D_{IO}\varepsilon_{t-1}/h_{t-1}$$

$$(.9) \qquad (24.1) \qquad\qquad (4.9) \qquad\qquad (2.1) \qquad\qquad (-.1)$$

$$-.69\text{E-}5D_{IO}\varepsilon_{t-1}/\sqrt{h_{t-1}} \quad +.93\text{E-}9\text{Trnd}$$

$$(-3.6) \qquad\qquad (1.9)$$

NAGARCH (1.1)

$$H_t = +.35\text{E-}5 \quad +.68H_{t-1} \quad +.37\varepsilon^2_{t-1} \quad -21.9\varepsilon_{t-1}/\sqrt{h_{t-1}} \quad -20.0D_{IO}\varepsilon_{t-1}/\sqrt{h_{t-1}} \quad -.74\text{E-}9\text{Trnd}$$

$$(4.3) \qquad (21.1) \qquad (9.9) \qquad (-6.5) \qquad\qquad (-.3) \qquad\qquad (-2.0)$$

AGARCH

$$H_t = +.32\text{E-}5 \quad +.61H_{t-1} \quad +.20\varepsilon^2_{t-1} \quad +.15D_{IO}\varepsilon^2_{t-1} \quad +.59\text{E-}3\varepsilon_{t-1} \quad -.19\text{E-}2D_{IO}\varepsilon_{t-1} \quad +.38\text{E-}9\text{Trnd}$$

$$(3.5) \qquad (17.9) \qquad (5.2) \qquad (1.6) \qquad (2.0) \qquad (-3.4) \qquad (.7)$$

Residual Statistics

	Best. eq.	Arch(5)	Garch(1.1)	SSwGarch	SSC-Garch	GJR	VGarch	NaGarch	AGarch
R^2	.43	.40	.40	.40	.40	.40	.41	.40	.40
Log Likelihood	9168	9512	9525	9530	9512	9498	9489	9503	9509
Kurtosis	16	23.8	23.8	23.8	23.2	23.4	22.5	22.9	23.2
Skewness	0.42	0.63	0.62	0.62	0.49	0.46	0.47	0.45	0.49
Kurtosis (standardised)		6.5	6.0	6.3	6.8	8.0	7.2	7.5	7.4
Skewness (standardised)		-0.11	-0.02	-0.06	-0.07	-0.10	-0.08	-0.04	-0.11
Positive sign bias test	2.98	1.1	1.1	.2	.3	.3	.5	.2	.7
Negative size bias test	-11.7	-.7	-1.0	-.6	-.5	-.3	-.9	-.4	-.4
Positive size bias test	5.9	-.2	-.1	-.0	-.2	-.3	.7	.4	-.2
Pagan-Sabau intercept		+.13E-4	+.11E-4	+.12E-4	+.17E-4	+.20E-4	-.15E-4	-.10E-4	+.12E-4
(std. error)		+.40E-5	+.40E-5	+.40E-5	+.39E-5	+.39E-5	+.49E-5	+.45E-5	+.40E-5
Pagan-Sabau coefficient		+1.16	+1.25	+1.22	+.93	+.81	+1.54	+1.30	+1.17
(std error)		+.08	+.08	+.08	+.07	+.06	+.16	+.13	+.08

Table 5.19: Akzo Nobel-1826 obs. - Sample Period: 01/01/73 - 31/12/79 - Opt. introd.

date: 26/6/78

D_{IO} = Option contract introduction dummy   Ssw = Sign switching dummy

Pr = Sign persistence variable   Trnd = Linear trend

ARCH (5)

Ht = +.13E-4	-.18E-4D_{IO}	+.14ε^2_{t-1}	+.07ε^2_{t-2}	+.06ε^2_{t-3}	+.01ε^2_{t-4}	+.14E-7Trnd
(9.6)	(-8.3)	(5.1)	(3.9)	(3.6)	(.9)	(8.5)

GARCH (1.1)

Ht = +.63E-5	-.95E-5D_{IO}	+.49H_{t-1}	+.15ε^2_{t-1}	+.71E-8Trnd	+.58E-6Pr	+.62E-6D_{IO}Pr
(5.2)	(-5.0)	(7.1)	(5.9)	(5.2)	(1.3)	(.6)

Sign Switching GARCH (1.1)

Ht = +.64E-5	-.99E-5D_{IO}	+.49H_{t-1}	+.15ε^2_{t-1}	+.73E-8Trnd	+.59E-6Pr	+.64E-6D_{IO}Pr
(5.2)	(-4.9)	(7.0)	(5.9)	(5.1)	(1.3)	(.7)
	+.25E-6Ssw					
	(.4)					

SSC-GARCH (1.1)

Ht = +.97E-5	+.38H_{t-1}	+.06$S^+_{t-1}\varepsilon^2_{t-1}$	+.28$S^-_{t-1}\varepsilon^2_{t-1}$	-.19E-5S^-_{t-1}	+.88E-8Trnd
(5.1)	(5.7)	(2.1)	(5.3)	(-1.2)	(4.7)
	-.16E-4$D_{IO}S^-_{t-1}$	-.09$D_{IO}S^+_{t-1}\varepsilon^2_{t-1}$	+.13$D_{IO}S^-_{t-1}\varepsilon^2_{t-1}$		
	(-6.3)	(-1.6)	(1.2)		

GJR

Ht = +.61E-5	+.58H_{t-1}	+.07ε^2_{t-1}	-.02$D_{IO}\varepsilon^2_{t-1}$	+.18$S^-_{t-1}\varepsilon^2_{t-1}$	-.17$D_{IO}S^-_{t-1}\varepsilon^2_{t-1}$	+.29E-8Trnd
(2.9)	(7.1)	(2.5)	(-.3)	(3.6)	(-1.4)	(1.8)

VGARCH (1.1) - Not estimated (collinearity problems)

NAGARCH (1.1)

$$Ht = +.47E\text{-}5 \quad +.65H_{t-1} \quad +.23\varepsilon^2_{t-1} \quad -11.4\varepsilon_{t-1}/\sqrt{h_{t-1}} \quad -17.0D_{IO}\varepsilon_{t-1}/\sqrt{h_{t-1}} \quad +.23E\text{-}8Trnd$$

$$\quad\;(1.9) \qquad\quad (7.2) \qquad\;\; (1.5) \qquad\qquad (-.4) \qquad\qquad\qquad\quad (-.1) \qquad\qquad\qquad (1.4)$$

AGARCH

$$Ht = +.17E\text{-}5 \quad +.62H_{t-1} \quad -.02\varepsilon^2_{t-1} \quad +.05D_{IO}\varepsilon^2_{t-1} \quad +.22E\text{-}2\varepsilon_{t-1} \quad -.14E\text{-}2D_{IO}\varepsilon_{t-1} \quad +.30E\text{-}8Trnd$$

$$\quad\;(.9) \qquad\quad (8.5) \qquad\;\; (-.4) \qquad\quad\;\; (.3) \qquad\qquad (4.3) \qquad\qquad (-1.3) \qquad\qquad (1.7)$$

Residual Statistics

	Best. eq.	Arch(5)	Garch(1.1)	SSwGarch	SSC-Garch	GJR	NaGarch	AGarch
R^2	.47	.47	.47	.47	.47	.47	.47	.47
Log Likelihood	6817	6866	6873	6873	6881	6875	6870	6878
Kurtosis	3.48	3.5	3.5	3.5	3.5	3.5	3.5	3.5
Skewness	0.12	0.11	0.11	0.11	0.12	0.12	0.12	0.12
Kurtosis (standardised)		3.0	3.0	3.0	3.1	3.5	3.5	3.1
Skewness (standardised)		-0.01	-0.02	-0.02	-0.03	-0.07	-0.07	0.01
Positive sign bias test	1.0	1.3	1.5	1.4	-.3	.8	1.2	1.3
Negative size bias test	-4.8	-1.2	-1.2	-1.2	.3	-.2	-1.2	-1.3
Positive size bias test	2.4	-1.1	-1.4	-1.4	.2	-.2	-1.1	-1.1
Pagan-Sabau intercept		+.27E-4	+.29E-4	+.30E-4	+.36E-4	+.32E-4	+.29E-4	+.66E-5
(std. error)		+.69E-5	+.68E-5	+.68E-5	+.61E-5	+.61E-5	+.68E-5	+.88E-5
Pagan-Sabau coefficient		1.04	+.98	+.95	+.78	+.90	+1.00	+1.71
(std error)		+.18	+.18	+.18	+.15	+.15	+.18	+.25

Table 5.20: Getronics -1761 obs.- Sample Period: 01/04/87-31/12/93 - Option introd.

date: 7/2/92

D_{IO} = Option contract introduction dummy   Ssw = Sign switching dummy

Pr = Sign persistence variable   Trnd = Linear trend

ARCH (5)

$Ht = +.41E-4$	$+.13E-4D_{IO}$	$+.33\varepsilon^2_{t-1}$	$+.01\varepsilon^2_{t-2}$	$+.15\varepsilon^2_{t-3}$	$+.05\varepsilon^2_{t-4}$	$+.02\varepsilon^2_{t-5}$
(21.1)	(7.5)	(9.4)	(1.2)	(6.5)	(3.5)	(1.6)
	$-.22E-7Trnd$					
	(-13.1)					

GARCH (1.1)

$Ht = +.18E-4$	$+.80E-5D_{IO}$	$+.48H_{t-1}$	$+.27\varepsilon^2_{t-1}$	$-.11E-7Trnd$	$+.29E-5Pr$	$-.13E-5D_{IO}Pr$
(10.0)	(5.0)	(15.0)	(9.9)	(-9.3)	(6.3)	(-1.4)

Sign Switching GARCH (1.1)

$Ht = +.18E-4$	$+.70E-5D_{IO}$	$+.49H_{t-1}$	$+.27\varepsilon^2_{t-1}$	$-.10E-7Trnd$	$+.25E-5Pr$	$-.97E-6D_{IO}Pr$
(9.9)	(4.3)	(15.8)	(10.0)	(-9.0)	(5.3)	(-.9)
	$+.12E-5Ssw$					
	(2.3)					

SSC-GARCH (1.1)

$Ht = +.24E-4$	$+.49H_{t-1}$	$+.17S^+_{t-1}\varepsilon^2_{t-1}$	$+.32S^-_{t-1}\varepsilon^2_{t-1}$	$-.89E-5S^-_{t-1}$	$-.75E-8Trnd$
(5.7)	(8.2)	(4.0)	(6.1)	(-5.4)	(-3.6)
	$-.18E-5D_{IO}S^-_{t-1}$	$-.16D_{IO}S^+_{t-1}\varepsilon^2_{t-1}$	$+.65D_{IO}S^-_{t-1}\varepsilon^2_{t-1}$		
	(-.6)	(-2.0)	(4.5)		

GJR

$Ht = +.20E-4$	$+.46H_{t-1}$	$+.25\varepsilon^2_{t-1}$	$-.10D_{IO}\varepsilon^2_{t-1}$	$+.04S^-_{t-1}\varepsilon^2_{t-1}$	$+.45D_{IO}S^-_{t-1}\varepsilon^2_{t-1}$	$-.76E-8Trnd$
(6.4)	(9.3)	(5.9)	(-1.2)	(.7)	(3.5)	(-4.2)

VGARCH (1.1)

$$H_t = +.18E\text{-}4 \quad +.62H_{t-1} \quad +.16E\text{-}4\varepsilon_{t-1}/h_{t-1} \quad -.78E\text{-}5\varepsilon_{t-1}/\sqrt{h_{t-1}} \quad -.20E\text{-}4D_{IO}\varepsilon_{t-1}/h_{t-1}$$
$$(5.2) \qquad\qquad (14.6) \qquad\qquad (7.1) \qquad\qquad\qquad (-2.1) \qquad\qquad\qquad (-7.4)$$
$$+.30E\text{-}4D_{IO}\varepsilon_{t-1}/\sqrt{h_{t-1}} \qquad -.11E\text{-}7Trnd$$
$$(6.7) \qquad\qquad\qquad (-5.6)$$

NAGARCH (1.1)

$$H_t = +.24E\text{-}4 \quad +.41H_{t-1} \quad +.18\varepsilon^2_{t-1} \quad 12.7\varepsilon_{t-1}/\sqrt{h_{t-1}} \quad -182.2D_{IO}\varepsilon_{t-1}/\sqrt{h_{t-1}} \quad -.11E\text{-}7Trnd$$
$$(7.7) \qquad (8.6) \qquad (2.1) \qquad\quad (1.1) \qquad\qquad (-4.6) \qquad\qquad (-6.3)$$

AGARCH

$$H_t = +.21E\text{-}4 \quad +.46H_{t-1} \quad +.27\varepsilon^2_{t-1} \quad -.42D_{IO}\varepsilon^2_{t-1} \quad +.32E\text{-}3\varepsilon_{t-1} \quad +.43E\text{-}2D_{IO}\varepsilon_{t-1} \quad -.11E\text{-}7Trnd$$
$$(6.2) \qquad (10.1) \qquad (4.7) \qquad (-5.1) \qquad\quad (.5) \qquad\qquad (5.5) \qquad\qquad (-5.8)$$

Residual Statistics

	Best. eq.	Arch(5)	Garch(1.1)	SSwGarch	SSC-Garch	GJR	VGarch	NaGarch	AGarch
R^2	.20	.20	.20	.20	.20	.20	.20	.20	.20
Log Likelihood	6088	6376	6379	6380	6375	6361	6354	6369	6382
Kurtosis	17.8	22.0	21.7	21.6	21.5	21.4	21.0	21.3	21.4
Skewness	0.45	0.62	0.59	0.58	0.66	0.65	0.63	0.64	0.64
Kurtosis (standardised)		5.2	4.7	4.8	5.2	6.0	5.5	5.5	5.3
Skewness (standardised)		0.34	0.27	0.25	0.37	0.41	0.36	0.33	0.33
Positive sign bias test	5.5	1.3	1.9	.9	.1	2.3	2.6	1.8	1.8
Negative size bias test	-18.3	-1.1	-1.8	-1.5	-.5	-1.5	-4.3	-1.0	-1.4
Positive size bias test	6.12	-1.0	-1.0	-.7	.0	-.9	-.1	-1.3	-1.1
Pagan-Sabau intercept		-.89E-5	-.93E-5	-.80E-5	-.33E-4	-.16E-4	-.49E-4	+.38E-4	-.10E-4
(std. error)		+.86E-5	+.88E-5	+.87E-5	+.86E-5	+.88E-5	+.11E-4	+.85E-5	+.88E-5
Pagan-Sabau coefficient		+1.36	+1.41	+1.38	+1.91	+1.58	+1.30	+.49	+1.45
(std error)		+.06	+.06	+.06	+.07	+.07	+.16	+.03	+.07

Table 5.21: Unilever - 1826 obs. - Sample Period: 01/01/73- 31/12/79 - Option introd. date: 4/4/78

D_{IO} = Option contract introduction dummy Ssw = Sign switching dummy
Pr = Sign persistence variable $Trnd$ = Linear trend

ARCH (5)

$Ht = +.12E-4$	$+.31E-5D_{IO}$	$+.15\varepsilon^2_{t-1}$	$+.23\varepsilon^2_{t-2}$	$-.74E-8Trnd$
(21.5)	(9.4)	(7.1)	(12.0)	(-16.1)

GARCH (1.1)

$Ht = +.70E-5$	$+.24E-5D_{IO}$	$+.43H_{t-1}$	$+.18\varepsilon^2_{t-1}$	$-.44E-8Trnd$	$+.41E-6Pr$	$-.51E-6D_{IO}Pr$
(7.1)	(7.8)	(7.2)	(8.0)	(-7.4)	(2.9)	(-3.3)

Sign Switching GARCH (1.1)

$Ht = +.59E-5$	$+.21E-5D_{IO}$	$+.51H_{t-1}$	$+.17\varepsilon^2_{t-1}$	$-.38E-8Trnd$	$+.32E-6Pr$	$-.43E-6D_{IO}Pr$
(7.4)	(7.6)	(9.9)	(8.3)	(-7.6)	(2.5)	(-3.0)
	$-.45E-6Ssw$					
	(-4.3)					

SSC-GARCH (1.1)

$Ht = +.23E-5$	$+.75H_{t-1}$	$+.10S^{+}_{t-1}\varepsilon^2_{t-1}$	$+.16S^{-}_{t-1}\varepsilon^2_{t-1}$	$-.80E-8S^{-}_{t-1}$	$-.14E-8Trnd$
(1.6)	(9.3)	(2.7)	(4.9)	(-.0)	(-1.9)
	$+.37E-6D_{IO}S^{-}_{t-1}$	$+.20D_{IO}S^{+}_{t-1}\varepsilon^2_{t-1}$	$+.03D_{IO}S^{-}_{t-1}\varepsilon^2_{t-1}$		
	(.8)	(2.2)	(.5)		

GJR

$Ht = +.39E-5$	$+.64H_{t-1}$	$+.09\varepsilon^2_{t-1}$	$+.18D_{IO}\varepsilon^2_{t-1}$	$+.05S^{-}_{t-1}\varepsilon^2_{t-1}$	$-.14D_{IO}S^{-}_{t-1}\varepsilon^2_{t-1}$	$-.18E-8Trnd$
(3.8)	(9.2)	(2.8)	(2.1)	(1.2)	(-1.3)	(-4.1)

207

VGARCH (1.1)

$$H_t = +.90E\text{-}5 \quad +.42H_{t-1} \quad +.25E\text{-}5\varepsilon_{t-1}/h_{t-1} \quad -.36E\text{-}5\varepsilon_{t-1}/\sqrt{h_{t-1}} \quad +.26E\text{-}6D_{IO}\varepsilon_{t-1}/h_{t-1}$$
$$(6.2) \qquad (4.8) \qquad\qquad (4.5) \qquad\qquad\qquad (-3.6) \qquad\qquad\qquad (.3)$$
$$-.20E\text{-}8D_{IO}\varepsilon_{t-1}/\sqrt{h_{t-1}} \qquad -.38E\text{-}8Trnd$$
$$(-.1) \qquad\qquad\qquad (-5.7)$$

NAGARCH (1.1)

$$H_t = +.18E\text{-}5 \quad +.80H_{t-1} \quad +.42\varepsilon^2_{t-1} \quad -92.6\varepsilon_{t-1}/\sqrt{h_{t-1}} \quad 40.0D_{IO}\varepsilon_{t-1}/\sqrt{h_{t-1}} \quad -.10E\text{-}8Trnd$$
$$(1.9) \qquad (12.6) \qquad (4.5) \qquad (-3.5) \qquad\qquad (.4) \qquad\qquad (-2.4)$$

AGARCH

$$H_t = +.11E\text{-}4 \quad +.18H_{t-1} \quad +.20\varepsilon^2_{t-1} \quad +.44D_{IO}\varepsilon^2_{t-1} \quad -.62E\text{-}3\varepsilon_{t-1} \quad -.12E\text{-}2D_{IO}\varepsilon_{t-1} \quad -.44E\text{-}8Trnd$$
$$(8.5) \qquad (2.3) \qquad (3.6) \qquad (3.1) \qquad (-1.8) \qquad (-2.4) \qquad (-7.1)$$

Residual Statistics

	Best. eq.	Arch(5)	Garch(1.1)	SSwGarch	SSC-Garch	GJR	VGarch	NaGarch	AGarch
R^2	.57	.57	.57	.57	.57	.57	.57	.57	.57
Log Likelihood	7944	8067	8070	8072	8063	8057	8050	8061	8050
Kurtosis	10.4	10.7	10.9	10.9	10.7	10.6	10.7	10.7	10.6
Skewness	-0.8	-0.82	-0.83	-0.83	-0.82	-0.82	-0.82	-0.82	-0.82
Kurtosis (standardised)		7.8	9.3	8.8	9.1	9.5	9.1	9.3	9.3
Skewness (standardised)		-0.75	-0.96	-0.88	-0.94	-0.98	-0.86	-0.95	-0.90
Positive sign bias test	-.4	-.6	-.7	-.0	-.5	-.7	-.8	-.5	-.8
Negative size bias test	-2.8	.4	.6	.4	.4	.4	.2	.2	.3
Positive size bias test	2.5	-.0	-.0	-.1	.1	.2	.6	.2	.4
Pagan-Sabau intercept		+.16E-4	+.13E-4	+.13E-4	+.14E-4	+.13E-4	+.14E-4	+.11E-4	+.15E-4
(std. error)		+.23E-5	+.26E-5	+.26E-5	+.25E-5	+.27E-5	+.26E-5	+.29E-5	+.26E-5
Pagan-Sabau coefficient		+.60	+.94	+.95	+.84	+.95	+.80	+1.17	+.73
(std error)		+.15	+.20	+.19	+.18	+.20	+.20	+.24	+.20

Table 5.22: Amstrad - 2170 obs. - Sample Period: 21/12/81 - 27/4/90 - Option introd. date: 23/4/87

D_{IO} = Option contract introduction dummy   Ssw = Sign switching dummy

Pr = Sign persistence variable   Trnd = Linear trend

ARCH (5)

$Ht = +.75E\text{-}4$	$-.46E\text{-}4D_{IO}$	$+.11\varepsilon^2_{t\text{-}1}$	$+.07\varepsilon^2_{t\text{-}2}$	$+.07\varepsilon^2_{t\text{-}3}$	$+.07\varepsilon^2_{t\text{-}4}$	$+.05\varepsilon^2_{t\text{-}5}$
(22.4)	(-4.7)	(7.3)	(4.8)	(4.6)	(5.7)	(3.5)
	$+.30E\text{-}7Trnd$					
	(4.7)					

GARCH (1.1)

$Ht = +.69E\text{-}5$	$-.66E\text{-}5D_{IO}$	$+.91H_{t\text{-}1}$	$+.05\varepsilon^2_{t\text{-}1}$	$+.73E\text{-}9Trnd$	$-.32E\text{-}5Pr$	$+.52E\text{-}5D_{IO}Pr$
(9.8)	(-6.6)	(140.1)	(11.0)	(1.4)	(-8.0)	(7.7)

Sign Switching GARCH (1.1)

$Ht = +.59E\text{-}5$	$-.70E\text{-}5D_{IO}$	$+.92H_{t\text{-}1}$	$+.05\varepsilon^2_{t\text{-}1}$	$+.13E\text{-}8Trnd$	$-.30E\text{-}5Pr$	$+.51E\text{-}5D_{IO}Pr$
(8.7)	(-7.4)	(144.3)	(11.1)	(2.6)	(-8.1)	(8.4)
	$+.23E\text{-}5Ssw$					
	(3.2)					

SSC-GARCH (1.1)

$Ht = +.31E\text{-}4$	$+.70H_{t\text{-}1}$	$+.14S^+_{t\text{-}1}\varepsilon^2_{t\text{-}1}$	$+.09S^-_{t\text{-}1}\varepsilon^2_{t\text{-}1}$	$-.15E\text{-}4S^-_{t\text{-}1}$	$+.24E\text{-}8Trnd$
(4.5)	(13.8)	(5.0)	(3.1)	(-3.1)	(.5)
	$-.10E\text{-}4D_{IO}S^-_{t\text{-}1}$	$-.12D_{IO}S^+_{t\text{-}1}\varepsilon^2_{t\text{-}1}$	$+.23D_{IO}S^-_{t\text{-}1}\varepsilon^2_{t\text{-}1}$		
	(-1.2)	(-3.2)	(3.2)		

GJR

$Ht = +.20E\text{-}4$	$+.74H_{t\text{-}1}$	$+.15\varepsilon^2_{t\text{-}1}$	$-.12D_{IO}\varepsilon^2_{t\text{-}1}$	$-.08S^-_{t\text{-}1}\varepsilon^2_{t\text{-}1}$	$+.23D_{IO}S^-_{t\text{-}1}\varepsilon^2_{t\text{-}1}$	$+.78E\text{-}9Trnd$
(3.3)	(13.4)	(6.3)	(-3.0)	(-2.5)	(3.7)	(.2)

VGARCH (1.1)

$$H_t = +.10E\text{-}4 \quad +.82H_{t-1} \quad +.20E\text{-}4\,\varepsilon_{t-1}/h_{t-1} \quad -.57E\text{-}5\,\varepsilon_{t-1}/\sqrt{h_{t-1}} \quad -.17E\text{-}4D_{IO}\varepsilon_{t-1}/h_{t-1}$$
$$\quad\;\;(2.0)\qquad\quad(15.7)\qquad\qquad(2.6)\qquad\qquad\qquad(-.4)\qquad\qquad\qquad(-1.9)$$
$$+.19E\text{-}4D_{IO}\varepsilon_{t-1}/\sqrt{h_{t-1}} \quad +.10E\text{-}9Trnd$$
$$(1.1)\qquad\qquad\qquad(.0)$$

NAGARCH (1.1)

$$H_t = +.17E\text{-}4 \quad +.75H_{t-1} \quad +.25\varepsilon^2_{t-1} \quad -11.1\varepsilon_{t-1}/\sqrt{h_{t-1}} \quad 36.5D_{IO}\varepsilon_{t-1}/\sqrt{h_{t-1}} \quad +.37E\text{-}8Trnd$$
$$\quad\;\;(2.9)\qquad\quad(13.2)\qquad(3.5)\qquad\quad(-1.7)\qquad\qquad\quad(2.1)\qquad\qquad\quad(1.1)$$

AGARCH

$$H_t = +.10E\text{-}4 \quad +.79H_{t-1} \quad +.05\varepsilon^2_{t-1} \quad -.04D_{IO}\varepsilon^2_{t-1} \quad +.16E\text{-}2\varepsilon_{t-1} \quad +.35E\text{-}3D_{IO}\varepsilon_{t-1} \quad -.11E\text{-}8Trnd$$
$$\quad\;\;(1.9)\qquad\quad(16.4)\qquad(1.2)\qquad\quad(-.6)\qquad\qquad(1.8)\qquad\qquad(.2)\qquad\qquad(-.2)$$

Residual Statistics

	Best. eq.	Arch(5)	Garch(1.1)	SSwGarch	SSC-Garch	GJR	VGarch	NaGarch	AGarch
R^2	.14	.14	.14	.14	.14	.14	.14	.14	.14
Log Likelihood	6518	6576	6622	6624	6594	6593	6599	6590	6603
Kurtosis	5.98	6.0	6.0	6.0	5.9	6.0	6.0	5.9	6.0
Skewness	0.84	0.85	0.86	0.87	0.85	0.85	0.85	0.85	0.85
Kurtosis (standardised)		6.3	5.8	5.7	5.6	5.9	6.3	6.6	6.3
Skewness (standardised)		0.84	0.72	0.71	0.80	0.79	0.84	0.81	0.87
Positive sign bias test	1.0	1.3	1.0	.9	-.1	.9	1.1	.9	.8
Negative size bias test	-2.9	-.3	-.6	-.7	.5	-.1	-.4	-.0	-.1
Positive size bias test	3.0	-.7	.1	.1	-.3	-.6	-.6	-.3	-.3
Pagan-Sabau intercept		+.73E-4	+.53E-4	+.55E-4	+.99E-4	+.83E-4	+.34E-4	+.66E-4	+.44E-4
(std. error)		+.21E-4	+.22E-4	+.22E-4	+.17E-4	+.18E-4	+.20E-4	+.20E-4	+.22E-4
Pagan-Sabau coefficient		+.62	+.77	+.76	+.44	+.55	+.91	+.68	+.84
(std error)		+.12	+.13	+.13	+.09	+.10	+.12	+.12	+.13

Table 5.23: British Petroleum-2088 obs.-Sample Period: 01/01/73-31/12/80-Opt. introd. date: 21/4/78

D_{IO} = Option contract introduction dummy   Ssw = Sign switching dummy
Pr = Sign persistence variable   Trnd = Linear trend

ARCH (5)

$Ht = +.18E\text{-}4 \quad -.41E\text{-}5D_{IO} \quad +.15\varepsilon^2_{t-1} \quad +.08\varepsilon^2_{t-2} \quad +.11\varepsilon^2_{t-3} \quad +.07\varepsilon^2_{t-4} \quad +.06\varepsilon^2_{t-5}$
(13.3)   (-1.4)   (7.5)   (3.6)   (5.8)   (3.6)   (3.7)
$+.49E\text{-}9Trnd$
(.2)

GARCH (1.1)

$Ht = +.42E\text{-}6 \quad +.37E\text{-}7D_{IO} \quad +.93H_{t-1} \quad +.05\varepsilon^2_{t-1} \quad -.26E10Trnd \quad +.15E\text{-}7Pr \quad -.10E\text{-}6D_{IO}Pr$
(3.4)   (.2)   (152.4)   (9.6)   (-.3)   (.1)   (-.7)

Sign Switching GARCH (1.1)

$Ht = +.43E\text{-}6 \quad +.35E\text{-}7D_{IO} \quad +.93H_{t-1} \quad +.05\varepsilon^2_{t-1} \quad -.24E10Trnd \quad +.11E\text{-}7Pr \quad -.10E\text{-}6D_{IO}Pr$
(3.3)   (.1)   (148.2)   (9.5)   (-.2)   (.1)   (-.7)
$-.28E\text{-}7Ssw$
(-.1)

SSC-GARCH (1.1)

$Ht = +.34E\text{-}5 \quad +.76H_{t-1} \quad +.10S^+_{t-1}\varepsilon^2_{t-1} \quad +.08S^-_{t-1}\varepsilon^2_{t-1} \quad +.30E\text{-}5S^-_{t-1} \quad -.77E\text{-}9Trnd$
(1.6)   (12.5)   (2.7)   (2.9)   (2.5)   (-.6)
$-.43E\text{-}5D_{IO}S^-_{t-1} \quad +.07D_{IO}S^+_{t-1}\varepsilon^2_{t-1} \quad +.22D_{IO}S^-_{t-1}\varepsilon^2_{t-1}$
(-2.1)   (1.1)   (3.6)

GJR

$Ht = +.55E\text{-}5 \quad +.74H_{t-1} \quad +.09\varepsilon^2_{t-1} \quad +.07D_{IO}\varepsilon^2_{t-1} \quad +.04S^-_{t-1}\varepsilon^2_{t-1} \quad +.05D_{IO}S^-_{t-1}\varepsilon^2_{t-1} \quad -.18E\text{-}8Trnd$
(2.8)   (11.6)   (2.6)   (1.0)   (.9)   (.6)   (-2.2)

VGARCH (1.1)

$$H_t = +.10E\text{-}4 \quad +.55H_{t-1} \quad -.20E\text{-}5\varepsilon_{t-1}/h_{t-1} \quad +.13E\text{-}4\varepsilon_{t-1}/\sqrt{h_{t-1}} \quad -.20E\text{-}5D_{IO}\varepsilon_{t-1}/h_{t-1}$$
$$(4.5) \qquad\quad (10.3) \qquad\quad (-1.5) \qquad\qquad\quad (5.1) \qquad\qquad\qquad\quad (-.8)$$
$$+.11E\text{-}4D_{IO}\varepsilon_{t-1}/\sqrt{h_{t-1}} \quad -.56E\text{-}8Trnd$$
$$(2.5) \qquad\qquad\qquad (-5.2)$$

NAGARCH (1.1)

$$H_t = +.23E\text{-}5 \quad +.85H_{t-1} \quad +.13\varepsilon^2_{t-1} \quad -6.6\varepsilon_{t-1}/\sqrt{h_{t-1}} \quad -23.4D_{IO}\varepsilon_{t-1}/\sqrt{h_{t-1}} \quad -.10E\text{-}8Trnd$$
$$(1.1) \qquad\quad (11.9) \qquad (1.3) \qquad\quad (-.3) \qquad\qquad\quad (-.5) \qquad\qquad\quad (-1.2)$$

AGARCH

$$H_t = +.48E\text{-}5 \quad +.73H_{t-1} \quad +.01\varepsilon^2_{t-1} \quad -.08D_{IO}\varepsilon^2_{t-1} \quad +.12E\text{-}2\varepsilon_{t-1} \quad +.15E\text{-}2D_{IO}\varepsilon_{t-1} \quad -.30E\text{-}8Trnd$$
$$(2.2) \qquad\quad (11.6) \qquad (.3) \qquad\quad (-.9) \qquad\qquad (2.6) \qquad\qquad (1.7) \qquad\qquad (-2.5)$$

Residual Statistics

	Best. eq.	Arch(5)	Garch(1.1)	SSwGarch	SSC-Garch	GJR	VGarch	NaGarch	AGarch
R^2	.45	.45	.45	.45	.45	.45	.45	.45	.45
Log Likelihood	7794	7863	7942	7942	7900	7898	7853	7912	7887
Kurtosis	4.06	4.1	4.4	4.4	4.2	4.2	4.1	4.2	4.2
Skewness	-0.12	-0.13	-0.13	-0.13	-0.12	-0.12	-0.12	-0.12	-0.12
Kurtosis (standardised)		5.0	3.7	3.7	4.3	4.6	4.5	4.6	4.8
Skewness (standardised)		-0.43	-0.15	-0.15	-0.40	-0.42	-0.30	-0.42	-0.45
Positive sign bias test	.04	-.7	-.2	-.2	.3	-.0	.8	.0	.3
Negative size bias test	-3.6	-.0	-.6	-.7	-.0	.3	-.7	-.2	-.3
Positive size bias test	4.2	-.3	.5	.5	-.2	-.1	.0	-.3	-.1
Pagan-Sabau intercept		+.15E-5	-.17E-4	-.17E-4	.13E-4	+.79E-5	-.29E-4	-.10E-4	-.33E-4
(std. error)		+.64E-5	+.59E-5	+.59E-5	+.61E-5	+.60E-5	+.11E-4	+.65E-5	+.88E-5
Pagan-Sabau coefficient		+1.74	+1.34	+1.34	+1.36	+1.53	+1.78	+2.12	+2.88
(std error)		+.16	+.14	+.14	+.14	+.14	+.34	+.16	+.25

212

Table 5.24: Cable - 1967 obs. - Sample Period: 05/11/81 - 30/12/88 - Option introd. date: 13/12/88

D_{IO} = Option contract introduction dummy Ssw = Sign switching dummy
Pr = Sign persistence variable $Trnd$ = Linear trend

ARCH (5)

$Ht = +.36E-4$	$+.14E-4D_{IO}$	$+.15\varepsilon^2_{t-1}$	$+.03\varepsilon^2_{t-2}$	$+.57E-2\varepsilon^2_{t-3}$	$+.07\varepsilon^2_{t-5}$	$-.13E-7Trnd$
(14.9)	(3.8)	(7.7)	(1.7)	(.4)	(4.2)	(-3.6)

GARCH (1.1)

$Ht = +.41E-6$	$.33E-6D_{IO}$	$+.98H_{t-1}$	$+.012\varepsilon^2_{t-1}$	$-.40E-9Trnd$
(4.6)	(5.07)	(322)	(5.5)	(-5.9)

Sign Switching GARCH (1.1)

$Ht = +.17E-4$	$+.11E-4D_{IO}$	$+.45H_{t-1}$	$+.13\varepsilon^2_{t-1}$	$-.61E-8Trnd$	$+.15E-5Pr$	$-.33E-5D_{IO}Pr$
(5.3)	(4.4)	(6.4)	(7.0)	(-2.8)	(2.4)	(-3.5)
	$-.39E-5Ssw$					
	(-5.3)					

SSC-GARCH (1.1)

$Ht = +.20E-4$	$+.21H_{t-1}$	$+.11S^+_{t-1}\varepsilon^2_{t-1}$	$+.10S^-_{t-1}\varepsilon^2_{t-1}$	$+.84E-5S^-_{t-1}$	$+.19E-8Trnd$
(4.1)	(1.7)	(3.3)	(2.2)	(3.4)	(.9)
	$-.37E-5D_{IO}S^-_{t-1}$	$+.22E-2D_{IO}S^+_{t-1}\varepsilon^2_{t-1}$	$+.13D_{IO}S^-_{t-1}\varepsilon^2_{t-1}$		
	(-1.1)	(.0)	(1.9)		

GJR

$Ht = +.26E-4$	$+.18H_{t-1}$	$+.07\varepsilon^2_{t-1}$	$+.01D_{IO}\varepsilon^2_{t-1}$	$+.09S^-_{t-1}\varepsilon^2_{t-1}$	$+.08D_{IO}S^-_{t-1}\varepsilon^2_{t-1}$	$+.24E-9Trnd$
(5.3)	(1.5)	(2.6)	(.2)	(1.8)	(1.0)	(.1)

VGARCH (1.1)

$$Ht = +.25E\text{-}4 \quad +.25H_{t-1} \quad +.44E\text{-}5\varepsilon_{t-1}/h_{t-1} \quad -.69E\text{-}6\varepsilon_{t-1}\sqrt{h_{t-1}} \quad -.39E\text{-}6D_{IO}\varepsilon_{t-1}/h_{t-1}$$

$$(4.9) \qquad (2.1) \qquad (1.7) \qquad\qquad (-.1) \qquad\qquad (-.1)$$

$$+.98E\text{-}5D_{IO}\varepsilon_{t-1}/\sqrt{h_{t-1}} \qquad -.26E\text{-}8Trnd$$

$$(1.4) \qquad\qquad (-1.0)$$

NAGARCH (1.1)

$$Ht = +.27E\text{-}4 \quad +.16H_{t-1} \quad +.45\varepsilon^2_{t-1} \quad -57.8\varepsilon_{t-1}/\sqrt{h_{t-1}} \quad 7.9D_{IO}\varepsilon_{t-1}/\sqrt{h_{t-1}} \quad -.16E\text{-}9Trnd$$

$$(6.4) \qquad (1.5) \qquad (5.7) \qquad (-5.9) \qquad\qquad (.2) \qquad\qquad (-.0)$$

AGARCH

$$Ht = +.25E\text{-}4 \quad +.22H_{t-1} \quad +.09\varepsilon^2_{t-1} \quad +.38E\text{-}2D_{IO}\varepsilon^2_{t-1} \quad +.23E\text{-}3\varepsilon_{t-1} \quad +.11E\text{-}2D_{IO}\varepsilon_{t-1} \quad -.19E\text{-}8Trnd$$

$$(4.9) \qquad (1.8) \qquad (1.4) \qquad (.0) \qquad (.3) \qquad (1.0) \qquad (-.8)$$

Residual Statistics

	Best. eq.	Arch(5)	Garch(1.1)	SSwGarch	SSC-Garch	GJR	VGarch	NaGarch	AGarch
R^2	.43	.43	.43	.43	.43	.43	.43	.43	.43
Log Likelihood	6790	6810	6830	6819	6817	6813	6810	6812	6811
Kurtosis	4.0	4.1	4.0	4.0	4.1	4.0	4.0	4.0	4.0
Skewness	0.09	0.09	0.10	0.10	0.10	0.10	0.10	0.11	0.10
Kurtosis (standardised)		3.5	3.1	3.1	3.3	3.4	3.5	3.5	3.5
Skewness (standardised)		0.20	0.23	0.20	0.19	0.23	0.23	0.23	0.23
Positive sign bias test	-.0	-1.0	-.7	.3	-.2	-1.2	-1.1	-1.0	-1.5
Negative size bias test	-4.3	-.2	-2.7	-.5	.2	.5	-.2	-.3	.0
Positive size bias test	2.3	-.2	1.9	-.1	.2	.5	-.1	-.0	.0
Pagan-Sabau intercept		-.26E-4	-.56E-4	-.29E-4	-.37E-4	-.34E-4	-.19E-4	+.66E-6	-.49E-4
(std. error)		+.11E-4	+.17E-4	+.12E-4	+.10E-4	+.10E-4	+.14E-4	+.13E-4	+.14E-4
Pagan-Sabau coefficient		+1.40	+2.30	+1.48	+1.70	+1.64	+1.25	+1.75	+1.99
(std error)		+.26	+.37	+.27	+.24	+.24	+.35	+.32	+.33

Table 5.25: General Elec.-1826 obs.-Sample Period: 01/01/73-31/12/79 -Opt.introd.
date: 21/04/78

D_{IO} = Option contract introduction dummy   Ssw = Sign switching dummy

Pr = Sign persistence variable   Trnd = Linear trend

ARCH (5)

Ht = +.22E-4	-.12E-4D_{IO}	+.14ε^2_{t-1}	+.13ε^2_{t-2}	+.04ε^2_{t-3}	+.10ε^2_{t-4}	+.04ε^2_{t-5}
(9.2)	(-5.5)	(6.7)	(5.1)	(2.3)	(5.1)	(2.2)
	-.11E-8Trnd					
	(-.4)					

GARCH (1.1)

Ht = +.42E-5	-.20E-5D_{IO}	+.73H_{t-1}	+.12ε^2_{t-1}	-.20E10Trnd	+.13E-5Pr	-.13E-5D_{IO}Pr
(3.4)	(-2.3)	(17.3)	(6.5)	(-.0)	(3.4)	(-2.8)

Sign Switching GARCH (1.1)

Ht = +.51E-5	-.18E-5D_{IO}	+.70H_{t-1}	+.13ε^2_{t-1}	-.34E-9Trnd	+.15E-5Pr	-.15E-5D_{IO}Pr
(3.7)	(-1.9)	(15.4)	(6.4)	(-.4)	(3.7)	(-2.8)
	+.13E-5Ssw					
	(3.2)					

SSC-GARCH (1.1)

Ht = +.13E-4	+.63H_{t-1}	+.22$S^+_{t-1}\varepsilon^2_{t-1}$	+.12$S^-_{t-1}\varepsilon^2_{t-1}$	-.45E-5S^-_{t-1}	-.43E-8Trnd
(2.6)	(8.0)	(5.3)	(3.2)	(-2.3)	(-1.5)
	+.31E-5$D_{IO}S^-_{t-1}$	-.25$D_{IO}S^+_{t-1}\varepsilon^2_{t-1}$	-.04$D_{IO}S^-_{t-1}\varepsilon^2_{t-1}$		
	(1.1)	(-4.1)	(-.5)		

GJR

Ht = +.56E-5	+.74H_{t-1}	+.22ε^2_{t-1}	-.21$D_{IO}\varepsilon^2_{t-1}$	-.14$S^-_{t-1}\varepsilon^2_{t-1}$	+.22$D_{IO}S^-_{t-1}\varepsilon^2_{t-1}$	-.14E-8Trnd
(1.4)	(10.2)	(5.2)	(-3.2)	(-2.9)	(2.6)	(-.7)

VGARCH (1.1): not estimated (collinearity problems)

NAGARCH (1.1)

$Ht = +.89E-5 \quad +.66H_{t-1} \quad -.01\varepsilon^2_{t-1} \quad 26.3\varepsilon_{t-1}/\sqrt{h_{t-1}} \quad -290.3D_{IO}\varepsilon_{t-1}/\sqrt{h_{t-1}} \quad -.24E-8Trnd$

$\quad(1.6)\qquad\quad(5.9)\qquad\quad(-.1)\qquad\qquad(1.4)\qquad\qquad\qquad(-1.3)\qquad\qquad\qquad(-1.0)$

AGARCH

$Ht = +.38E-5 \quad +.79H_{t-1} \quad +.13\varepsilon^2_{t-1} \quad -.05D_{IO}\varepsilon^2_{t-1} \quad -.71E-4\varepsilon_{t-1} \quad -.31E-3D_{IO}\varepsilon_{t-1} \quad -.51E-9Trnd$

$\quad(.9)\qquad\quad(9.1)\qquad\quad(2.7)\qquad\quad(-.3)\qquad\qquad(-.1)\qquad\qquad(-.2)\qquad\qquad(-.2)$

Residual Statistics

	Best. eq.	Arch(5)	Garch(1.1)	SSwGarch	SSC-Garch	GJR	NaGarch	AGarch
R^2	.56	.56	.56	.56	.56	.56	.56	.56
Log Likelihood	6759	6879	6890	6894	6887	6886	6881	6886
Kurtosis	5.7	5.8	5.8	5.8	5.8	5.8	5.8	5.7
Skewness	0.15	0.14	0.14	0.14	0.14	0.14	0.13	0.13
Kurtosis (standardised)		3.2	3.2	2.9	3.4	3.6	4.5	4.1
Skewness (standardised)		0.11	0.15	0.11	0.12	0.16	0.19	0.18
Positive sign bias test	.5	1.1	1.3	.6	.7	1.6	1.5	1.3
Negative size bias test	-3.0	-.1	-.1	-.0	-.3	-.7	-.0	-.1
Positive size bias test	4.4	.0	-.1	-.0	-.5	-.9	-.4	-.2
Pagan-Sabau intercept		+.26E-4	+.16E-4	+.16E-4	+.31E-4	+.34E-4	+.37E-4	+.23E-4
(std. error)		+.61E-5	+.65E-5	+.65E-5	+.59E-5	+.57E-5	+.52E-5	+.61E-5
Pagan-Sabau coefficient		+1.49	+1.82	+1.82	+1.36	+1.26	+1.14	+1.58
(std error)		+.13	+.15	+.15	+.12	+.11	+.10	+.13

References

Antoniou, A. and Holmes, P. (1992), "The Relationship between Future Trading and Spot Price Volatility: Distinguishing Between the Message and the Messenger", *Brunel University, Discussion Paper,* 82-102.

Baldauf, D. and Santoni, F. (1991), "Stock Price Volatility: Some Evidence from an ARCH Model", *Journal of Future Markets,* vol.11, pp.191-200.

Becchetti, L. and Caggese, A. (1995), "Effect of Index Option Introduction on Stock Index Volatility: A Procedure for an Empirical Testing Based on SSC-Garch Models", *Working Paper C.E.I.S. 46.*

Bera, A.K. and Higgins M.L. (1993), "ARCH Models; Properties, Estimation and Testing", *Journal of Economic Surveys,* Vol. 7 pp.305-62.

Black, J.M. and Tonks, I. (1992), "Asset Price Variability in a Rational Expectation Equilibrium", *European Economic Review,* vol. 36, pp. 1367-1377.

Bollerslev T. (1986), "Generalized Autoregressive Conditional Heteroskedasticity", *Journal of Econometrics,* No. 1, pp.307-27.

Bollerslev, T., Chou, R.Y. and K .Kroner (1992), "ARCH Modeling in Finance: A Review of the Theory and Empirical Evidence", *Journal of Econometrics,* No. 1-2, pp.5-60.

Danthine, J.P.(1978), "Information, Futures Prices, and Stabilizing Speculation",*Journal of Economic Theory,* Vol 17, 79-98

Edwards, F.R. (1988), "Does Future trading Increase Stock Market Volatility?", *Financial Analysit Journal,* vol.44, n. 1 pp.63-69.

Engle, R.F. (1982), "Autoregressive Conditional Heteroskedasticity with Estimates of the Variance of UK Inflation", *Econometrica,* No. 4, pp. 987-1008.

Engle, R.F., and Ng, V. (1993), "Measuring and Testing the Impact of News on Volatility", *Journal of Finance,* No. 5, pp. 1749-78.

Fornari, F., Mele, A. (1994), "Asymmetries and Nonlinearities in Economic Activity", *Banca d'Italia Working Paper, n. 230.*

French, K. and Roll, R. (1986), "Stock return variances: the arrival of information and the reaction of the traders", *Journal of Financial Economics,* 17.

Glosten, L., Jagannathan, R. and Runkle, D. (1989), "Relationship between the Expected Value and the Volatility of the Nominal Excess Return on Stocks", *Working Paper, Department of Finance, Columbia University.*

Grossman, S.J., and Stiglitz, J.E. (1980), "The Impossiblity of Informationally Efficient Markets", *American Economic Review,* vol. 70, pp. 393-408.

Hull, J.C. (1993), *Options, futures and other derivative securities,* Prentice Hall, Englewood Cliffs, NY.

217

Klemkosky, R.C. and Maness, T.S. (1980), "The impact of options on the underlying securitiers", *Journal of Portfolio Management*, Winter.

Lee, S.B. and Ohk, K.Y. (1992), "Stock Index Future Listing and Structural Change in Time-Varying Volatility", *Journal of Future Markets*, Vol. 12, n. 5, pp. 493-509.

Nelson, D. (1990), "ARCH Models as Diffusion Approximations", *Journal of Econometrics*, 45, pp. 7-38.

Pagan, A. and Sabau, H. (1988), "Consistency Tests for Heteroskedasticity and Risk Models", University of Rochester, mimeo.

Robinson, G. (1993), "The effect of Future Trading on Cash Market Volatility: Evidence from London Stock Exchange", *Bank of England Working Paper* n. 19.

Seguin, P.J., (1990), "Stock Volatility and Margin Trading" *Journal of Monetary Economics 26*, 101-121.

Skinner, D.J. (1989), "Option market and stock return volatility", *Journal of Financial Economics*, Vol. 23.

Stein, J.C. (1987), "Informational Externalities and Welfare-reducing Speculation", *Journal of Political Economy* 95, 1123-1145.

Stoll, H.R. and Whaley, R.E. (1990), "The Dynamics of Stock Index and Stock Index Future Returns", *Journal of Financial and Quantitative Analysis*, Vol. 25, pp. 441-68.

Trennepohl, G.L. and Dukes, W.P. (1979), "CBOE options and stock volatility", *Review of Business and Economic Research*, Vol. 14.

Turnovsky, S.J. (1983), "The Determination of Spot and Futures Prices with Storable Commodities",*Econometrica* , Vol 51, 1363-87.

Wang, Y. (1993), "Near-Rational Behaviour and Financial Market Fluctuations", *The Economic Journal*, Vol. 103, pp. 1462-1478.

Whiteside, M.M., Dukes, W.P. and Dunne, P.M. (1983), "Short term impact of option trading on the underlying securities", *Journal of Financial Research*, 6.

6 Finance, investment and innovation: a theoretical and empirical comparative analysis in Japan and the UK[*]

Leonardo Becchetti

1. Introduction

The aim of this section is to propose a comparative view of panel data econometric estimates testing the existence of informational asymmetries and financial constraints at firm level. To this purpose, separate estimates for two countries (Japan and the UK) are performed under three different specifications (Arellano-Bond (1988) GMM, fixed and random effect estimates).

The underlying ambitious and only partially attainable target would be that of examining how differences in leverage and in the sensitivity of investments to liquidity, for subgroups of firms in different countries, depend on the differences in country financial and industrial structures. These two countries have been chosen because of their peculiar and different financial features, widely acknowledged by the existing literature on finance and innovation systems (among others by Nelson, 1993; Ferguson, 1988; Florida-Kenney, 1988; Borrus, 1988; Sakakibara-Westney, 1985). Japan has followed a peculiar method for organizing the relationship between the financial and the real sector and, for historical reasons (government regulations imposing interest rate ceilings and the impossibility of raising money abroad during the 1970s), many firms are part of groups (keiretsu) in which banks play an important role (Takagi, 1993). The main features of the Japanese system are: i) extensive cross-holdings of shares with a group of "stable shareholders" including banks, insurance companies and non financial corporations accounting for 64% of listed shares; ii) high participation

[*] Republished from *Empirica*, 22, 1995, Kluwer.

of banks in firm equity (around 22% in 1990) (Hodder-Tschoegl, 1993); iii) external financing sources under the form of loans representing a high percentage of total financing sources (around 35% as the 1970-87 average) with internal finance representing around 53% in the same period (Corbett, 1987).

The UK system presents, instead, i) a dispersed ownership structure with 2/3 of 200 larger firms with no single shareholder possessing an ownership share higher than 10% in 1989 (Takagi, 1993); ii) a lower bank-firm participation compared to Japan, with banks possessing only 4.8% of firm shares (Edwards-Fisher, 1993); iii) a relatively higher reliance on internal financing sources (around 87% as the 1970-87 average) and a lower reliance on bank loans (around 15%) with respect to Japan (Corbett, 1987). The idea of the chapter is that higher bank-firm cross-holdings and higher reliance on bank loans as a financing source reveal that Japanese firms suffer from lower imperfect information and lower lemons' costs.

This hypothesis is empirically tested with panel data in the chapter which is structured in three sections. The first section is a survey of the empirical literature that tests informational asymmetries using panel data at firm level. In this context, previous contributions are critically evaluated and some crucial methodological issues arising in panel data estimates are discussed, such as those concerning choice between fixed and random effects, the opportunity of performing mean group estimators, the solutions for endogeneity and the choice between level and differenced specifications.

The second section of the chapter presents and comments on UK sample estimates and tries to evaluate the efficacy of different country systems in reducing informational asymmetries with a panel data econometric analysis. Several problems arise in this attempt of a comparative evaluation of the efficiency of the different systems. Even though most data come from the same source (Datastream) there is only partial homogeneity among variables of different countries and, more important, among their accounting procedures. For this reason the liquidity measures adopted are not the same, given that Japanese firms and German firms do not give any information related to several account items like profits, R&D expenditures and all proxies of capital intensity.

As a consequence, the possibility of a comparative analysis arises (more than from direct intercountry analysis) from intracountry subgroup analysis which allows us to infer some conclusions on the different degrees of sensitivity of investments to liquidity within groups of firms in each countries.

The third section presents and comments on Japanese sample estimates. The split variables used to create the subsample are firm size, firm q, the sectorial level of technology and the recent sector performance on the stock market. The comparison between Japanese and British results mainly evidences that the "keiretsu" model with strong vertical (between banks and firms) and horizontal (among banks) integration sensibly reduces the cost differential between internal and external sources and it determines substantial invariance in sensitivity to financial constraints across different subgroups of firms.

These results seem consistent with the "short-termist" hypothesis saying that the Japanese system, with a closer connection of banks and firms within keiretsus and with less severe regulation against insider trading, is more capable of reducing problems caused by informational asymmetries (Cosh-Hughes-Singh, 1990; Frank-Mayer, 1990; Hamid-Singh, 1992; Aaker-Jacobson, 1993).

2. The analysis of financial constraints on firm investments: theoretical microfoundations and empirical problems

Several attempts to microfound the incidence of financial intermediaries in the real sector have been made (Jensen-Meckling, 1976; Greenwald-Stiglitz and Mayers-Majluf, 1984) and some empirical contributions have empirically tested their conclusions (Fazzari-Hubbard-Petersen; 1988; Gertler-Hubbard, 1988 and Whited, 1992 for the US; Hayashi-Inoue, 1988 and Hoshi-Kashyap-Sharfstein, 1992 for Japan; Devereux-Schiantarelli, 1990 and Bond-Meghir, 1994 for the UK).

All these papers, excepting Withed, assume the same "hierarchy of finance" theoretical approach. The approach developed by Fazzari et al. (1988) starts from an intertemporal maximisation of firm present value subject to a capital depreciation constraint and to an additional source of fund constraint where the firm can fund investments by borrowing, by issuing new shares or by using after tax retained profits. While in the full-information model the final specification of the demand for investments is only function of the Tobin q, the "hierarchy of finance" approach originally introduces a lemons' problem between the firm and market financiers that significantly changes the picture. In this case, first order conditions from the modified maximisation show that, for an intermediate group of firms whose investment demand is higher than retained after tax profits, it is not convenient to issue new shares. This is because the "lemons' premium" cost of equity underpricing is higher than expected profits from marginal, bond or equity financed, investments.

As a result of the Fazzari et al. model, the standard equation, tested in all empirical papers - though each author adds to this initial specification other regressors or adopts different divisional criteria based on additional theoretical assumptions - is the following:

$$(I/K)_t = \alpha_0 + \alpha_1 q_{t-1} + \alpha_2 (CF/K)_{t-1} \qquad (1)$$

The hypothesis to be tested is the sensitivity of investments to cash-flow where the two variables are divided by capital to avoid the influence of scale effects. As is well known, in a neoclassical framework, firm investments depends from the ratio between firm value and the replacement cost of capital stock. If informational problems arise as in "hierarchy of finance" models, investments are sensitive to other variables, access to external financing sources is rationed, or has additional costs, and investment plans are decisively influenced by yearly liquidity[1].

Some authors (Devereaux-Schiantarelli, 1990) modify the standard specification adding debt and assets variables as regressors. The underlying assumptions are that: i) total debt, debt seniority or the debt/equity ratio increasing bankruptcy risks should increase agency costs and that: ii) an increase in total assets should reduce informational and external financing costs because more collateral may be provided as a guarantee for money lending[2].

The first empirical problem in the estimates provided by all the authors previously quoted is the evaluation of capital, for which replacement cost and not book value has to be considered. The procedure for the evaluation of the replacement cost of capital is nowadays quite standard (it is defined as the "perpetual inventory method") and it requires only the initial book value of the capital stock, to which subsequent inflation-corrected yearly investments are added.

A more controversial problem is the evaluation of Tobin's q. An average q is the usually adopted proxy for marginal q, and the two variables coincide only under some particular conditions (constant returns of scale, perfect competition and a single quasi-fixed factor). The estimated q variable is then likely to be seriously biased (Chirinko, 1993)[3]. A solution for this problem, as observed by Hoshi et al. (1992), is the division of the sample into subgroups. The differences in liquidity coefficients (and in sensitivity to cash flow) for firms belonging to different subgroups should be unbiased given that the q bias is the same for the two groups of estimates[4]. Even for these solutions, though, an important caveat exists, since the assumption that q mismeasurement is equally severe in both subgroups is debatable. This is because future profits of firms less tightly integrated in the financial system tend to be more misvalued by the market. The answer to this objection is that no empirical evidence of first order relevance of the three biases has so far been found (Blanchard-Ree and Summers, 1993; Hoshi and Kashyap, 1990) and that, comparing first and longer differences of investment equations in our sample shows the irrelevance of the q measurement error.

The simple advice of dividing into subsamples is implicitly followed by all other authors in previous contributions without additional control for the seriousness of the measurement error. Hoshi et al. (1992) opt for a "keiretsu"/"no keiretsu" division, trying to test if Japanese firms, which are parts of a large group containing banks, may mitigate in this way agency costs. Hubbard et al.(1988) adopt a dividend payout and firm size split criteria, while Devereaux-Schiantarelli (1989) use firm size, firm age, investment perspectives (proxied with Tobin q) and firm industry.

What is interesting in these results is the difference in the modifications of the basic model tested, in the criteria adopted to split samples, and in the interpretations of the obtained findings.

This last point (result interpretation) is particularly important because empirical testing of informational asymmetries through panel data is still at its beginning and several problems of observational equivalence have still not been solved.

It is then quite important to define, according to different agency cost hypotheses presented in the literature, which conclusions may be drawn from results on different liquidity coefficient magnitudes on subgroup estimates. The "keiretsu" approach results are less subject to criticism than others. The only problems may be those of different accounting procedures between group and no group firms (with intragroup transactions taking place at no market values) and of endogenous group membership. Both of these objections are rejected by the authors with reasonable arguments.

Many more problems arise in the interpretation of results obtained using divisional criteria. A general objection to all of them is that of the "reverse causation" phenomenon. Firm investments may be more sensitive to internal liquidity just because these firms are those with better investment perspectives and tend consequently to increase their debt exposition to finance their projects. It is then necessary to introduce some more control for firm investment perspectives and this can be done in several ways. First is the one followed by Fazzari et al. (1988) and by Becchetti (1994), selecting a sample of firms with positive performance for the time period considered in the analysis. Contemporary performance should be a reasonably good proxy for future investment performance. Second is the method of dividing a group by q values, which should themselves be good proxies for future investment performance. If firms with higher q are more sensitive to cash flow than those with lower q this should be seen as an empirical validation of the "reverse causation" hypothesis.

The results obtained on the size divisional criteria may have two main interpretations: a higher sensitivity of small firms with respect to larger ones indicates a classical credit rationing result. Banks run larger risks with small firm financing than with large firm financing because, in the first case, the project risk coincides with (or is next to) firm risk, while, in the second case, there is less risk of firm insolvency due to a project failure.

223

In a well-developed financial market with "fragmented ownership", the results may be completely different. In this case, an agency problem between managers and ownership is more likely to arise in large companies where the manager's stake is low relative to overall firm capital (Harris-Raviv, 1991). These managers may care more for firm growth than for firm profitability, trying to increase investment quantity rather than quality. In this case overinvestment may occur and large firms may become more sensitive to cash flow than small ones.

Another controversial divisional criterion adopted in empirical research is based on dividend payout ratio. Modigliani and Miller state that dividend policies are irrelevant and may even have negative effects because they are usually taxable, while taxes could be reduced by retaining and reinvesting profits. Nonetheless the phenomenon of dividend payment often combined with an increase in new capital occurs, and does not appear to be explained by these kinds of theories.

Imperfect information theories may provide better explanations (Easterbrook, 1987) assuming that dividend payments are a signal of the well-being of a firm though not, perhaps, the most convenient one. Efficient auditing procedures or raising money regularly on the capital market are cheaper signals, while the decision of preferring a dividend distribution to retained earning reinvestment may also have the negative effect of increasing firm leverage.

If capital markets are well developed, high dividends should be associated with low growth firms with poorer investment perspectives, while if, as in the Italian case, an insufficiently developed capital market reduces the availability of cheaper signal, high dividend policies should be adopted by high growth firms to signal their well-being.

Another divisional criterion of less debatable interpretation is firm age. In this case, the fact that firms of more recent stock market quotation are more sensitive to cash flow should validate the Myers-Mayluf hypothesis that "debt dominates equity by minimizing lemons' problems" (Withed, 1992), and that newer firms are more equity constrained than older ones because of lack of reputation.

A final important divisional criterion is that of analysing the different sensitivity of firms belonging to high-tech sectors. These firms should face more longer-term risky investment projects and need therefore a lower short term-long term indebtedness ratio and a lower debt-equity ratio. In a well developed financial system they should find in closed-end funds and venture capital funds the sources for adequate equity financing, and for reducing their dependence from short term interest payments. A lower sensitivity of their investment to cash flow should then indicate that the financial structure of the country supports innovation in the right way, though the usual control for the "reverse causation"

224

phenomenon must be introduced in the empirical test to avoid low sensitivity as a signal of low performance and not of a better capacity to overcome financing constraints.

In conclusion, the considerations developed in this section suggest that relevant split criteria to test the existence of financial constraints on investments should be the following: firm age, firm size, firm q, firm bankruptcy risk, firm collateral, firm belonging to declining/non declining sectors, firm belonging to high-tech/non high tech sectors.

3. The results of the UK firm sample

For the empirical analysis of the UK, the Fazzari-Hubbard-Petersen (1988) approach is followed. The sample is taken from Datastream and includes 127 firms whose balance sheets have been reported on for 7 years (1986-1992). Firms whose financial constraints may be caused by poor economic performance (a non positive net sales rate of growth) more than from informational asymmetries and firms presenting incomplete balance sheets or evident accounting irregularities have been dropped.

We estimate the sensitivity of investment plans to liquidity as a proxy of financial constraints arising from informational asymmetries on the financial markets, and try to distinguish this rationale from the alternative one of overinvestment. The sample has been divided according to 8 divisional criteria that may help us to test the unbiased differences in cash flow sensitivity in spite of the possible existence of a measurement error in other explanatory variables. Details over the data set including the list of the firms in the panel are presented in the Appendix.

The basic variables used for estimates are: investment over the replacement cost of capital as a dependent variable, Tobin q and cash-flow over the replacement cost of capital as regressors. The replacement cost of capital has been evaluated according to the perpetual inventory method that keeps the book value of capital for a base year and reevaluates adding year by year investment and considering depreciation and inflation.

The Tobin-q has been computed, dividing the market value of shares plus debt minus inventories divided by capital evaluated at its replacement cost.

The 8 divisional criteria adopted are respectively: i) firm size calculated considering the values of capital stock; ii) firm age measured from the first day of quotation in the stock market; iii) the membership of the firm to declining or to growing sectors, where sector performance has been calculated from the stock market sectorial index compared with the total market index for the period 1985-1990; iv) the membership of a firm to high-tech or to non high-tech sectors; v) a proxy for firm bankruptcy risk calculated as a ratio between firm total current liabilities and firm net profits; vi) a proxy for firm capacity to collateralise calculated as a ratio of total gross fixed assets minus asset depreciation to total debt current liabilities; vii) a dividend payout indicator given by the ratio of dividend paid on net profits; viii) the Tobin's q considered as a proxy for investment perspectives.

Descriptive statistics on UK data (Table 6.1) provide a perspective on the total sample giving also the percentage of firms falling in the subgroups created according to the 8 divisional criteria. New firms are 23% of the sample, those belonging to declining sectors are 45%, those belonging to high-tech sectors are 31%, those with poor collateral are 39%, those at higher relative risk of bankruptcy are 30%. About the dividend payout ratio, the Tobin-q and firm size four classes have been created, though econometric estimates will be performed on two subsamples containing the lower or the higher two subclasses.

The table also provides information on the average level and standard deviation of the main relevant accounting variables considered in the analysis. What can be noted about these variables is the relatively small difference between capital per worker and reevaluated capital stock. This can be explained by the fact that the first item is calculated as based on nominal gross capital values, while the second is an approximation of the real value of net capital computed following the perpetual inventory method. The interpretation of the ratio between these two magnitudes is interesting as we can say generally that, if in a subgroup the capital per worker is near or even higher than the reevaluated capital, the renewal of the existing capital stock through investment is particularly urgent for the relevant subgroup.

The correlation matrix (Table 6.2) among all dummy variables provides other important information about subgroup features. The strongest correlation appears to be the positive one between high tech sectors and declining ones confirmed by the analysis of stock exchange sector performances described in Table 6.3 A well characterised "cluster" seems to be the one of new small firms in the highest q class, with a low ratio between assets and liabilities (lowcoll) and between net profits and liabilities (bankr): these firms also tend to have a low dividend payout ratio.

To provide details of the criteria followed for the division of growing and declining sectors, Table 6.6 gives the percentage relative performance of the *Financial Times* sectorial index on FT500 with health and breweries among the best performers and electricals, electronics and constructions among the worst performers.

The technique adopted for econometric estimates is chosen by discriminating between one-way and two-way models and between fixed effect and random effect models. Given the results of the test used to discriminate among the different specifications, the final estimates reported are always two-way estimates where both time and firm dummies are included. This choice avoids some econometric problems given that, if one-way estimates are in the presence of firm specific effects, estimates would be biased (Devereaux-Schiantarelli, 1990).

The additional choice between random effect and fixed effects is less clear cut. Random effects should be generally preferred in cases, such as this one, when average subgroup variable values deviate from total group variable means (Johnston 1991). Moreover, GLS estimation has the advantage of orthogonalising the variance-covariance matrix, removing not only the panel data specific problem of longitudinal error correlation, but also eventual problems of heteroskedasticity and autocorrelation.

While Mundlak (1978) affirms that random effects should always be preferred, Green (1993) reminds us that random effect models assume that individual effects are uncorrelated with regressors and this is often not so.

What is more important, anyhow, is that the estimates obtained are quite robust across the two different specifications and a comparison between fixed effects and random effect coefficients presents very small differences, and always gives the same qualitative results for the significance of the cash-flow coefficient and for its ordering within subgroups.

A synthetic table (Table 6.4) indicates coefficients and significance to allow the reader to compare the results for different estimates (a detailed description of each subgroup estimate is provided in the Appendix). Low values of the Hausman test indicate indifference between fixed and random effect model, while high values of the Hausman test indicate preference for fixed effect model as random effect coefficient and t-test are biased (the maximum difference between the two models estimates is, anyhow, never higher than .04-.05). The test checks for the orthogonality of the random effects and the regressors and when the null hypothesis of orthogonality is rejected OLS is consistent and GLS is not, while under the alternative case OLS and GLS are consistent but OLS is inefficient.

The only problem that may remain is the eventual endogeneity between variables. A problem of endogeneity occurs if good firms are those who generate higher cash flows and also those who have more and better investment projects. In this case higher investment with higher cash flows would not mean financial constraint but would just be a reflexion of a "separating equilibria" between good firms (high level of investment and high level of cash flow) and bad firms (low level of investment and low level of cash flow).

There are two ways to face the problem in literature. Fazzari et al. (1988) and Hoshi et al. (1992) ignore it (given that, concerning the relative coefficient ordering between subsamples, they assume that the bias acts in the same way for

227

the coefficient of the same regressor in different subsamples). Devereaux and Schiantarelli (1989) propose to avoid it, with instrumental variables in first differences, and lagged dependent variables, using as instruments the variable values in levels. We will follow a similar approach using lagged regressors in levels and first differences.

The robustness of results from level estimates with lagged regressors will be checked against estimates in first difference using the Arellano-Bond (1991) GMM approach. The one-step estimates calculated are robust to heteroskedasticity and use the GMM instrumental variable approach. For each subsample the instruments used (lagged levels of the regressors $dcfk_{t-1}$ and dq_{t-1}) are indicated. Tests for first and second order autocorrelation (AR1 and AR2) and tests for the validity of instruments (Sargan) give the expected results. The possibility that the estimates in first differences are sensitive to inclusion of lagged dependent variables as regressors has been considered. The coefficient of dik_{t-1} has proved to be not significant across all subgroups, and the results from this specification have been omitted, given that estimates on other parameters remain unaltered.

A first general result for the five split criteria giving clearer results (firm size, firm age, firm sector performance and firm sector level of technology) is that higher sensitivity to cash flows coincides with lower impact of Tobin's q on investments according to the theoretical idea that financial constraints reduce the possibility of exploiting opportunities of investment profitability. Moreover, the q coefficient is always weakly significant but never significant with the wrong (negative) sign. This indicates financial constraints, but also measurement difficulties met by all previous empirical works and described in previous sections.

If we look at the split by size we may observe that small firm investments are more sensitive to liquidity measures than large firm ones, as shown by cash flow and q coefficients significance and magnitude in the two subsamples. The interpretation is straightforward. Given the existence of capital market imperfections, a large firm financing a project will run a lower risk, as compared with a small firm, and the single project failure will have minor effects on the capacity of paying outstanding debt[5].

Also the results from the subsample divided by firm age, indicating financial constraints for new and not for old firms, seem to confirm the Myers-Majluf version of the informational asymmetry problem. In fact, firms recently quoted on the stock market are expected to suffer from higher cost of external financing because shareholders have less knowledge of their market performance, and their equity issues or dividend policies are more likely to be misinterpreted as "bad signals". But what must be considered in the analysis of these results is the high correlation between new and small firms. The

228

dimensional result could be conditioned by the fact that large firms are highly correlated with old ones. What has been done then is an estimate for firm age within firm size. Even when this estimate is performed and only the subset of small firms is considered, old small firms remain less sensitive to cash flow than new small ones.

In a "thick market" model the capacity of reducing informational asymmetries on the stock market is a fundamental resource. Firms in declining sectors are revealed to be more sensitive than firms in the growing sector and this is also consistent with the imperfect information theoretical hypotheses and with the fact that membership of a declining sector is a bad signal for equity investors. The fact is confirmed if the estimate of the model in levels is repeated given firm size and if the model is estimated in first differences with the GMM-instrumental variable procedure.

Another interesting result is that firms' investments in high-tech sectors seem almost insensitive to liquidity, contrary to what happens in low-tech sectors. The result is valid in both the level and the difference specifications and appears independent of firm size given that high-tech firms are almost equally distributed among dimensional classes. This result seems to confirm that the UK structure of the "technological district" and its "thick market" feature sensibly reduce informational asymmetries for high-tech firms (Cary, 1989; Gladstone, 1988).

A split that does not yield clear-cut results is the dividend payout one (Tabs. A6.11.1 and A6.11.2). The difference between liquidity coefficients in the estimated levels is quite small as in first difference coefficients and the dividend payout ratio has very small variation across firm subgroups. Our interpretation is that, for quoted firms in a context of imperfect information, changes in dividend payments are not a "cheap" signal. A firm which is more rationed might have, in principle, an interest in retaining dividends to increase internal finance because it has a positive cost differential between external and internal finance. But, in reality, the reduction of dividend payments is a very bad signal for the market and its costs (reduction in firm market value) may increase the cost of external finance.

On the other hand, firms who are less rationed if they have good investment perspectives, should increase dividend payments to signal this to the market, but, according to what Easterbrook stated (1986) in his survey, dividends are an inefficient signal because firms may send information to the market in a less expensive way. For these two reasons neither the firms who are more rationed nor those who are less rationed have an incentive to divert from a fixed common dividend policy when the market provides them with more efficient signals.

The same problems seem to arise for the interpretation of the q-split where there is no clear difference between the two subgroups. Here problems in q-estimation may substantially affect the relevance of the results obtained.

Clearer indications come from the bankruptcy risk split and from the collateral availability split. Firms with a relatively high bankruptcy risk and lower capacity to collateralise are more credit constrained, given that ratios between assets and liabilities and between liquidity and liabilities are signals clearly interpretable by investors. These results hold even for a given firm dimension but the relative estimates are omitted.

In conclusion, a synthetic consideration of the situation of the UK firms is the following: the English institutional relationship between investors and financiers with dispersed ownership and higher relative external financing from non bank intermediaries seems to limit credit constraint problems, above all for firms that are less sensitive to informational asymmetries on the stock marke; these are large firms which may send good signals to shareholders like an established stock market reputation, a good financial situation and the belonging to a growing sector. When these firms are in need of some form of financing they may easily go public because, due to their good reputation, the cost differential of equity financing with respect to self-financing is highly reduced.

Unlike Japan, the presence of several financial intermediaries determines a quite dispersed distribution of agency costs across firms. Informational asymmetries seem to persist anyway for firms that are smaller, have less collateral, more bankruptcy risk and belong to low-tech sectors or declining sectors.

4. The results from the Japanese firm sample

The Japanese sample includes 157 firms with a positive growth rate of net sales throughout the 1986-1992 period, nonzero investments and complete balance sheet for the same period (see Appendix).

Some methodological problems occur when estimating the Japanese sample because of different accounting procedures in the UK and Japan. Japanese firms appear more indebted than UK firms. This is because, due to differences in accounting conventions, land and securities in Japan are registered in the balance at their original value and assets of associated companies are not consolidated. Moreover, intercountry differences in leverage may sensibly vary reflecting the effect of bearish or bullish stock exchange behaviour (Hodder-Tschoegl, 1993).

Another problem is that many items (and mainly all those related to technology measures) are not available and a different proxy for liquidity has to be found. Therefore, among many others, it is not correct to make direct comparisons of coefficient magnitudes across countries, while some comparative insights may be provided confronting intracountry subgroup estimates when homogeneous split criteria are adopted.

Lack of detail on the available data, here, allows us to create only four divisional criteria: firm size, belonging to declining/non declining sector, belonging to high-tech/non high-tech sector, low/high q ratio.

The two most interesting results from Japanese analysis (Tables 6.5-6.7) (a detailed description of each subgroup estimate is provided in the Appendix) are: i) the sensitivity of investment to cash flow is quite invariant across firm subgroups contrary to the results obtained in the UK case; ii) the only significant difference is the one between large and small firms with fixed effect estimates with larger firms that appear more sensitive than smaller ones.

The plausible interpretations for these two results are that the extensive cross-holdings of shares between firms and between firm and banks reduces inequalities in the access to credit among firms that differ in size, investment perspective, capital intensity and belong to growing or declining groups. The small dimensional inequality seems to suggest that there could be a situation of overinvestment even in Japanese firms, given that the group of larger ones seems also, from the correlation matrix reported, to be generally in a more favourable position, having high q and being part of growing high-tech sectors.

Given that the dimensional effect is quite weak the most interesting hypothesis drawn from the results is the one that intragroup participation may reduce firm inequalities in access to credit.

A further result is that the "vertical and horizontal integration", determined by equity participation between banks and firms belonging to the same group, seems to sensibly reduce financial constraints. This could be explained by the fact that banks are part of all important Japanese "keiretsu", greatly reducing external financing costs for all firms being part of the group.

5. Conclusions

The analysis of the econometric results obtained, together with the knowledge of the institutional systems and the hypotheses supported in the theoretical model, allow us to formulate some tentative conclusions on the comparative efficiency of the different "national models" of finance, investment and innovation.

In "thick markets" where financial markets are well developed and several different types of financial intermediaries exist, but information is nonetheless imperfect and costly, the empirical relation between investment and liquidity shows, both from estimates in levels and in differences, that large and high-tech firms benefit more from the advantages of the systems reducing their cash constraint problems. The groups that are more penalised from imperfect information and financial constraints are those of small and new firms, firms belonging to declining sectors and low-tech sectors, firms that have a higher bankruptcy risk and less capacity to provide collateral. This hypothesis seems to be confirmed by the results on UK firms' data.

In "horizontally integrated markets", like the Japanese one, the share participation of banks and real investors seems to reduce the agency costs imbalance across groups of firms divided in terms of size and different measures of financial wealth. The cost differential between internal and external financing appears to be quite small and seems to be reduced. This might be explained by the fact that the "preference link" between firms and banks in Japan includes a closer relationship with some advantages such as extensive formal and informal monitoring of banks on firm activities and presence of bank personnel among firm key executives.

These empirical results seem to provide the following implications: i) the increase in the quantity and in the quality of financial intermediaries may reduce informational asymmetries for those groups of firms that benefit from the information provided to investors by the stock market; ii) "horizontal" (firm-firm cross holdings) and "vertical" (bank-firm cross-holdings) integration may equate agency costs across firms reducing the costs of external financing. This last empirical finding is consistent with the assumption of the "short-termist" hypothesis saying that "greater information asymmetries with respect to long-term business performance induce US stock market participants to attach greater importance to current-term results than their foreign counterparts" (Aaker-Jacobson, 1993).

All these findings should be the basis for further analysis trying to establish a higher level of consistency between empirical evidence, theoretical assumptions and institutional features of finance and innovation national systems.

Table 6.1 Statistics on the overall UK sample

Item	Mean Value (% of the group on the overall sample for subgroup dummies)	Standard Deviation	Item	Mean Value (% of the group on the total sample for subgroup dummies)
Market value	3,476,340	23,009,000	DIVC1	.11
Net revenues	847,430	2,119,800	DIVC2	.34
IK	.074	.137	DIVC3	.37
CFK	.213	.247	DIVC4	.14
Debt margin	.691	.547	QC1	.18
Total assets	495,110	1,191,000	QC2	.28
Dividends paid over revenues	.156	.073	QC3	.25
Capital per worker	166,230	1,227,200	QC4	.28
Rivaluated capital stock	674,380	1,927,300	DECLINE	.45
DIMC1	.290		NEW	.23
DIMC2	.300		BANKR	.30
DIMC3	.230		TECH	.31
DIMC4	.160		LOWCOLL	.39

Variable legend for subgroup dummies:

BANKR = firms with higher bankruptcy risk (measured as a ratio between total liabilities and net sales)

NOCOLL = firms with lower capacity to provide collateral (measured as a ratio between assets and liabilities)

NEW = firms with more recent first market listing (less than 14 years)

TECH = firms belonging to high-tech sectors

DECLINE = firms belonging to declining sectors

QC1..QC4 = firms ranked according to their q-Tobin value (QC1 indicates the group with lowest q-Tobin value)

DIMC1...DIMC4 = firms ranked according to their size (DIMC1 shows the smallest size group)

DIVC1...DIVC4 = firms ranked according to the dividend/revenue ratio (DIVC1 shows the lowest ratio group)

Note: for the subgroup classes indicated in the legend only the mean value is provided and it shows the percentage of the class considered on the overall group.

Table 6.2 Correlation matrix among UK firm subgroups

	New	Lowcol	Decline	Tech	DimC1	DimC2	DimC3	DimC4
New	1.00							
Lowcoll	0.03	1.00						
Decline	-0.10	-.00	1.00					
Tech	-.02	.09	.33	1.00				
DimC1	.25	-.05	.07	.09	1.00			
DimC2	.07	-.07	.17	-.05	--	1.00		
DimC3	-.17	.16	-.17	.10	--	--	1.00	
DimC4	-.19	-.04	-.11	-.16	--	--	--	1.00
QC1	.02	-.24	-.06	-.18	.01	.04	-.02	-.04
QC2	-.18	-.09	.02	-.01	.02	-.00	-.06	.05
QC3	-.10	-.08	-.02	.11	-.05	.01	.02	.03
QC4	.26	.38	.05	.06	.01	-.04	.06	-.04
BANKR	.19	.31	.11	.06	-.01	.11	-.008	-.11
DIVC1	.04	-.06	.13	-.02	-.06	.09	-.02	-.02
DIVC2	.14	-.01	-.13	-.10	.08	.02	-.01	-.10
DIVC3	-.16	-.03	.00	.10	-.03	-.09	.06	.09
DIVC4	-.13	.16	.03	-.03	-.30	.07	-.06	.06

Table 6.2 (con't) Correlation matrix among UK firm subgroups

	QC1	QC2	QC3	QC4	BanKR	DIVC1	DIVC2	DIVC3	DIVC4
QC1	1.00								
QC2	--	1.00							
QC3	--	--	1.00						
QC4	--	--	--	1.00					
BanKR	.04	-.08	-.22	.26	1.00				
DIVC1	.09	-.05	-.03	.00	.14	1.00			
DIVC2	-.08	.56	-.00	.02	-.09	--	1.00		
DIVC3	-.07	-.06	.10	.01	-.03	--	--	1.00	
DIVC4	.10	-.01	-.07	-.01	.02	--	--	--	1.00

Table 6.3 Relative sectorial stock exchange performance (sectorial FT-index percentage relative performance with respect to FT500 - 1985-90)

Sectorial index	Relative performance on FT500 (%)	Sectorial index	Relative performance on FT500 (%)
Building materials	+ 2.68	Paper	+ 10.73
Construction	- 41.21	Newspaper printing	- 34.28
Electricals	- 31.37	Health	+ 30.09
Electronics	- 40.66	Chemicals	- 24.62
Mechanical engineering	- 15.99	Store	- 2.11
Motors	+ 13.24	Textiles	- 6.58
Breweries	+ 33.83	Electric machines	- 0.55
Leisure goods	- 19.42	Oil	- 5.60
Food	+ 4.97	Transport	+ 24.05

Table 6.4 Synthesis of the econometric results on the UK sample

Subgroup division	Cash flow coefficient			Tobin's q coefficient			(Random vs. fixed)
	Random Effects	Fixed Effects	GMM	Random Effects	Fixed Effects	GMM	
Large	.04*	.04*	.0006**	.0009***	.001***	-.04*	4.03
Small	.19***	.17***	.15***	.001**	.0006*	-.002*	12.71
New	.21***	.18***	.16***	.001*	-.0005*	-.003***	24.05
Old	.12***	.12***	-.18*	.001***	.002***	.001*	9.28
Declin.	.19***	.18***	.16***	-.001*	-.0002*	-.003***	14.07
Not decl.	.15***	.13***	-.09*	.001***	.002***	.001**	9.64
High tech	.02*	.05*	-.09*	.002***	.002***	.0005**	2.59
Low tech	.20***	.18***	.15***	.007**	.006**	.0003*	10.34
High q	.20***	.17***	.14**	.001*	.001**	.002**	12.59
Low q	.17***	.17***	.13**	.008**	.006**	.007**	1.75
High coll.	.13**	.13**	.13***	.0001*	.0003*	.001*	.30
Low coll.	.17***	.16***	.02*	.002***	.002**	.003***	7.00
High BR	.18***	.17***	.15***	.002***	.0005*	-.002*	13.47
Low BR	.15***	.16***	.02	.0009***	.001***	.0003**	4.39
High div.	.16***	.16***	.09***	.0003*	.0004*	.0006**	.37
Low div.	.18***	.17***	.13***	.002***	.001**	-.001*	11.10

Legend:
*** coefficient significantly different from zero at 99%
**coefficient significantly different from zero at 91%
* coefficient not significantly different from zero
Instruments used for the GMM analysis: cf/k$_{t-i}$, cf/k$_{t-2}$, q$_{t-1}$, q$_{t-2}$

Small firms: firms whose market value is lower than 1,000,000 pounds in 1986 (75 firms);
Large Firms: firms whose market value is higher than 1,000,000 pounds in 1986 (52 firms);
Old firms: firms whose first market quotation is before 1-1-1980 (98 firms); *New firms*: firms

whose first market quotation is after 1-1-1980 (29 firms); *Declining sectors*: average negative relative performance of the sectorial index over stock market index (57 firms); *Non declining sectors*: average positive relative performance of the sectorial index over stock market index (70 firms); *Low bankruptcy risk firms*: those with total current liabilities/net sales higher than 4 (89 firms); *High bankruptcy risk firms*: those with total current liabilities/net sales lower than 4 (38 firms); *High-tech sectors*: Electronics, Mechanical Engineering, Chemicals, Pharmaceuticals, Oil Extraction (39 firms); *Low-tech sectors*: all the other sectors (88 firms); *High q*: firms with market value/revaluated capital stock higher than 2 (58 firms); *Low q*: firms with market value over revaluated capital stock lower than 2 (69 firms); *Low collateral firms*: those with total current liabilities/total assets > .70 (50 firms); *High collateral firms*: those with total current liabilities/total assets < .70 (77 firms); *Low dividend payout ratio*: firms with a ratio of dividend paid/revenues lower than .152 (57 firms); *High dividend payout ratio*: firms with a ratio of dividend paid/revenues higher than .152 (70 firms).

Table 6.5 Statistics on the overall Japanese sample

Item	Mean (% of the group on the overall sample for subgroup dummies)	Standard deviation
IK	.26	.69
CASH	46,464,000	85,653,000
Capital stock	75,007,000	173,480,000
Investments	10,315,000	26,496,000
Total liabilities*	88,586,000	22,1980,000
Total sales	183,220,000	362,940,000
MVK	5.25	7.53
TECH	.36	.48
DECLINE	.18	.38
QC1	.26	.44
QC2	.27	.44
QC3	.24	.42
QC4	.23	.42
DIMC1	.13	.34
DIMC2	.32	.47
DIMC3	.33	.47
DIMC4	.20	.40

Variable Legend for dummy variables:
TECH: high-tech firms
DECLINE: firms belonging to low performing sectors
QC1..QC4:firms ranked according to their q-Tobin value (QC1 indicates the group with lowest q-Tobin value)
DIMC1...DIMC4: firms ranked according to their size (DIMC1 indicates the smallest size group)

Table 6.6 Correlation matrix for the overall sample

	TECH	DECL	DIM C1	DIM C2	DIM C3	DIM C4	QC1	QC2	QC3	QC4
TECH	1.00									
DECLINE	.08	1.00								
DIMC1	.09	.10	1.00							
DIMC2	.07	.05	--	1.00						
DIMC3	-.08	-.09	--	--	1.00					
DIMC4	-.05	-.04	--	--	--	1.00				
QC1	.03	.01	.06	.08	-.20	.09	1.00			
QC2	-.01	.15	.06	-.11	.00	.08	--	1.00		
QC3	.01	.05	.08	.-03	.08	-.13	--	--	1.00	
QC4	-.04	-.18	-.21	.07	.12	-.05	--	--	--	1.00

Table 6.7 Econometric results on Japanese sample

	Cash flow coefficient			Tobin's q coefficient			Hausman test
Subgroup division	Random Effects	Fixed Effects	GMM	Random Effects	Fixed Effects	GMM	(Random vs. fixed)
Large	.06***	.06***	.009*	-.01**	-.03**	-.02*	46.46
Small	.06***	.05***	.01*	-.003**	.002*	-.006*	29.57
Declin.	.02**	.005*	-.008*	.02**	.03**	-.03*	3.25
Not decl.	.06***	.06***	.01*	-.009**	-.02**	-.03*	66.16
High tech	.10***	.07***	.017**	.002***	.02**	.05**	15.71
Low tech	.03***	.06***	-.003*	.03***	.01***	-.04*	69.88
High q	.05***	.06***	.06**	-.009*	-.003**	.006*	49.44
Low q	.08***	.07***	.03*	.02**	.01**	.003*	2.81

Legend:
*** coefficient significantly different from zero at 99%
**coefficient significantly different from zero at 91%
* coefficient not significantly different from zero
Instruments used for the GMM analysis: cf/k_{t-1}, cf/k_{t-2}, q_{t-1}, q_{t-2}

Large firms: firms whose total fixed assets in 1986 are higher than 10,000,000 Yen
Small firms: firms whose total fixed assets in 1986 are lower than 10,000,000 Yen
Declining sectors: average negative relative performance of the sectorial index over stock market index (29 firms)
Non declining sectors: average positive relative performance of the sectorial index over stock market index (127 firms)
High-tech sectors: Electronics, Mechanical Engineering, Chemicals, Pharmaceuticals, Oil Extraction (57 Firms)
Low-Tech sectors: all the other sectors (99 firms)
High q: firms whose market value/revaluated capital stock is higher than 2 (69 firms)
Low q: firms whose market value/revaluated capital stock is lower than 2 (87 firms)

Appendix

127 selected UK firms

Selection criteria:

From an original group of 500 quoted firms with positive net sales rates of growth for each year in the sample period (1986-1992), 127 firms were selected having available balance sheets and nonzero investments for each year.

Firms included in the sample

Laser Scan Hdg, Guinness, Marston Thompson, Whitbread, Wolverhampton & Dudley, Highland Distilleries, T & N, Blue Circle Industries, RMC Group, BPB Industries, Morgan Crucible, Laporte, BTR, Glaxo Holdings, London International, Smith Nephew, Molins, Thorn EMI, Perkins Food, Home Counties Newspapers, Stanley Leisure Org., Weir Group, Adwest, T I Group, Bibby, Unilever, Tesco, Assd. British Food, United Biscuits, Security Services, Dixons, Photo Me, Rank Organisation, Smiths Industries, Premier Cons. Oil, Booker, Charter Consolidated, Dalgety, James Finley, Inchape, Bowater, Boots, Great Universal Stores, Lasmo, Allied Textile Cos., W.H.Smith Group, Courts, Scapa Group, Manchester Ship Canal, De La Rue, Ocean Group Plc, Haynes Publishing, Cable & Wireless, Watts, Blake, Bearne & Co., Morland, TT Group, Hanson, Scottish T.V., British Vita, R.E.A. Holdings, EIS Group, Ports. Sund. Nwsp., Wolstenholme Rink, Jones Stroud, Anglia T.V., J.W. Spear, Ellis & Everard, Control Techniques, Nurdin & Peacock, Coats Viyella, Sema Group, Hardys & Hansons, Verson International, Heywood Williams Grp, Ulster Television, Burtonwood Brewery, Attwoods, Beales Hunter, Brent Chemicals, EMAP, Ladbroke Group, Leslie Wise Group, Leeds Group, Rotork, Corp. Svs. Gp., Tomkins, Wace Group, Owners Group, Mai, Jarvis Plc, Lambert Howarth, Castings, Chemring, T.Cowie, Davenport Knitwear, Leigh Interests, N.Brown Group, Holt Joseph, Ross Group, Burdene Invs., British Airways, Aegis Group, Bulmer H.P., Sainsbury J., Mcleod Russel, Wellcome, Bespak, Clyde Petroleum, Sidney C. Banks, Christian Salvesen, Reuters Holdings, B A A, Asprey, British Borneo, Trafalgar House, Wembley LPC, Cape, Glesson MJ, AAH Holdings, Clayhithe, Pentos, Badar GB, WM Morrison Supermarket, BettBros, Spirax.

Table A6.1.1 Econometric results - overall UK sample - 998 observations

Variable	Coefficient	T-test	Variable	Coefficient	T-test
Random effects			**Fixed effects**		
CF/K_{t-1}	.26	15.24	CF/K_{t-1}	.26	14.63
Q_{t-1}	-.0006	-2.67	Q_{t-1}	-.008	-3.56
const.	.02	1.75	const.	.002	4.49
R^2 (fixed eff.)	--		.57		
L (1)	--		647.88		
L (2)	--		562.08		
L (3)	--		749.80		
L (4)	--		758.27		
LM(2w vs 1w)	317.13 (.00)				
Hausman (Fx. vs Rn.)	15.48 (.00)				

Legend:
(1) = Firm effects only; (2) = X-variables only; (3) = X-variables and firm effects; (4) = X-variables, time and firm effects; 2w = Two-way model; 1w = One way model; Fx. = Fixed effect model; Rn. = Random effect model; L = Log likelihood; LM = Lagrange Multiplier

Table A6.1.2 Econometric results - overall UK sample

Variable	Coefficient	T-test	Variable	Coefficient	T-test
One step est.			**Two-step est.**		
$d(cf/k)_{t-1}$	.14	4.14	$d(cf/k)_{t-1}$	.14	27.53
dq_{t-1}	-.0008	-.73	dq_{t-1}	-.0009	-3.83
const	-.01	-1.41	const	-.01	-2.05
AR(1)	-.88 (.37)		AR(1)	-1.50 (.13)	
AR(2)	-2.31 (.02)		AR(2)	-1.60 (.10)	
Sargan	80.34		Sargan	16.44	
Instruments	cf/k_{t-1}, cf/k_{t-2}, q_{t-1}, q_{t-2}		Instruments	cf/k_{t-1}, cf/k_{t-2}, q_{t-1}, q_{t-2}	

(time dummy coefficients are omitted)

Table A6.2.1 Split by size - econometric results

Variable	Coefficient	T-test	Variable	Coefficient	T-test
Large firms	rnd. e. (fix. e.)		**Small firms**	rnd. e. (fix. e.)	
CF/K_{t-1}	.04 (.04)	.90 (.81)	CF/K_{t-1}	.19 (.17)	10.95 (10.10)
Q_{t-1}	.001 (.001)	3.33 (3.87)	Q_{t-1}	.001 (.0006)	2.07 (1.04)
const.	.05 (.05)	3.18 (4.65)	const.	.02 (.03)	1.75 (6.04)
R^2	-- (.83)		R^2	-- (.84)	
L (1)	529.29		L (1)	534.34	
L (2)	275.77		L (2)	323.62	
L (3)	540.77		L (3)	598.92	
L (4)	542.83		L (4)	610.57	
LM(2w vs 1w)	457.93 (.00)		LM(2w vs 1w)	444.18 (.00)	
Hausman (Fx. vs Rn.)	4.03 (.13)		Hausman (Fx. vs Rn.)	12.71 (.00)	

Legend:
(1) = Firm effects only; (2) = X-variables only; (3) = X-variables and firm effects; (4) = X-variables, time and firm effects; 2w = Two-way model; 1w = One way model; Fx. = Fixed effect model; Rn. = Random effect model; L = Log likelihood; LM = Lagrange Multiplier

Table A6.2.2 Split by size -econometric results

Variable	Coefficient	T-test	Variable	Coefficient	T-test
Large firms	1-step		**Small firms**	1-step	
$d(cf/k)_{t-1}$	-.04	-.34	$d(cf/k)_{t-1}$	.15	8.15
dq_{t-1}	.0006	2.52	dq_{t-1}	-.002	-1.81
const	.0009	.07	const	-.01	-1.18
AR(1)	-1.71 (.087)		AR(1)	-1.46	
AR(2)	-.53 (.59)		AR(2)	-1.20	
Sargan	14.94		Sargan	16.44	
Instruments	cf/k_{t-1}, cf/k_{t-2}, q_{t-1}, q_{t-2}		Instruments	cf/k_{t-1}, cf/k_{t-2}, q_{t-1}, q_{t-2}	

(Time dummy regressor coefficients are omitted)

Table A6.3.1 Split by age - econometric results

Variable	Coefficient	T-test	Variable	Coefficient	T-test
New firms	rnd. e. (fix. e.)		**Old firms**	rnd. e. (fix. e.)	
CF/K_{t-1}	.21 (.18)	10.34 (8.48)	CF/K_{t-1}	.12 (.12)	3.42 (3.61)
Q_{t-1}	.001 (-.0005)	1.79 (-0.71)	Q_{t-1}	.001 (.002)	5.82 (5.00)
const.	.01 (.04)	.83 (3.78)	const.	.03 (.03)	4.18 (2.65)
R^2	-- (.87)		R^2	-- (.82)	
L (1)	166.92		L (1)	903.43	
L (2)	121.93		L (2)	463.14	
L (3)	206.24		L (3)	940.11	
L (4)	210.96		L (4)	954.00	
LM(2w vs 1w)	80.64 (.00)		LM(2w vs 1w)	808.21 (.00)	
Hausman (Fx. vs Rn.)	24.05 (.00)		Hausman (Fx. vs Rn.)	9.28 (.00)	

Legend:
(1) = Firm effects only; (2) = X-variables only; (3) = X-variables and firm effects; (4) = X-variables, time and firm effects; 2w = Two-way model; 1w = One way model; Fx. = Fixed effect model; Rn. = Random effect model; L = Log likelihood; LM = Lagrange Multiplier

Table A6.3.2 Split by age - econometric results

Variable	Coefficient	T-test	Variable	Coefficient	T-test
New firms	1-step		**Old firms**	1-step	
$d(cf/k)_{t-1}$	.16	29.95	$d(cf/k)_{t-1}$	-.18	-.98
dq_{t-1}	-.003	-8.19	dq_{t-1}	.001	1.29
const	.01	.76	const	.0004	1.24
AR(1)	-1.74 (.08)		AR(1)	-.047 (.96)	
AR(2)	-1.14 (.25)		AR(2)	-.36 (.71)	
Sargan	21.08		Sargan	32.68	
Instruments	cf/k_{t-1}, cf/k_{t-2}, q_{t-1}, q_{t-2}		Instruments	cf/k_{t-1}, cf/k_{t-2}, q_{t-1}, q_{t-2}	

Table A6.4.1 Split by sector performance - econometric results

Variable	Coefficient	T-test	Variable	Coefficient	T-test
Declining sector firms	rnd. e. (fix.e.)		**Growing sector firms**	rnd. e. (fix. e.)	
CF/K$_{t-1}$	.19 (.18)	11.25 (10.69)	CF/K$_{t-1}$	.15 (.13)	3.99 (3.18)
Q$_{t-1}$	-.001 (-.0002)	-.39 (-1.73)	Q$_{t-1}$	.001 (.002)	5.07 (5.77)
const.	.04 (.05)	2.30 (8.50)	const.	.02 (.02)	1.29 (1.88)
R^2	-- (.87)		R^2	-- (.78)	
L (1)	414.56		L (1)	618.86	
L (2)	216.61		L (2)	372.08	
L (3)	474.41		L (3)	649.80	
L (4)	487.07		L (4)	652.32	
LM(2w vs 1w)	419.77 (.00)		LM(2w vs 1w)	431.20 (.00)	
Hausman (Fx. vs Rn.)	14.07 (.00)		Hausman (Fx. vs Rn.)	9.64 (.00)	

Legend:
(1) = Firm effects only; (2) = X-variables only; (3) = X-variables and firm effects; (4) = X-variables, time and firm effects; 2w = Two-way model; 1w = One way model; Fx. = Fixed effect model; Rn. = Random effect model; L = Log likelihood; LM = Lagrange Multiplier

Table A6.4.2 Split by sector performance-econometric results

Variable	Coefficient	T-test	Variable	Coefficient	T-test
Declining sector firms	1-step		**Growing sector firms**	1-step	
$d(cf/k)_{t-1}$	.16	28.44	$d(cf/k)_{t-1}$	-.09	-1.34
dq_{t-1}	-.003	-6.89	dq_{t-1}	.001	1.84
const	-.01	-1.62	const	.004	.40
AR(1)	-1.48 (.13)		AR(1)	-.62 (.53)	
AR(2)	-1.63 (.10)		AR(2)	1.00 (.31)	
Sargan	16.28		Sargan	13.65	
Instruments	cf/k_{t-1}, cf/k_{t-2}, q_{t-1}, q_{t-2}		Instruments	cf/k_{t-1}, cf/k_{t-2}, q_{t-1}, q_{t-2}	

Table A6.5.1 High-tech/low-tech split - econometric results

Variable	Coefficient	T-test	Variable	Coefficient	T-test
High-tech sector firms	rnd.e. (fix.e.)		**Low-tech sector firms**	rnd.e. (fix.e.)	
CF/K_{t-1}	.02 (.05)	.78 (1.32)	CF/K_{t-1}	.20 (.18)	12.00 (10.51)
Q_{t-1}	.002 (.002)	5.32 (4.96)	Q_{t-1}	.007 (.006)	2.05 (1.46)
const.	.02 (.02)	1.91 (2.31)	const.	.04 (.04)	2.78 (8.01)
R^2	-- (.78)		R^2	-- (.84)	
L (1)	426.66		L (1)	632.99	
L (2)	283.34		L (2)	345.58	
L (3)	448.67		L (3)	702.49	
L (4)	459.02		L (4)	709.28	
LM(2w vs 1w)	278.03 (.00)		LM(2w vs 1w)	569.45 (.00)	
Hausman (Fx. vs Rn.)	2.59 (.27)		Hausman (Fx. vs Rn.)	10.34 (.00)	

Legend:
(1) = Firm effects only; (2) = X-variables only; (3) = X-variables and firm effects; (4) = X-variables, time and firm effects; 2w = Two-way model; 1w = One way model; Fx. = Fixed effect model; Rn. = Random effect model; L = Log likelihood; LM = Lagrange Multiplier

Table A6.5.2 - High-tech\low-tech split - econometric results

Variable	Coefficient	T-test	Variable	Coefficient	T-test
High-tech sector firms	1-step		**Low-tech sector firms**	1-step	
$d(cf/k)_{t-1}$	-.09	-.63	$d(cf/k)_{t-1}$	.15	(3.56)
dq_{t-1}	.0005	.70	dq_{t-1}	.0003	(1.01)
const	-.009	-1.08	const	.004	(1.20)
AR(1)	-1.18 (.23)		AR(1)	-1.03 (.59)	
AR(2)	-1.82 (.06)		AR(2)	-1.14 (.29)	
Sargan	24.42		Sargan	27.85	
Instruments	cf/k_{t-1}, cf/k_{t-2}, q_{t-1}, q_{t-2}		Instruments	cf/k_{t-1}, cf/k_{t-2}, q_{t-1}, q_{t-2}	

Table A6.6.1 Dividend payout split - econometric results

Variable	Coefficient	T-test	Variable	Coefficient	T-test
High dividends firms	rnd.e. (fix.e.)		**Low dividend firms**	rnd.e. (fix.e.)	
CF/K_{t-1}	.16 (.16)	3.81 (3.44)	CF/K_{t-1}	.18 (.17)	11.02 (9.09)
Q_{t-1}	.0003 (.0004)	.76 (.93)	Q_{t-1}	.002 (.001)	5.06 (2.93)
const.	.04 (.047)	2.43 (4.36)	const.	.01 (.01)	.88 (3.22)
R^2	-- (.86)		R^2	-- (.82)	
L (1)	545.48		L (1)	492.59	
L (2)	226.88		L (2)	374.78	
L (3)	556.50		L (3)	559.41	
L (4)	565.73		L (4)	564.88	
LM(2w vs 1w)	579.65 (.00)		LM(2w vs 1w)	253.42 (.00)	
Hausman (Fx. vs Rn.)	.37 (.82)		Hausman (Fx. vs Rn.)	11.10 (.003)	

Legend:
(1) = Firm effects only; (2) = X-variables only; (3) = X-variables and firm effects; (4) = X-variables, time and firm effects; 2w = Two-way model; 1w = One way model; Fx. = Fixed effect model; Rn. = Random effect model; L = Log likelihood; LM = Lagrange Multiplier

Table A6.6.2 Dividend payout split - econometric results

Variable	Coefficient	T-test	Variable	Coefficient	T-test
High-dividend firms	1-step		**Low dividend firms**	1-step	
d(cf/k)$_{t-1}$	.09	1.44	d(cf/k)$_{t-1}$	.13	3.83
dq$_{t-1}$	.0006	2.82	dq$_{t-1}$	-.001	-1.01
const	-.001	-.13	const	-.01	-1.92
AR(1)	-1.22 (.22)		AR(1)	-1.64 (.09)	
AR(2)	-1.33 (.18)		AR(2)	-1.03 (.30)	
Sargan	15.25		Sargan	17.58	
Instruments	cf/k$_{t-1}$, cf/k$_{t-2}$, q$_{t-1}$, q$_{t-2}$		Instruments	cf/k$_{t-1}$, cf/k$_{t-2}$, q$_{t-1}$, q$_{t-2}$	

Table A6.7.1 Investment perspective performance split - econometric results

Variable	Coefficient	T-test	Variable	Coefficient	T-test
Firms with low q	rnd.e. (fix.e.)		**Firms with high q**	rnd.e. (fix.e.)	
CF/K_{t-1}	.17 (.17)	3.88 (3.74)	CF/K_{t-1}	.20 (.17)	11.16 (8.83)
Q_{t-1}	.008 (.006)	2.72 (2.02)	Q_{t-1}	.001 (.001)	3.31 (2.23)
const.	.02 (.03)	1.57 (3.12)	const.	.01 (.02)	1.01 (2.70)
R^2	-- (.90)		R^2	-- (.81)	
L (1)	686.02		L (1)	442.93	
L (2)	296.98		L (2)	277.09	
L (3)	703.43		L (3)	497.45	
L (4)	710.43		L (4)	503.21	
LM(2w vs 1w)	677.61 (.00)		LM(2w vs 1w)	302.23 (.00)	
Hausman (Fx. vs Rn.)	1.75 (.41)		Hausman (Fx. vs Rn.)	12.59 (.001)	

Legend:
(1) = Firm effects only; (2) = X-variables only; (3) = X-variables and firm effects; (4) = X-variables, time and firm effects; 2w = Two-way model; 1w = One way model; Fx. = Fixed effect model; Rn. = Random effect model; L = Log likelihood; LM = Lagrange Multiplier

Table A6.7.2 - Investment perspective performance split - econometric results

Variable	Coefficient	T-test	Variable	Coefficient	T-test
High-q firms	1-step		**Low-q firms**	1-step	
$d(cf/k)_{t-1}$	.14	2.44	$d(cf/k)_{t-1}$	.13	2.83
dq_{t-1}	.002	2.22	dq_{t-1}	.007	-2.31
const	-.004	-.23	const	-.005	-1.92
AR(1)	-1.46 (.15)		AR(1)	-1.60 (.09)	
AR(2)	-1.33 (.11)		AR(2)	-1.09 (.27)	
Sargan	25.43		Sargan	18.72	
Instruments	cf/k_{t-1}, cf/k_{t-2}, q_{t-1}, q_{t-2}		Instruments	cf/k_{t-1}, cf/k_{t-2}, q_{t-1}, q_{t-2}	

Table A6.8.1 Bankruptcy risk split - econometric results

Variable	Coefficient	T-test	Variable	Coefficient	T-test
Low risk firms	rnd.e. (fix.e.)		**High risk firms**	rnd.e. (fix.e.)	
CF/K_{t-1}	.15 (.16)	4.43 (4.52)	CF/K_{t-1}	.18 (.17)	8.37 (7.34)
Q_{t-1}	.0009 (.001)	3.38 (3.94)	Q_{t-1}	.002 (.0005)	3.46 (.66)
const.	.03 (.02)	2.03 (3.07)	const.	.03 (.04)	1.69 (4.65)
R^2	-- (.86)		R^2	-- (.82)	
L (1)	923.79		L (1)	212.91	
L (2)	450.65		L (2)	144.57	
L (3)	948.07		L (3)	248.07	
L (4)	958.14		L (4)	253.66	
LM(2w vs 1w)	857.88 (.00)		LM(2w vs 1w)	133.75 (.00)	
Hausman (Fx. vs Rn.)	4.39 (.11)		Hausman (Fx. vs Rn.)	13.47 (.00)	

Legend:
(1) = Firm effects only; (2) = X-variables only; (3) = X-variables and firm effects; (4) = X-variables, time and firm effects; 2w = Two-way model; 1w = One way model; Fx. = Fixed effect model; Rn. = Random effect model; L = Log likelihood; LM = Lagrange Multiplier

Table A6.8.2 Bankruptcy risk split - econometric results

Variable	Coefficient	T-test	Variable	Coefficient	T-test
Low risk firms	1-step		**High risk firms**	1-step	
$d(cf/k)_{t-1}$	.02	.21	$d(cf/k)_{t-1}$	.15	7.25
dq_{t-1}	.0003	1.40	dq_{t-1}	-.002	-.190
const	-.001	-.20	const	-.02	-1.30
AR(1)	-.67 (.10)		AR(1)	-1.63 (.50)	
AR(2)	-1.59 (.28)		AR(2)	-1.06 (.11)	
Sargan	19.14		Sargan	19.54	
Instruments	cf/k_{t-1}, cf/k_{t-2}, q_{t-1}, q_{t-2}		Instruments	cf/k_{t-1}, cf/k_{t-2}, q_{t-1}, q_{t-2}	

Table A6.9.1 Collateral capacity split - econometric results

Variable	Coefficient	T-test	Variable	Coefficient	T-test
High-collateral firms	rnd.e. (fix.e.)		**Low-collateral firms**	rnd.e. (fix.e.)	
CF/K_{t-1}	.13 (.13)	2.85 (2.66)	CF/K_{t-1}	.17 (.16)	8.51 (7.67)
Q_{t-1}	.0001 (.0003)	.47 (.69)	Q_{t-1}	.002 (.002)	3.84 (2.38)
const.	.03 (.03)	3.02 (4.33)	const.	.03 (.02)	1.20 (3.72)
R^2	-- (.70)		R^2	-- (.84)	
L (1)	705.19		L (1)	290.53	
L (2)	433.43		L (2)	168.92	
L (3)	710.60		L (3)	335.80	
L (4)	715.10		L (4)	340.90	
LM(2w vs 1w)	467.07 (.00)		LM(2w vs 1w)	269.04 (.00)	
Hausman (Fx. vs Rn.)	.30 (.86)		Hausman (Fx. vs Rn.)	7.00 (.03)	

Legend:
(1) = Firm effects only; (2) = X-variables only; (3) = X-variables and firm effects; (4) = X-variables, time and firm effects; 2w = Two-way model; 1w = One way model; Fx. = Fixed effect model; Rn. = Random effect model; L = Log likelihood; LM = Lagrange Multiplier

Table A6.9.2 Collateral capacity split - econometric results

Variable	Coefficient	T-test	Variable	Coefficient	T-test
High-collateral firms	1-step		**Low-collateral firms**	1-step	
$d(cf/k)_{t-1}$	.13	3.69	$d(cf/k)_{t-1}$	.02	.90
dq_{t-1}	-.001	-.96	dq_{t-1}	-.003	3.04
const	-.01	-1.20	const	.10	4.35
AR(1)	-2.90 (.01)		AR(1)	-1.97 (.05)	
AR(2)	-2.12 (.02)		AR(2)	-1.65 (.24)	
Sargan	60.23		Sargan	45.67	
Instruments	cf/k_{t-1}, cf/k_{t-2}, q_{t-1}, q_{t-2}		Instruments	cf/k_{t-1}, cf/k_{t-2}, q_{t-1}, q_{t-2}	

156 selected Japanese firms

Selection criteria:

i) available balance sheets for each year in the period 1986-1992
ii) positive net sales rate of growth for each year in the period 1986-1992
iii) nonzero investments for each year in the period 1986-1992

Firms included in the sample

Miyaji Construction, Sekisui Jushi, Yurtec, Tostern Viva, Kawasumi Laboratories, Sagami Rubber, Sakata Seed, TKC, Asatsu, Yamato Setrubi, L&M Foods, Kyokuto Boeki, Toa Valve, Miyairi, Kawasaki Electric, Fushiki Kairiku Unso, Hinode Keisen, Tohoku Telecom, Toyobo Suifu, Dainippon Printing, Ajinomoto, Kajima, Sankyo, Banyu Pharmaceiutical, Canon, Daiwa House Industry, J.G.C. Corporation, Mitsubishi Heavy Industries, Tsukishima Kinai, Nippon Nodo, Yamanouchi Pharmaceutical, Nitto Denko, Kinden, Daiwa Seiko, Taisei Prefab., Daiichi Pharmaceutical, Mikuni, Calpis Food Industry, Wakachiku Construction, Shionogi, Nippon Road, Casio Computer, Faisei Rotec, Ito Yokado, Takuma, Daiho Constructions, Toa Corporation, Bull-Dog Sauce, Seiki Tokyo Kogyo, Nissin Food Products, Bunka Shutter, Tobishima Corporation, Taisho Pharmaceutical, Nissan Construction, Totetsu Kogyu, Chudenko, Kandenko, Nippon Densetsu, Todentu, Sanki Engineering, Takasage Therm., Hitachi Plant, Yamataki Baking, Sapporo Breweries, Chukyo Coca Cola, Q.P., Miyuki Keori, Ishihara Sangyo, Sekisui Chemical, Dainippon Pharmaceutical, Yoshitomi Pharmaceutical, Chugai Pharmaceutical, Kaken Pharmaceutical, Hisamitsu Pharmaceutical, Kansai Paint, Takasago International, Inax, Nippon Hume Pipe, Kurimoto Iron, Yokogawa Bridge Works, Kawada Industries, Sankyo Aluminium, Tsudakome, Teijin Seiki, Mitsubishi Kakoki, Chiyoda, Toyo Kanetsu, Mitsubishi Electric, Nissin Electric, Toko Electrical, Yamatane Honeywell, Koito Mnftg., Aichi Machine, Calsonic, Toyo Radiator, Stanley Electric, Takara Standard, Nishi-Nippon Railroad, Toyo Wharf & Wharehouse, Sumitomo Wharehouse, Kansai Niken, Fukuyama Transport, Nippon Express, Kyudenko, Seiken Co, Toshoku, Tsunamoto Shoji, Tokai Kanko, Nichirenchi Chemical, Fujitec, Topre, Dainei Telecom, Kinki Nippon Tourist, Jusco, Mochida Pharmaceuticals, Miura, Denki Kogyo, Tabai, Kasumi, Kodensha, Koyo Iron Works, Koa, Unicharm, Hagataninen, Seyo Food Systems, Nintendo, Nippon Koei, Sonton Food, Tokyo Denki Komushi, Showa Manuf., Fuji Oil, Horiba, Sankei Building, Yamato Transport, Skylark, Inageya, Santen Pharm., Torishima Pump, Gunei Chemical, Kinugawa Rubber, Sanyo Engineering, Taikisha, Myojo Foods, Organo, Tonami Transport, Wakodo,

Nissha Printing, Seven Eleven Japan, Toshiba Engineering, Yondenko, Shimachu, Kanto Natural Gas, Kawagishi Bridge Works, Okan Valve, CSK.

Table A6.10.1 Estimates results for Japan - overall sample

Variable	Coefficient	T-test	Variable	Coefficient	T-test
Random effects			Fixed Effects		
CF/K_{t-1}	.05	6.64	CF/K	.06	7.05
Q_{t-1}	-.08	-2.13	Q	-.02	-6.09
const.	.27	3.62	const.	.39	13.44
R^2	--			.91	
L (1)	--			14.80	
L (2)	--			-655.96	
L (3)	--			65.16	
L (4)	--			75.73	
LM(2w vs 1w)	740.00 (.00)				
Hausman (Fx. vs Rn.)	79.91 (.00)				

Legend:
(1) = Firm effects only; (2) = X-variables only; (3) = X-variables and firm effects; (4) = X-variables, time and firm effects; 2w = Two-way model; 1w = One way model; Fx. = Fixed effect model; Rn. = Random effect model; L = Log likelihood; LM = Lagrange Multiplier

Table A6.10.2 Estimates results for Japan - overall sample

Variable	Coefficient	T-test	Variable	Coefficient	T-test
One-step			**Two-step**		
$d(cf/k)_{t-1}$	.01	.50	$d(cf/k)_{t-1}$	.01	6.16
dq_{t-1}	-.03	.02	dq_{t-1}	-.03	-19.23
const	.04	.02	const	.005	.92
AR(1)	7.05 (.00)		AR(1)	.95 (.34)	
AR(2)	-5.18 (.00)		AR(2)	-1.07 (.28)	
Sargan	90.56		Sargan	16.16	
Instruments	cf/k_{t-1}, cf/k_{t-2}, q_{t-1}, q_{t-2}		Instruments	cf/k_{t-1}, cf/k_{t-2}, q_{t-1}, q_{t-2}	

Table A6.11.1 Split by firm dimension - econometric results

Variable	Coefficient	T-test	Variable	Coefficient	T-test
Large firms	rnd.e. (fix.e.)		**Small firms**	rnd. e. (fix.e.)	
CF/K_{t-1}	.06 (.06)	5.07 (5.46)	CF/K_{t-1}	.06 (.05)	5.09 (3.40)
Q_{t-1}	-.01 (-.03)	-2.07 (-4.96)	Q_{t-1}	-.003 (.002)	-.41 (.97)
const.	.35 (2.57)	2.57 (10.18)	const.	.13 (.17)	4.54 (6.99)
R^2	-- (.91)		R^2	-- (.82)	
L (1)	-130.97		L (1)	428.85	
L (2)	-468.39		L (2)	166.33	
L (3)	-102.62		L (3)	451.55	
L (4)	-97.09		L (4)	483.34	
LM(2w vs 1w)	287.22 (.00)		LM(2w vs 1w)	431.44 (.00)	
Hausman (Fx. vs Rn.)	46.46 (.00)		Hausman (Fx. vs Rn.)	29.57 (.00)	

Legend:
(1) = Firm effects only; (2) = X-variables only; (3) = X-variables and firm effects; (4) = X-variables, time and firm effects; 2w = Two-way model; 1w = One way model; Fx.= Fixed effect model; Rn. = Random effect model; L = Log likelihood; LM = Lagrange Multiplier

Table A6.11.2 Split by firm dimension - econometric results

Variable	Coefficient	T-test	Variable	Coefficient	T-test
Large firms	1-step		**Small firms**	1-step	
$d(cf/k)_{t-1}$	.009	.46	$d(cf/k)_{t-1}$	.01	.76
dq_{t-1}	-.02	-1.33	dq_{t-1}	-.006	-.71
const	.07	1.39	const	.03	3.50
AR(1)	1.17 (.24)		AR(1)	2.55 (.01)	
AR(2)	-.71 (.47)		AR(2)	.67 (.50)	
Sargan	23.86		Sargan	43.65	
Instruments	cf/k_{t-1}, cf/k_{t-2}, q_{t-1}, q_{t-2}		Instruments	cf/k_{t-1}, cf/k_{t-2}, q_{t-1}, q_{t-2}	

Table A6.12.1 Investment perspective performance split - econometric results

Variable	Coefficient	T-test	Variable	Coefficient	T-test
High-q firms	rnd.e. (fix.e.)		**Low-q firms**	rnd.e. (fix.e.)	
CF/K_{t-1}	.05 (.06)	4.43 (4.69)	CF/K_{t-1}	.08 (.07)	5.31 (4.02)
Q_{t-1}	-.009 (-.03)	-1.65 (-4.18)	Q_{t-1}	.02 (.01)	2.61 (1.34)
const.	.44 (.63)	2.81 (8.99)	const.	.04 (.06)	1.28 (1.81)
R^2	-- (.91)		R^2	-- (.81)	
L (1)	-149.98		L (1)	640.08	
L (2)	-448.83		L (2)	330.48	
L (3)	-126.39		L (3)	670.52	
L (4)	-119.02		L (4)	695.42	
LM(2w vs 1w)	108.91 (.00)		LM(2w vs 1w)	494.38 (.00)	
Hausman (Fx. vs Rn.)	49.44 (.00)		Hausman (Fx. vs Rn.)	2.81 (.24)	

Legend:
(1) = Firm effects only; (2) = X-variables only; (3) = X-variables and firm effects; (4) = X-variables, time and firm effects; 2w = Two-way model; 1w = One way model; Fx.= Fixed effect model; Rn. = Random effect model; L = Log likelihood; LM = Lagrange Multiplier

Table A6.12.2 Investment perspective performance - econometric results

Variable	Coefficient	T-test	Variable	Coefficient	T-test
High-q firms	1-step		**Low-q firms**	1-step	
d(cf/k)$_{t-1}$	.06	1.95	d(cf/k)$_{t-1}$	.03	.57
dq$_{t-1}$	.006	.74	dq$_{t-1}$	.003	.85
const	.03	1.65	const	.002	.34
AR(1)	-2.97 (.02)		AR(1)	-1.55 (.12)	
AR(2)	.006 (.99)		AR(2)	.008 (.99)	
Sargan	21.81		Sargan	35.46	
Instruments	cf/k$_{t-1}$, cf/k$_{t-2}$, q$_{t-1}$, q$_{t-2}$		Instruments	cf/k$_{t-1}$, cf/k$_{t-2}$, q$_{t-1}$, q$_{t-2}$	

Table A6.13.1 Split by sector performance - econometric results

Variable	Coefficient	T-test	Variable	Coefficient	T-test
Declining sector firms	rnd.e. (fix.e.)		**Growing sector firms**	rnd.e. (fix.e.)	
CF/K_{t-1}	.02 (.005)	1.06 (.23)	CF/K_{t-1}	.06 (.06)	6.25 (6.60)
Q_{t-1}	.02 (.03)	2.97 (2.05)	Q_{t-1}	-.009 (-.02)	-2.31 (-5.79)
const.	.11 (.10)	1.97 (1.57)	const.	.29 (.42)	3.16 (12.02)
R^2	-- (.83)		R^2	-- (.91)	
L (1)	143.68		L (1)	-52.02	
L (2)	35.47		L (2)	-589.20	
L (3)	147.53		L (3)	-9.65	
L (4)	167.26		L (4)	-2.12	
LM(2w vs 1w)	180.76 (.00)		LM(2w vs 1w)	536.25 (.00)	
Hausman (Fx. vs Rn.)	3.25 (.19)		Hausman (Fx. vs Rn.)	66.16 (.00)	

Legend:
(1) = Firm effects only; (2) = X-variables only; (3) = X-variables and firm effects; (4) = X-variables, time and firm effects; 2w = Two-way model; 1w = One way model; Fx. = Fixed effect model; Rn. = Random effect model; L = Log likelihood; LM = Lagrange Multiplier

Table A6.13.2 Split by sector performance - econometric results

Variable	Coefficient	T-test	Variable	Coefficient	T-test
Declining sector firms	1-step		**Growing** sector firms	1-step	
$d(cf/k)_{t-1}$	-.008	-.27	$d(cf/k)_{t-1}$	.01	.45
dq_{t-1}	-.03	-1.7	dq_{t-1}	-.03	-1.71
const	.02	1.61	const	.05	1.56
AR(1)	.69 (.48)		AR(1)	1.19 (.23)	
AR(2)	-.95 (.33)		AR(2)	-.72 (.46)	
Sargan	23.86		Sargan	43.65	
Instruments	cf/k_{t-1}, cf/k_{t-2}, q_{t-1}, q_{t-2}		Instruments	cf/k_{t-1}, cf/k_{t-2}, q_{t-1}, q_{t-2}	

Table A6.14.1 High-tech/low-tech split - econometric results

Variable	Coefficient	T-test	Variable	Coefficient	T-test
High-tech sector firms	rnd.e. (fix.e.)		**Low-tech sector firms**	rnd.e. (fix.e.)	
CF/K_{t-1}	.10 (.07)	7.65 (5.23)	CF/K_{t-1}	.03 (.06)	3.83 (6.15)
Q_{t-1}	.002 (.02)	6.56 (6.17)	Q_{t-1}	.03(.01)	8.18 (5.91)
const.	-.004 (-.006)	-.10 (-.21)	const.	.05(.05)	1.11 (11.85)
R^2	-- (.93)		R^2	-- (.91)	
L (1)	321.60		L (1)	-108.07	
L (2)	23.69		L (2)	-510.96	
L (3)	358.09		L (3)	-68.28	
L (4)	380.06		L (4)	-62.02	
LM(2w vs 1w)	585.14 (.00)		LM(2w vs 1w)	134.48 (.00)	
Hausman (Fx. vs Rn.)	15.71 (.00)		Hausman (Fx. vs Rn.)	69.88 (.00)	

Legend:
(1) = Firm effects only; (2) = X-variables only; (3) = X-variables and firm effects; (4) = X-variables, time and firm effects; 2w = Two-way model; 1w = One way model; Fx. = Fixed effect model; Rn. = Random effect model; L = Log likelihood; LM = Lagrange Multiplier

Table A6.14.2 High-tech/Low-tech split - econometric results

Variable	Coefficient	T-test	Variable	Coefficient	T-test
High-tech sector firms	1-step		**Low-tech sector firms**	1-step	
$d(cf/k)_{t-1}$	.017	1.18	$d(cf/k)_{t-1}$	-.003	-.23
dq_{t-1}	.05	1.67	dq_{t-1}	-.04	-2.17
const	.04	2.26	const	.05	1.33
AR(1)	.93 (.34)		AR(1)	1.16 (.24)	
AR(2)	-1.5 (.13)		AR(2)	-.67 (.49)	
Sargan	23.86		Sargan	43.65	
Instruments	cf/k_{t-1}, cf/k_{t-2}, q_{t-1}, q_{t-2}		Instruments	cf/k_{t-1}, cf/k_{t-2}, q_{t-1}, q_{t-2}	

Legend:
(1) = Firm effects only; (2) = X-variables only; (3) = X-variables and firm effects; (4) = X-variables, time and firm effects; 2w = Two-way model; 1w = One way model; Fx. = Fixed effect model; Rn. = Random effect model; L = Log likelihood; LM = Lagrange Multiplier

Notes

[1] The objection made by Chirinko (1993) is not clear on this point. The author argues, on the basis of the theoretical results of an unpublished paper (Chirinko, 1992), that measures of cash flow need not appear in the tested equations as Tobin's q also captures liquidity constraint effects. Against this assumption there are the results of several published theoretical models such as Fazzari et al. (1988) and Bond-Meghir (1994) and all the previously mentioned empirical results that show the theoretical and emprical relevance of cash flow when a lemons' problem exists.

[2] We prefer to use pre sample values of these two variables to create sample subgroups rather than additional regressors in the model, given that, according to the "agency cost" explanations provided, they should affect the degree of firm financial constraints. This is straightforward in models (Fazzari et al. 1988) where a maximum debt to equity ratio dictated by lenders exists.

[3] Chirinko (1993) identifies three main sources of bias saying that: i) divergence between market sentiments and fundamentals creates distortions when marginal q is influenced by excess volatility giving a biased measure of firm fundamentals which determine investments decisions; ii) the generalisation of applying fixed depreciation rates in the perpetual inventory method adopted for measuring capital stock may not be appropriate in times of rapid technological evolution with time changing rates of capital depreciation; iii) tax and non tax components of the price of capital may also distort the evaluation of capital stock.

[4] Hoshi-Kashyap and Scharfstein (1992) to support their approach affirm that: "the advantage of this approach is that, even though the individual estimate of the liquidity coefficients may be biased (say because Tobin's q is mismeasured), provided that the bias is to be the same for two sets of firms, the estimated difference in the coefficients will be an unbiased estimate of the true difference" and again: "This approach is useful even if the estimated coefficients on liquidity are biased. This is because the difference in the estimated coefficients is an unbiased estimate of the true difference as long as the biases are the same for the two sets of firms"

[5] This "size effect" is consistent with the results of coordination failure finance and innovation theoretical models (Becchetti, 1995): large firms are less likely to suffer from weak and strong cash constraint that can reduce innovator and investor property rights, generating "equity dilution" problems and reducing the incentive to invest and to innovate. The "long purse" of these firms and the multiplicity of financial intermediaries that may reduce coordination costs are factors that may markedly reduce the significantly of their investment and innovation plans from current liquidity.

References

Aaker, D. and Jacobson, R. (1993), "Myopic management behaviour with efficient but imperfect financial markets: a comparison of information asymmetries in the US and Japan", *Journal of Accounting and Economics*.

Arellano, M. and Bond, S.R. (1991), "Some tests of specifications for panel data: Monte Carlo evidence and an application to employment equation", *Review of Economics and Statistics*.

Becchetti, L. (1995), "Finance Nonneutrality in Technological Venturing: three Coordination Inefficiencies", paper presented at the 1995 Conference of the Royal Economic Society.

Becchetti, L. (1994), "Finance, Investments and Innovation: an empirical analysis of the Italian case", *Sviluppo Economico*, forthcoming.

Bernanke, B.S. and Gertler, M. (1987), "Financial Fragility and Economic Performance", NBER, Working Paper 2318.

Blanchard, O.J., Rhee, C., and Summers, L. (1993), "The Stock Market, Profit and Investment," *Quarterly Journal of Economics*, 108.

Bond S. and Meghir C. (1994), "Dynamic Investment Models and the Firm's Financial Policy", *Review of Economic Studies*, 61.

Borrus, M.G. (1988), *Competing for Control*, Cambridge, Ballinger.

Calomiris, C. and Hubbard, G. (1988), Firm Heterogeneity, Internal Finance, and Credit Rationing NBER, Working Paper 2497.

Cary, L. (1989), *The Report Guide to Venture Capital in the UK*, London: Pitman, 4th edn.

Chirinko, R.S., 1987, "Tobin's q and Financial Policy", *Journal of Monetary Economics*, 19.

Chirinko, R.S. (1993), Business Fixed Investment Spending, *Journal of Economic Literature* Vol. 31.

Cosh, A., Hughes, A. and Singh, A. (1990), "Takeovers and short termism in the UK: analyitical and policy issues in the UK economy", *Institute for Public Policy Research*, London.

Devereaux, M. and Schiantarelli, F. (1990), "Investment, Financial Factors, and Cash Flow: evidence from UK Panel Data", in R.G. Hubbard ed. *Asymmetric Information, Corporate Finance and Investment*, Chicago, University of Chicago Press.

Easterbrook, F.H. (1986), "Two Agency-Cost Explanations of Dividends", *American Economic Review*, Vol. 74, N. 4.

Edwards, J. and Fischer, K. (1993), *Banks Finance and Investment in Germany*, Cambridge University Press.

Fazzari S.M., Hubbard, G.R. and Petersen, B.C. (1988), "Financing Constraints and Corporate Investments", *Brooking Papers on Economic Activities*.

273

Florida, R. and Kenney, M. (1988), "Venture Capital and High Technology Entrepreneurship", *Journal of Business Venturing*, Vol. 3.

Frank, J. and Mayer, C. (1990), "Capital Market and Corporate Control: a Study of France, Germany and UK", *Economic Policy*, 1990.

Gladstone, D. (1988), *Venture Capital Investing*, Prentice Hall.

Green, W.G. (1993), *Econometric Analysis*, Mc Millan, New York.

Hamid, J. and Singh, A. (1992), "Corporate Financial Structure in Developing Countries", Technical Paper IFC.

Hodder, J.E. and Tschoegl, A.E. (1993), *An Overview of Japanese Financial Structure, in Japanese Capital Markets*, Takagi S. (eds.) Basil Blackwell, Oxford.

Hoshi, T., Kashyap, A.K. and Scharfstein, D. (1992), "Corporate Structure, Liquidity and Investment: Evidence from Japanese Industrial Groups", *Quarterly Journal of Economics*, Vol. 90.

Hoshi, T. and Kashyap, A.K. (1994), "Evidence on Q and Investment for Japanese Firms", *Journal of Japanese International Economies*, 4.

Hubbard, G.R. and Kashyap, A.K. (1992), "Internal Net Worth and the Investment Processes: an Application to US Agriculture", *Journal of Political Economy*, Vol. 100.

Jorgenson, D.W. and Siebert, C.D. (1958), "A Comparison of Alternative Theories of Corporate Investment Behaviour", *American Economic Review*, Vol. 58.

Myers, S.C. and Majluf, N.S. (1984), "Corporate Financing Decisions When Firms Have Investment Information That Investment Do Not", *Journal of Financial Economics*, Vol. 13.

Nelson, R. (1993), *National Innovation Systems*, Oxford University Press, New York.

Sakakibara, K. and Westney, D.E. (1985), "Comparative Study of the Training, Careers and Organization of the Engineers in the Computer Industry in the United States and in Japan, Hitotsoubashi", *Journal of Commerce and Management* 20 (1).

Whited, T.M. (1992), "Debt, Liquidity Constraints, and Corporate Investment: Evidence from Panel Data", *The Journal of Finance*, Vol. XLVII, n. 4, September.

7 High-tech firms, asymmetric information and credit rationing

Luigi Guiso

1. Introduction

The efficient allocation of funds among projects or firms can be severely limited by informational problems. By its very nature, the extension of credit is subject to informational asymmetries, with the lenders playing the role of the less informed agent. In these circumstances, as shown by Jaffee and Russell (1976) in a consumption-loan model and by Stiglitz and Weiss (1981) in a general credit-to-firms model, a limit on the amount of credit extended might turn out to be the optimal policy for the financial intermediary.

It is also intuitively plausible that informational problems are more severe with regard to high-tech (H-T) firms. Innovative projects are much less understood by outside observers, since past experience or observed past realisations can offer little guidance in assessing the prospects of truly new projects; whereas, the entrepreneur undertaking the innovative project is likely to have, if not more knowledge, at least a better perception of its likelihood of success. Thus, sorting out good and bad projects is more difficult than in more traditional fields. Furthermore, as pointed out by Bhattacharya and Ritter (1983), H-T firms have little incentive to communicate information on their innovative projects to the intermediary since this might also reveal useful information to the firm's competitors. This, in turn, lowers the value of innovative firms' signals about their quality, making credit rationing more probable. Finally, it is likely that intermediaries prefer to secure their loans with physical assets and are reluctant to lend when the project involves substantial investment in R&D rather than in plant and equipment. Unlike investment in equipment and machinery which can offer as collateral the same good purchased, expenditure on R&D can only be backed by the (highly uncertain) revenue that it generates: thus, if the R&D project fails and the firm defaults, there is no collateral to protect the creditor. As a consequence, financial intermediaries may end up allocating less to the high-tech-high-growth projects than they would if informational problems in the H-T sector were not more severe than in the traditional, low-tech (L-T) sector. Since innovative projects are the main engine of economic growth the lack of financing can severely constrain the speed of development of the economy[1]. This is an example of the efficiency loss induced by asymmetric information.

In this chapter I want to discuss the question of whether access to credit is empirically more difficult for H-T firms than for those undertaking traditional investment projects. The idea that market financing of innovative projects is likely to encounter severe obstacles is not new. Indeed, it dates back at least to Schumpeter's defence of monopoly power since not only does it guarantee that innovative firms can internalise the benefits of their innovations, but also it provides funding for future innovative projects. Clearly, this requires that firms faced with a contraction in cash flow cannot maintain their expenditure in innovative investment by raising external funds. Arrow (1962) was among the first to notice that moral hazard problems can hamper the external financing of innovative investment. More recently, Stiglitz (1993) has explored the cyclical and growth consequences of cash constraints on innovative firms arising from moral hazard or adverse selection in credit and equity markets. Implicit in his analysis is that firms engaging intensively in innovative investment are more likely to be credit constrained than firms undertaking investment in traditional fields, so that expenditures on innovative activities are tied to the availability of internal funds.

Empirical evidence of the effects of financial markets imperfections on innovation has so far been based on the sensitivity of R&D expenditure to the firm's cash flow, in analogy with the empirical studies of investment and financial constraints[2]. In spite of the strong a priori beliefs, it has often been difficult to find an effect of internal funds on R&D expenditures; with the exception of Grabowski's (1968), tests based on cross sectional data, as those by Hamburg (1966), Mueller (1967) and Scherer (1965) found no significant effect of the firm's cash flow on R&D. One possible explanation is that the R&D-cash-flow relationship is affected by a firm's unobservable characteristics that cannot be easily eliminated in cross sectional data. More recent studies based on panel data have been more successful. Hall (1992), using a large panel of US manufacturing firms, finds a strong effect of cash flow on R&D expenditures and interprets this as evidence that innovative firms are credit constrained[3]. Himmelberg and Petersen (1994) concentrate their analysis on a short panel of US small firms in high-tech industries and find that R&D expenditure is positively and significantly related to the firm's cash flow. Hao and Jaffe (1993) obtain a similar result using a relatively small panel of US firms but with a long time series dimension. One problem with these studies is that the effect of the firm's cash flow on current expenditure for R&D might reflect gloomy expectations of future profits rather than current liquidity constraints. To avoid this problem, Greenwald, Salinger and Stiglitz (1992) look at the behaviour of R&D expenditure in the automobile industry and in the airline industry following specific episodes which are likely to be characterised by the fact that the induced changes in the firm's cash flow can reasonably be expected to be uncorrelated (or negatively correlated) with future expectations. They find that the decrease in cash flow was followed by a parallel decrease in R&D expenditure, with sharper decreases among those firms for which the decrease in cash flow was larger.

While these findings are consistent with investment in innovative activities being subject to severe borrowing constraints, they cannot establish whether the sensitivity of R&D expenditure to cash flow reflects a general difficulty in obtaining access to external funds or whether raising external funds is more problematic for highly innovative firms, as implicitly assumed[4]. Testing this proposition requires information on the innovative content of a given firm and on the limits to borrowing it encounters. In Section 2, a sample of Italian manufacturing firms is described, which allows the identification of credit-constrained firms. This information can be used to make inferences on bank's lending strategies towards firms whose investment projects differ according to expected return and riskiness. In Section 3 direct information on firms' subjective probability distribution of demand growth is used to compare the risk-return relationship of H-T firms with that of L-T firms and it is shown that, ceteris paribus, H-T firms are riskier. Section 4 comments on the results of estimating a probit model that relates the probability of being credit-constrained to observable characteristics of the firm, including whether it belongs to the H-T group or not. The estimates show that H-T firms are more likely to be constrained in credit markets than firms undertaking traditional investment projects. This suggests that the sensitivity of R&D to the firm's cash flow found in the recent literature reflects severe obstacles in the access to credit by firms undertaking innovative investment rather than unobserved future expectations. Section 5 summarises the main findings and draws conclusions.

2. Credit-constrained firms: when and how many?

To define credit-constrained firms I have used the Bank of Italy Survey on Investment in Industry (INVIND), which, at the beginning of each year, collects information on investment made, employment, sales, and investment and employment plans, together with a set of characteristics on a representative sample of about 1,000 Italian manufacturing firms with 50 or more employees. Appendix 1 contains a more detailed description of the sampling methodology and outlines the main features of the survey. Since 1988 INVIND has also collected direct information on the access of firms to bank credit. This information is used to identify credit-constrained firms.

2.1 Defining credit-constrained firms

According to our definition, a firm is said to be liquidity-constrained if, at the rate of interest prevailing in the loan market, it wishes to obtain a larger amount of loans but cannot. In other words, if the firm is credit-constrained there must be excess demand in the loan market and the market rate must be below its clearing level. In these circumstances financial intermediaries are actually rationing credit. Furthermore, at the current level of debt, the firm's marginal productivity of capital exceeds the rate of interest on loans. Hence, a credit-constrained firm would be willing to pay a slightly higher interest rate in order to obtain a larger amount of credit.

Figure 7.1 illustrates these points. It shows the demand for loans (the schedule of the marginal product of capital) as a downward sloping function of the market rate of interest. When the latter is equal to r, the notional demand is L^* but the firm can only obtain $\bar{L} < L^*$. At $\bar{L}$, the marginal product of capital, $mpk(\bar{L})$, exceeds r.

Both $L^* - \bar{L}$ and $mpk(\bar{L}) - r$ measure the constraint on borrowing. Empirically, however, neither the notional demand for credit, L^*, nor the marginal product of capital, $mpk(\bar{L})$, is observed. This is what makes it difficult to state whether a firm is liquidity constrained or not. Thus, to identify credit-constrained firms, one has to resort to indirect indicators or proxies. For instance, Petersen and Rajan (1994) rely on the fact that credit-constrained firms are willing to pay a higher price to raise additional funds and define as constrained in the bank-loan market those firms that borrow from non-institutional lenders at abnormally high rates; Gertler and Gilchrist (1994) use firm size as the identification criterion on the assumption that larger firms have easier access to credit; Hoshi, Kashyap and Scharfstein (1991) use as an identification device the strength of ties between the firm and the banks and consider firms with close ties as less likely to be credit-constrained, on the assumption that this mitigates informational and incentive problems; Fazzari, Hubbard and Petersen (1988) separate firms on the basis of their dividend policy, arguing that firms that retain more of their earnings are more likely to be liquidity-constrained.

While indirect indicators are useful, they still are based on an untestable assumption, namely that the indicator is a good gauge of the firm's access to the loan market. Furthermore, while the indicator might be correlated with the firm's access to credit, it could also pick-up other effects that have little or nothing to do with liquidity constraints. I will return to this point later.

Information from the INVIND Survey offsets these objections. Firms in the sample are asked three questions on access to credit, which are used to identify the location of the notional demand for loans: i) whether at the current market interest rate they wish a larger amount of credit; ii) whether they would be willing to accept a small increase in the interest rate charged in order to obtain more credit; iii) whether they have applied for credit but have been turned down by the financial intermediary. In our definition, a firm is credit-constrained if, given a positive answer to the first *or* second question, it answers "yes" to the third[5]. Table 7.1 shows the share of credit-constrained firms according to this definition. It also reports the rate of growth of industrial production and bank credit as measures of the cyclical pattern of the expected return from investment projects and of credit availability: rationing credit makes sense only if total available credit is scarce.

The pattern of the share of credit-constrained firms seems to imply that banks' lending policy fluctuates markedly over the cycle: in years of fast growth and easy credit supply, the share of credit-constrained firms is rather small (around 3%). However, with the start of the recession and the restrictive monetary policy adopted at the end of 1992, the share of credit-constrained firms jumped to 9% and rose further to almost 13% in 1993[6]. Thus, credit constraints have a highly counter-cyclical pattern, rising with the downturn and almost disappearing when the economy experiences high growth.

The study of credit rationing cyclical behaviour is beyond the scope of this paper. It is worth noticing, however, that the pattern shown in Table 7.1 is consistent with the recent literature on credit cycles and with the existence of a credit multiplier formalised by Bernanke and Gertler (1989), Bernanke and Blinder (1992) and Kiyotaky and Moore (1993). It is also consistent with credit-supply-induced business cycles as formalised by Rajan (1994). One implication of this literature is that banks' credit policy tends to exacerbate demand expansions by easing access to credit in "good" times and to accentuate contractions by limiting credit in "bad" times.

Having assessed the extent of credit rationing among industrial firms we now turn to the next question: which firms are credit-constrained?

2.2 Credit-constrained firms

In answering this question reference is made to the 1993 survey only, rather than using the whole panel; 1993 is in fact the year with the highest share of credit-constrained firms and this makes it most suitable to identify their characteristics;

279

furthermore I wanted to avoid facing the problem of persistence in credit rationing: this issue is sufficiently important to deserve a separate paper.

Table 7.2 shows the sample means of a set of variables for the rationed and non-rationed firms respectively, in the year 1993. A commonly held opinion is that bank credit rationing is less likely among "large" firms, partly because they can more easily raise funds directly on the market, partly because large firms are thought to be able to offer better collateral, partly because they have more "visibility" which reveals to financial intermediaries their quality and allows them to charge the proper interest rate on the loan instead of cutting its amount. These considerations underpin the use of firm size as a proxy for financial "quality" in most of the recent empirical work on the transmission mechanism of monetary policy (see Gertler and Gilchrist 1993, 1994; Rondi, Sack, Schiantarelli and Sembenelli, 1993). This presumption is contradicted by Table 7.2. The share of credit-constrained firms is in fact lower among the smaller firms by a significant margin.

Being credit-rationed is more likely in the South than in the North: among the credit-constrained firms, the share of firms located in the South is 20%, compared with only 9% among the non-rationed. Credit-constrained firms are also younger and have changed ownership more frequently over the 10 years before the survey. Interestingly, rationed firms are less likely to belong to a group, while, for those that do, the size of the group, measured by the number of firms in it, is significantly smaller. This suggests that borrowing and lending between firms belonging to the same group might allow to ease (or even overcome) borrowing constraints.

The last row shows the share of H-T firms in the two groups, using two different definitions to partition the sample into innovative and traditional firms. To identify H-T firms I use information drawn from the Istat Survey on Technological Innovation in Italian Industry (1990). The first indicator is based on the share of innovative firms in each branch of economic activity, while the second relies on the amount of total expenditure on innovative activities across sectors. The methodology used is described in more detail in Appendix 2. The share of H-T firms appears to be somewhat smaller among the rationed according to both definitions. This could, prima facie, be taken as evidence that banks are able to discriminate efficiently among firms and that the more innovative firms and investment projects are not penalised by their intrinsically higher riskiness. Before jumping to this conclusion, however, one must consider that, as shown in Table 7.3, H-T firms have characteristics that may lower the probability of being liquidity-constrained, irrespective of the nature of their investment projects. For instance, besides being on average larger, they are more likely to be located in the North and to belong to a group, two factors that appear to lower the probability of being denied credit. Firms operating in the North deal with more efficient financial intermediaries and have easier access to extra sources of external finance; if a firm belongs to a group it can raise funds from other firms in the group that have cash in excess of their needs. Thus, a proper test of whether being a highly innovative firm (as well as of having any other characteristic) makes it more difficult to obtain bank credit, requires controlling for all these factors. Section 4 presents a formal test based on a probit model.

3. Risk, return and H-T and L-T firms

The main proposition to be tested - banks are more likely to limit access to credit to H-T firms - rests on the assumption that the more severe information problems within the group of H-T firms makes them riskier. Before testing this proposition it is of interest to look at the relative riskiness and expected "return" of high-tech and low-tech firms as measured by expected medium-term growth and its variance.

The 1993 INVIND collects information on each firm's subjective probability distribution of the growth rate of demand for its products over the three years following the survey (i.e. over the period 1994-1996). More specifically, each firm is required to assign weights, summing up to 100, to given intervals of the firm's real demand growth three years ahead. This distribution can be used to compute measures of expected growth and of its uncertainty, which are reported in Table 7.4.

It might be argued that what distinguishes high-tech from low-tech firms is not the uncertainty associated with product demand but technological uncertainty related, for instance, to the experimentation of new products or production processes or to investment in research for new products, the demand for which in case of success can be easily foreseen. Although this is a possibility, it is also reasonable for high-tech firms to be more uncertain about the demand for their products: most innovations concern the introduction of new goods and firms have to guess at what the buyers' reactions will be at the time (uncertain as well) when the product will be marketable. Furthermore, even when the innovation concerns mainly the production process, it is unlikely to leave the firm's product unaffected[7].

It is interesting to note that subjective uncertainty (measured by the mean variance of the expected growth rate of demand over the three years following the survey) increases substantially as one moves from the L-T to the H-T group. The "return" (i.e. the subjective average expected growth of demand) is also increasing with the technological content, although to a lesser extent. The average expected growth rate is 6.86% over a 3 year period for L-T firms and 7.11 for H-T firms: the difference, however, is not statistically significant (p

281

value = 0.761); on the other hand, uncertainty appears to be increasing substantially as one moves from the L-T to the H-T group. The mean variance of the expected growth of the demand for the firm's product rises from 10.7 among the L-T firms to 16.3 among H-T firms; measuring uncertainty in terms of the conditional standard error, it is on average 2.4 percentage points among the L-T firms and rises to 2.8 percentage points among the H-T firms. In both cases the difference is statistically significant (the p-value is 0.042 for the conditional variance and 0.06 for the conditional standard deviation).

To get a better understanding of the factors affecting this relationship I posit that the risk-return relation can be described by the following regression equation:

$$\sigma_i = \alpha\mu_i + \beta\mu_i^2 + \gamma Z_i + \delta Htech + u_i \tag{1}$$

where σ is the conditional standard error of the expected growth of demand, μ the conditional expected growth rate of demand, Z a vector of firms' characteristics, $Htech$ an indicator variable for high-tech firms and u a random shock; firms in the sample are indexed by i. To capture the likely non-linear nature of the risk-return relationship a quadratic term in μ has been inserted. The results are reported in Table 7.5.

The higher the expected growth, the higher the subjective conditional standard error of demand growth, i.e. a higher return is expected only at the cost of a greater uncertainty as well: a 1 percentage point increase in expected growth leads - ceteris paribus - to an increase in the subjective standard deviation of about 1/5 of a percentage point. Since the relationship is moderately convex, the higher the initial value of the expected return, the greater is the increase in uncertainty. The risk-return relation appears to be unaffected by the size, the age or the geographical source of the firm's demand measured by the share of exports in total sales; it is, however, affected by location: firms in the North and in the Centre face a lower level of demand uncertainty, which is about half the sample mean value of the subjective standard deviation. Uncertainty is also lower for public companies (perhaps because a significant part of the demand for their product comes from the government) and for corporations, although the coefficient for the last variable is only significant at the 10% confidence level. Finally, the dummy variable for H-T firms has a positive and statistically significant coefficient; its size implies that, other things being equal, the level of demand uncertainty associated with them is about half a percentage point higher than that associated with L-T firms[8].

4. Are innovative firms more likely to be credit-constrained?

To test whether banks' rationing behaviour is affected by the innovative nature of investment projects, I assume that the decision to grant or refuse credit depends on a set of observable characteristics of the firm, identified by the vector X_{it}, where the index i ($i=1,2 \ldots N$) refers to the firm and t to the year (1993 in our case).

One can imagine that the bank observes X and on the basis of the observed characteristics infers the quality (riskiness and return) of the project (firm). Let P_{it}^* be the latent variable for the bank decision whether to finance firm i or not. When $P_{it}^* > 0$ the signals received are such that they lead the bank to classify the firm as belonging to a group which is likely to have a high share of "lemons" and to ration the credit extended to it. I assume that P_{it}^* depends linearly on X:

$$P_{it}^* = \beta X_{it} + u_{it} \tag{2}$$

where β is a vector of coefficients and u_{it} an error term. Let P_{it} be a dummy variable which takes value 1 if firm i is credit-constrained at t and zero otherwise. Then

$$prob\,(P_{it} = 1) = prob\,(P_{it}^* > 0) = prob\,(u_{it} \geq -\beta X_{it}) \tag{3}$$

Assuming that u_{it} is normally distributed, the vector of parameters β can be estimated (up to a constant of proportionality) by maximum likelihood.

Since subjective expected growth and subjective demand uncertainty are not observed by the financial intermediaries but are private knowledge of the firm, the bank cannot make its decision conditional on these variables. More generally, the vector X includes only variables that can be observed by the bank at the time it decides whether to extend credit. These include publicly available information, like firm characteristics and published balance sheet information.

Banks are also likely to have additional information on the firm either gathered directly at a cost or inferred by observing other banks' behaviour with respect to the firm. The INVIND survey contains information on a number of variables for both the current and the previous year some of which is also available in official balance sheets and some of which is not but is likely to be known by banks, such as the firm's ownership and control structure.

INVIND, however, does not provide information on most balance sheet items - including assets, liabilities and their composition - which are likely to be relevant in bank credit decisions. To overcome this problem I have used information from the Company Accounts Data Service (CADS, Centrale dei Bilanci) which has been filing the balance sheets of over 30,000 Italian firms since 1982. I first singled out firms in the 1993 INVIND that are also in the 1992 CADS by matching their tax code numbers (available in both surveys). Over 78 percent of the firms in the 1993 INVIND sample are also present in the 1992 Company Accounts reports. This reduces the sample from 995 to 779 observations. After deleting missing values it is further reduced to 608 firms.

Table 7.6 reports the results of the estimation of the probit model. In column 1 the vector of explanatory variables includes several performance indicators, firms' measures of indebtedness and collateralisable wealth; since these variables refer to 1992 and are published in the firm's balance sheet, they are (in principle) in the bank's information set. Thus, the bank decision can be conditioned upon them. Out of three performance indicators, only the number of hirings has a significant negative effect on the probability of rejecting a loan application. Since in the presence of adjustment costs hiring decisions are highly forward looking, this is consistent with banks looking far into the firm's future when deciding credit to the firm[9]. The effect of sales per worker is negative but not statistically different from zero, while gross operating surplus as a share of total sales has a negligible positive effect.

The probability of rationing is strongly affected by present liabilities: the ratios of long-term and short-term debt to total net liabilities have both a positive and statistically very significant effect on the probability of being liquidity-constrained. Particularly strong is the effect of short-term liabilities; its coefficient is almost three times as high as that of long-term debt. At sample means, an increase of 10 percentage points in the ratio of short term liabilities to total liabilities raises the probability of being credit-constrained by 2 percentage points (that is 17% of the unconditional probability).

The two measures of collateral given by the share, in total assets, of real and financial assets respectively, do not affect the probability of a firm being denied credit. While this result may seem surprising, it is not inconsistent with the theory. As pointed out by Stiglitz and Weiss (1981, 1986) collateral requirements have a positive incentive effect but they also have a negative selection effect. Firms with larger amounts of marketable wealth are likely to be more prone to take larger risks, assuming entrepreneurs are risk averse. Furthermore, among the high-collateral firms there is likely to be a larger proportion of risk-takers, that is of firms that undertook risky projects which by chance were successful. Hence, raising collateral requirements might bring in a higher-than-average proportion of bad risks.

The probability that a firm will be rationed is markedly affected by the firm's geographical location: firms in the North or in the Centre are less likely to suffer from lack of credit than those in the South. This is consistent with banks in the South being less skilled at screening; but it is also consistent with firms in the South facing riskier projects as shown in the estimation of the risk-return

284

relationship reported in table 7.5. Everything else constant, moving a firm from the South to the North would lower its probability of being denied credit by almost 4 percentage points.

To test for the disclosure of information deriving from the existence of the firm in the market over a long period of time, I have included as a regressor the firm's age, measured from its year of foundation. If the observation of the firm over a long time span leads to a reduction in the degree of informational asymmetry, younger firms should have a higher probability of being denied credit. This implication does not receive support from the data. However, this result is likely to be due to the fact that most firms in the sample are long established: only 3.5% of the firms are less than 10 years old and only 0.5% (4 firms) are really young (5 years old or younger).

The regression results confirm the descriptive analysis of Table 7.2: contrary to what is commonly asserted in the literature, firm size is not a good predictor of difficulty in obtaining credit. Being a small firm significantly reduces the probability of being credit-constrained by almost 3.5 percentage points. On the other hand the probability of being credit constrained is higher for state-owned firms and lower if the firm is a limited company, belongs to a group or sells a high share of its output abroad.

Our indicator for H-T firms, based on the share of innovative firms present in each branch of economic activity, has a positive effect but its coefficient is not statistically different from zero. Furthermore, the size of the coefficient implies that the probability of being credit-constrained is increased by a negligible amount (0.2%) if the firm belongs to the H-T group. The same result is obtained using the second indicator (based on the share of expenditure on innovation in each sector). This invalidates the idea that informational problems are more severe among H-T firms. Before reaching this conclusion it has to be realised that indicators for H-T firms are likely to be affected by measurement errors, since L-T firms can be classified as H-T simply because they belong to a branch that is defined *a priori* high-tech. On the assumption that high-tech status raises the probability of being denied credit, the estimated coefficient is biased downwards and its standard error is overestimated if the indicator variable for H-T firms is affected by measurement error. To verify the robustness of the result at least partially, column 2 shows the estimates of the probit model using as a measure of the firm's technological inclination the share in total assets of capitalised expenditure on a number of items including R&D and patents. Interestingly, the effect of this variable on the probability of the firm being liquidity-constrained is positive and sizeable (10 percentage points increase in the share of capitalised expenditure raises the probability of being liquidity-constrained by 1.5 percentage points). However its coefficient has a high standard error and the hypothesis that it is equal to zero can only be rejected at the 20% confidence

285

level. Furthermore, since the R&D variable also includes other items, this measure too is subject to error. Unfortunately the Company Accounts database does not provide distinct information for the capitalised value of R&D expenditure and patents.

In an attempt to solve these measurement problems, I have run instrumental variable estimates of the probability of a firm being liquidity-constrained. To this end I have instrumented the high-tech dummy and the R&D variable running a first stage probit and an OLS regression against a list of instruments[10]. The fitted values are then used in a second stage probit regression of the probability of a firm being liquidity-constrained. The results are reported in Table 7.7. Most coefficients are unchanged with respect to those shown in Table 7.6, except that in both regressions the size of the coefficient of the indicator for high-tech firms increases considerably; that of the dummy for high-tech firms more than doubles and that of the R&D asset share in total assets trebles. Although this reveals that measurement errors are likely to be important, it has to be pointed out that the first stage regressions are unlikely to provide good instruments for detecting H-T firms. Their fit is in fact rather poor, particularly for the R&D assets regression[11].

In summary, there is some evidence that due to more severe informational problems, credit rationing is more likely among H-T-high-risk firms; this evidence, however, is blurred by measurement problems in the proxies used to identify high risk firms.

5. Conclusions

The idea that information problems may be more severe when a financial intermediary is faced with a high-tech-high-risk firm carries the implication that banks are prone to cut credit to the most innovative firms in the economy. There is some evidence that this is indeed the case. Cross-sectional data on a sample of Italian manufacturing firms reveal that if a firm is in the high-tech category it is more likely to be denied credit. Unfortunately, measurement problems in the proxies for high-tech firms do not allow a precise estimate of the size of the effect. More definite conclusions on this point can be reached if better measures of the indicator for high-tech firms are found. One such possibility is to estimate a probit model for the probability that a firm is H-T using the individual data of the survey on technological innovation (Istat, 1990) and conditioning on a set of firms' characteristics which are observed both in the Istat survey and in the INVIND survey. The estimated model could than be used to impute to *each* firm in the INVIND survey a probability of being of the H-T type. This variable could than be used as a regressor in the probit model for the probability of being liquidity constrained.

The results also shed light on the determinants of credit rationing. The probability that a firm will be denied credit does not appear to depend on the amount of collateralisable assets (either real or financial); while this is in contrast with what one might expect a priori, it is not necessarily inconsistent with theory: a high level of collateral might signal that the firm is in the high risk category if high levels of wealth are the consequence of a lucky sequence of good draws. In deciding their credit policy banks seem to react to the level and composition of firms' liabilities: a large share of short-term financial liabilities considerably increases the probability of a firm being credit-constrained. Interestingly, small and private firms are less likely to be liquidity-constrained. These results are consistent with those of Rondi, Sembenelli and Zanetti (1994) who estimate Euler equations for investment on a panel of Italian industrial firms and find that investment is more responsive to cash flow in the sub-samples of large firms and state-owned firms. Finally, the probability of liquidity constraint is markedly affected by geographical location: firms in the South are much more likely to be denied credit than firms with similar characteristics located in the North or in the Centre. While this result might reflect differences of riskiness in the two areas, it may also be due to a lesser ability of banks in the South to discriminate efficiently among their clients. A third possibility is that the geographical dummies are proxying for differences across regions in the efficiency of courts, and hence in the cost of repossessing credit in case of default. Disentangling these alternative explanations is of importance but is left for future research.

Appendix 1: The INVIND survey

Since the early 1980s the Bank of Italy has run a yearly survey on a sample of industrial firms. The main purpose is to collect information on investment made and investment and employment plans. It also collects information on a set of "demographic" characteristics (geographical location of the firm, ownership structure, sector, year of foundation), qualitative information on production capacity, reasons for revising investment plans, expected variations in costs, total sales and export sales. The number of firms in the sample, which functions as a panel, is around 1,000. Interviews are conducted at the beginning of the year by well trained officials of the Bank of Italy.

Table A7.1 compares the sample and population frequency distributions by firm size (number of employees), sector of activity and regional location. It is clear that the structure of the sample virtually reproduces that of the population.

In order to ensure a good degree of representativeness, the sample is stratified by sector of activity, firm size and geographical location across the Italian regions. Since 1987 the stratification has referred to the joint frequency distribution of the firms population in September 1987 according to the mentioned criteria provided by Istat, the National statistical institute. Prior to 1987 the unit surveyed was the plant; since 1987 it is the firm. Small firms (less than 50 employees) are excluded in order to keep sample size under control; 282 firms have been present over the whole 10 survey years, 784 for at least 7 years, while more than 1,100 for at least 4.

In case of mergers, acquisitions and break-ups, information is collected in order to account for these phenomena.

Data are subject to extremely detailed controls of correctness and consistency; any time doubts arise on a specific variable, the firm is contacted again and the data adjusted. This, together with the relatively small size of the sample, and the professional qualification of the interviewers, who have established long-term relations with the firms' managers, guarantee high quality data.

Since 1988 a questionnaire on access to credit has been added to the survey while in 1992 detailed information on the structure of firm's ownership and control was collected.

Appendix 2: The identification of high-tech firms

INVIND has no direct information on the nature of investment projects or the firm in general. To distinguish high-tech from "traditional" firms I have constructed two proxies, based on sectors, using information drawn from a survey on technological innovation in Italian industry run by Istat (1990). The first proxy is based on the share of firms in each sector that can be classified as innovative according to Istat criteria[12] .

The sector (and hence the firms belonging to it) has been considered high-tech if the share of innovative firms in the Istat samples exceeds 40%. If the share is between 20 and 30% the sector is considered as medium-tech and is classified as low-tech if less than 20% of the firms are innovative.

The second proxy is based on information on the allocation of total expenditure over the period 1981-1985 among three types of innovation activities: R&D, projecting and engineering and productive investment.

For each type of activity, the sector was given a score of 1 if the expenditure share on that activity was below 20%; a score of 2 if it was between 20 and 30% and of 3 if it exceeded 30%. I then classified a sector (and hence the firms in it) as high-tech if, after giving weight equal to 2 to the scores attributed to expenditures in R&D and weight equal to 1 to the scores attributed to the other types of activities, the weighted sum of scores given for expenditure in R&D and in projecting and engineering exceeded 6; as average-tech if the score was between 4 and 6 and low-tech if the total score was equal to 3.

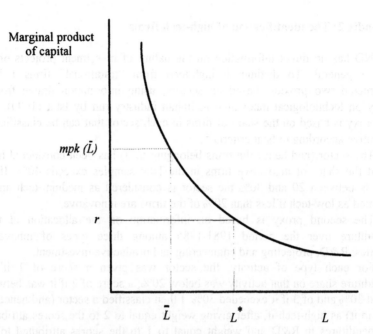

Figure 7.1 Demand for loans and credit rationing

Table 7.1 Credit-constrained firms over the business cycle

Year	Share of credit-rationed firms	Growth rate of industrial production	Bank loans growth rate(a)
1988	2.7	6.0	15.57
1989	3.5	3.1	18.67
1990	3.4	0.2	15.98
1991	4.3	-2.0	13.99
1992	9.0	-0.6	6.97
1993	12.8	-2.8	1.67

Source: Istat for industrial production and Bank of Italy for bank loans

(a) Rate of growth of end-of-period total loans to the private sector.
A firm is defined as credit rationed if, at the interest rate prevailing in the loan market it would like to obtain a larger amount of loans but has been turned down by a financial intermediary.

Table 7.2 Sample characteristics among rationed and non rationed firms in 1993

	Credit-rationed	Non-rationed
Firm size (0,1)		
≤ 200 employees	0.38	0.44
> 200 employees	0.62	0.56
Geographical location (0,1)		
North	0.59	0.69
Centre	0.22	0.22
South	0.20	0.09
Shares of exports in total sales	0.25	0.31
Belongs to a group (0,1)	0.71	0.73
Ltd (0,1)	0.75	0.80
Status of ownership (0,1)		
Public firms	0.18	0.05
Private firms	0.82	0.95
Firm's age	41.39	42.20
Ownership structure (a)		
Number of firms in the group	3.30	5.20
Number of control changes	0.87	0.57
since 1982	1.48	1.68
Number of persons	0.27	0.25
exercising control	0.14	0.09
Parental relationships (b)		
Companies with minority		
control		

Table 7.2 (con't) Sample characteristics among rationed and non rationed firms in 1993

Real collateral / total assets (c)	0.24	0.23
Long term debt / total liabilities (c)	0.24	0.22
Short term debt / total liabilities (c)	0.60	0.50
Htech 1 (0,1) (d)	0.29	0.35
Htech 2 (0,1) (d)	0.28	0.34

The (0,1) notation means that the variable is a dummy equal to 1 if the firm has the specified characteristic and equal to zero otherwise. For these variables the table reports the share of firms in the sample with the given characteristic.

(a) Information on ownership structure refers to the year 1992

(b) Dummy equal to 1 if there are parental relationships among those with control power within the firm.

(c) Computed for the subsample of 694 firms which are simultaneosly present in the INVID survey and in the CADS sample in 1992. Figures refers to the year 1992.

(d) The identification of high-tech firms is based on information drawn from the Survey of Technological Innovation in the Italian Industry conducted by Istat (1990). The first indicator (Htech1) is based on the share of innovative firms, according to the Istat classification, in each branch of economic activity; the second indicator (Htech2) relies on the amount of total expenditure on innovative activities across sectors. See Appendix 2 for details.

Table 7.3 H-Tech and L-Tech firms: sample means for selected variables

	High-Tech	Low-Tech
Firm size (0,1)		
≤ 200 employees	0.31	0.48
> 200 employees	0.69	0.52
Geographical location (0,1)		
North	0.79	0.65
Center	0.17	0.23
South	0.04	0.12
Firms age	44.60	41.10
Sales per worker (a)	1021.50	411.60
Ltd (0,1)	0.80	0.80
Status of ownership (0,1)		
Public firms	0.07	0.06
Private firms	0.93	0.94
Belongs to a group (a)	0.84	0.68

Table 7.3 (con't) H-Tech and L-Tech firms: sample means for selected variables

Structure of firms control		
Number people exercizing control	1.47	1.73
Maximum share of stock	0.80	0.72
held by the person exercizing	0.85	0.10
control	0.70	0.56
Companies with the minority	0.14	0.30
control		
Number of control changes since 1982		
Parental relationship (b)		
Liquidity constrained firms (0,1)	0.11	0.14
Shares of R&D assets (c)	0.03	0.02
Collateral / total assets (c) (d)	0.23	0.24
Long term debt / total liabilities (c)	0.22	0.23
Short term debt / total liabilities (c)	0.49	0.50

The (0,1) notation means that the variable is a dummy equal to 1 if the firm has the specified characteristic and equal to zero otherwise. For these variables the table reports the share of firms in the sample with the given characteristic.To identify high-tech firms the definition based on firm's sector (Htech 1) has been used (see the note to Table 7.2)
(a) Thousands of 1992 lire.

(b) Dummy = 1 if there are parental relationships among those with control power within the firm.
(c) Computed for the subsample of 694 firms which are simultaneosly present in the INVID survey and in the CADS sample in 1992. Figures refers to the year 1992.
(d) Real assets as a share of total assets.

Table7.4 Risk and return for H-T and L-T firms

	Low-tech firms	High-tech firms
Mean expected growth rate of demand (1993/1996)	6.86	7.11
Mean conditional variance of demand growth	10.07	16.32
Mean conditional standard error of demand growth	2.40	2.83

The identification of high-tech firms is based on the firm's sector according to the first definition (Htech 1) described in the note to Table 7.2. The expected growth rate of demand and its variance are based on the subjective probability distribution of demand growth reported three years in advance by the firms in the 1993 INVID sample. In particular, each firm in the sample was asked to attribute weights (summing to 100) to a set of intervals for the growth rate of demand for its product(s) three years ahead. The mean expected growth rate of demand and the conditional variance are computed from this subjective probability distribution using the methodology described in Guiso and Parigi (1995).

295

Table 7.5 OLS estimates of the risk return relationship. Dependent variable: conditional subjective standard deviation of firm's demand growth

Variable	Coefficient	t-statistic	Coefficient	t-statistic
Expected growth	0.1414	6.994	0.1206	5.771
(Expected growth)^2	0.0008	1.388	0.011	1.729
Firm's age	0.0040	1.142	0.0054	1.463
Regional location (0,1)				
North	-1.0183	-2.790	-0.9745	-2.302
Centre	-1.3350	-3.347	-1.2378	-2.695
Small (0,1)	-0.0839	-0.377	-0.0684	-0.286
Share of exports in total sales	0.2063	0.540	-0.5997	1.468
Number of plants (a)	-0.0229	-0.452	-0.0209	-0.394
Ltd (0,1)	-0.4132	-1.645	-0.3769	-1.307
Public (0,1)	-0.9764	-2.168	-0.6726	-1.336
Belongs to a group (0,1)	-0.2850	-1.172	-0.0394	-0.154
Htech (0,1) (b)	0.4256	1.926		
R&D and patents			0.4937	1.415
Constant	2.8320	5.735	2.5982	4.534
Number of observations (η)	634		534	
F(12, η-k)	19.35		14.04	
Prob > F	0.00		0.00	
Adjusted R-square	0.25		0.23	
RMS	2.50		2.39	

The (0,1) notation means that the variable dummy is equal to 1 if the firm has the specified characteristic and equal to zero otherwise.
(a) Number of the plants with more than 5 employees.
(b) Based on the firm's sector (see the note to table 7.2 and Appendix 2).

Table 7.6 Probit estimates. Probability of a firm being liquidity constrained
Dependent variable: dummy = 1 if the firm is liquidity constrained

Variable	Coefficient	t-statistic	Coefficient	t-statistic
Firm's age	0.0007	0.263	0.0005	0.190
Sales per worker	-0.0001	-0.607	-0.0007	-0.633
Number of hirings	-0.0068	-2.501	-0.0067	-2.502
Gross oper. surplus/sales	0.0127	0.373	0.0125	0.360
Long term debt (a)	1.0879	2.786	0.9780	2.456
Short term debt (a)	2.8151	5.357	2.7829	5.308
Real assets (b)	-0.4393	-0.699	-0.3567	-0.562
Long term financial assets (b)	0.1344	0.156	0.2159	0.247
Short term financial assets (b)	-0.7749	-1.283	-0.6483	-1.058
North (0,1)	-0.5618	-2.152	-0.5571	-2.111
Centre (0,1)	-0.8096	-2.711	-0.8170	-2.702
Small (0,1)	-0.5194	-2.796	-0.5350	-2.866
Share of export in total sales	-0.6139	-1.971	-0.5563	-1.847
Number of plants	0.0041	0.074	0.0015	0.027
Ltd (0,1)	-0.3448	-1.739	-0.3332	-1.688
Public (0,1)	0.4697	1.742	0.4680	1.730
Belongs to a group (0,1)	-0.3065	-1.665	-0.2945	-1.601
Htech (0,1) (c)	0.0502	0.294		
R&D and patents			2.7054	1.562

Table 7.6 (con't) Probit estimates. Probability of a firm being liquidity constrained. Dependent variable: dummy = 1 if the firm is liquidity constrained

Constant	-1.0721	-1.833	-1.1698	-1.971
Number of observation	608		608	
chi2 (18)	76.30		78.54	
Prob > chi^2	0.00		0.00	
Log likelihood	172.78		151.23	
Pseudo R^2	0.18		0.18	

The (0,1) notation means that the variable dummy is equal to 1 if the firm has the specified characteristic and equal to zero otherwise.
(a) As a share of total liabilities.
(b) As a share of total assets.
(c) Based on the firm's sector (see the note to Table 7.2 and Appendix 2).

Table 7.7 Second stage Probit estimates of the probability of a firm being liquidity constrained. Dependent variable: dummy = 1 if the firm is liquidity constrained

Variable	Coefficient	t-statistic	Coefficient	t-statistic
Firm's age	-0.0001	-0.030	-0.0001	-0.235
Sales per worker	-0.0001	-0.504	-0.0001	-0.507
Number of hirings	-0.0065	-2.411	-0.0065	-2.419
Gross oper. surplus/sales	0.134	0.401	0.0131	0.393
Long term debt (a)	1.0485	2.638	1.0351	2.600
Short term debt (a)	2.6957	4.999	2.6990	5.002
Real assets (b)	-0.5073	-0.794	-0.4868	-0.760
Long term financial assets (b)	0.1549	0.181	0.1573	0.183
Short term financial assets (b)	-0.8427	-1.386	-0.8301	-1.364
North (0,1)	-0.5773	-1.855	-0.5694	-2.134
Centre (0,1)	-0.7938	-2.552	-0.7758	-2.554
Small (0,1)	-0.5297	-2.301	-0.5438	-2.582
Share of export in total sales	-0.5629	-0.720	-0.4366	-1.331
Number of plants	0.0082	0.152	0.0065	0.120
Ltd (0,1)	-0.3840	-1.276	-0.3473	-1.617
Public (0,1)	0.4908	1.628	0.4954	1.813
Belongs to a group (0,1)	-0.3407	-1.795	-0.3407	-1.795
Htech (0,1) (c)	0.1207	0.062		

Table 7.7 (con't) Second stage Probit estimates of the probability of a firm being liquidity constrained. Dependent variable: dummy = 1 if the firm is liquidity constrained

R&D and patents			8.1490	0.642
Constant	-0.9166	-1.428	-1.1266	-1.634
Number of observation	590		590	
chi^2 (18)	70.87		71.72	
Pseudo R^2	0.17		0.17	

The (0,1) notation means that the variable dummy is equal to 1 if the firm has the specified characteristic and equal to zero otherwise.
(a) As a share of total liabilities.
(b) As a share of total assets.
(c) Based on the firm's sector (see the note to Table 7.2 and Appendix 2).

Table A7.1 Population and sample marginal frequency distribution by firm's size, sector of activity and geographical location

	Popula-tion	Sample
Firm's size (number of employees)		
50-99	22.7	19.8
100-199	20.2	20.2
200-499	21.3	26.4
500-999	17.5	17.0
over 900	18.3	16.7
Branch of economic activity		
Metallurgy	4.6	4.6
Non-metallic mineral products	7.8	8.5
Chemical products	8.2	9.2
Ferrous and non-ferrous ores and metals	8.8	7.4
Agricultural and industrial machinery	11.3	12.5
Office and data processing machines; precision	1.8	2.4
and optical instruments	10.1	9.0
Electrical goods	3.0	2.4
Cars	2.6	2.9
Trains, ships, airplanes and motor vehicles	8.7	9.2
Food products, beverages and tabacco	9.4	8.4
Textiles	3.9	4.3
Leather and footwear	6.1	6.6
Clothing	3.4	3.6
Timber and furniture	5.2	4.4
Paper, products of printing and publishing	4.2	4.1
Rubber and plastic products	1.0	0.7
Other manufacturing products		

Table A7.1 (con't) Population and sample marginal frequency distribution by firm's size, sector of activity and geographical location

Geographical location (regions)		
Piemonte and Valle d'Aosta	12.7	10.4
Lombardia	33.8	31.3
Liguria	2.5	2.3
Trentino Alto Adige	1.1	1.2
Veneto	8.9	9.0
Friuli Venezia Giulia	2.4	2.8
Emilia romagna	10.1	11.1
Toscana	6.3	10.7
Umbria	1.6	1.6
Marche	2.4	2.5
Lazio	3.4	3.4
Abruzzi	2.1	2.3
Molise	0.6	0.4
Campania	3.9	3.5
Puglia	2.0	2.1
Basilicata	0.4	0.4
Calabria	0.6	0.7
Sicilia	1.9	1.9
Sardegna	3.2	2.2

Notes

[1] The relationship between financial intermediation and development has been thoroughly studied in recent years (see Pagano (1993) for an overview of the literature). The literature has shown that financial development can increase growth through several channels. Financial intermediaries can promote growth because the size of their portfolio allows them to be better informed than individual investors about the nature of shocks (aggregate versus firm-specific) to each single firm, implying that they can allocate funds more efficiently to the most productive projects (Greenwood and Jovanovic, 1990). Alternatively, banks can promote growth because, as in Bencivenga and Smith (1991), they can offer liquidity insurance to each single consumer, allowing them to channel more funds to illiquid, high-return technology and to reduce the losses due to earlier liquidation of investment in order to face consumers' liquidity needs. Finally, financial intermediation transfers funds from households to firms at lower costs than would be incurred by individual investors. The more efficient the process of channelling funds, the larger the share of households' saving which can be used to finance firms' investment projects, and the higher the economy's growth rate. This literature is concerned with the efficiency gains deriving from financing through intermediaries compared with arm's length financing; we are interested instead in assessing the reaction of intermediaries to investment projects characterised by different degrees of informational asymmetry. King and Levine (1993b) analyse the role of financial intermediation in financing innovative activities in an endogenous growth model, but assume that information is symmetrically distributed between firms and intermediaries.

[2] See, among others, Fazzari, Hubbard and Petersen (1988), Hoshi, Kashyap and Sharfstein (1991) and Bond and Meghir (1994).

[3] In a previous related study, Hall (1990) shows that corporate restructuring that involved a substantial increase in leverage was followed by a decline in R&D expenditure. He interprets this as evidence of firms being cash constrained since a higher share of gross profits is used to service the debt. An alternative interpretation is that intermediaries have become less prone to finance the firm since a higher leverage implies a higher probability of default.

[4] Himmelberg and Petersen (1994) find indeed that, contrary perhaps to what one might expect, the effect of cash flow on physical investment is considerably larger than that on investment in R&D. On the other hand, Hao and Jaffe (1993) by splitting the sample according to firm size, find that current liquidity has a positive effect on R&D expenditure only in the subsample of smaller firms while it is statistically insignificant for larger firms. This last result is consistent with the cash flow effects on R&D arising from binding liquidity constraints if access to external funds is, as is commonly held, easier for larger firms. Another interpretation, as the authors recognise, is that the result reflects larger adjustment costs for R&D expenditure in large firms than in small ones.

[5] It might be argued that a firm is credit constrained if it answers "yes" to the third question and has given a positive answer to *both* the first two. That is, only those firms that want more credit *and* are willing to pay a higher rate should be considered as credit-rationed once they have been turned down for credit. While it is true that a credit-constrained firm is willing to trade a higher rate for a larger loan, this, strictly speaking, is only true for small increases in the interest rate. If the increase in the rate is large enough, the increase in total cost can

outweigh the increase in revenue so that profits could decline with respect to the initial position where only τ is obtained. For example, if output is produced with capital, k, according to the production function $k^{0.2}$, the profit-maximising demand for loans, on the assumption that all capital is financed with borrowing, is $k = (5p)^{-1.25}$, where p is the cost of capital in units of output. If $p=1$, the notional demand for loans is $k*=0.1337$. Suppose that the bank lends only 0.10, so that firm's profit is 0.5309. Clearly the firm is credit-constrained. However if it were offered as much money as desired while accepting a "slight" increase in the cost of borrowing of only 4 percent, it would prefer to produce at $k=0.10$, since its profits would otherwise decline to 0.5298. Since what is meant by "small" in the question raised in the survey is left unspecified; there are instances where a positive answer is given to the first question and a negative to the second. I have retained these firms in the sample and considered them as rationed if they were turned down for credit (they account for about half the credit-rationed firms in the 1993 sample).

[6] The INVIND sample includes only firms with 50 employees at least; thus, it may be argued that the figures in Table 7.1 considerably underestimate the extent of credit rationing if, as is commonly held, this is more likely to be applied to small firms. Here and in Section 4, however, it is shown that liquidity constraints are more likely among larger firms.

[7] The following figures support the above statements: in the Istat (1990) survey, after taking out the firms with less than 50 employees to make the comparison with INVIND meaningful, out of 8,281 innovative firms 933 only (22% of the sample) realised innovations which affected only the production process over the period 1981-1985; the remaining 78% realised innovations which concerned both the firm's product and its production process (61% of the firms) or only the product (17%).

[8] In Table 7.5 we have used the first definition to identify H-T firms. Results are unaffected if the second definition is used to construct the dummy *Htech*.

[9] I have also included investment made in the past year as an additional regressor. Its coefficient is negative as expected but is imprecisely estimated (t statistic = 1.20).

[10] The same set of variables was included in the first stage of the two regressions, namely: firm's age, a firm's size dummy, two regional location dummies, an ownership status dummy, a dummy for corporations, a set of variables for the structure of control (number of persons exercising control, maximum share of total stock held by the person exercising control, a dummy for companies with minority control), the share of export sales and the number of hours per employee spent in training activities.

[11] The pseudo R^2 in the first stage probit of the *Htech* indicator is 0.09, while the R^2 at the OLS regression of or R&D assets is only 0.03.

[12] The Istat survey was run over a sample of about 35,000 firms with more than 20 employees. A first stage of interviews led to the identification of 16,701 firms which in the period 1981-1985 introduced technological innovations. These firms are classified as innovative. They were further partitioned into two groups. The first (3,200 firms) included those that reported having introduced new products or new productive processes on the basis of R&D and projects conducted *within* the firm or based on their own patent. The second

group (13,000 units) included those that introduced innovations based on the acquisition of new technologies from outside. Firms in the first group are considered as highly innovative.

References

Arrow, K.J. (1962), "Economic Welfare and the Allocation of Resources for Invention" in R.R. Nelson (ed.), *The Rate and Direction of Inventive Activity: Economic and Social Factors*, Princeton University Press, Princeton.

Bencivenga, V. R. and Smith, B.D. (1991), "Financial Intermediation and Endogenous Growth", *The Review of Economic Studies*, 58: 195-209.

Bernanke, B. and Gertler, M. (1989), "Agency Costs, Net Worth and Business Fluctuations", *American Economic Review*, LXXIX: 14-31.

Bernanke, B. and Blinder, A.S. (1992), "The Federal Funds Rate and the Transmission of Monetary Policy", *American Economic Review*: 901-922.

Bhattacharya, S. and Ritter, J.R. (1983), "Innovation and Communication: Signalling with Partial Disclosure", *The Review of Economic Studies*, 50: 331-346.

Bond, S. and Meghir, C. (1994), "Dynamic Investment Models and the Firm's Financial Policy", *The Review of Economic Studies*, 207: 197-222.

Fazzari, S., Hubbard, R.G. and Petersen, B. (1988), "Investment and Finance Reconsidered", *Brookings Paper* on *Economic Activity*: 141-195.

Gertler, M., and Gilchrist, S. (1993), "The Role of Credit Market Imperfections in the Monetary Transmission Mechanism: Arguments and Evidence", *Scandinavian Journal of Economics*: 43-64.

Gertler, M., and Gilchrist, S. (1994), "Monetary Policy, Business Cycles and the Behaviour of Small Manufacturing Firms", *The Quarterly Journal of Economic*, 3: 309-334.

Grabowski, H. (1968), "The Determinants of Industrial Research and Development", *Journal of Political Economy*, 76: 292-306.

Greenwood, J. and Jovanovic, B. (1990), "Financial Development, Growth and the Distribution of Income", *Journal of Political Economy*, 98: 1076-1107.

Guiso, L. and Parigi, G. (1995), "Investment and Demand Uncertainty. Evidence from a Cross-Section of Italian Firms", paper presented at the CEPR European Summer Symposium in Macroeconomics, 28 June/2 July, Perugia, Italy.

Hao, K.Y. and Jaffe, A.B.(1993), "Effect of Liquidity on Firm's R&D Spending", *Economic Innovation and New Technology*, 2: 275-282.

Hall, B. (1990), "The Impact of Corporate Restructuring on Industrial Research and Development", *Brookings Papers on Economic Activity*, 1: 85-136.

Hall, B. (1992), "Investment in Research and Development at the Firm Level: Does the Source of Finance Matters?", NBER Working Paper No. 4096.

Hamburg, D. (1966), *Essays on the Economics of Research and Development*, Random House, New York.

Himmelberg, C.P. and Petersen, B.C. (1994), "R&D and Internal Finance: A panel Study of Small Firms in High- Tech Industries", *Review of Economics and Statistics,*

Hoshi, T., Kashyap, A. and Scharfstein, D. (1991), "Corporate Structure, Liquidity and Investment: Evidence from Japanese Industrial Groups", *The Quarterly Journal of Economics,* 56: 33-60.

Istat (1990), "Indagine statistica sull'innovazione tecnologica nell'industria italiana", Collana d'informazione, n. 14.

Jaffee, D. and Russell, T. (1976), "Imperfect Information, Uncertainty and Credit Rationing", *The Quarterly Journal of Economics,* 90: 651-666.

King, R. and Levine, R. (1993a), "Finance and Growth: Schumpeter Might be Right", *Quarterly Journal of Economics.*

King, R. and Levine, R. (1993b), "Finance, Entrepreneurship and Growth. Theory and Evidence", *Journal of Monetary Economics,* 32: 513-542.

Kiyotaky, N. and Moore, J. (1993), "Credit Cycles", Paper presented at the CEPR conference on "Corporate Finance", Sesimbra, Portugal, October 29-30.

Mueller, D. (1967), "The Firm Decision Process: An Econometric Investigation", *The Quarterly Journal of Economics,* 81: 58-87.

Petersen, M., Rajan, A. and Rajan, R.G. (1994), "The Benefits of Lending Relationships: Evidence from Small Business Data", *The Journal of Finance,* 1: 3-37.

Rajan R.G. (1994), "Why Bank Credit Policies Fluctuate: A Theory and Some Evidence", *The Quarterly Journal of Economics,* 2: 395-442.

Rondi, L., Sembenelli, A. and Zanetti, G. (1994), "Is Excess Sensitivity of Investment to Financial Factors Constant Across Firms?", *Journal of Empirical Finance,* 1: 365-383.

Rondi, L., Sack, B., Schiantarelli, F. and Sembenelli, S. (1993), "Firm's Financial and Real Responses to Business Cycle Shocks and Monetary Tightening Evidence for Large and Small Italian Companies", *CERIS Working Paper* n. 5/1993.

Scherer, F.M. (1965), "Firm Size, Market Structure, Opportunity and the Output of Patented Inventions", *American Economic Review,* 55:1097-1125.

Stiglitz, J.E. and Weiss, A. (1981), "Credit Rationing in Markets with Imperfect Information", *American Economic Review,* 71: 393-410.

Stiglitz, J.E. (1993) "Endogenous Growth and Cycles", NBER Working Paper No. 4286.

8 New technology investment and financial development: cross-country evidence

Boyan Jovanovic

1. Introduction

Panel data from the U.S. and other countries show that firms' investment decisions are often constrained by their cash flow and that relaxing finance constraints will therefore raise investment. As a result, better finance could lead to greater real activity and possibly to more growth.

The connection between R&D and finance is twofold. First, finance is especially important for small firms, and there is considerable evidence that small firms account for a disproportionately large number of innovations[1]. And second, regardless of firm size, R&D activity is the most difficult to monitor since inventive activity is not usually routinely observable. This means that informational asymmetries are the biggest in R&D investments, and developments in the financial system apt to overcome this asymmetry will be especially helpful in increasing the volume of R&D spending.

Of course, small firms are the ones that grow the fastest, and they are the ones that need external finance the most. Therefore, when a country develops financially, its small firms will benefit the most, since they are the most cash-constrained. (A theoretical and empirical analysis of the small, cash-constrained entrepreneur is in Evans and Jovanovic, 1989).

On the other hand, not everyone believes that better financial markets will speed development. First, DeLang (1992) argues that the advent of complex financial markets in the US has contributed to a decline in the importance of banks and in particular, a decline of concentrated ownership by bankers like J.P. Morgan, whose non-banking activities seemed to raise the level of performance in firms in which they held a high stake[2]. And Lichtenberg and Pushner (1992) show that in Japan firms with more concentrated bank ownership perform better than other firms. Second, Meyer (1990) has shown that stock markets have at times been a negative source of net finance for the business sector[3], and Japelli and Pagano (1992) have argued that better consumer loan possibilities reduce saving and can therefore harm growth.

All these are valid points, but several remarks can be made about them. First, it has not been established that concentrated ownership by banks actually raises firms' performance. It could simply be that banks identify "winners" and acquire a larger stake in them. What is needed is evidence that performance improves after concentrated bank ownership is put into effect. Second, while net stock finance may be negative in some periods, typically it is the fast growing firms that issue shares, and the big slow-growing firms that retire them. Hence it is gross finance that matters, rather than net. And third, when consumers can borrow more easily, this makes them better off. And since this withdraws funds from business investors only if the economy is closed, even in this case one needs some sort of positive externality to business investment before one can conclude that easier consumer finance is bad for welfare.

This report looks at several different ways of measuring the way that financial development affects investment in new technology. Data on the adoption of specific new technologies, and two datasets on total factor productivity, all indicate that there is a positive relation between finance and technology. The relation is especially strong when one disaggregates by sector so as to eliminate noise from composition effects. We use cross-country data on financial development compiled by Atje and Jovanovic (1993), some of which are reported in the Appendix. The paper also discusses some statistical biases that may arise because of reverse causation - feedback effects from technology to finance at firm level and country level.

2. Finance and the allocation of capital

The basic idea af this section is that the extent and quality of financial intermediation will affect the efficiency with which factors are allocated within the firm. This argument can apply to variable factors such as labour and raw materials, but only physical capital will be dealt with here. The analysis easily extends to other factors of production. The starting point of the analysis is the assumption that the value, V, of the firm's assets depends on the firm's capital stock, K, and on the efficiency, X, with which this capital stock is allocated:

$$V = G(K, X) \tag{1}$$

The function G is increasing in both arguments.

The Greenwood-Jovanovic (1990) model rests on the assumption that the efficiency with which the firm's capital stock is allocated depends on the way in which it is financed. The greater the amount of intermediation, the greater the efficiency with which the capital stock is allocated. The reason is that more intermediation brings more information to bear on the investment decision. The idea is that, because intermediaries lend to a lot of people, they may know more about general business conditions than any one borrower does. More generally, and particularly in the US, a lot of investment bankers and some specialised banks are experts in the businesses that they fund.

Suppose, therefore, an increasing relation between X and the extent of intermediation, F. The exact nature of this relation will depend on how familiar each firm is with the technology embodied in its capital stock. If the technology is new, it is especially important that an informed allocation decision is made, and in such an industry the allocative effect of financial intermediation will be larger. Let F denote the extent to which the capital stock is intermediated (we shall specify how to measure F later on). Then we assume that

$$X = H(F, T) \tag{2}$$

where T is the degree of the technological newness of the capital decision; a bigger T means roughly "more high-tech". This relation is drawn in Figure 8.1. The idea here is simple: If a technology is old, then everyone understands how it should be used, and the capital stock is allocated efficiently even in the absence of intermediation. But when the technology is new, there is a lot of uncertainty about it, and pooling information will help allocate capital better[4].

The properties of H highlighted in Figure 8.1 are

$$\frac{\partial X}{\partial F} > 0 \quad \text{and} \quad \frac{\partial^2 X}{\partial F \partial T} > 0 \tag{3}$$

The second property (i.e., that the slope is greater for technologically intensive processes) is the one that we wish to focus on: the beneficial effects of finance are stronger in high-tech industries and in high-tech firms.

Now suppose that we restrict matters further as in Lucas and Prescoot (1971). These authors make assumptions that guarantee constant returns to scale in K^5. This means that the value of the firm is proportional to its capital stock:

$$V(K, X) = q(X)K \tag{4}$$

This means that Tobin's average q and marginal q are the same, and that both are equal to

$$\frac{V(K, X)}{K} = q(X) \qquad (5)$$

So we have Tobin's q depending on the efficiency of allocation, X, and X in turn depending on F via equation (2).

Under further assumptions, we will be able to derive a testable restriction on the relationship between q(X) and F illustrated in Figure 8.2.

In testing for the impact of finance or allocative efficiency, it is important to single out the effect of education on human capital more generally. There is an older literature in development economics and labour economics - see Griliches (1958) for example - which emphasises that more educated people make better decisions, especially when it comes to implementing new tecnnology[6]. Since countries with more financial developmend typically also have more human capital[7], the latter should be held constant. I try to do so in some of the empirical work reported below.

3. Finance and diffusion of new innovations: the Nabseth-Ray data

Nabseth and Ray (1974, p. 17) summarise the post-war diffusion of 10 innovations in six European countries. Some of the information from that table is reproduced in Table 8.1. The numbers in the first 10 rows denote the fraction of all potential adopters that have already adopted the new invention. Row 11 shows the country average - the country-specific diffusion rates averaged over the 10 innovations. It shows that Sweden was the fastest adopter, Italy the slowest.

The question we ask next is: are these country-specific speeds of diffusion related to the level of each country's financial development? The data on financial development are taken from Atje and Jovanovic (1993). They are described and reported in Appendix 1 and in Table 8.2.

Figure 8.3 reports the plot of diffusion speed on the level of financial development. With the exception of Sweden, an outlier, the other countries are arranged in a fairly strong positive relation[8].

3.1 Summary of the Nabseth-Ray study

For some of the inventions that they studied, Nabseth and Ray made the explicit observation that financial constraint was an important restriction on the adoption of new technology. The page number references in the next 4 paragraphs are to the Nabseth-Ray study.

3.1.1 Numerically Controlled Machines (NCMs) Transition to capital-intensive production seemed easier with this technology when: (i) the rate of self-financing was high; or (ii) firms had easy access to outside financing. (p. 41). The first of these findings agrees with Himmleberg and Petersen's (1991).

NCMs were expensive and the decision to install them depended on the access to capital. The implication of this was that a large fraction of NCMs were installed by large and medium sized firms. These were firms that found it easier to finance investment, and the capital needed to install NCMs was usually a minor part of their total investment. Smaller firms may be better suited to numerically controlled machines, and some small firms were among the early adopters. But they may have been facing liquidity constraints in that the price of a single NCM might have been higher than their total average investment in a year (p. 52).

3.1.2 Special presses in paper-making Once again confirming Himmelberg and Petersen's conclusions, the self-financing ratio (annual average cash flow measured as a percentage of the annual average of gross investment - p. 65) was an important correlate of adoptions. Data were available only for the UK and Sweden. For Sweden, the average self-financing ratio was higher for early adopters and decreased for later adopters (the table on p. 77). But then the self-financing ratio of the non-adopters was also high (pp. 77-8).

3.1.3 Tunnel kilns Of the 94 firms in the sample, almost half financed all of their investment from retained profits, and a further third financed over 50% of their investment in this way. The stock exchange or other external sources of funds played a limited role. According to Nabseth and Ray, the reason was partly that, for many firms with unconvincing prospects, especially the smaller ones, raising funds in the stock market could only be done at punitive cost. Thus low profit levels could well act as a constraint on adoption (p. 123). These remarks are probably relevant to many small Italian firms today.

3.1.4 Shuttleless looms Some firms in Italy, UK and Germany cited high capital costs as a reason for not installing shuttless looms. Fewer firms in these countries and in the US mentioned funds being unobtainable as a reason for not adopting them (Table 10.12, p. 269).

3.2 Conclusion

The overall conclusion from the case studies gathered by Nabseth and Ray is that the method of investment financing in the introduction of a new process is a factor that accounts for the differences in the diffusion of technology among firms. Firms face at least two problems with financing: (i) capital markets may be imperfect so that it is impossible to borrow more than a certain amounts, and (ii) having borrowed the money, investments in new technology involve high risks, especially because relevant experience is scarce. Firms may therefore be reluctant to borrow money for this purpose. The implication is that a greater willingness to invest in new processes might be expected if they could be financed out of the firms' own resources (pp. 306-7). Therefore liquidity constraints, either through credit rationing or because of inability to issue equities, are an important factor bearing upon firms' decision whether to adopt new production processes. If this is indeed the case, one could try and see whether the introduction of junk bonds, for example, has any impact on the adoption of inventions or, for that matter, on R&D financing. The main reason for the introduction of junk bonds in the US in the 1980s after all, was, initially at least, to finance risky projects that otherwise would never be financed in a more conventional way. The analysis of the 1980s' experience in the US, however, is still under way[9].

Table 8.1 Cross-country diffusion of 10 post-war products

Diffusion by 1966	Austria	France	Italy	Sweden	UK	W. Germany
NC machine tools (1955) (a)	n.a.	.08	.03	n.a.	.09	.04
Special presses (1964)	35	25	4	52	24	15
Tunnel kilns (1948)	58	31	45	59	12	48
Basic oxygen steel (1952)	67	17	27	33	28	32
Float glass (1958)	0	7	6	0	25	6
Giberellic acid (1959)	0	n.a.	0	48	70	0
Continuous casting (1952)	1.2	0.6	2.0	2.2	1.6	2.4
Shuttleless loom (1953)	5	8.5	3	2.4	8	9.5
Plate cutting method (1950)	0	68	48	80	36	66
Automatic transfer lines (1947)	0	n.a.	39	97	52	81
Country average over products (R)	18.5	19.7	17.4	41.5	25.6	26
Rank of country's average	5	4	6	1	3	2

Source: Nabseth and Ray (1974, p. 17, table 2.1).

(a) Figure in parenthesis gives the year when initially introduced.

Table 8.2 Financial data for the Nabseth-Ray countries

	Country	D/K	B/K	S/K	F
1	United States	37.6	10.1	30.3	78.0
2	United Kingdom	12.5	1.6	18.7	32.8
3	Austria	25.9	0.0	1.0	26.9
6	France	18.2	1.4	3.3	22.9
7	Germany	26.9	0.1	3.5	30.5
8	Italy	17.0	0.1	2.4	19.5
11	Sweden	16.3	2.3	4.2	22.9
14	Japan	31.3	1.2	11.2	43.8

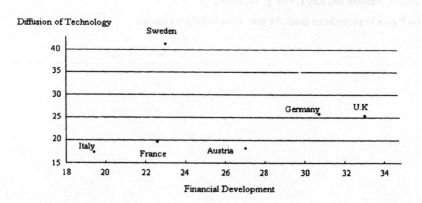

Figure 8.1 Speed of diffusion and financial development

4. Finance and total factor productivity: cross-country evidence

The previous section looked into the diffusion of specific innovations in different countries. This was a direct way of measuring the technological progress of a country's production methods, and we concluded that, with the exception of Sweden, there was a direct relation between the diffusion of technology in a country and its level of financial development. But there are also less direct ways of measuring technical progress. One way to view new technology is in terms of the output increase which can be produced with a constant amount of resources. An often used measure of technological advancement is total factor productivity, sometimes called the Solow residual. If financial development does speed up the adoption of technology, then our measure of financial development should be positively related to measures of total factor productivity.

Figure 8.2 shows that in cross-country data there is indeed a positive relation between F and TFP. The data cover 74 countries, and are reported in Table A.1 of Appendix 2. TFP was calculated by the formula

$$\text{Ln TFP}_i = \ln Y_i - (1/3)\ln K_i - (2/3)\ln_i$$

where Y, is country is output, K_i its capital stock and L_i its population, all measured in 1980. Log TFP is reported in Appendix Table A.1, where there are further details about how it was calculated.

While Figure 8.2 suggests a strong positive relationship, our finance variable may actually be a proxy for something else, possibly human capital in the workforce. To get a rough measure of human capital, we obtained data on secondary enrolment in 1970 in the 74 countries.

317

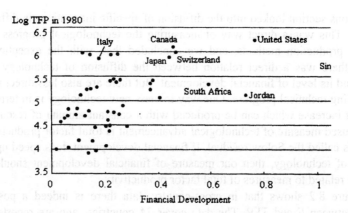

Figure 8.2 The positive relation between financial development and total factor productivity

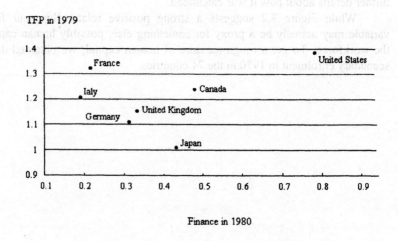

Finance in 1980

Figure 8.3 Financial development and TFP - The Wolff data

This variable is defined as H. We then ran the following least squares regression:

$$\ln TFP = (4.42 + 0.78 \, F) + 1.57 \, H$$
$$(57.91)\,(3.52) \quad (10.71) \qquad\qquad (6)$$

$n = 74$, $R^2 = 0.68$, t-values in parentheses. So, while our measure of H is highly significant (as one would expect if human capital mattered to production), it does not drive out our measure of financial development.

4.1 Wolff's data on TFP

In the above calculations, the regression (6) and the scatterplot in Figure 8.2 are all based on data from Summers and Heston: in particular, the data on physical capital that are needed for the calculation of TFP were compiled by Benhabib and Spiegel (1992) using the Summers-Heston database and the perpetual inventory method. Wolff (1991) uses different data on physical capital, compiled by Goldsmith and others, which are arguably of higher quality, even though the number of countries in his sample is small (seven). For the seven countries in question, the correlation coefficient between Wolff's data and ours is 0.75, and the scatterplot of the two sets of numbers is in Figure A1 of the Appendix. It shows that Italy looks more technologically advanced in Wolff's data than in ours.

Figure 8.3 shows a fairly weak but positive relationship between finance and TFP. However, the analog of the regression in equation (6) shows rather puzzling results:

$$\ln TFP = 0.18 + 0.24F - 0.13H$$
$$(0.53) \ (0.59) \ (0.22) \qquad\qquad (7)$$

$n = 7$, $R^2 = 0.12$, t-values in parentheses. It's hard, however, to draw any definite conclusion from such a small sample.

5. Sectorial analysis of total factor productivity (TFP) and finance

This section reports on some preliminary datawork which will be extended in future work. The data contain estimates of TFP by sector and for many of the OECD countries. The aim is to see if in each sector, countries with better financial arrangements also have higher TFP. The answer is "Yes" for almost all sectors. The next task is to break up the effect into two parts.

(a) The direct effect of finance on TFP through improved allocation of capital. This is the effect emphasised in the model of Greenwood and Jovanovic (1990).

(b) The indirect effect of finance on TFP through increased R&D spending (which better financial arrangements make possible).

Two authors have recently studied TFP for several OECD countries: Costello (1993) and Wolff (1993). They are commented upon both, although the Costello data is not available in level form and only the Wolff data can therefore be analysed.

5.1 Costello's sectorial TFP data

Costello (1993) carries out a cross-country study of technical change in which several sectors of the economy are considered. In Table 3 she reports the growth of Solow residuals (i.e., TFP) for 1960-88 for the following sectors: Food, Textiles, Chemicals, Basic Metals, and Metal Manufacturing. The correlation between TFP growth of a sector in a country and its finance shows for the most part a negative relationship, which is not surprising given that the OECD countries show strong convergence, and that richer countries are financially more developed. Table 8.6 shows the plots, and the correlation coefficients, denoted by ρ. The negative ρ's documents that the technological catch-up has been taking place at the sectorial as well as at the aggregate level.

5.2 Wolff's sectorial TFP data

These data are partly reported in Wolff (1993), but Table 8.7 reports them in greater detail for the year 1988[10]. There are 14 OECD countries and for most of them there is information on 11 sectors. The Manufacturing sector is then broken down into 9 subsectors. All the numbers are expressed in terms of US TFP and most of them are therefore less than unity.

We do not have a measure of finance for Finland, which was omitted from the analysis. Table 8.8 reports the cross-country correlations of these TFP numbers with our finance measure. Most of them are large and some are highly significant, in spite of the rather small sample size. Following Table 8.8, I report, in Table 8.9, cross-country plots that belong to each sector and to each manufacturing industry. Italy is marked on each figure, and the US is easily identifiable because its TFP is equal to one in each graph.

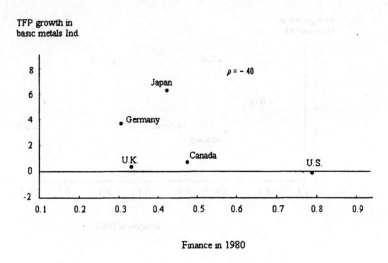

Figure 8.4a Finance vs TFP growth in the basic metal industry

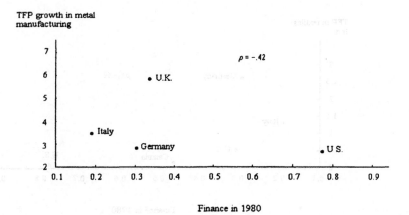

Figure 8.4b Finance vs TFP growth in metal manufacturing

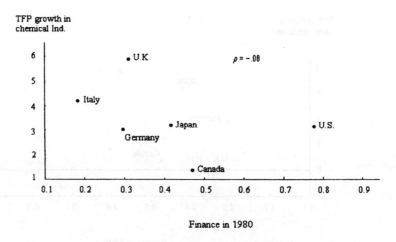

Figure 8.4c Finance vs TFP growth in the chemicals industry

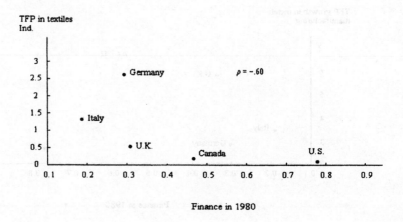

Figure 8.4d Finance vs TFP in the textiles industry

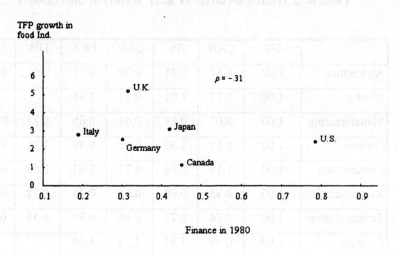

Figure 8.4e Finance vs TFP growth in the food industry

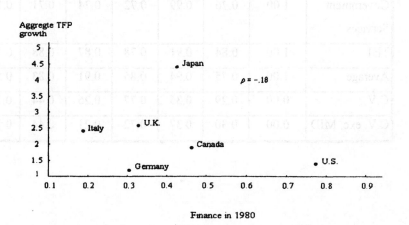

Figure 8.4f Finance vs aggregate TFP growth in 1960-88

Fig 8.4 Annualized TFP growth 1960-88 and finance (Costello data)

Table 8.7a Wolff's sectorial TP data: sectors of the economy

	US	CAN	JPN	GER	FRA	ITA	UK
Agriculture	1.00	0.51	0.34	0.39	0.97	0.51	0.65
Mining	1.00	0.72	1.01	0.27	1.38		
Manufacturing	1.00	0.67	0.88	0.61	0.65	0.72	0.56
Utilities	1.00	0.55	1.50	0.82	0.99	1.16	0.56
Construction	1.00	1.19	0.66	0.73	0.63	0.56	0.69
Restaurants	1.00	0.93	0.90	0.62	0.75	0.79	0.55
Transportation	1.00	0.74	0.72	0.65	0.74	0.56	0.70
Finance, Insurance, Real Estate	1.00	0.98	1.47	2.72	1.10		
Social Services	1.00	0.45	0.97	1.00	1.13	1.66	0.41
Government Services	1.00	0.76	0.99	0.72	0.74	0.71	0.54
TET	1.00	0.84	0.91	0.78	0.87	0.88	0.74
Average	1.00	0.75	0.94	0.85	0.91	0.83	0.58
C.V.	0.00	0.29	0.35	0.77	0.26	0.44	0.15
C.V. exc. MID	0.00	0.30	0.37	0.72	0.21	0.44	0.15

Table 8.7a (con't) Wolff's sectorial TP data: sectors of the economy

	AUS	NLD	BEL	DNK	NOR	SWE	FIN	C.V
Agriculture	0.81	0.77	1.06	0.60	0.35	0.47	0.43	0.380
Mining	1.29	3.33	0.32	2.82	2.28	0,33	0.62	0.758
Manufacturing	0.64	0.62	0.74	0.44	0.43	0.49	0.61	0.235
Utilities	0.58	0.67	1.02	0.48	0.60	0.84	0.63	0.345
Construction	0.76	0.89	0.88	0.49	0.43	0.78	0.62	0.267
Restaurants		0.69	0.80		0.56	0.64	0.55	0.202
Transportation	0.69		0.70	0.52	0.56	0.57	0.59	0.179
Finance, Insurance, Real Estate	0.87		1.37	0.79	0.77	0.67	0.71	0.494
Social Services	1.19		0.64	1.29	0.70	0.60	0.64	0.391
Government Services	0.91	1.05	0.72	0.58	0.57	0.64	0.57	0.222
TET	0.79	0.89	0.85	0.65	0.71	0.66	0.64	0.131
Average	0.86	1.15	0.83	0.89	0.73	0.60	0.60	0.347
C.V.	0.26	0.79	0.32	0.82	0.73	0.23	0.12	0.43
C.V. exc. MID	0.22	0.19	0.25	0.41	0.23	0.18	0.12	0.29

Tab 8.7b TFP of nine manufacturing industries

	US	CAN	JPN	GER	FRA	ITA	UK
All of manufacturing	1.00	0.67	0.88	0.61	0.65	0.72	0.56
Food	1.00	0.66	0.54	0.59	0.62	0.78	0.93
Textiles	1.00	0.88	0.52	0.63	0.78	0.77	0.58
Wood products	1.00	0.82		0.52	0.58		
Paper, print	1.00	0.74	0.71	0.61	0.73	0.90	0.78
Chemicals	1.00	0.50	1.44	0.70	0.76	0.81	1.18
Non-metal mining	1.00	0.75	0.63	0.63	0.83	0.82	0.76
Basic metals	1.00	0.91	1.91	0.60	0.63	0.91	0.58
Machinery and equipment	1.00	0.77	0.88	0.51	0.54	0.69	0.47
Other	1.00	0.46	0.52	0.39		0.25	1.68
Average	1.00	0.72	0.89	0.57	0.68	0.74	0.87
C.V (AVG ex US)		0.20	0.53	0.15	0.14	0.27	0.43

Tab 8.7b (con't) TFP of nine manufacturing industries

	AUS	NLD	BEL	DNK	NOR	SWE	FIN	C.V.
All of manufacturing	0.64	0.62	0.74	0.44	0.43	0.49	0.61	0.235
Food			0.95	0.58	0.21	0.48		0.337
Textiles			0.58	0.53	0.52	0.54		0.235
Wood products				0.42	0.47	0.63		0.302
Paper, print			0.76	0.49	0.46	0.50		0.234
Chemicals			0.90	0.50	0.39	0.53		0.386
Non-metal mining			0.50	0.37		0.51		0.262
Basic metals			0.86	0.48	0.91	0.48		0.454
Machinery and equipment			0.79	0.33	0.42	0.43		0.331
Other			0.58	0.37		0.23		0.715
Average			0.74	0.45	0.48	0.48		0.278
C.V (AVG ex US)			0.21	0.17	0.41	0.21		0.27

Table 8.7c Coefficient of variation of relative TFP levels across countries, 1970-1988 for six sectors

	1970	1979	1988
Agriculture	0.28	0.29	0.38
Mining	0.63	1.00	0.76
Manufacturing	0.19	0.20	0.23
Utilities	0.59	0.39	0.35
Construction	0.31	0.24	0.27
Restaurants	0.25	0.22	0.20

Table 8.8 Sectorial TFP correlations with F

Sector	Cross-Country correlation of TSP with F	Number of countries covered	Significance level
Agriculture	.16	13	.60
Mining	-.20	11	.55
Manufacturing	.73	13	.00
Utilities	.22	13	.46
Construction	.61	13	.11
Restaurants	.68	11	.02
Transportation	.86	12	.00
Finance, Insurance,	.07	10	.85
Real estate	-.13	12	.68
Social services	.58	13	.04
Government services TET	.63	13	.02
Manufacturing Food	.42	11	.20
Textiles	.68	11	.02
Wood products	.94	7	.00
Paper, print	.61	11	.04
Chemicals	.41	11	.20
Non-metal minings	.66	10	.04
Basic metals	.38	11	.25
Machinery and equipment	.71	11	.02
Other	.38	9	.32

Table 8.9a Aggregate

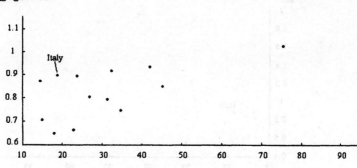

Finance vs
Aggregate TFP

Finance in 1980

Table 8.9b Agriculture

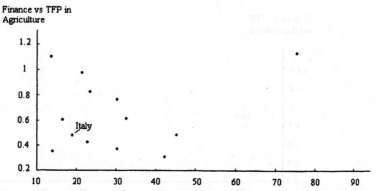

Finance vs TFP in
Agriculture

Finance in 1980

Table 8.9c Basic metal industries

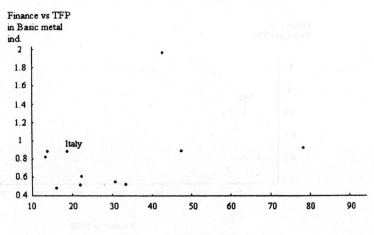

Finance vs TFP
in Basic metal
ind.

Finance in 1980

Table 8.9d Chemical industry

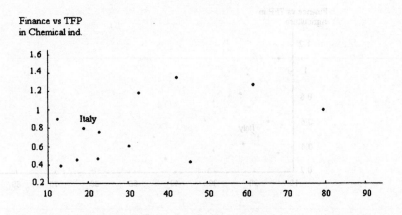

Finance vs TFP
in Chemical ind.

Finance in 1980

330

Table 8.9e Construction

Finance vs TFP
in Construction

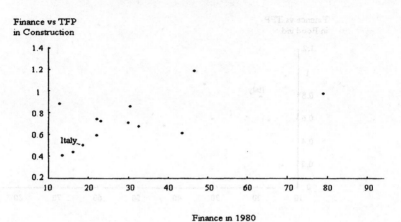

Finance in 1980

Table 8.9f Finance, insurance and real estate

Finance vs TFP in
FIRE

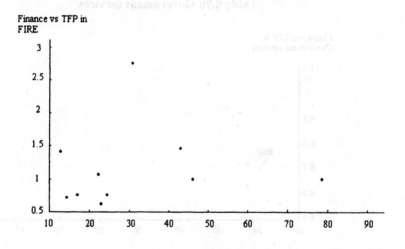

Finance in 1980

331

Table 8.9g Food industry

Finence vs TFP
in Food ind.

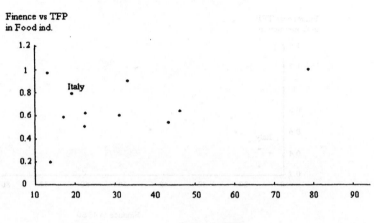

Finance in 1980

Table 8.9h Government services

Finance vs TFP in
Government services

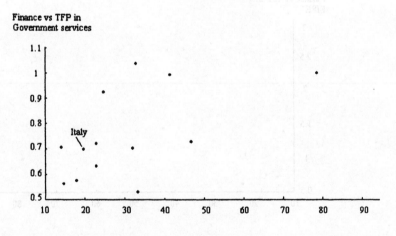

Finance in 1980

Table 8.9i Machinery industry

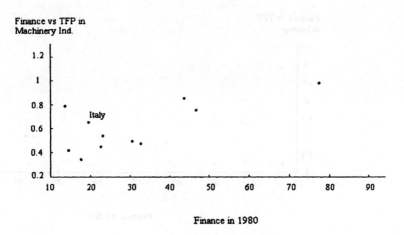

Finance vs TFP in
Machinery Ind.

Italy

Finance in 1980

Table 8.9j Manufacturing

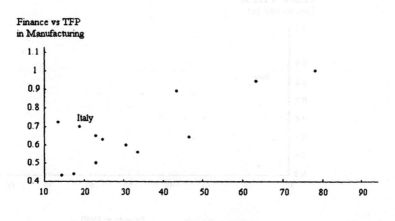

Finance vs TFP
in Manufacturing

Italy

Finance in 1980

Table 8.9k Mining

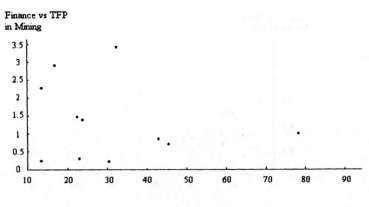

Finance vs TFP
in Mining

Finance in 1980

Table 8.9l Non-metallic industry

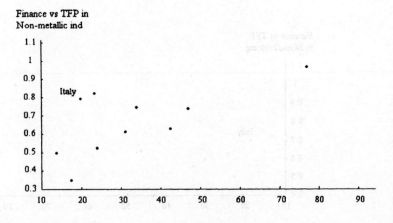

Finance vs TFP in
Non-metallic ind

Italy

Finance in 1980

Table 8.9m Other industries

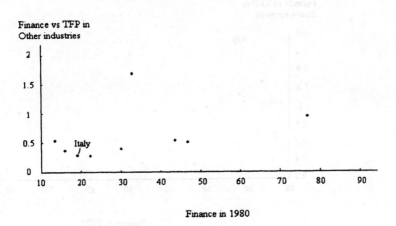

Table 8.9n Paper industry

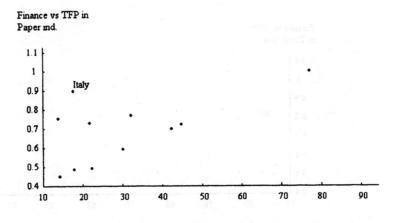

Table 8.9o Social services

Finance vs TFP in
Social services

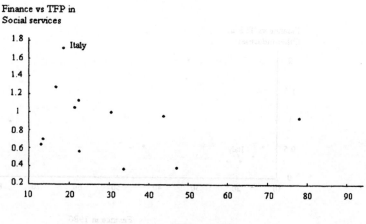

Finance in 1980

Table 8.9p Textile industry

Finance vs TFP
in Textile ind.

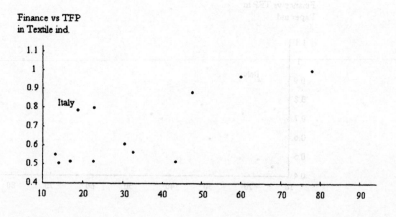

Finance in 1980

336

Table 8.9q Trade

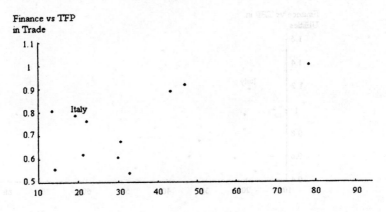

Finance vs TFP
in Trade

Finance in 1980

Table 8.9r Transportation

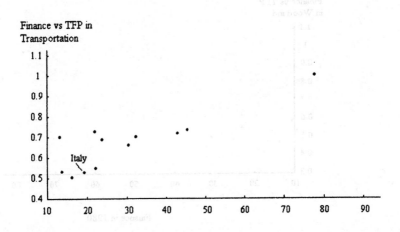

Finance vs TFP in
Transportation

Finance in 1980

Table 8.9s Utilities

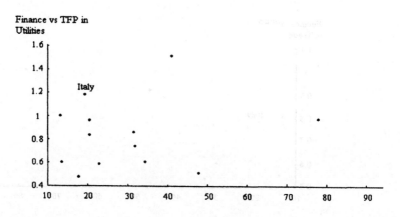

Finance vs TFP in Utilities

Italy

Finance in 1980

Table 8.9t Wood industry

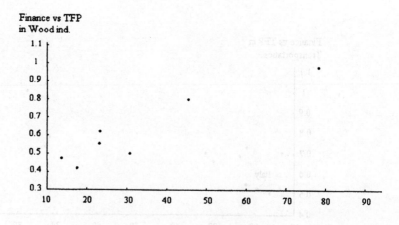

Finance vs TFP in Wood ind.

Finance in 1980

6. Reverse causation between technology adoption and finance

The effect of finance on technology adoption, especially in small firms, may be overestimated for one important reason: successful R&D programmes are likely to lead to more external financing. This at least has been found to be true in the US which is a relatively developed financial market: Lerner (1993) looks at the relationship between financing and oversight of privately-held firms by venture capitalists (venture capitalists usually know something about the business they are financing.) Lerner uses a sample of 271 biotechnology firms between 1978 and 1989. He finds that technological progess, as measured by a firm's patent applications, increases the probability of a new financing round (by the venture capitalist) by 75%. This suggests that venture capitalists' financing of firms is an important oversight mechanism, in that withdrawal of funds can serve as an important punishment device. But, more importantly, it shows that successful implementation of high-tech methods by a firm will make it easier for the firm to get more financing. This means that the causal effect of finance on R&D is likely to be overstated unless this feedback is taken into account.

This phenomenon is likely to be true in relations between borrowers and lenders everywhere. In Germany and Japan, banks often work closely with the businesses they lend to and a firm's success is likely to make financing easier[11]. Moreover, the success could be something that the lender anticipates and that is reflected in the size of the loan. This means that firms expected to succeed are given bigger loans. Since unsuccessful firms may do more R&D, the causation again is running in the reverse direction.

These feedback effects are present not just at the firm level, but also at country level: when a country attains a higher level of income, this leads to more investment in the country's financial infrastructure. This backward link was emphasised in the Greenwood-Jovanovic (1990) model. Atje and Jovanovic (1993) find, however, that the beneficial effect of finance on real activity remains strong even after one controls for the reverse causation present in the data.

7. R&D intensity and type of investment financing

The matter will not be analysed in the present report, but deserves being discussed in the future. The question to focus on: "what is the nature of funding in (a) R&D intensive firms and (b) R&D intensive industries or sectors"? Specifically, one can go into bank involvement to see whether it is heavier in R&D intensive sectors, where the need to monitor is clearly greater.

In the US, the COMPUSTAT files have information about the composition of firms' liabilities, and also about their R&D intensity. The Global Vantage

Tapes have similar information for firms in other countries, but sample sizes are too small to allow country-by-country analysis over sectors[12]. Nevertheless the data could be pooled over all countries.

For certain other countries, sectorial information on bank lending is available. For example, it is possible to know what fraction of total investment, by sector, is financed by banks[13]. These figures should then be correlated with sectorial R&D/sales ratios. In principle, one would expect debt to be a more important source of external finance in R&D-intensive sectors than commercial paper or equity. Other sectorial characteristics, such as physical capital intensity, should be checked for in such a cross-sector analysis.

Appendix 1

The measurement of financial development at country level

We shall measure financial development as follows:

$$F = \frac{D+B+E}{K}$$

where

      D = cumulative credit to domestic residents issued by private and government banks averaged over 1975-1980 to eliminate transitory variation within countries[14]

      B = privately issued bonds outstanding in 1980

      E = value of shares outstanding in 1980

      K = the physical capital stock in 1980[15]

The year 1980 was the earliest for which we have E for enough countries. For most countries B is either negligible or equal to zero, and for roughly half of them, which have no stock market, E is equal to zero[16].

    The data for K come from Benhabib and Spiegel (1992) who geometrically depreciate the Summers-Heston investment numbers at a constant rate.

    In countries that do have stock markets, some of the capital stock is in privately held firms. Such firms do not issue bonds either, so E =- B = 0 for them. For publicly traded firms, the ratio (D + B + E)/K is essentially Tobin's q.

    Table 8.2 describes the financial data for the 6 European countries in Nabseth and Ray's sample (plus the US and Japan for reference). The data for all countries are reported in Table A.1 in this Appendix.

Table Al Financial Data and TFP

	Country	D/K	B/K	S/K	F	log TFP
1	United States	37.6	10.1	30.3	78.0	6.23
2	United Kingdom	12.5	1.6	18.7	32.8	5.89
3	Austria	25.9	0.0	1.0	26.9	5.80
4	Belgium	10.5	0.0	3.6	14.1	5.89
5	Denmark	14.6	0.0	2.7	17.3	5.78
6	France	18.2	1.4	3.3	22.9	5.89
7	Germany	26.9	0.1	3.5	30.5	5.88
8	Italy	17.0	0.1	2.4	19.5	5.84
9	Netherlands	23.1	0.0	7.7	30.8	5.90
10	Norway	12.1	0.0	2.0	14.4	5.90
11	Sweden	16.3	2.3	4.2	22.9	5.91
12	Switzerland	33.6	0.0	12.9	46.5	6.01
13	Canada	19.4	5.6	21.5	46.4	6.10
14	Japan	31.3	1.2	11.2	43.8	5.78
15	Greece	18.3	0.0	3.1	21.3	5.43
16	Iceland	12.3	0.0	0.0	12.3	5.98
17	Ireland	11.3	0.0	0.0	11.3	5.50
18	Malta	11.8	0.0	0.0	11.8	5.44
19	Portugal	32.2	0.0	0.4	32.6	5.37
20	Spain	29.0	0.0	3.2	32.2	5.53
21	Australia	10.0	0.0	13.9	23.9	5.91
22	South Africa	11.0	0.0	47.9	58.9	5.32
23	Bolivia	6.1	0.0	0.0	6.1	4.82
24	Brazil	17.3	0.0	2.4	19.6	5.45
25	Chile	13.6	0.0	24.3	37.9	5.46
26	Colombia	9.0	0.0	3.3	12.3	5.28
27	Dominican Republic	14.5	0.0	0.0	14.5	5.05
28	Ecuador	8.4	0.0	0.0	8.4	5.12

Table Al (con't) Financial Data and TFP

	Country	D/K	B/K	S/K	F	log TFP
29	El Salvador	36.7	0.0	0.0	36.7	5.04
30	Guatemala	15.2	0.0	0.0	15.2	5.30
31	Haiti	19.7	0.0	0.0	19.7	4.72
32	Honduras	18.2	0.0	0.0	18.2	4.76
33	Mexico	7.2	0.0	4.1	11.2	5.61
34	Paraguay	14.0	0.0	0.0	14.0	5.28
35	Uruguay	15.7	0.0	1.1	16.9	5.23
36	Venezuela	23.1	0.0	2.5	25.6	5.61
37	Guyana	3.1	0.0	0.0	3.1	5.74
38	Jamaica	8.1	0.0	0.7	8.9	4.57
39	Cyprus	18.6	0.0	0.0	18.6	4.85
40	Israel	23.2	0.0	14.9	38.1	5.43
41	Jordan	39.9	0.0	36.0	75.9	5.75
42	Syrian Arab Republic	4.8	0.0	0.0	4.8	5.12
43	Egypt	40.1	0.0	2.2	42.3	5.64
44	Yemen	16.5	0.0	0.0	16.5	5.14
45	India	12.7	0.0	2.5	15.2	4.77
46	Indonesia	8.5	0.0	0.1	8.6	4.11
47	Korea, Rep. of	19.2	0.0	2.8	22.0	4.74
48	Malaysia	15.3	0.0	25.4	40.8	5.08
49	Pakistan	14.3	0.0	1.9	16.2	5.37
50	Philippines	16.0	0.0	5.6	21.6	4.59
51	Singapore	27.1	0.0	85.3	112.4	4.89
52	Thailand	23.6	0.0	3.0	26.6	5.72
53	Algeria	32.4	0.0	0.0	32.4	5.05
54	Burundi	7.3	0.0	0.0	7.3	5.12
55	Cameroon	31.1	0.0	0.0	31.1	4.20
56	Central African Rep.	12.5	0.0	0.0	12.5	4.45

Table AI (con't) Financial Data and TFP

	Country	D/K	B/K	S/K	F	log TFP
57	Zaire	11.7	0.0	0.0	11.7	3.89
58	Benin	38.0	0.0	0.0	38.0	4.76
59	Ghana	4.3	0.0	0.0	4.3	4.65
60	Madagascar	16.9	0.0	0.0	16.9	4.47
61	Malawi	10.9	0.0	0.0	10.9	4.18
62	Mauritania	24.4	0.0	0.0	24.4	4.49
63	Mauritius	20.7	0.0	0.0	20.7	5.36
64	Morocco	23.6	0.0	3.5	27.1	5.14
65	Niger	15.5	0.0	0.0	15.5	4.46
66	Nigeria	9.8	0.0	2.3	12.2	4.79
67	Rwanda	10.2	0.0	0.0	10.2	4.66
68	Senegal	37.2	0.0	0.0	37.2	4.76
69	Sudan	43.1	0.0	0.0	43.1	5.11
70	Tanzania	1.5	0.0	0.0	1.5	4.00
71	Togo	16.5	0.0	0.0	16.5	4.35
72	Tunisia	32.3	0.0	0.0	32.3	5.27
73	Burkina Faso	13.6	0.0	0.0	13.6	3.94
74	Zambia	4.4	0.0	0.0	4.4	4.03
75	Papua New Guinea	4.8	0.0	0.0	4.8	4.70

Sources:

D is taken from various issues of the International Monetary Fund's *International Financial Statistics*, line 32d.

B is taken from OECD Financial statistics Part 2, *Financial Accounts of OECD Countries*, various issues.

S is taken from International Finance Coporation, *Emerging Stock Market Factbook* (1989).

In the calculation of TFP, the capital stock data are taken from Benhabib and Spiegel (1992), and Gross Domestic Product and Population are taken from the data base compiled by Summers and Heston (1991).

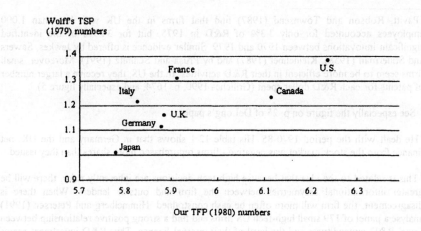

Figure A.1 Wolff's TFP data on our TFP data

Notes

[1] Pavitt, Robson and Townsend (1987) find that firms in the UK with less than 1,000 employees accounted for only 3.3% of R&D in 1975, but for 34.9% of the identified significant innovations between 1970 and 1979. Similar evidence is offered by Jewkes, Sawers and Stillerman (1958), Kleinchnet (1987) and by Prusa and Schmitz (1991). Moreover, small firms seem to be more efficient in their R&D activities: In the US, they receive a larger number of patents for each R&D dollar spent (Griliches 1990, p. 1674, and especially figure 5).

[2] See especially the figure on p. 25 of DeLong's paper.

[3] He dealt with the period 1970-85. His table 12.1 shows that in Germany and the UK, net finance from the stock market was negative - firms repurchased more shares than they issued.

[4] This is related to the idea that because high-tech decisions are inherently risky, there will be greater informational assymetries between the firm and outside lenders. When there is disagreement, the firm will more often be cash constrained. Himmelberg and Petersen (1991) analyse a panel of 179 small high-tech US firms and find a strong positive relationship between firms' R&D expenditures and the level of their internal finance. Thus R&D investment seems to be cash-constrained. The point is that if this is true in a financially developed economy such as the US, we expect even greater constraints to be likely to occur in financially less developed economies like Italy.

[5] This rests on the assumption that both firm's production function and its costs of adjusting K, are both homogeneous of degree one in K and in investment.

[6] Grilieches (1957) studied the adoption of new improved seeds by farmers and found that educated farmers adopted the new seeds faster.

[7] The cross-country correlation between F and either the primary or secondary enrolment rate is positive.

[8] The outlier observation (Sweden) is perhaps due to unusually high spending on R&D. In a sample of firms from Standard and Poor's Compustat services, the Swedish companies in the sample spent 5.8% of their sales revenues on R&D in 1992, compared with 5.5% in Germany, 5.2% in Canada, 3.8% in France, 3.7% in US, and 2.7% in the UK (*Business Week*, June 28, 1993).

[9] Hall (1990) provides an example of recent work on understanding the impact of the recent merger waves on finance and R&D.

[10] These data are provided by Ed Wolff. Table 8.7C is relevant for TFP convergence among countries, for 6 sectors. It shows convergence only for utilities.

[11] When lenders do not observe the shocks that influence borrowers' payoffs, borrowers of course have an incentive to misrepresent these shocks, always claiming the adverse outcome. But optimal contracts will tend to have the "reinforcement" property: in a repeated situation borrowers who perform well are better treated by lenders. See Atkeson and Lucas (1992) for recent work an this subject, and for further references.

[12] The best represented are Japan with 82 firms and the UK with 75 firms.

[13] Information on bank lending by sector for the UK, for example, can be found in the *Quarterly Bulettin*, Bank of England, August 1991, table 5. In the US, such information is on the Citibase database and elsewhere.

[14] Some of this credit is extended to consumers, not firms, and should not be counted, but the data does not distinguish consumer credit from business credit.

[15] Except that in computing the D/K ratio, we use the ratio D_t/K_t averaged over t ranging between 1975 and 1980.

[16] Foreign holdings of domestic firms' bonds and equities are included, as they should be, and so are foreign bank loans. Since B, D and E are all measured in 1980 or earlier, however, their foreign components are negligible.

References

Atkeson, A. and Lucas, R.E. (1992), "On Efficient Distribution with Private Information," *Review of Economic* Studies 59, no. 3 (July): 427- 53.

Atje, R. and Jovanovic, B. (1993), "Finance and Development", unpublished paper, New York University, April.

Benhabib, J. and Spiegel, M. (1992), "Growth Accounting with Physical and Human Capital Accumulation", unpuhlished paper, New York University, March.

Costello, D. (1993), "A Cross-Country, Cross-Industry Comparison of Productivity Growth", *Journal of Political Economy* 101, no. 2 (April): 207-23.

DeLong, B. (1992), "What Morgan Wrought", WQ (Autumn): 17-30.

Evans, D. and Jovanovic, B. (1990), "An Estimated Model of Entrepreneurial Choice under Liquidity Constraints", *Journal of Political Economy* 97, no. 4 (August): 808-27.

Greenwood, J. and Jovanovic, B. (1990), "Financial Development, Growth, and the Distribution of Income", *Journal of Political Economy* 98, no. 5, pc. 1 (October): 1076-1107.

Griliches, Z. (1990), "Patent Statistics as Economic Indicators: A Survey", *Journal of Economic Literature* 28 (December): 1661-1707.

Griliches, Z, (1957), "Hybrid Corn: An Exploration in the Economics of Technical Change", *Econometrica* 25, no. 4 (October).

Hall, B. (1990), "The Impact of Corporate Restructuring on Industrial R&D" Brookinzs Papers on Economic Activity: Microeconomics: 85-124.

Himmelberg, C. and Petersen, B. (1991), "R&D and Internal Finance: A Panel Study of Small Firms in High-Tech Industries", unpublished paper, Stern School of Business, New York University, June.

Jappelli, T. and Pagano, M. (1992), "Saving, Growth and Liquidity Constraints", CEPR Discussion Paper no. 652.

Jewkes, J., Sawers, D. and Stillerman, R. (1987), *The Sources of Invention*, London: MacMillan.

Kleinchnecht, A. (1987), "Measuring R&D in Small Firms: How Much are we Missing?" *Journal of Industrial Economics* 36, no. 2: 253-56.

Lerner, J. (1993), "Venture Capitalists and the Financing of Privately Held Firms", unpublished paper, Graduate School of Business, Harvard University, April.

9 Financing technological innovation in Italy: sources, governmental support and productivity growth

Giuliana Battisti

1. Introduction

The aim of this chapter is to test the efficiency of Italian investments in R&D with respect to the introduction of new ways of employing human and capital resources. The analysis tries to quantify the correlation between the amount of financial resources devoted to inventive activity and the introduction rate of innovations into the production system.

In this framework the governmental policy plays a fundamental role both in terms of choice of eligible sectors and modality of the interventions.

The Total Factor Productivity represents the contribution of the innovative activity it has been introduced into the economic system. However controversial, this indicator has been chosen on account of the many different and changing ways technical progress affects the combination of human and capital inputs in the production process.

A brief historical and political excursion summarises the Italian economic path in the last three decades. The composition of public and private financing sources for industrial R&D are analysed with particular attention to the governmental intervention in favour of this high risk activity.

The link between invention and innovation, in terms of technological independence from abroad, is measured by two proxies: the amount of R&D

carried out by the industrial laboratory of research (input) and the efficiency, i.e. TFP, reached by the economic system (output)[1].

The chapter concludes by focusing attention on the productivity path of the sectors mainly supported by the government such as: Electrical-Electronics, Chemical-Pharmaceuticals, Mechanical and Transportation.

A final section summarises the main findings, providing an overall view of the economic, financial and political difficulties the Italian economy should overcome to get closer to the frontier of technological independence from abroad.

2. Productivity and factor substitution: the Italian economic background

The capacity of the economic system to transform available resources is measured by the Total Factors Productivity (TFP) in terms of reduction of real net costs for unit of production. Supposing the presence of only two factors of production (labour and capital), the comparison between potential and actual products is the indicator for the efficiency of the means of production.

This approach can be summarised as relative differences[2] and it is similar to the well-known Solow aggregate production function model (Solow, 1957) and also to the Bank of England capital utilisation model in manufacturing industry (Bank of England, 1971).

This methodology applied to the Italian case indicates that the contribution to economic growth is due, for almost 40%, to capital input changes, for 50%, to a reduction in the labour input and, for about 80%, to a change in the organisation of the production also including improvements in the quality of factors and prices changes.

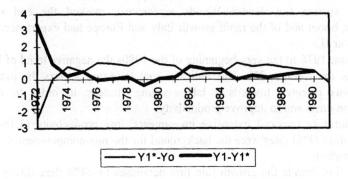

* The Industrial production has been disaggregated into two components according to definition [7] given in the Methodological Note, i.e. (Y1-Yo) = (Y1*-Yo) + (Y1-Y1*). Italian economic growth (Y1-Yo) is explained by the percentage contribution of factor utilisation (Y1*-Yo) and by the productivity or TFP (Y1-Y1*).

Graph 9.1 Total factors productivity and factors utilisation of the Italian manufacturing industries

Graph 9.1 shows productivity trends and the technical progress contribution to Italian economic development. Furthermore it underlines the reduction in the labour units employed in the production process, the decrease of capital accumulation rate, especially during oil crises, and the high discontinuity with which such structural changes took place.

Since the information this level of aggregation provides is very poor, in the following part the determinants of economic growth are analysed over time together with some brief recollection of main historical and political events.

During the 1970s Italy experienced a very unstable economic period. In order to face this difficult time several companies tried to reduce costs by looking for a more flexible structure and committing part of their production to external small firm and home workers. For the whole period the factors' contribution is systematically greater than their productivity.

In Graph 9.2 this relevant factor mobilisation contrasts the negative trend of the system's total efficiency, confirming production reorganisation. "Entrepreneurs tried to improve static efficiency, e.g. costs reduction through the rationalisation of existing capital assets, rather than dynamic efficiency, e.g. the introduction rate of technological innovation" (Malerba, 1991).

In 1973 the first economic crises (Kippur war) and the crisis of the financial system (i.e. Bretton-Woods agreement), marked the end of the economic boom and of the rapid growth Italy and Europe had experienced after World War II.

From 1976 to the very beginning of the 1980s the negative trend of labour input was on average -2%. This indicates that for many sectors the industrial policy was oriented towards a labour-saving strategy in order to reduce production costs and to improve productivity.

Therefore previous extensive investments, low productivity (3.1%) and accumulation (1%) rates were the background for the non-competitiveness of the Italian products.

In this decade the growth rate first decreases to -60% then slowly starts growing again, despite being interrupted by the two oil crises. Investments dramatically decrease and so does the productivity of the system (-26.9%). Difficulties also arise from a lack of flexibility of the production process in the short run, as machinery becomes suddenly obsolete due to the rapid growth of the incorporated technical progress.

In this period firms made a big effort in R&D activities but in the wrong direction, far away from the technological frontier. The difficulties they met on financial ground were notable and the total absence of economic incentives led them to abandon any large scale planning.

The fact that there was no governmental intervention whatsoever to stimulate R&D in advanced high-tech areas did not help to overcome this difficult period (Belvisi, Carnazza, 1988).

These were the main causes for contraction in labour supply and willingness to invest, especially for firms already experiencing difficulties in self-financing their activity (Valli, 1989).

Towards the end of the 1970s this situation led an increasing number of small firms to characterise the Italian economic scenario. Some of them were highly dependent on the large ones while others became highly independent, dynamic and innovative.

Late in the 1980s, the Italian manufacturing sector experienced the positive effects of production re-organisation, despite difficulties due to high unemployment rate and tax evasion, the Lira depreciation against the Dollar, the raw materials and labour cost increase and the high inflation rate, further aggravated by high interest rates and capital costs.

From 1985 the TFP started growing again, as well as investments in R&D. Italy looked for a higher competitiveness of its products.

At the beginning of the 1990s the economic scenario does not seem to be much different. Typical of this period is the growth of multinational groups and the tendency towards an industrial concentration by which firms try to incorporate into their system small firms specialised on a particular step of the production process. Time saving and costs reduction are the rationale for this phenomenon (Malerba, 1988).

Italian firms have to face external competition to maintain their market share and their economic autonomy. The economic background has to be highly efficient, dynamic and with an avant-garde technology. The low labour cost of the newly industrialised countries forces traditionally labour intensive Italian production to be more and more efficient and to improve the quality of its products (ICE, 1993)[3].

In the following paragraphs the analysis focuses on investment in R&D for industrial innovation and on its effects on the system productivity growth both at national and sectorial level.

3. Financing sources of technical progress and the role of governmental support

Technical progress usually stands for know-how acquisition leading to new production processes and to the production of new consumer goods. According to Schumpeter, technical progress might be divided into three different stages: invention, innovation and diffusion. These three stages range from the discovering of new goods or new ways of producing and processing them, to the launch of the product and its diffusion process (Schumpeter, 1943).

There is an extensive literature in this field referring to different and sophisticated definitions of technical progress. Sherer, for example, recognises four stages in the innovation process: invention, developing/execution, entrepreneurship and investments (Sherer, 1985).

This approach underlines the costly research activities behind industrial R&D programs, while management in terms of innovation methodologies and costs, plays a major role also. Innovations are in fact possible because of the external financing available to the "innovative entrepreneurs" and should provide profits that highly contribute to increase savings. Although this process is one of the firm's main targets, the associated risk is very high.

To be completed the innovative process requires a consistent amount of financial resources and sometimes this is a real constraint for the firm. In fact the associated risk is double: (i) economic risks due to the characteristics of the invention itself and (ii) financial risks due to the ex-post financial returns of investments (Isa Marchini, 1985).

The first type of risks can be summarised in the following three cases:
a) temporal risk of introducing the innovation too early or too late (depending on the willingness of the market to assimilate it);

b) technological or technical risk of the inventive activity after years of unsuccessful research;

c) market risk in terms of insufficient competitiveness of costs, volumes, profits, cash flow or simply in terms of general scarce profitability of the innovation.

Financial risks include: uncertainty about profitability (profitability risk), debt solvency (solvency risk), time length of returns, or gaps before a successful economic performance (time lag risk). This points out the innovative firm's difficulties in finding the necessary financial resources to support its high risk project. This is particularly true for traditional sources external to the firm, such as banks and Special Credit Institutes, that are notoriously risk averse.

Using a simple classification, financing sources can be classified into:

a) external sources, i.e. leasing society, factoring, merchant banks, venture capital society, stock market and foreign sponsors;

b) internal source, i.e. self-financing;

c) governmental source, i.e. subsidised loans including 100% subsidy promoted by regional, national or European programmes.

In order to have a complete picture of Italian firms' financial management of innovation, the composition of R&D expenditure is examined according to origin.

Table 9.1 shows the percentage of funds internal to the firm (self-financing). The second group includes public administration funds (Italian Personal/Movable Institution (IMI) and governmental support). In the third group public, private enterprises and credit institutions funds are grouped, followed by foreign financiers.

For each of the four categories the partial total is presented at the bottom of the table. The total amounts of funds for each year are summed up in the last column. Data has been deflated to allow comparisons over time[4].

In 1994 even if the Public Administration carried out 41.2% of the national research activity, it did finance 49.5%. This shows that a significant amount of industrial research is funded by the government.

From 1979 to 1992 an average of 70% of the industrial research costs have been financed by firms themselves. The remainder has been financed by public administration (16%), public and private enterprises (9%) and from abroad (5%).

A trend worthy of note is the increasing rate of total industrial expenditure in R&D, indicating that firms recognise the strategic role of innovation in their production management. This relevant increase has been higher than the average rate of the G7 and was particularly marked in the 1980s for high-tech sectors, such as aerospace, electronics, mechanics and pharmaceuticals[5].

The growth rate of the total expenditure was about 7.2% and it involved a change in its composition.

Table 9.1 Composition of the industrial R&D financing sources

(a) Percentage shares as a proportion of total annual R&D

	Self-financing	Public administration			Enterprises				Foreign sector	
		Public support	IMI	Total	Public	Private	Credit instit.	Total		TOTAL financ.
1979	75.2	1.57	4.25	5.82	5.89	7.89	3.09	16.86	2.12	100
1980	70.1	5.20	4.08	9.27	4.45	6.27	6.02	16.74	3.96	100
1981	72.1	4.99	3.82	8.80	7.20	7.27	0.33	14.80	4.26	100
1982	72.0	5.36	6.38	11.74	6.58	4.66	0.25	11.49	4.71	100
1983	68.4	9.34	8.70	18.1	5.57	3.18	0.52	9.27	4.27	100
1984	69.8	5.84	12.14	17.97	3.40	2.45	0.16	6.01	6.17	100
1985	71.2	7.35	9.56	16.91	3.42	2.27	0.12	5.81	6.08	100
1986	62.5	13.63	11.17	24.81	2.86	2.51	0.03	5.42	7.32	100
1987	66.0	7.38	13.97	21.35	2.79	2.83	0.10	5.74	6.90	100
1988	68.7	6.29	12.59	18.89	3.11	2.74	0.03	5.89	6.56	100
1989	71.4	5.25	11.06	16.31	3.06	2.51	0.22	5.79	6.46	100
1990	67.4	6.79	12.55	19.35	2.98	1.82	0.23	5.03	7.24	100
Average	*69.6*	*6.58*	*9.19*	*15.78*	*4.28*	*3.87*	*0.93*	*9.07*	*5.50*	*100*

(b) Annual growth rate of financing sources at real prices (base=1985)

	Self-financing	Public administration			Enterprises				Foreign sector	TOTAL financing
		Public support	IMI	Total	Public	Private	Credit Instit.	Total		
1980	-0.58	70.11	2.40	253.9	-19.32	-15.17	108.38	5.98	99.80	6.77
1981	15.78	6.72	5.17	7.95	82.06	30.41	-93.92	-0.60	20.99	12.40
1982	4.10	38.93	74.21	11.93	-4.78	-33.27	-19.45	-19.12	14.98	4.19
1983	1.12	64.35	45.40	86.91	-9.81	-27.34	121.42	-14.04	-3.39	6.58
1984	10.11	7.33	50.67	-32.82	-34.00	-16.51	-67.31	-29.89	56.37	8.07
1985	17.83	8.72	-8.98	45.50	16.29	6.75	-10.23	11.70	13.90	15.58
1986	-6.74	55.10	24.32	97.17	-11.02	18.23	-71.15	-0.89	27.99	6.32
1987	11.26	-9.42	31.57	-43.02	2.66	18.36	231.17	11.39	-0.77	5.26
1988	12.52	-4.25	-2.421	-7.70	20.58	4.71	-64.86	11.15	2.82	8.20
1989	10.67	-8.21	-6.65	-11.33	4.66	-2.77	599.59	4.64	4.83	6.36
1990	0.49	26.46	21.02	37.90	3.57	-22.56	10.82	-7.45	19.58	6.58
1991	n.a.	n.a.	n.a	n.a.	n.a.	n.a.	n.a.	n.a.	n.a.	2.95
1992	n.a.	n.a.	n.a	n.a.	n.a.	n.a.	n.a.	n.a.	n.a.	5.49
average	6.99	23.34	21.52	40.58	4.63	-3.56	67.68	-2.47	23.37	7.29

Source: personal elaboration of ISTAT data

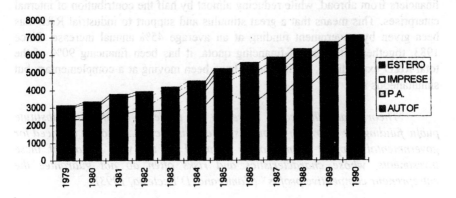

Graph 9.2 Composition of industrial R&D financing sources*: 1979-1992
Source: personal elaboration of ISTAT data
* data are in millions of 1985 Italian Liras.

From Graph 9.2 we can see that the self-financing quota is systematically the most relevant source growing at a rate of 6.7%. The second main source was the public administration fluctuating from 5.8% in 1979 to 24.8% in 1986. It contributes on average to 16% of the total financing.

Almost 42% of this source has been managed by IMI, the most important medium term Credit Institute of the country, its discontinuity is clearly visible over the whole period, ranging from 50% at the beginning of 1980s to almost one third at the end. This means that over the last decade in Italy the financial effort moved toward a diversification of financial instruments. Total governmental support has been growing at a rate of 23.5%, while IMI at 40% shows a positive trend over the whole period.

The quota from abroad shows a strictly positive trend. Its contribution has been about 5%, growing at an average rate of 23.37%.

The peculiar aspect of the evolution of the financial system concerns external sources that systematically decrease over time at a rate of -2.46%. A better understanding of this phenomenon is here given once again by the internal composition of the aggregate. Public and private enterprises have been financing 50.8% and 42.5%, respectively, while the remaining 6.7% has been financed by Credit Institutes. A dramatic change in sources composition at the beginning of the 1980s is particularly evidenced by the last one, whose quota has been decreasing after the large amount of money dispensed during the 1970s.

In this context the general features of the Italian credit system for high risk investments can be summarised in a growing role for public administration and financiers from abroad, while reducing almost by half the contribution of internal enterprises. This means that a great stimulus and support to industrial R&D has been given by government funding at an average 45% annual increase. Since 1983, together with the self-financing quota, it has been financing 90% of the total R&D expenditure. Both sources have been moving at a complementary but simultaneous rate.

"Theoretically this could represent the tendency of firms to substitute public funding for their own resources, when this occurs...although the need for governmental support seems to be required by the very nature of these investments, whose characteristics and risks often do not guarantee the entrepreneur competitive profits" (Camerano, D'Ecclesia, 1993).

Despite its discontinuity, the public intervention has been showing the highest growth rate. With respect to international market challenges, the timing of this instrument seems to be lost.

In fact it was only in 1963 that the need for an institutional co-ordinator of innovation supporting policies led to the Institution of the Ministry for the co-ordination of Technological and Scientific Research (Law 283/63). The first complex and programmed political action appeared in 1968 only, when so-called Law 1089 was passed giving rise to the first Italian Fund for Applied Research (FRA). From 1970 to 1975, a number of laws modified the fund, especially its financial budget. However, the real change occurred in 1982 when Law 46/82 was passed, introducing radical changes in the management of FRA and also giving rise to the institution of a new Fund for Technological Innovations (FIT). This law still is the pivot of governmental intervention in favour of industrial research in Italy.

Among other legislative instruments operating in this direction, the most important is Law 1328/65, the so-called Sabbatini Law, created to encourage the acquisition of tools machinery. At present this law, FIT and FRA are the main instruments to promote industrial investments in R&D and technological innovations, ranging from applied research to industrial development of innovation and to the diffusion of endorsed technological knowledge to the other firms, especially the small and medium sized. During the 1980s the above instruments played an increasing role in the process of transferring funds from government to firms and it is possible to say that all three of them have become pivot of the government's role in this field (OCSE, 1992).

Graph 9.3 confirms the high correlation between financial support and economic performance of the Italian manufacturing sector. This means that firms have been ready to transform external financing resources into R&D investments, even if their desultory availability could not guarantee any continuity in industrial research planning and financing.

Research, being the first stage of the process, has been suffering from this randomness. Which testifies to the fact that financial constraints are serious barriers to the introduction of new technologies.

Italian firms, because of the long, costly and uncertain result of research, find it really difficult to weigh up the financial guarantee against the risk of failure.

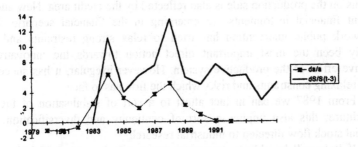

Graph 9.3 Annual growth rate of technical progress (da/a) and R&D expenditure (dS/S) of Italian manufacturing firms*
* Series have been lagged in order to maximise the degree of correlation

Such problems markedly affected Italian technological performance. In fact, since the Second World War the country developed its own peculiar attitude towards importing machinery already equipped with new technology.

Masahiro Kuroda in 1994 tried to measure Japanese degree of technological independence from abroad. We compared figures based on TFP Divisia index for Japan and Italy. This study is not fully reported here, but the result until 1975 was anyway a marked similarity in their imitative strategy and TFP growth rate. After that period the Japanese economy started using its available resources in a very efficient way, and developed its own attitude towards endogenous innovations and inventions.

As for Italy, only in recent years it seems to show the hoped for change in the slope of the technological independence growth path. This means that the demand for financial resources or for the equivalent amount of industrial R&D expenditure has been increasing over the last decade.

Nowadays technical progress and innovation are synonyms for competitiveness. To be efficient means in fact to gain or to maintain an adequate market share of the national and international trade. In this framework one of the main obstacles the Italian system has to face is finding enough resources to guarantee the continuity of the innovative process. This is mainly due to the financial sector inefficiency where economic agents' savings are still subject to many transactions before reaching the firm. Furthermore the high interest rate caused by public deficit, economic recession, overall negative conjuncture and institutional crises do not favour the rising of high risk activity but rather credit rationing and adverse selection of eligible investors.

Anyway, pressure from abroad in terms of lower labour costs and better resource allocation are forcing Italy to face the problem with no delay. This stimulus on the production side is also reflected by the credit area. New and more efficient financial instruments are emerging in the financial scenario. In this framework public intervention has tried to relax strong restraints and it has actually been the most important direct action towards the innovative and inventive effort of the productive system. However irregular, it has succeded in partly relaxing constraints and risks which the firm has to face.

From 1987 we can in fact attest to a sort of stabilisation of the R&D expenditure; this also implies a sort of continuity and diversification of the financial stock flow directed to industrial research.

If Italy will be able to guarantee this continuity and availability of risk capitals, the qualitative and quantitative improvement in the production organisation and management will certainly have greater chances not to suffer from pressing international competitiveness.

Once observed the composition of financial sources, i.e. the composition of industrial R&D, their impact on the productivity of the system will be investigated.

Relevant methodologies and main results are presented in the following section.

4. Impact analysis of R&D investment: 1980-1992

The effect of the increasing R&D expenditure is here measured in terms of its impact on the technical progress growth rate. Research activity being the first stage of the innovation process, will be used to test for the presence of any endogenous technological independence from abroad, in terms of correlation with the increase in the efficiency with which human and capital resources are combined in the production process.

In this context the relative variation approach provides a measure of the contribution given to the productivity changes by factors not exclusively related to the stock of inputs.

This specification can be easily related to Solow's aggregated production function; in fact the productivity annual growth rate, or relative change of the technical progress index, is measured as follows:

$$da/a = (Y1-Y1^*)/Yo = dY/Yo - B\ dK/Ko - A\ dL/Lo$$

where K is capital stock, i.e. number of durable/capital goods, L is labour stock, i.e. annual working units, "a" is the index of technical progress, A and B (assumed as constant over the period) are labour and capital shares of industry value added, Y. This provides the relative change of 'innovation' from one year to the next[6].

Although criticised by a wide economic literature, this indicator is used to pick up the broad perspective which technological progress can entail, i.e. organisational, managerial and structural changes, etc. That is why the words "innovation", "efficiency" and "productivity" are often preferred to the sometimes misleading and restrictive "technological progress".

To avoid comparability problems, growth rates instead of levels will be used for both R&D expenditure and innovation introduction rate, providing a measure of their sensitiveness to unit change of their growth rates, i.e. elasticity. Graph 9.7 gives an idea of the dissimilarity of incremental changes in the two variables[7].

Between 1972 and 1992, while R&D expenditure grew by 6.46% efficiency grew by 2.27%. These figures, surprising as they are, condense more than 20 years of Italian economic history. This high level of aggregation does not provide any serious conclusion, so the whole period has been divided into two phases, according to the relevance of governmental intervention, i.e. before and after 1982.

During the 1970s the average growth rate is 5.77 for industrial R&D expenditure and 2.375 for performance. In the following decade these values do not change very much being on average 6.87 and 2.206 respectively, and their differences rely on the variables behaviour from one period to another. The high fluctuation typical of the 1970s has led to an almost negative sensitiveness (-0.17) of TFP incremental variations to relative changes in R&D expenditures. The complete lack of any symmetric lagged response confirms the almost total absence of R&D planning and programming, especially in the years of transition towards a new efficient production system.

Firms were actually facing inflation and a recession phase at the time, and were trying to reach a static rather than a new dynamic efficiency[8]. Consequently innovations passed only marginally through firms' R&D laboratories. The absence of any correlation between expenditure and efficiency confirms the peculiar adaptive and imitative capability of the Italian system.

Typical of this period are the new production assets developed with strong local peculiarities such as the so-called "diffused economy" and industrial districts[9]. These new industrial organisations were mainly based on small and medium sized firms along the whole supply chain. As a result innovations were more often the result of entrepreneurial intuitions than the result of years of scientific research carried out in industrial R&D laboratories.

Only towards the end of 1970s did the increase in R&D expenditure indicate the Italian willingness to abandon its imitative and adaptive strategy. The government tried to encourage those changes with several laws and funds, i.e. Law 1089/68.

At the beginning of 1980s the result of the new policy was an increase in industrial R&D.

However, the desired launch of the Italian endogenous technological independence was delayed because of slow industrial take-off (i.e. capital life cycle, second-hand asset value and general start-up costs). With respect to the previous decade, the cross elasticity between productivity and the amount of industrial R&D expenditure rose from 0.17% to 4.15% and the strategic role of innovation and technology management was particularly relevant in the aerospace, electrical, mechanical and pharmaceutical sectors (Malerba, 1987).

In the following part the sectorial analysis will try to highlight the characteristics of productivity growth in more detail. Four sectors, that is the ones receiving most public funding, will be considered.

Unfortunately before 1980 data on capital stock are not available at sectorial level, so the analysis covers twelve years only, i.e. 1980-1992.

5. Impact analysis on selected sectors

The substantial industrial reorganisation occurring during 1980s in the manufacturing sector was supported by growing, though questionable, public support in favour of industrial investments in R&D and technological innovation.

The main government instruments were: (i) Law 1089/68 modified by Law 46/82 and the institution of the Funds for Applied Research (FRA), (ii) Law 46/82 and the institution of the fund for Technological Innovation (FIT) and (iii) Law 696/83, updated by Law 399/87 for high tech tools machinery acquisition by artisans and small firms.

The first one (i) aims at guaranteeing applied research, the second, (ii) should assist industrial transformation and the last (iii) should provide incentives for the diffusion of knowledge embodied in the new high-tech machinery.

The Law 46/82 scheme has been mainly used by science oriented sectors, such as electronics, pharmaceuticals and aerospace. They are all characterised by the presence of large industrial firms capable of administrating and creating innovation autonomously.

From 1982 to 28/02/93 the Fund for Technological Innovation sponsored 300 projects submitted by the automobile sector. This accounted for almost 24% of governmental resources available (Bemporad, Bencini and Tuzi, 1993). This means that this policy has matched the needs of many innovative companies with a very high and diversified volume of production. Firms belonging to this sector are large scale economy based and their innovations mainly concern new processes and engineering activity, whose introduction into the production system occurs in the short-medium run. These are also very large firms and their competitiveness is based on prices. Consequently their willingness to adopt new technology and a new production organisation, in order to reduce costs, is very high[10].

The users of the funds for the acquisition of high tech machinery, (iii) are very different from the previous ones. Significant examples are textile and mechanical industries, characterised by small, highly specialised firms in particular areas of the market and whose competitiveness is based on flexibility, reliability, post-sale assistance. Their innovation comes from new machinery acquisition and this means that they depend on some other sectors of R&D activity, such as electrical-electronics.

Amongst several governmental funds, the so called Sabbatini Law (i.e. Law 1329/65) plays a key role in the range of interventions favouring the acquisition and diffusion of tools machinery. Since 1985 the demand for financial support has increased at a very fast rate mainly because of the improvements in the bureaucracy of the project evaluation and submission (OECD, 1993).

Mediocredito Centrale is the Italian Credit Institute in charge of the fund administration. The efficiency improvement in the procedure adopted by the bank has encouraged the acquisition of new machinery from abroad without any restriction on buyers and sellers. In this way several small-size firms have been easily able to access the public fund.

A CNR/ISTAT survey states that five sectors out of 62 in the manufacturing sectors absorbed about 60% of public funds and they are: electronics, pharmaceutical products, data-processing machinery, aerospace and automobile industries.

A further characteristic common to those sectors is that, since the end of 1970s and for all the 1980s, they all experienced a relevant and growing R&D and added value ratio (Malerba, 1988).

In the following sections four sectors are analysed in more detail being the most representative of the different financing modalities. To have a complete picture of the efficacy and efficiency of governmental and industrial policies, the mechanical sector will also be included.

Unfortunately sectorial figures for capital stock are available at a very high degree of aggregation and only for the period 1980-1992. This has reduced the analysis to few macrosectors including different industries. Problems related to time series shortness have already been overcome by means of an index instead of econometric modelling.

5.1 Chemical pharmaceutical sector

Graph 9.4 shows that, for the chemical-pharmaceutical sector, the firms' effort in R&D has had a relevant impact on their productivity growth.

In the last decade, despite the crises experienced by the chemical sector, the technological level has been particularly high. This is mainly due to big firms' internationalisation and to the presence of highly innovative and permanent pharmaceutical research laboratories.

It is noteworthy that the average growth rate of firms' R&D expenditures (9.93%) has been maintained on average above the national one (6.67%).

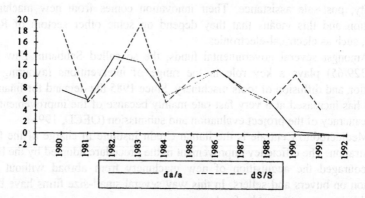

Graph 9.4 Annual growth rate of technical progress (da/a) and total R&D expenditure (dS/S) of chemical pharmaceutical firms in Italy

Over the same period productivity has been rising at 6.75% per year, well above the national growth rate (2.206%). The sensitiveness of the system to changes in R&D expenditure has been 3.982. The efficacy of the innovative effort can be seen from the congruence of the two time series over time (see Graph 9.4). The high elasticity shows the dynamic and successfully innovative strategy of the sectors.

Looking at financial sources for industrial research activity, it is possible to notice the relevance of public support in this area. From 1980 to 1992 it has been growing at a rate of 8.014% and has activated, after proper lag, a 4.02% productivity growth rate. This means that on average a 4.02% increase of public funds has been necessary to activate one unit of TFP growth. Government timeliness is pointed out by the short time lag before successful research activity is introduced into the system. About 60% of the public administration source has been administrated by IMI (Istituto Mobiliare Italiano), growing at an average rate of 14.03% per annum.

Since Law 42 was passed, the government has been financing almost 10% of the total industrial research (see Table 9.2). Surprisingly enough, the productivity path has been fluctuating with a slightly negative trend. IMI guaranteed some support, fluctuating around an average of 14.03% per annum. The productivity growth has been much lower at 6.74% per annum. In this framework government intervention in favour of industrial innovation, i.e. Law 46/82, was introduced at the beginning of 1980s in order to stimulate the slowly growing sectorial productivity.

Comparing both annual growth rates, their correspondence, although with different intensity and lags, amounts to almost 3.769, and shows a very high response by the traditionally big firms with their own industrial laboratories of research.

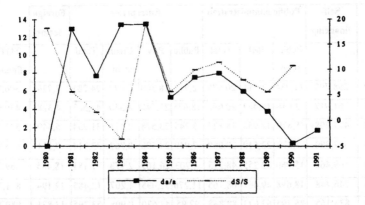

Graph 9.5 Annual growth rate of technical progress (da/a) and sources administrated by IMI (dS/S): 1980-1991

The presence of a small time lag between government intervention and success of innovation, after its introduction into the system, can be explained by the modifications made to FRA and the introduction of FIT in 1982.

According to those changes, firms could ask for public support for programmes already undertaken or projects subject to industrial introduction in

365

the medium run. Chemical-pharmaceuticals was one of the top five favoured areas of intervention, receiving almost the 20% of total IMI availability (Temporad, Bencini and Tuzi, 1993).

Within this sector public support has been able to interpret the real needs of its firms that, especially at the beginning of 1980s, were experiencing difficult times facing strong competitiveness from abroad.

Up to 1992 this policy stimulated investment in R&D, relaxing financial constraints associated to this high risk activity. It has also been a sort of buffer against decreasing productivity, although it has not been able to promote the hoped for technological take-off. Undoubtedly the general economic crisis, especially in the chemical sector, contributed to slowing down a promising sectorial performance.

Table 9.2 Composition of industrial R&D financing sources: the chemical-

pharmaceutical sector

(a) Current values in million Lira

	Self-financing	Public administration			Enterprises				Foreign sector	
		Public supp.	IMI	Total	Public	Priv.	Credit instit.	Total		TOTAL financing
1980	258,795	11,234	9,344	20,578	2,911	18,300	2,990	24,281	2,729	306,383
1981	361,917	3,634	16,464	20,098	18,675	21,548	4,340	44,563	4,328	430,906
1982	477,208	5,879	12,958	18,837	5,245	23,578	2,431	31,254	5,449	532,748
1983	562,390	7,379	22,610	29,989	7,949	24,598	0,767	33,314	0,214	625,907
1984	569,466	15,960	32,255	48,215	4,203	26,169	2,978	7,181	18,485	669,516
1985	746,448	18,698	49,467	68,165	11,276	32,095	1,207	12,483	12,194	871,385
1986	833,165	25,195	63,673	88,868	97,95	42,630	0,908	53,295	13,831	989,159
1987	965,121	43,265	69,219	112,484	15,110	40,793	3,214	59,117	24,736	1,161,458
1988	1,195,729	37,013	62,731	99,744	17,763	39,975	1,625	59,363	17,397	1,372,233
1989	1,367,306	52,944	73,205	126,149	32,178	29,934	2,984	65,096	18,080	1,576,631
1990	1,484,440	68,013	61,522	129,535	63,689	12,855	2,955	79,499	86,070	1,779,544
1991*	n.a.	n.a.	n.a.	n.a.	n.a.	n.a.	n.a.	n.a.	n.a.	2,115,751
1992*	n.a.	n.a.	n.a.	n.a.	n.a.	n.a.	n.a.	n.a.	n.a.	2,309,105

(b) Real value in million Lira (base year=1985)*

	Self-financing	Public Administration			Enterprises				Foreign sector	TOTAL financing.
		Public support	IMI	Total	Public	Private	Credit instit.	Total		
1980	504.650	21.906	18.220	40.127	5.676	35.685	5.830	47.347	5.321	597.446
1981	593.543	5,959	27.000	32.960	30.627	35.338	7,117	73.083	7.097	706.685
1982	668.091	8.230	18.141	26.371	7.343	33.009	3,403	43.755	7,628	745.847
1983	680.491	8.928	27.358	36.286	9.618	29.763	0,928	40.309	0,258	757.347
1984	620.717	17.396	35.157	52.554	4.581	28.524	3,246	7.827	20.148	729.772
1985	746.448	18.698	49.467	68.165	11.276	32.095	1,207	12.483	12.194	871.385
1986	774.843	23.431	59.215	82.647	9.109	39.645	0,844	49.564	12.862	919.917
1987	839.655	37.640	60.220	97.861	13.145	35.489	2,796	51.431	21.520	1.010.468
1988	980.497	30.350	51.439	81.790	14.565	32.779	1,332	48.677	14.265	1.125.231
1989	1.052.825	40.766	56.367	97.134	24.777	23.049	2,297	50.123	13.921	1.214.005
1990	1.068.796	48.969	44.295	93.265	45.856	9,255	2,127	57.239	61.970	1.281.271
1991*	n.a.	n.a.	n.a.	n.a.	n.a.	n.a.	n.a.	n.a.	n.a.	1.417.5531
1992*	n.a.	n.a.	n.a.	n.a.	n.a.	n.a.	n.a.	n.a.	n.a.	1.477.827

* Data have been deflated by the GNP deflator in order to make comparisons over time. i.e. constant purchasing power.
Sources: Personal processing of ISTAT data

5.2 Electrical-electronic sector

Table 9.3 shows that over the last decade the electrical-electronic sector self-financed on average 69% of the total R&D expenditure. The remaining part has come from public administration (18%), external companies including public, private companies and ICS (10%) and from abroad (3%). The composition of financing sources outlines the peculiarity of this sector where continuity and length of innovative projects requires an enormous amount of money. The high risk and the length of time required for outstanding credits from those investments is shown by the marginal support from external sources.

For this sector, to be competitive and to maintain its market share, it means that it must be on the technological frontier of knowledge; that is, being highly innovative. In particular, the electronic sector plays a fundamental role in the automation process, services and industrial organisations. On its innovation depends most of the national technological independence. As technological inputs supplier for many sectors, it actually plays a strategic role for the whole Italian economic system (Camerano, D'Ecclesia, 1993).

The composition of R&D financing sources was almost the same over the decade, with the exception of contributions from sources external to the firm, in particular public ones, whose quota starting in 1982 systematically decreased from 19% to 7%.

This sector has been considered by government intervention as one with first priority and it has been included amongst the top five sectors favoured by Law 46/82. The electronic sector was accordingly granted a relevant quota from FIT which was mainly for planning, development, experimentation and pre-industrialisation of innovative projects and inventions.

The analysis of financial sources (Table 9.3) confirms that government support, even though amounting to 15% only, and regardless of its wide fluctuations, has been the major contribution in support of industrial research. IMI, which from 1968 also administrated the Fund for Applied Research (FRA), managed almost the 47% of total public support, although its continuity over time has never been guaranteed (Marchini, 1993).

The discontinuity of research financing has been mainly due to several modifications of Law 46 and to the exploitation of the Fund, such as in 1984 (Momigliano and Antonelli, 1986).

These interruptions slowed down the efficacy of public interventions in promoting the necessary technological launch of the sector.

Table 9.3 Composition of industrial R&D financing sources: the electrical-electronic sector

(a) Percentage shares as a proportion of total annual R&D expenses

	Self financing	Public administration		Enterprises				Foreign sector	
		Public support	IMI	Public	Private	Credit inst.	Total		TOTAL financing
1979	69.66	8.04	2.57	10.11	3.03	5.76	18.91	3.37	100
1980	53.26	18.48	13.99	6.84	2.68	15.73	25.25	2.99	100
1981	63.87	15.62	11.45	13.69	4.95	0.27	18.92	1.57	100
1982	65.11	14.13	9.18	17.83	0.18	0.25	18.26	2.47	100
1983	69.67	21.57	14.90	5.63	0.04	0.22	5.90	2.84	100
1984	76.18	14.74	8.44	5.73	0.22	0.24	6.19	2.87	100
1985	74.03	15.73	9.66	4.98	0.82	0.16	5.96	4.27	100
1986	67.38	23.47	16.55	4.23	0.25	0.01	4.50	4.63	100
1987	69.84	21.42	12.79	4.70	0.63	0.02	5.35	3.37	100
1988	68.41	21.40	12.17	5.61	0.88	-	6.50	3.67	100
1989	69.43	20.34	9.19	5.04	0.67	0.42	6.15	4.06	100
1990	73.92	20.04	9.82	1.12	0.46	0.12	1.70	4.31	100
1991	71.82	16.77	-	-	-	-	7.43	3.96	100
1992	71.68	17.53	-	-	-	-	7.01	3.77	100
Avg.	68.88	17.81	10.89	7.13	1.24	2.11	9.86	3.44	100

(b) Annual growth of electrical-electronic R&D financing sources, i.e. ds/s (percentages)

	Self financing	Public administration		Enterprises				Foreign sector	TOTAL financing
		Public supp.	IMI	Public	Private	Credit instit.	Total		
1980	-23.11	131.13	445.94	-31.95	-10.96	174.23	34.25	-10.62	0.56
1981	38.58	-2.29	-5.41	131.19	113.01	-97.96	-13.38	-39.3	15.56
1982	-30.41	-38.24	-45.27	-11.16	-97.45	-36.20	-34.11	7.25	-31.74
1983	14.50	63.29	73.70	-66.16	-73.08	-8.61	-65.41	23.34	7.019
1984	20.97	-24.35	-37.31	12.47	427.62	21.06	16.06	11.51	10.63
1985	12.03	23.02	31.92	0.18	328.64	-22.11	11.06	71.49	15.28
1986	-1.64	61.18	85.05	-8.15	-66.25	-90.18	-18.41	17.20	8.06
1987	6.32	-6.39	-20.70	14.02	152.64	6.64	21.92	-25.20	2.57
1988	2.00	4.06	-0.87	24.33	46.06	-	26.54	13.19	4.13
1989	7.92	1.07	-19.74	-4.52	-18.70	-	0.54	17.62	6.33
1990	10.95	2.68	11.34	-76.79	-29.41	-69.34	-71.04	10.73	4.21
1991	-7.68	-20.47	-	-	-	-	313.09	-12.61	-4.97
1992	6.35	11.33	-	-	-	-	0.54	1.30	6.55
Avg.	4.36	15.84	47.15	-1.50	70.19	-13.61	17.05	6.60	3.40

Source: Personal processing of ISTAT data

The comparison between government expenditure and technical progress growth rate provides a clear perception of the irregularity of the interventions both in time and magnitude.

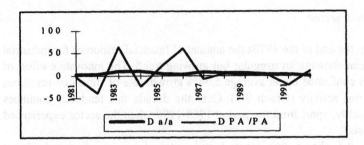

Graph 9.6 Technical progress (da/a) and governmental support (dS/S) to industrial research (growth rates)

The quota administered by IMI has been even more irregular than the total one. In spite of this, considering two time lags as stated by Law 46, it is still possible to detect a small correlation between funds received from these sources and improvements in the production means.

Far from being a spurious result the two years lag actually represents the objective of Law 46: the medium run industrial introduction of innovations.

In general this instrument seems to have only partially contributed to the productivity growth of the system. In fact, the high degree of internationalisation of the sector and the high technological dependence from abroad only marginally lead innovation to pass through the national research laboratories. This is also confirmed by the negative Italian technological balance especially during the first half of 1980s when the electronic sector amounted to 8% of the manufacturing sector negative balance (respectively 7% of cash outlay and 3% of the receipts) (Camerano, D'Ecclesia, 1993).

In the 1980s the government financing growth rate was 6.24% with a fluctuation of about ± 6.24%. Productivity has grown at an average of 4.269% with a much lower variability (±2.86). With respect to the 3.639% annual growth rate of the total sectorial expenditure in R&D, with a variability of ± 11.9%, the IMI quota has been the highest in absolute terms with an annual growth rate of 7.27% but at the same time it has been the most discontinuous source with a standard deviation equal to 44.19.

As a final remark, the analysis confirms that over the last decade there has been a growing government intervention which, despite its irregularity, constituted a real attempt to support and partly to compensate the sector's high and risky investments in industrial research.

5.3 Mechanical sector

Starting from the end of the 1970s the amount of financial resources for industrial R&D has been showing an irregular but growing trend. The innovative effort of this sector is confirmed by an average 5.34% growth rate of financial resources invested in this activity (Graph 9.7). Over the decade this tendency continues almost invariably, apart from the period 1988-1990 when the sector experienced a serious crisis.

Table 9.4 shows that internal and external sources financed almost constantly 86% of total research. Self-financing has been increasing over time up to 70%, showing a symmetric path to the public funds quotas. In this case also, firms seem to have been able to suddenly substitute their self-financing quota to the governmental one, when the latter was available (Camerano D'Ecclesia, 1993).

Apart from the high discontinuity of the IMI quota its contribution to project development and realisation on average amounted to 20% on average. The remaining support from Public Administration is surprisingly stable over time with an average contribution of 6%.

The composition of the remaining sources is 10% from enterprises and 4% from abroad. Over the years the first one registered a remarkable reduction while the second one increased systematically. An explanation for this comes from the effect of the reduction of the Special Credit Institutes whose contribution starting in 1981 has been almost nil. The contribution of public and private enterprises has been decreasing by half, becoming a negligible source.

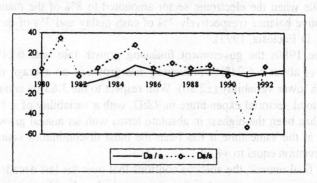

Graph 9.7 Technical progress (da/a) and governmental support (dS/S) to the industrial research: mechanical sector (growth rates)

Graph 9.7 shows that over the years the degree of activation of R&D expenditure has been highly positive, apart from the negative peak in 1991 (-53%). On average it has been necessary a 3.5% increase in R&D investments in order to have a unit change in the total productivity of the sector.

Table 9.4 Composition of the industrial R&D financing sources: mechanical sector

(a) Percentage shares as a proportion of total annual R&D expenses

	Self financing	Public administration			Enterprises				Foreign sector	
		Public support	IMI	Total	Public	Private	Credit inst.	Total		TOTAL financing.
1979	59.14	5.68	9.449	3.76	4.34	9.12	15.66	29.13	2.27	100
1980	36.36	2.80	38.47	35.66	4.37	6.91	12.67	23.96	0.29	100
1981	70.76	5.45	14.01	8.55	3.41	6.87	0.38	10.63	0.45	100
1982	62.85	5.89	19.49	13.60	5.15	6.43	0.01	11.60	6.04	100
1983	42.86	6.79	40.84	34.04	3.88	4.87	0.65	9.41	6.87	100
1984	71.42	5.03	14.62	9.58	3.31	3.34	0.15	6.81	7.14	100
1985	67.20	5.68	22.22	16.53	3.69	2.86	0.38	6.94	3.62	100
1986	65.87	5.92	24.28	18.35	2.18	3.433	0.10	5.72	4.11	100
1987	72.96	8.31	17.14	8.83	1.39	3.46	0.12	5.02	4.89	100
1988	73.85	8.01	15.36	7.35	1.75	3.75	0.08	5.59	5.11	100
1989	77.00	7.02	13.03	6.00	1.46	3.24	0.34	5.05	4.90	100
1990	60.29	6.93	27.29	20.35	1.11	3.42	1.14	5.68	6.73	100
1991	71.31	n.a.	19.07	n.a.	n.a.	n.a.	n.a.	5.24	4.31	100
1992	70.99	n.a.	19.30	n.a.	n.a.	n.a.	n.a.	5.64	4.04	100
media	64.49	6.13	21.044	15.22	3.01	4.81	2.64	9.75	4.34	100

(b) Annual growth rate of R&D financing, i.e. ds/s (percentages)

	Self financing	Public administration			Enterprises				Foreign sector	TOTAL financing
		Public supp.	IMI	Total	Public	Private	Credit institutes	Total		
1980	-35.64	-37.90	-21.80	326.55	5.37	-20.62	-15.31	-13.88	-86.53	4.68
1981	163.01	212.38	162.72	-50.78	5.58	33.43	-95.85	-40.02	108.83	35.15
1982	-13.45	23.23	5.20	35.58	46.98	-8.18	-96.50	6.32	1202.9	-2.56
1983	-16.99	40.30	507.59	131.28	594.53	-20.21	4853.92	-14.60	19.64	5.20
1984	68.42	-3.80	-82.70	-60.11	-88.62	-19.78	-72.53	-15.42	21.46	16.94
1985	20.92	58.21	45.14	95.36	43.36	10.03	216.62	30.91	-34.81	28.50
1986	3.10	17.78	9.54	14.91	-37.80	26.01	-69.75	-13.19	19.32	5.18
1987	22.38	65.79	55.10	-21.96	-29.54	11.66	25.20	-3.11	31.67	10.50
1988	6.38	7.47	1.29	-5.82	32.67	13.73	-24.07	17.14	9.76	5.10
1989	12.92	1.17	-4.99	-8.11	-9.75	-6.38	313.56	-2.23	3.73	8.29
1990	-23.08	3.72	-3.01	105.70	-25.43	3.71	228.39	10.46	34.94	-1.75
1991	-44.03	n.a.	n.a.	-66.94	n.a.	n.a.	n.a.	-56.31	-69.67	-52.68
1992	49.96	n.a.	n.a.	8.24	n.a.	n.a.	n.a.	15.18	0.32	6.94
Avg.	16.45	35.31	61.28	38.76	48.85	2.13	478.51	-6.05	97.1	5.34

Source: Personal processing of ISTAT data

In this framework government intervention has not played a major role. The amount of its financial resources, even if consistent, is not significantly correlated to the efficiency reached in time by the system. Furthermore, as shown by Graph 9.8, the discontinuity of its support seems to be the cause for this. This could be interpreted as public administration inefficiency, but further analysis confirmed the opposite, since the total value is only smoothing each single source. Both the graphical inspection (Graph 9.9) and the degree of correlation between annual productivity and financing sources confirm the efficacy of Law 46 and in particular of the Funds for Technological Innovation (FIT). In general there has been a necessary 7% increase in R&D to stimulate a unit positive change in the sectorial Total Factor Productivity.

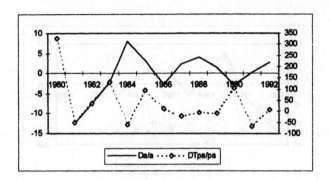

Graph 9.8 Technical progress (da/a) and public administration support (dPAtot / PA tot) to industrial research: mechanical sector (growth rates)

Apart from IMI, the remaining public support has been showing an even higher growth rate (60%) but a lower degree of activation (10.34).

This suggests that different government interventions other than Law 46 have been effective, with differing timing and modalities, on the mechanical sector.

A further point to stress is that in recent years a large amount of IMI resources has been mainly awarded to three industrial sectors: Electronics, Mechanical, Chemicals. According to ISTAT these quota amounted respectively to 30%, 38% and 10% of total financial sources administrated by IMI (ISTAT, 1993).

According to IMI data set the number of projects adopted between the institution of the Law in 1982 and 10/9/92 are respectively: (i) 16.3%, 25.4% and 15.5% of total FIT resolutions, and (ii) 20%, 15% and 19% of total FRA resolutions (IMI data set, 1992).

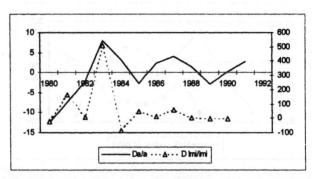

Graph 9.9 Technical progress (da/a) and IMI support (dImi/Imi) to industrial research: mechanical sector (growth rates)

The congruency of the Electrical-electronic and Chemical-pharmaceutical number of projects supported by both FRA and FIT funds is one of the peculiarities of those two sectors. Often the same project is presented to the two sources to guarantee the complete execution of the project. This means that firms applying for support are large firms capable of managing all the research necessary for successful completion.

Contrary to this, the mechanical sector is characterised by firms which are relatively small, highly specialised, dynamic and highly flexible. The composition of the project awarded by Law 46/82 indicates a high demand for funding product and process innovation (projecting, experimentation, development and pre-industrialisation), rather than their Applied Research activity. In fact projects approved by FIT are double the ones awarded by FRA.

For further understanding and clarification of these results it is important to keep in mind that the Mechanical sector also includes the production of machinery and equipment for agriculture, food-industry and other industries, tools and computer science machinery, etc. In this framework the diffusion speed of innovation and the degree of internationalisation are further relevant determinants of the productivity growth of the sector.

5.4 Transport sector

In this case the characteristics of statistical sources, i.e. capital stock, did not allow the disaggregation of the aerospace and automobile sector to analyse the impact of financial sources on productivity growth. The following paragraph focuses only on the investigation of the transport sector as a whole, including vehicles and materials for railways production, transport by land, sea and air. In this case also, self-financing and government resources for industrial innovation are the most important for firm borrowing decisions.

Over the last decades, they sum up to 84%, showing a sort of complementary path, especially after the second half of the 1980s. It is noteworthy that over the same period the increase of resources from abroad has been constant and particularly high (10.3%).

Tables 9.5a and 9.5b show a negligible contribution from private enterprises (1%) and ICS (0.4%). Also the public enterprises quota, whose average was about 3.5%, after 1985 decreased to an almost stationary 1.5%. The relevance of IMI is marginal and accounts only for an average 4% of the total cost of research activity, even if it is possible to notice a modest and irregular increase after 1982. The rest of public administration financed the 16% of the total expenditure.

The picture these figures draw indicates the complete absence of any articulated financial market in support of this high risk activity. Apart from financing from abroad, Public Administration is almost the only investor external to the firm. From 1983 onwards its contribution to the efficiency of the sector seems to have become particularly relevant, (see Graph 9.10).

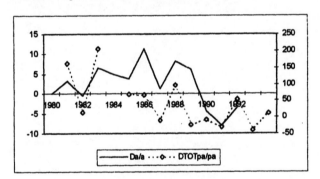

Graph 9.10 Technical progress (da/a) and public administration support (dPAtot / PA tot) to industrial research: transport sector (growth rates)

IMI administrated only 16% of those sources, and its share was higher in 1985-87 and 1989. This means that the government strongly supported industrial R&D.

This sectorial aggregation includes several different activities, both large scale economy (i.e. automobile) and high tech firms (i.e. aerospace). The first group seems to be the more suitable for support by FIT, the second by FRA.

At aggregate level the strong correspondence of TFP (5.7%) and industrial research (7.7%) growth rates indicates that transport in Italy reached a high degree of technological independence. It seems in fact that inventions and innovations are completely manageable by national firms. The governmental role has been fundamental even though decreasing over time. IMI and so the Law 46/82, showed a discrete degree of activation.

The system's production sensitivity to changes in financial support has been negligible on average, but relevant in some years such as 1985, 1986 and 1990.

Despite its relevance, it accounted for only 3.8% of the total expenditure in industrial research. Since 1983 other measures have been adopted to support this high risk activity and they are the most frequently used by firms to finance their innovative projects.

Table 9.5 Composition of industrial R&D financing sources: transport sector

(a) Percentage shares as a proportion of total annual R&D expenses

	Self-financing	Public administration			Enterprises				Foreign sector	TOTAL financing
		Public Support	IMI	Total	Public	Private	Credit institutes	Total		
1979	83.82	1.50	0.40	1.90	0.75	12.01	0.55	13.30	0.95	100
1980	78.61	4.25	0.06	4.32	0.84	7.14	0.51	8.50	8.56	100
1981	75.41	4.21	0.43	4.64	0.99	7.92	0.01	8.92	11.01	100
1982	73.02	10.99	2.72	13.71	0.46	3.67	-	4.13	9.11	100
1983	65.36	16.86	3.54	20.40	0.99	4.19	1.33	6.52	7.69	100
1984	57.06	25.21	4.33	29.54	0.56	2.89	-	3.46	9.92	100
1985	60.26	21.33	3.82	25.15	0.95	1.86	-	2.81	11.76	100
1986	37.90	25.81	18.96	44.77	0.99	1.41	-	2.40	14.91	100
1987	48.54	29.16	4.37	33.54	0.95	1.40	-	2.35	15.55	100
1988	55.34	25.15	2.54	27.69	0.57	1.42	-	1.99	14.96	100
1989	64.02	16.30	2.29	18.60	0.74	1.56	0.08	2.39	14.97	100
1990	59.08	22.09	2.78	24.88	0.70	1.74	0.02	2.48	13.55	100
1991*	69.07	n.a.	n.a.	15.37	n.a.	n.a.	n.a.	9.81	5.75	100
1992*	66.65	n.a.	n.a.	16.66	n.a.	n.a.	n.a.	10.78	5.89	100
media	63.87	16.91	3.85	20.09	0.79	3.94	0.42	5.71	10.33	100

* Data are forecasts

(b) Annual growth rate of R&D financing, i.e. ds/s (percentages)

	Self-financing	Public administration			Enterprises				Foreign sector	
		Public Support	IMI	Total	Public	Private	Credit institutes	Total		TOTAL finacing
1980	8.41	227.54	-80.94	161.72	30.30	-31.22	7.48	-26.15	933.63	15.59
1981	1.46	4.78	580.4	13.72	23.97	17.30	-97.88	11.01	36.02	5.76
1982	0.66	171.20	554.92	206.86	-51.65	-51.73	-	-51.78	-13.96	3.95
1983	17.04	73.29	47.30	68.13	144.6	28.85	-	78.26	-4.51	13.02
1984	-13.59	71.25	39.86	65.80	-34.90	-20.84	-	-39.22	47.59	14.50
1985	11.35	-10.81	-6.95	-10.24	77.92	-32.30	-	-14.30	24.98	5.43
1986	-30.31	34.07	449.57	97.21	15.41	-15.91	-	-5.29	40.46	10.79
1987	31.49	15.96	-76.28	-23.10	-1.7	1.80	-	0.33	7.06	2.65
1988	25.70	-4.88	-35.99	-8.94	-33.1	11.85	-	-6.37	6.05	10.26
1989	18.53	-33.55	-7.528	-31.16	33.06	12.79	-	22.95	2.60	2.47
1990	5.07	54.25	38.43	52.30	6.52	26.95	-62.25	17.94	3.02	13.85
1991	17.02	n.a.	n.a.	-38.16	n.a.	n.a.	n.a.	295.4	-57.52	0.09
1992	48.21	n.a.	n.a.	10.96	n.a.	n.a.	n.a.	12.51	4.98	2.38
media	10.85	54.82	136.62	43.46	19.07	-4.77	-50.88	22.71	79.262	7.75

Source: Personal processing of ISTAT data

6. Concluding remarks

Italy is clearly looking for its technological independence and an increasing amount of industrial research confirms this. The programming activity of Public Administration has been responding to market requests, refining and improving its interventions from time to time.

In the past, funds allocation was often criticised, especially on account of its high concentration on a small group of large firms, which did not seem proper given the large number of small-medium firms of the Italian economic system. Innovation, for them, is often the result of entrepreneurial intuition or developments of existing technologies, while a great deal of industrial research comes from permanent laboratories of large industrial groups that can afford financial costs, as well as economic and financial risks.

That is the main reason why it is easier for large firms to get support. Besides, since the beginning of 1970s main government interventions have been oriented towards key sectors in the Italian economy, such as large firm based chemicals, mechanical, electronics, automobile and aerospace. Nevertheless, almost in each programme special quotas were reserved for small-medium firms to guarantee their smaller project financing (Annunziato, 1993).

The analysis described in this paper has not always been able to measure the direct impact on each of those sector, due to the high aggregation level of statistical figures (especially on capital stock), so definitions could not go deeper than the sectorial classification adopted in the National Economic Accounts.

Each of the four sectors considered so far showed different responses to financial incentives.

The government support for R&D expenditure in the chemical-pharmaceutical sector has been able to sustain productivity growth, compensating for difficulties experienced by the chemical sector.

Very different results have been found for electrical-electronics. Also in this case the total amount of R&D expenditure has been relevant, but its irregularity has not allowed to detect any significant correlation with the productivity growth of the sector. Its relevant technological dependence from abroad indicates that innovations, as well as management, production organisation and assimilation of new technologies, are only partly the outcome of Italian industrial laboratory research. A high degree of internationalisation and a tendency to adopt co-operative strategy have led Italian firms to share innovative risks with foreign companies.

In spite of the low correlation with R&D it is possible, for this sector, to detect some increase in the dynamic of resource transformation.

The mechanical sector has shown a very high correlation between R&D expenses and productivity growth. Public administration financed on average

26% of this high risk investments, confirming the efficacy of its support to innovative activity.

A similar situation has been detected for Transport. Also in this case the role of the public administration has been very important. Excluding the quota from abroad (10%), it has been the main external financing source (20%).

Overall it is possible to say that governmental interventions have been able to interpret the needs of innovative industries. Unfortunately its irregularity and its delays slowed down its potential.

The financial system surrounding innovative firms has greatly contributed to the Italian "technological gap" with respect to foreign industries.

The complexity of capital market and the number of transactions required for funds to reach the firm, are another restraint on efficient resource allocation. This lack of financial instrument diversification makes it particularly difficult for innovative firms to find external sources to sponsor their high-risk investments. On average in Italy almost 70% of innovative investments is self-financed by the firm itself, 20% comes from public administration and the remaining 10% from external enterprises and from abroad. This should be sufficient to confirm the real need for a more efficient financial market able to increase and to diversify its services in support of high risk areas. Anyhow, in recent years, the slight stabilisation and convergence of the actual supply and demand for financial support in these areas seem to indicate a certain degree of planning and continuity in research activity, overcoming the high instability and randomness of previous years. This can also been interpreted as an increasing industrial R&D activity carried out by national research laboratories, which implies that the strategic role of innovation has been well understood by Italian entrepreneurs and by government.

In fact the Italian high tech sectors considered in this chapter showed a considerable increase in their total factor productivity. Most of their industrial research seems to be carried out by their industrial R&D laboratories. The chemical-pharmaceutical (6.75%) and the electrical-electronic (4.27%) sectors have registered a much higher TFP than national average (2.206%). Transport, despite its similarity to the latter, has shown a dynamic and continuos effort in endogenous R&D.

The government, without guaranteeing any continuity, increasingly supported industrial research. Its financial aids have partly reduced the main restraints on the innovative process caused by both economic and financial risks. The transport and mechanical sectors have greatly benefited from its interventions, especially those concerned with the diffusion of new innovations and inventions. The relevant dynamics and the increasing financial efforts confirm this recent industrial policy.

The present analysis probably does not put enough emphasis on the complexity of new technologies, or on innovation spreading, such as lags caused by life cycles of technical progress adopted by the production system; but time series shortness has not allowed any cycle and trend measurement or any other econometric estimation.

Results presented so far shed some light on public policy, financial system and sectorial performance in terms of financial investments, success of the research, intra and inter firm diffusion of innovations and their economic performance.

Methodological note

A) ECONOMIC GROWTH AND INDEX OF TECHNICAL PROGRESS
Because of the shortness of some of the annual time series, i.e. capital input, the analysis is based on index instead of traditional econometrics.

This statistical procedure moves from the comparison between actual and potential product and it is usually referred to as "Metodo delle variazioni Relative" (i.e. Relative Variations/Changes methodology).

Assuming the existence of only two production inputs, i.e. labour and capital, the following variables have been used:
L = labour stock, i.e. number of employees according to the Annual Working Unit definition
v = average unit value of employees in monetary value, i.e. labour cost per hour
K = capital stock, i.e. number of capital goods
p = price per unit of capital

Assuming that labour and capital can be defined in terms of human and assets value, it is possible to define specific productivity in terms of:

$$_LP_o = A * Y_o / L_o v_o \qquad\qquad _KP_o = B * Y_o/K_o\, p_o$$
$$\text{Labour Specific Productivity} \qquad\qquad \text{Capital Specific Productivity}$$

where A and B are shares of national income of the two factors. They are supposed to be constant over the current year, and Y_o is the actual net product that can be expressed as:

$$Y_o = {_L}P_o * L_o\, v_o + {_K}P_o * K_o\, P_o \qquad\qquad (t=0)$$

Assuming that in the short run (i.e. one year) factors cost, v_t and p_t and specific productivity are constant, the theoretical production function at time 1 becomes:

$$Y_1{}^* = {_L}P_o * L_1\, v_o + {_K}P_o * K_1\, p_o \qquad\qquad (t=1)$$

or equivalently:

$$Y_1{}^* = A\, Y_o * L_1/L_2 + B Y_o * K_1/K_2 \qquad\qquad (t=1)$$

This formulation allows to specify the stock of the two factors keeping constant their current prices.

The efficiency of the economic system or Total Productivity Index can be easily derived from the comparison between actual and theoretical production, such that:

$$_0I_{p1} = Y_1 / Y_1^*$$

Furthermore considering Labour (DL) and Capital (DK) constant increments, from period 0 to 1, with some manipulation it is easy to obtain:

$$Y_1^* = Y_0 + DL_0 * A \, Y_0 / L_0 + Dk_0 * B \, Y_0 * BY_0 / K_0$$

from which

$$Y_1 - Y_0 = (Y_1^* - Y_0) + (Y_1 - Y_1^*)$$

where:
$(Y_1^* - Y_1)$ is current labour remuneration times labour stock relative increment/variation plus capital remuneration times capital stock relative increment/variation and $(Y_1 - Y_1^*)$ is income variation due to joint factors productivity, i.e. increasing efficiency in resource transformation and allocation. Equivalently this can be rewritten as:

$$Y_1 - Y_0 = A \, Y_0 * DL_0 / L_0 + B \, Y_0 * DK_0 / K_0 + (Y_1 - Y_1^*)$$

This means that at the end of the year the production growth is composed of:
1) labour stock *increment*, keeping constant specific productivity, monetary value, age structure and labour forces qualification
2) capital stock *increase*, keeping constant productivity, capital prices and capital structure
3) joint factors productivity *increase*, i.e. increase of the efficiency of the economic system or technical progress.

This methodology tries to take into account all technical progress effects, related to any changes in the production function. These include: slow-down, acceleration, organisational improvements, changes in the qualitative composition of labour forces, impact of new technologies and new geographical inter/intra-sector resources allocation, etc. (Giusti Vitali, 1988). This approach is consistent with what is ment by technological progress.

As mentioned in this chapter (paragraph 3), it considers all the impacts on production process of invention, innovation, development, diffusion and management. The generality of the Total Productivity Index makes this indicator the most suitable instrument to take into account all those steps. Besides, it is possible to show that the same results can be found using the Solow's production function specification, i.e.

$$Y = a(t) F(L; K)$$

where t is time, L and K are labour and capital production inputs and "a" measures the annual impact of technical progress. In fact, supposing a linear homogeneous function and a competitive market, such that input costs equal marginal products, we can differentiate and divide by Y, obtaining:

$$dY/Y=da/a+(K/L*dK/dL)*dK/K+(L/K*dL/dK)*dL/L=da/a+B*dK/K+A*dL/L$$

that is exactly equivalent to the previous model. The residual is called technical progress growth rate:

$$da/a=(Y1-Y1*)/Yo=dY/Yo-BdK/Ko-A*dL/Lo$$

Information given by the previous analysis is very limited as it combines several sectorial performances in a unweighted smoothed average.

In order to overcome this limitation the methodology has been applied to observe the performance of selected sectors, those receiving highest quota of government support.

B) IMPACT ANALYSIS: THE EFFECTS OF INDUSTRIAL R&D EXPENDITURES

Impact analysis has been performed to measure the effects of the increasing innovative effort on Italian industrial performance.

According to the definition given so far, the effects of the innovative activity can be measured by:

$$da/a = (Y1-Y1^*)/Yo = dY/Yo - B\ dK/Ko - A * dL/Lo$$

where "a" is the so called "index of technical progress". It measures the annual growth rate of improvements in transforming the same amount of inputs into product.

Using industrial R&D expenditures (S) as a proxy for the research carried out by Italian firms it is possible to define dS/S as the index measuring the national inventive effort.

This "relative indicators", i.e. growth rate instead of levels, have been used to avoid measurement problems due to the two different data series.

Plotting the two indexes over time has been the first step of the analysis. This gave an idea of time lags and of the presence of any correspondence between the two growth rates.

A more accurate statistical procedure has been applied to quantify the degree of sensitiveness of da/a to unit changes of dS/S. The optimal lag, calculated by maximising the correlation between the two measurements, stands for the delay occurring between inventions (or innovations) and the effects of their industrial realisations. Furthermore, the ratio of the two growth rates, corresponding to the highest covariation and optimal lag, has been used to measure the relative elasticity of technical progress to unit changes of R&D expenses, i.e. volume of industrial research.

This methodology has been applied at both national and sectorial level.

Notes

[1] At the time the paper was written the data set was extremely unexplored. Data on capital stock for the last decade was confidentially provided by the Italian Institute of Statistics. Data on financial sources has been carefully collected from several issues of ISTAT *Statistical Bulletin*. The remaining figures refer to the Italian National Accounts.
The quantitative analysis of economic growth for the period 1970-80 refers to the "relative difference" method suggested by Franco Tassinari (1990). A relevant contribution to the analysis of economic growth and technological achievements came in the past from Masahiro Kuroda (1993) and Jorgerson, Gollop and Fraumeni (1987) respectively for Japan and the United States.
A methodological note at the end of the paper gives more details on the statistical technique and the necessary caveats adopted.
The overall analysis relies on a wide literature and on a prior hypothesis dictated by the peculiarity of the Italian system.

[2] A detailed description of statistical methodologies and time series definitions and sources are reported, in the Methodological Note, at the end of the paper.

[3] For a deeper analysis of the Italian sectorial specialisation and international performances see the Annual Reports of the Italian Institute of Foreign Trade (ICE)

[4] Data source is ISTAT. Annual figures at current value were initially published in *Supplemento al Bollettino Mensile di Statistica* and subsequently in *Collana d'Informazione: Statistiche della Ricerca Scientifica*.

[5] Camerano, R. D'Ecclesia, *Incentivi Finanziari per l'Innovazione Industriale, un Confronto tra gli Interventi nei Paesi OCSE*, contribution to *Rinnovamento e Ristrutturazione Aziendale; il Ruolo Svolto dallo Stato nel Mercato*, edited by G. Szego, Franco Angeli, Milano, 1993.

[6] See note 2 and Methodological Note at the end of the paper.

[7] The covariation measures the lagged impact of the unit increase of the R&S expenses over the Total Factors Productivity. Lags correspond to the gap between invention and benefits of its introduction into the system. The Methodological Note, section c), describes the procedure adopted.

[8] Malerba F. and A. Falzoni *Tecnologia e Dinamica Settoriale nello Sviluppo Economico Italiano: 1951-81*; *Una Prima Esplorazione Grafica Attraverso I Dati Censuari*, edited by Filippini C. (1993); *Innovazione Tecnologica e Servizi alle Imprese* Progetto Finalizzato CNR, Franco Angeli, Milano.

[9] A wide literature describes the peculiarity of italian industrial districts, original contributions are:
Becattini G. (1975) a cura di *Lo sviluppo economico della Toscana* IRPET, Firenze;
Becattini G. (1979) "Dal settore industriale al distretto industriale. Alcune considerazioni sull'unitá di indagine dell'economia industriale", in *Rivista di Economia e Politica Industriale* n.1; Becattini G. (1989) *Modelli locali di sviluppo*, Il Mulino, Bologna; etc.

[10] Malerba F. and A. Falzoni *Tecnologia e Dinamica Settoriale nello Sviluppo Economico Italiano: 1951-81. Una Prima Esplorazione Grafica Attraverso I Dati Censuari*, edited by Filippini C. (1993) *Innovazione Tecnologica*.

References

Annunziato, P. (1993), "Confronti internazionali dei sistemi di sviluppo tecnologico", Centro Studi della Confindustria-Ricerche, n. 80, Roma.

Archibugi, D., Cesaratto, S. and Sirilli, G. (1988), "Fonti delle conoscenze tecnologiche e organizzazione industriale: una riconsiderazione critica", *Rivista di Economia Politica*, fasc. 4.

Archibugi, D. and Santarelli, E. (1989), "Tecnologia e struttura del commercio internazionale: la posizione dell'Italia", *Ricerche Economiche*, XLIII, n. 4, pag. 427-455.

Bagella, M. (1987), "Istituti di credito speciale ed il mercato finanziario- 1947-62", Franco Angeli, Milano.

Banca d'Inghilterra (1971), "Capital Utilization in Manifactury Industry", Bollettino Trimestrale, December.

Beccattini, G. (1975), a cura di "Lo sviluppo economico della Toscana" IRPET, Firenze.

Beccattini, G. (1979), "Dal settore industriale al distretto industriale. Alcune considerazioni sull'unità di indagine dell'economia industriale", in *Rivista di Economia e Politica Industriale* n. ,1.

Beccattini, G. (1989), "Modelli locali di sviluppo", Il Mulino, Bologna.

Belvisi, P.L. and Carnazza, P. (1988), "La piccola e media impresa nel cambiamento strutturale dell'economia italiana: un'analisi empirica", *Rivista di Politica Economica*, fasc. 2.

Bemporad, E., Bencini, I. and Tuzi, F. (1993), "Il finanziamento pubblico della ricerca industriale: analisi degli strumenti e dei risultati", *Studio & Ricerca* n. 12, CNR, Roma.

Bentivogli, C. and Rossi, G., (1993) "Crediti commerciali e strategie aziendali di finanziamento degli scambi con l'estero", rapporto sul Commercio Estero, ICE.

Cbr -Centrale dei Bilanci- (1993), "Banca dati dei Bilanci Contabili delle Imprese Italiane Pubbliche, Private e a Partecipazione estera", Roma.

CEE, (1991), "Indagine conoscitiva sui sistemi creditizi nell'ambito della comunità europea" a cura di Onida F., Franco Angeli, Milano.

Falzoni, (1993), "Investimenti diretti e commercio internazionale complementi o sostituti?", Rapporto sul commercio estero, ICE.

FAST - Federazioni delle Associazioni Scientifiche e Tecniche- (1984), "L'incentivazione ed il finanziamento dell'innovazione", Franco Angeli, Milano 1984.

Filippini, C. (1993), "Innovazione tecnologica e Servizi alle Imprese", Progetto finalizzato del CNR, Franco Angeli, Milano.

Graziani, A. (1989), "L'economia Italiana dal '45 ad oggi", *La Nuova Italia Scientifica*, Roma.

Guarini Tassinari G., (1988), "Statistica Economica, Problemi, Metodi ed Analisi", Il Mulino, Bologna.

Guarini Tassinari, G. (1990), "Statistica Economica: problemi, metodi ed analisi", Il Mulino, Bologna.

ICE (years 1989-1992), "Rapporto sul Commercio Estero", Roma.

ISTAT (years 1960-1993), "Conti Economici Nazionali", Roma.

ISTAT (years 1979-1992), "Indagine Statistica sulla Ricerca Scientifica", supplemento al Bollettino Mensile di Statistica; Collana di Informazione, Roma.

ISTAT (1986), "Indagine sulla diffusione dellInoovazione nell'Industria Manifatturiera Italiana", *Notiziario Statistico*.

ISTAT (various years), "Tavole Intersettoriali dell'Economia Italiana", *Bollettino Mensile di Statistica*.

ISTAT, "Statistiche della ricerca scientifica", *Collana d'Informazione* n. 19, 1993.

Krugman-Obstfeld (1991), "Economia Internazionale", Hoepli.

Kuroda, M. (1993), "Economic Growth and Structural Change in Japan: 1960-1985", Working Paper n. 14, Progetto Strategico "Cambiamento tecnologico e Sviluppo industriale", CNR.

Malerba, F. (1991), "L'attività di ricerca e sviluppo nell'industria italiana", L'idustria, pag.66-67.

Malerba, F., (1988), "Note su sviluppo finanziario e crescita economica locale", *Note Economiche*, Monte dei Paschi di Siena, n. 2.

Malerba, F. (1991), "Italy: the national system of innovation", *Quaderno Cespri*, n. 45.

Marchini, I., (1985), "Il finanziamento dell'innovazione nelle imprese industriali", Facoltà di Economia e Commercio di Urbino, Franco Angeli, Milano.

Mariotti, S. (1993), "L'internazionalizzazione dei servizi in Italia: analisi degli investimenti diretti esteri", Rapporto sul Commercio Estero, ICE.

Milana, C. (1992), "Processi di accumulazione e politica industriale in Italia", Franco Angeli, Milano.

Momigliano, F. (1986), "Le leggi della politica industriale in Italia", Il Mulino, Bologna.

OCSE (1992), "Politiche nazionali della scienza e della tecnologia: Italia", supplemento al Bollettino Università Ricerca, Ed. Italiana a cura del Ministero dell'Università e della Ricerca Scientifica, Istituto Poligrafico Zecca di Stato, Roma.

Onado, M. (1986), "Sistema finanziario ed industria", Il Mulino, Bologna.

391

Papi, L. (1992), "Debito delle Imprese e Rischio Economico delle banche", *Note Economiche*, n. 1/2.

Pittaluga, G.B. (1987), "L'evoluzione recente della teoria del razionamento del credito", serie 3, fasc. 7.

Predetti, A. (1988), "L'informazione economica di base", Giuffrè Editore, Milano.

Prosperetti, L. (1993), "Gli effetti della svalutazione della lira: un'analisi intersettoriale", *Rapporto sul Commercio Estero*, ICE.

Salvatore, D. (1992), "Economia Internazionale", La Nuova Italia.

Schumpeter, J.A. (1977), "Teoria dello sviluppo economico", Sansoni, Firenze; trad. da "The Theory of Economic Development", Harvard University Press, (1934).

Sherer, F.M. (1965), "Invention and Innovation in the Watt-Boulton Steam-Engine Venture, Technology and Culture".

Sherer, F.M. (1985), "Economia industriale, strutture di mercato, condotta delle imprese e performance", Ed. Unicopoli.

Solow, R.M. (1957), "Techynical change and the Aggregate production Function", *Review of Economics and Statistics*, August.

Sylos Labini, P. (1993), "Why the interpretation of the Cobb-Douglas production function must be radically changed", Working Paper.

Szego, G. (1993), "Rinnovamento e ristrutturazione industriale il ruolo dello stato del mercato", Franco Angeli, Milano.

Tamburini, G. (1986), "Occupazione e tecnologie avanzate", Il Mulino, Bologna.

Tamburini, G. (1988), "Verso l'economia dei nuovi servizi: il settore finanziario", Il Mulino, Bologna.

Tronti, L. (1987), "Slowdown e aggiustamento: la produttività nel sistema economico italiano a confronto con quella dei maggiori concorrenti-1960-1984-", *Rivista di politica Economica*, fasc. 3.

Valli, V. (1982), "L'economia e la Politica economica italiana dal '45 ad oggi", Etas Libri, Milano.

Valli, V. (1989), "Politica economica: i modelli, gli strumenti, l'economia italiana", La Nuova Italia Scientifica, Roma.

10 The structure of financing and intellectual property rights

Pasquale Lucio Scandizzo

1. Introduction

The uncertainty surrounding investment returns is at the basis of the financial structure of both the firm and the project. This structure, in turn, may give origin to conflicts of interest between stockholders and bond-holders with ensuing suboptimal investment decisions. The resulting deadweight losses, known as agency costs of debt, have been the subject of several studies (Jensen and Meckling, 1976; Myers, 1977; Fama, 1980; Myers and Majluf, 1984; Berkovitch and Han Kim, 1990).

At the most elementary level, agency costs arise because different types of "stake-holders", under different conditions and expected payoffs, agree to share the risks involved in the operation of the firm. While the basic distinction applies to bondholders as senior claimants and to stockholders as residual claimants, the structure of risk sharing can be complicated at will by differentiating the claimants on the basis of the seniority of their claim.

If the financial structure of the firm can be more or less complex depending on how finely it is risk spread over different types of claimants, the question arises as to whether: (i) the firm value depends in a predictable way on the complexity and other characteristics of such a financial structure and, (ii) the structure has any influence on the firm's capacity to undertake risky projects involving intellectual property rights.

The standard framework of agency costs of debt assumes that investment decisions are prior to firm financing strategy and that operating decisions are taken by shareholders (or managers) in order to maximise the value of equity. When there is no debt in the financial structure, an equity maximising policy is equivalent to a firm value maximising policy. When debt is present, on the contrary, investment incentives can be distorted by the conflict of interests that originates when the project NPV is shared between claimants according to their relative "seniority". This distortion of incentives induces suboptimal investment decisions that result in a difference between leveraged firm and unleveraged value of the firm (agency costs of debt).

The impact of the agency costs of debt have been envisaged in situations like "asset substitution" (Jensen and Meckling, 1976), "over-investment" and "under-investment" (Myers, 1977; Berkovitch and Kim, 1990).

Jensen and Meckling show how shareholders of a leveraged firm have incentives to increase the riskiness of the firm's assets, thus increasing the risk for debtholders, even if the greater risk is associated with lower present values of future cash flows. Shareholders are in fact interested only in the "upper" side of the probability distribution of firm results, that is in the part where cash flows are greater than the face value of debt. Debtholders, on the opposite, receive only the full payment of debt as specified in the contractual provision but nothing of the cash flows which are greater than the face value of debt. Therefore, they are interested in the "lower" part of the probability distribution of firm results: the addition of risk increasing projects to the firm reduces the expected value of their claim. In this case, the agency cost of debt consists in the increased cost of financing that debtholders require when they assess the shareholders incentive to accept a risk-increasing investment project.

Myers shows how shareholders of a leveraged firm can have incentives not to accept a positive NPV project: the "under-investment" incentive arises because existing debtholders get a share of the project NPV while shareholders bear the investment cost. In presence of risky debt in the financial structure, debtholders appropriate the positive results of the project financed with internal funds up to the face value of their claim, leaving to shareholders only the residual. The agency cost of debt is directly related to the change in firm value that the project would have produced if adopted, but that was lost because of the decision to reject the project.

While in the Myers contribution, the agency costs of debt are due to the under-investment incentives that origin from risky debt, Berkovitch and Kim (1980) show that risk-shifting incentives can also produce significant deviations from the NPV rule. Using a model based on a different probability level for each state (high and low) and on a project entirely financed with an exogenous specified amount of debt, the authors show how under- and overinvestment incentives can arise from the "seniorship" of debt. In particular, the issuance of senior debt to finance a new investment project can have two effects on the shareholders' investment incentives. On the one hand, a greater seniority of new debt with respect to existing debt makes the former less risky because it increases its probability to be paid back in case of default. This reduces the cost of new debt and makes it easier to use senior debt to finance the investment, thus reducing underinvestment incentives. On the other hand, however, the low cost of new debt, if senior to the existing one, can generate incentives for excessive investment expenses and can result in the acceptance of negative NPV projects (overinvestment). Also in this case, the agency costs of debt depend on the relative weight of the two incentives and can be defined as the difference between the firm values that originate from the acceptance/rejection of the project.

In this paper, I examine these issues within a theoretical framework which is similar, but more general than the one used by Berkovitch and Kim. In addition to the structure of the firm, in the usual case of private production, I shall study the case of intellectual property.

In this case, the financing structure of the firm appears a potentially relevant variable in determining both the size and the input mix of the enterprise. Two main issues in this regard appear worthy of consideration. First, the initiator of the intellectual project, i.e. the inventor or the artist, may hope to appropriate a substantial fraction of work proceeds only if he creates an organisation capable of protecting his property rights. In fact, existing legislation often only provides a framework within which protection of intellectual property rights may be pursued.

In the United States, for example, patent law cannot be applied unless the invention is considered sufficiently unrelated to "prior art", and even if applied, in many cases "...would be held invalid if ever litigated". Trade secret law (protection against the theft of ideas) is also difficult to implement because of the strategies used by firms to avoid legal challenges and the difficulty to establish legal proof (Anton and Yao, 1994, p.191).

Second, the undertaking of a project that may result in an invention or a work of art is often a repeated activity operated under a thick veil of uncertainty. This is specially true for R&D activities, which may be the riskier part of a portfolio of activities of a firm that otherwise operates a different kind of business. Even in the case of more specific products, such as an art performance, a movie or a show, resources have to be committed long before project completion not only to direct project activities, but also to activities aimed at protecting property rights in the event of success.

Activities to protect their dominant position in a market may also be undertaken by firms threatened by the entry of a potential challenger engaged in a project that may yield significant technology improvements. For a competitive market, for example, W. Nordhaus (1969) shows that the decision to commit resources to research a single cost reducing invention is unaffected by the decision to license the invention at the profit maximising licence fee.

S. Salant (1984) demonstrates that, in a market with one incumbent, licensing after the innovation can encourage potential competitors to research in anticipation of future earnings from licensing. N. Gallini (1984) shows, on the other hand, that pre-commitment of resources to licensing may discourage further research both by the entrant and by the incumbent.

The main result of this paper is that the combination of limited liability and financial structure gives rise to incentives for the shareholders to over- as well as to under-invest in almost all circumstances. Where projects with intellectual property are at stake, however, diversifying their financial structure tends to discourage levered firms from engaging in licensing and similar *ex ante* activities to secure property rights. In turn this may lessen incentives to engage in pre-emptive activities to discourage potential entrants from undertaking research.

2. The financing structure of the firm

Consider a firm whose cash flow has a present value of Y, where Y is a random variable distributed in the interval $[-\infty, Y_M]$ with a known distribution function F(Y). Assume that the firm lasts only one period and is financed with a zero coupon bond of face value D, which is discounted at the market value at the beginning of the period and is due for repayment at the end of the period.

Proposition 1 - The value to the shareholders of a firm with one type of debt-financing is independent of the debt-equity ratio and always greater than the net present value of the firm.

Proof: If, for a given investment level of I, financing is obtained floating zero coupon notes of nominal value equal to D, the value to the shareholders, because of limited liability is:

$$V_A = \max [0, Y - D] \tag{1}$$

and the expected value is:

$$EV_A = \int_D^{Y_M} (Y - D) \, dF(Y) = [1 - F_1 (D)] EY - [1-F(D)] D \tag{2}$$

where F(Y) is the distribution of cash flow, in the interval $[-\infty, Y_M]$, and $F_1 (D)$ is the ordinate of the Lorenz curve defined (Kakwani 1980) as:

$$F_1 (Y) = \frac{\int_{-\infty}^{Y} v \, dF(v)}{\int_{-\infty}^{\infty} v \, dF(v)} \tag{3}$$

396

The market value of debt, on the other hand, is:

$$V_D = \max \{ \min [D, Y], 0 \} \qquad (4)$$

and its expected value is:

$$EV_D = \int_0^D v dF(v) + D (1-F(D)) = [F_1 (D) - F_1 (0)] EY + (1-F(D)) D \qquad (5)$$

In order to finance the investment I, $EV_D = I$, i.e., substituting into (5) and solving for D:

$$D = \frac{I - [F_1(D) - F_1(0)]EY}{1 - F(D)} \qquad (6)$$

Substituting this expression for D into (2), we readily obtain:

$$EV_A = EY - I + | F_1 (0) | EY \qquad (7)$$

where $| F_1 (0) | \,>/\, 0$ denotes the absolute value of $F_1 (0)$.

q. e. d.

Comment: Expression (2) states that the expected value of the stock of a firm is made of two parts: (a) the share of the cash flow expected value in the states of nature where income exceeds debt payment and, (b) the cost of paying the debt obligations in the same states of nature. Expression (5), on the other hand, states that the market value of the firm's bonds is also made of two parts: (a') the share of the cash flow expected value in the states complementary to (a) and, (b') the value of debt payment in the same states as in (a). Thus, as Modigliani and Miller noted, a larger amount of debt financing will have two effects that will exactly counterbalance each other: (i) the amount financed by stockholders will decline, giving a boost to the net cash flow accruing to them, (ii) bonds market value will also decline forcing the firm to issue more bonds for the same amount of investment. Note also that the creation of a firm with limited liability creates a distribution effect in favour of both stockholders and at the expenses of the owners of wealth external to the firm. The term $| F_1 (0) |$ EY represents in fact the expected destruction of wealth not sustained by the stakeholders. The deadweight loss can be eliminated by an appropriate *ad valorem* tax on cash flow

Y. Such a tax should be raised at a rate equal to $|F_1(0)|/(1+|F_1(0)|-i)$ where i=I/EY. It would have to be, therefore, a function of the investment financed with debt.

Proposition 2 - The shareholders' value of a project financed through sale of junior debt may be greater, equal or lower than its net present value (NPV).

Proof: Denote with D_1 the senior notes and with D_2 the junior notes. The expected value of the firm for the shareholders is:

$$EV_A^* = \int_{D_1+D_2}^{\infty} zdG(z) - (D_1 + D_2)(1 - G(D_1 + D_2)) \tag{8}$$

where $z = x + y$, y being the cash flow from existing activities and x the cash flow from the project. G(z) is the distribution function of z.

The face value of the senior notes is the same as in (5) with $D=D_1$, while the value of the junior notes is:

$$EV_{D_2} = \int_{D_1}^{D_1+D_2} (z - D_1)dG(z) + D_2(1 - G(D_1 + D_2)) = I_x \tag{9}$$

where I_x denotes investment costs of the new project, while the investment cost originally borne to create the firm is $I_y = EV_{DI}$.

Substituting into (8) expressions (5) and (9) yields:

$$EV_A^* = \left[\int_0^{\infty} zdG(z) - I_y - I_x \right] + \left[\int_0^{D_1} ydF(y) - \int_0^{D_1} zdG(z) \right] + D_1(G(D_1) - F(D_1)) \tag{10}$$

Developing the integrals in the second square parenthesis by parts, we obtain:

$$EV_A^* = \left[\int_0^{\infty} zdG(z) - I_y - I_x \right] + \int_0^{D_1} (G(u) - F(u))du \tag{11}$$

Subtracting the expression for EV_A:

$$EV_A^* - EV_A = (EX - I_x) + \int_0^{D_1} (G(u) - F(u))du \tag{12}$$

398

or, developing again by parts:

$$EV_A^* - EV_A = NPV + [G(D_1) - F(D_1)] \quad D_1 + [F_1(D_1)EY - G_1(D_1)E(Y + X)] \quad (13)$$

q. e. d.

Comment: The first term in square brackets in expression (13) measures the extent to which the project changes the probability of default for senior debt. If such a probability increases, the burden that falls on senior debt constitutes an incentive to undertake the project even where NPV is negative (over investment). The second term in square brackets, on the other hand, measures the extent to which the project changes the expected value of cash flow. If this change is negative (the term in square brackets is positive), an additional burden of cost may be shifted from shareholders to senior creditors, providing further incentives to undertake the project. Conversely, if either the probability of default for senior debtors decreases or their expected share of the cash flow increases, shareholders will count this as an increase in cost, and may reject projects that cause these effects even though their NPV may be positive.

Corollary 2.1 - For risk averse shareholders, the value of a project financed through sale of junior debt will be greater, equal or lower than NPV according to whether the project increases, leaves unchanged or decreases the risk of the firm in default towards senior shareholders according to the criterion of second degree stochastic dominance (SSD).

Proof: The result follows directly from expression (12).

Comment: While Proposition 2 holds for risk neutral shareholders also, the corollary implies that risk-averter shareholders will always experience a benefit if the risk share of senior debt increases, while its face value remains unchanged. For a project that increases the value of expected cash flow, risk neutral shareholders must compare the cost given by the leakage of cash flow increase to senior debt holders with the possible benefit given by their additional shouldering of the burden of default. For risk averse shareholders, on the other hand, this is equivalent to a reduction of risk, since the existence of senior debt allows them to shift some of the project risks to senior creditors costlessly.

Because senior creditors might anticipate the firm expansion at their expenses, Proposition 2 implies the further corollary:

Corollary 2.2 - The shareholders' value of a firm financed by senior debt may be lower, equal or greater than its net present value if creditors anticipate its intention to expand through junior debt.

Proof: If the creditors who finance the firm perfectly anticipate its expansion, the market value of the debt originally issued will be:

$$EV_{D_1} = \int_0^{D_1} vdF(v) + (1 - F(D_1))D_1 - \int_0^{D_1} (G(u) - F(u))du \qquad (14)$$

Integrating by parts the first integral on the right and simplifying yields:

$$EV_{D_1} = \int_0^{D_1} (1 - G(u))du = \int_0^{D_1} udG(u) + D_1(1 - G(D_1)) \qquad (15)$$

Equating to I_y and substituting in (15), for $D = D_1$, we obtain:

$$EV_A = \left[\int_0^{Y_M} vdF(v) - I_y \right] - \int_0^{D_1} (G(u) - F(u))du = (EY - I_y) - \int_0^{D_1} (G(u) - F(u))du$$

$$(16)$$

Comment: Even perfect anticipation on the part of creditors of future expansion and financing plans of the firm will not solve the over-under investment problem. If senior creditors will anticipate a loss, in fact, they will increase the price of credit (the ratio between face value and market value of the note floated) and, as a result, the value of the firm will fall below its net present value. In this case, to prevent a future overinvestment, creditors may discourage the firm from investing at all. Vice versa, if creditors predict that the firm will engage in projects that increase its value and/or decrease the danger of default, they will concede more generous credit terms to prevent future underinvestment. But again, this will be self-defeating since it will encourage the firm to start operations at a larger scale than it would be optimal.

The results obtained can be extended *a fortiori* to the case where new creditors have the same rights of the previous ones:

Proposition 3 - The shareholders' value of a project financed through additional debt may be greater, equal or lower than its net present value (NPV).

Proof: Proceeding as before, we find:

$$EV_A^* = \int_{D_1+D_2}^{Y_M} vdG(v) - (D_1 + D_2)(1 - G(D_1 + D_2)) \qquad (17)$$

$$EV_{D_2} = \frac{D_2}{D_1 + D_2} \int_0^{D_1+D_2} vdG(v) + D_2(1 - G(D_1 + D_2)) \qquad (18)$$

while EV_{D1} is as in (5) with $D=D_1$.

Substituting (18) and (5) into (17) ~ and setting $EV_{D1} = I_y$ and $EV_{D2} = I_x$, we find:

$$EV_A^* - EV_A = NPV + \int_0^{D_1} (\alpha G(u) - F(u))du + \alpha \int_{D_1}^{D_1+D_2} \alpha G(u)du \qquad (19)$$

$$where \quad \alpha = \frac{D_1}{D_1 + D_2}$$

Integrating by parts, we obtain:

$$EV_A^* - EV_A = NPV + (G(D_1) - F(D_1))D_1 + F_1(D_1)EY - \alpha G_1(D_1 + D_2)E(Y + X) \qquad (20)$$

q.e.d.

Comment: The result in (20) closely parallels the result in (13) for junior debt. In the case of new debt versus older debt, the difference between NPV and shareholders' value is still due to the two components identified for junior debt versus senior debt, i.e. (i) variation in the probability of default and, (ii) variation in the expected value of cash flow. It is this second term that carries the main difference with the junior-senior case, since the expected value "with the project" concerns older debt only for its share of total debt of the firm.

3. Intellectual property and agency costs

A first characterisation of a project aimed at producing an intellectual product is its lack of protection from appropriation. In general, we can assume that only a share θ of the output X may be retained by the firm, while $(1-\theta)$ will leak out to non intended beneficiaries. I also assume that the firm can protect its property (and increase θ) before project completion by purchasing a "protection input" z at a price r, such that $\theta = \theta(z)$, $\theta_z = \partial\theta / \partial z > 0$ and $\theta_{zz} = \partial^2\theta / \partial z^2 \le 0$.

Given these assumptions, we can state the following:

Proposition 4 - A firm financing a project aimed at producing an intellectual product (IP) with junior debt tends to underprotect its future property rights, and the greater the degree of underprotection, the greater will be the amount of outstanding senior debt.

Proof: From expression (13), we directly find:

$$EV_A^* - EV_A = \theta EX - I_x + [G(D_1) - F(D_1)]D_1 - [G_1(D_1)E(Y + \theta X) - F_1(D_1)EY] - rz]$$
(21)

where $\theta = \theta(z)$.

Differentiating with respect to z and equating to zero:

$$\theta_z(1 - G_1(D_1))EX - r = 0$$
(22)

q.e.d.

Comment: A non leveraged firm, or a firm without outstanding senior debt ($D_1 = 0$ and $G_1(D_1) = 0$) would equate the marginal productivity of z in terms of protection delivered $\theta_z EX$ to the price of the input. The greater the already existing amount of leverage, vice versa, the higher will be the opportunity costs of engaging in protection activities, because some of the payoff from these activities will accrue to senior debt-holders. Note that, while the existence of leverage may increase or decrease project attractiveness, it will always reduce the extent to which shareholders will be willing to spend money to protect their expected product. In this case, if debtholders lower the price that they are willing to pay for the bond to reflect this cost of underprotection, the firm will always be underpriced by initial creditors. As creditors learn to deduct from the expected proceeds of their loan the costs due to the firm suboptimal behaviour, new firms that might engage in IP projects will be progressively discouraged to go into business or they will be encouraged to enter the market with a smaller size than it would be optimal.

Proposition 5 - A firm financing an IP project with new debt tends to underprotect its future property rights on the project, and the degree of underprotection will be greater: (i) the greater the absolute amount of outstanding debt, (ii) the lower its relative share of total debt.

Proof: From expression (20), for a project yielding $\theta(z) X$ at a cost $I_x + rz$:

$$EV_A^* - EV_A = \theta EX - I_x + [G(D_1) - F(D_1)]D_1 + [F_1(D_1)E(Y) - \alpha G_1(D_1)(EY + \theta EX)] - rz \quad (23)$$

Differentiating w.r.t. z and equating to zero:

$$\theta_z(1 - \alpha G_1(D_1))EX - r = 0 \quad (24)$$

q.e.d.

Comment: The degree of underprotection will now also depend on the relative amount of old debt $\alpha = D_1/(D_1 + D_2)$. The reason is that the cost incurred in purchasing protection for future property rights does not go completely wasted in the case where $X < D_1$. New debt will be benefited for a share $1-\alpha$ and this will be reflected in better terms for the new loan.

4. Some empirical evidence

In order to test the hypothesis that the level of R&S activity is affected by the financial structure of the firm, I analyse a DATASTREAM sample of 74 US firms belonging to four sectors, where R&S has an important role: (i) chemical-pharmaceutical products, (ii) aerospace, (iii) electronics, (iv) precision mechanics. For each firm I have utilised budget data for a period of 14 years (1980-1993) for a total of 1036 observations.

The variables included in the first regression (Model I) are the following:

RS (dependent variable):   Expenditure for research and development in each year
DLOAN   Yearly variation of total debt
EQUISSU   Yearly variation of total equity
LTD   Share of debt to be reimbursed beyond a five year horizon
CF   Cash flow

DUM   Dummy to account for asymmetric effects of the "bottom line"
           outcome. The dummy equals 1 if income this year is higher than last
           year and zero otherwise.
CFD   Interaction between cash flow and dummy (DUM x CF).

I expect a positive sign for the variable DLOAN, since, by propositions 2
and 3, a firm whose leverage is growing will show a preference for risky
enterprises. For the same reason, I expect a negative sign for EQUISSU and
DUM and a positive sign for all other variables, except for CFD, for which either
sign should be equally acceptable on a priori grounds.

Table 10.1 Regression results for Model I

LS// Dependent Variable is RS
SMPL range: 1 - 1036
Number of observations: 1036

VARIABLE	COEFFICIENT	STD. ERROR	T-STAT.	2-TAIL SIG.
C	21357.381	8013.0842	2.6653135	0.0078
DLOAN	0.0360350	0.0165333	2.1795448	0.0295
EQISSU	-0.0820067	0.0235894	-3.4764182	0.0005
LTD	0.0926649	0.0156405	5.9246714	0.0000
CF	0.0895900	0.0058771	15.244028	0.0000
CFD	0.0456544	0.0075486	6.0480394	0.0000
DUM	-25995.976	9652.0088	-2.6933229	0.0072

R-squared	0.574951	Mean of dependent var	0.000328
Adjusted R-squared	0.572473	S.D. of dependent var	216949.2
S.E. of regression	141853.5	Sum of squared resid	2.07E+13
Log likelihood	-13756.11	F-statistic	231.9829
Durbin-Watson stat	0.673591	Prob (F-statistic)	0.000000

In the second regression (Model II), I have used the same variables of
model I, but the variable DUM has been re-defined as equal to 1 when the debt-

404

equity ratio is above the average for the period considered and zero otherwise. As Table 2 shows, only the coefficient of the dummy variable shows a negative sign (higher R&S expenditures when "risk" increases) while the interaction variable CFD shows a positive sign (a higher risk makes less sensitive the investment in R&S to variations of cash flow).

Table 10.2 Regression results for Model II

LS// Dependent Variable is RS				
SMPL range: 1 - 1036				
Number of observations: 1036				
VARIABLE	COEFFICIENT	STD. ERROR	T-STAT.	2-TAIL SIG.
C	12934.497	5929.2690	2.1814658	0.0294
DLOAN	0.0313023	0.0167598	1.8677022	0.0621
EQISSU	-0.0938923	0.0235762	-3.9824972	0.0001
LTD	0.1058856	0.0163755	6.4660965	0.0000
CF	0.1353857	0.0061876	21.880047	0.0000
CFD	-0.0348218	0.0075931	-4.5859984	0.0000
DUM	-26896.710	9545.8872	-2.8176228	0.0049
R-squared	0.570281	Mean of dependent var		0.000328
Adjusted R-squared	0.567775	S.D. of dependent var		216949.2
S.E. of regression	142630.7	Sum of squared resid		2.09E+13
Log likelihood	-13761.77	F-statistic		227.5977
Durbin-Watson stat	0.686543	Prob (F-statistic)		0.000000

5. Conclusions

The financing structure of the firm may give rise to agency costs because of the uncertainty surrounding the firm's future prospects at the time when the conditions on the firm's debt are being negotiated. Each creditor of the firm is the holder of a promise to pay, whose value will be contingent on the state of nature and on the value of other claims against the firm. The interdependent nature of the problem and the imperfection of information will generally prevent shareholders from facing project prospects without over-investment or under-investment incentives.

By applying the results on the agency costs of debt to the case of intellectual property, I have shown that the financial structure of the firm has the further consequence to discourage firms from engaging in *ex ante* licensing and other activities to protect future property rights. The results obtained also imply that unleveraged firms, and project financing, may be the more appropriate financial structure for R&D projects and generally for activities involving intellectual property. On the other hand, in the case where invention or artistry generates some form of market power, a more diversified financial structure may lessen the incentive to pre-empt future research by over-investing in *ex ante* licensing or other protection activities.

In general, the effects described will tend to reinforce each other. Thus, the incentive to use junior debt or new debt to finance new projects will encourage firms to undertake risky projects of the R&D variety over and above what would be optimal, *coeteris paribus*. On the other hand, the incentive to underprotect future property rights in this area will make these projects less costly than they would be if the firm's financial structure were not taken into consideration. Both effects may thus work as incentives partly counteracting phenomena such as risk aversion and free riding that tend instead to discourage R&D projects.

The empirical evidence examined also suggests that the incentives provided by an expanding financial leverage tend to dominate underincentives from risk aversion and fear of loss of property rights. Firms whose leverage increases more rapidly tend to expand R&D activities and more so in years where debt grows faster than equity or is at levels higher than average. While the data do not allow a direct test of a tendency to underprotect intellectual property rights on the part of firms whose leverage increases at higher rate, the results obtained by econometric analysis could be consistent both with over-incentives in investing in R&D and with under-incentives in requiring *ex ante* protection.

References

Amit, Raphael; Glosten, Lawrence and Muller, Eitan (1990), "Entrepeuneurial Ability, Venture Investments, and Risk Sharing", *Management Science*, October, 36(10) pp. 1232-45.

Anton, J.J., Yao, Dennis, A. (1994), "Expropriation and Inventions: Appropriable Rents in the Absence of Property Rights", *The American Economic Review*, March, 84(1), pp. 190-209.

Berkovitch, E. and Kim, E.H. (1990), "Finance Contracting and Leverage Induced over-and Incentives", *Journal of Finance*, July, XLV, n.3, pp. 765-794.

Fama, E.F. (1980), "Agency Problem and the Theory of the Firm", *Journal of Political Economy*, vol. 88, n. 2, pp. 288-298.

Gallini, N.T. (1984), "Deterrence by Market Sharing: A Strategic Incentive for Licencing", *The American Economic Review*, December, 74(5), pp. 931-941.

Jensen, M.C. and Meckling, W. (1976), "Theory of the Firm: Managerial Behaviour, Agency Costs and Ownership Structure", *Journal of Financial Economics*, n. 3, pp. 305-360.

Kakwani, C. (1980), *Income Inequality and Poverty, Methods of Estimation and Policy Applications*, Oxford University Press.

Myers, S.C. (1977), "Determinants of Corporate Borrowing", *Journal of Financial Economics*, vol. 5, pp. 147-175.

Myers, S.C. and Majluf N. (1984), "Corporate Finance and Investment Decisions when Firms have Informations that Investors do not have", *Journal of Financial Economics*, n. 13, pp. 187-221.

Nordhaus and William, D. (1969), *Invention, Growth and Welfare*, Cambridge: MIT Press.

Salant and Sthephen (1984), "Preemptive Patenting and the Persistence of Monopoly: Comment", *American Economic Review*, March, 74(3), pp. 247-50.

For Product Safety Concerns and Information please contact our
EU representative GPSR@taylorandfrancis.com Taylor & Francis
Verlag GmbH, Kaufingerstraße 24, 80331 München, Germany